# RAND McNALLY
# WORLD FACTS & MAPS

**RAND McNALLY**
Chicago/New York/San Francisco

# Contents

**Hot Spots: Current Events in Focus**

## Europe and the Soviet Union  6
Soviet Union: Empire in Crisis  8
Estonia: The Flag Flies Again  10
Armenia: War with Azerbaijan  11
Poland: Solidarity Takes Over  12
Romania: Nowhere to Go But Up  14
Czechoslovakia: Prague Spring Returns  16
Hungary: Communism Bows Out  17
East Germany: Reviving the German Question  18
European Community: Establishing a Single Market Economy  20

## North America  22
The United States: War on Drugs  24

## Latin America  26
Nicaragua: Defeat of the Sandinistas  28
El Salvador: War Games in Central America  30
Haiti: Poverty and Repression  32
Panama: The Fall of a Despot  33
Brazil: Saving the Rain Forest  34
Colombia: Cocaine, Corruption, and Chaos  36
Argentina: A Fragile Democracy  38

## East Asia and the Pacific  40
New Caledonia: Rocky Road to Independence  41
China: Reform and Repression  42
China: Tibetan Nationalism  44
Hong Kong: Awaiting the Dragon  45
Cambodia: Casualty of the Vietnam War  46
Japan: Entering a New Era  48

## South Asia  50
Sri Lanka: Ethnic Rivalry Explodes  51
Afghanistan: Civil War and Turmoil  52
India: Conflict over Sikh Nationalism  54

## The Middle East and North Africa  56
Lebanon: Politics, Religion, and Demographics  58

---

*World Facts & Maps* was produced and edited by the staff of Rand McNally. The views expressed are the authors' and not necessarily those of the publisher.

*Photo Credits*
5: UPI (street scene, San Salvador, El Salvador).
81: J.B. Cuny/FPG International (flags outside United Nations headquarters, New York City).

Copyright © 1990 by Rand McNally & Company.
All rights reserved.
Printed in the United States of America.
Library of Congress Catalog Card Number: 90-53192
ISBN: 0-528-83420-7

Cyprus: An Island Divided   60
Libya: The Enigmatic Qadhafi   62
Iran: The Tide Turns   64
*Legacies of the Six-Day War*   66
   Jerusalem   67
   Gaza Strip   68
   Golan Heights   69
   West Bank   70

**Sub-Saharan Africa**   71
South Africa: Apartheid and the Homelands   72
Namibia: The Struggle for Independence   74
Mozambique: Renamo's Reign of Terror   76
Ethiopia: The Politics of Famine   78
Sudan: A Country Divided   80

**World Gazetteer: Profiles of Nations and Places**

Afghanistan   82
Albania   82
Algeria   83
American Samoa   84
Andorra   84
Angola   84
Anguilla   85
Antarctica   85
Antigua and Barbuda   85
Argentina   86
Aruba   86
Ascension Island   86
Australia   87
Austria   88
Azores   88

Bahamas   88
Bahrain   89
Balearic Islands   89
Bangladesh   89
Barbados   90
Belgium   91
Belize   91
Benin   92
Bermuda   93
Bhutan   93
Bolivia   94
Botswana   94
Brazil   95
British Indian Ocean
   Territory   96
Brunei   96
Bulgaria   96
Burkina Faso   97
Burma   98
Burundi   98

Cambodia   99
Cameroon   100
Canada   101
Canary Islands   101
Cape Verde   101
Cayman Islands   102

Central African Republic   102
Chad   103
Channel Islands   103
Chile   103
China   104
Christmas Island   105
Cocos Islands   105
Colombia   105
Comoros   106
Congo   106
Cook Islands   107
Corsica   107
Costa Rica   107
Cuba   108
Curaçao   108
Cyprus   108
Cyprus, North   109
Czechoslovakia   109

Denmark   110
Djibouti   111
Dominica   111
Dominican Republic   112

Ecuador   112
Egypt   113
El Salvador   114
Equatorial Guinea   115
Ethiopia   115

Faeroe Islands   116
Falkland Islands   116
Fiji   117
Finland   117
France   118
French Guiana   119
French Polynesia   120

Gabon   120
Galápagos Islands   121
Gambia   121
Germany, East   122
Germany, West   122

| | | |
|---|---|---|
| Ghana 123 | Mexico 155 | Seychelles 179 |
| Gibraltar 124 | Micronesia, Federated | Shetland Islands 180 |
| Greece 124 | States of 155 | Sierra Leone 180 |
| Greenland 125 | Midway Islands 155 | Singapore 181 |
| Grenada 126 | Monaco 155 | Solomon Islands 181 |
| Guadeloupe 126 | Mongolia 156 | Somalia 182 |
| Guam 126 | Montserrat 157 | South Africa 183 |
| Guatemala 126 | Morocco 157 | South Georgia 183 |
| Guernsey 127 | Mozambique 157 | Soviet Union 183 |
| Guinea 127 | | Spain 184 |
| Guinea-Bissau 128 | Namibia 158 | Sri Lanka 185 |
| Guyana 128 | Nauru 159 | Sudan 186 |
| | Nepal 159 | Suriname 187 |
| Haiti 129 | Netherlands 160 | Swaziland 187 |
| Honduras 130 | Netherlands Antilles 161 | Sweden 188 |
| Hong Kong 130 | New Caledonia 161 | Switzerland 188 |
| Hungary 131 | New Zealand 161 | Syria 189 |
| | Nicaragua 162 | |
| Iceland 132 | Niger 163 | Taiwan 190 |
| India 132 | Nigeria 164 | Tanzania 191 |
| Indonesia 133 | Niue 164 | Tasmania 191 |
| Iran 134 | Norfolk Island 164 | Thailand 191 |
| Iraq 135 | Northern Mariana | Togo 192 |
| Ireland 135 | Islands 164 | Tokelau 193 |
| Isle of Man 136 | Norway 164 | Tonga 193 |
| Israel 136 | | Trinidad and |
| Italy 137 | Oman 165 | Tobago 193 |
| Ivory Coast 138 | Orkney Islands 166 | Tunisia 194 |
| | | Turkey 194 |
| Jamaica 139 | Pacific Islands, Trust | Turks and Caicos |
| Japan 139 | Territory of the 166 | Islands 195 |
| Jersey 140 | Pakistan 166 | Tuvalu 195 |
| Jordan 140 | Palau 167 | |
| | Panama 167 | Uganda 195 |
| Kenya 141 | Papua New Guinea 167 | United Arab |
| Kerguelen Islands 142 | Paraguay 168 | Emirates 196 |
| Kiribati 142 | Peru 169 | United Kingdom 197 |
| Korea, North 142 | Philippines 169 | United States 198 |
| Korea, South 143 | Pitcairn 170 | Uruguay 200 |
| Kuwait 143 | Poland 170 | |
| | Portugal 171 | Vanuatu 200 |
| Laos 144 | Puerto Rico 172 | Vatican City 201 |
| Lebanon 145 | | Venezuela 201 |
| Lesotho 145 | Qatar 172 | Vietnam 202 |
| Liberia 146 | | Virgin Islands, |
| Libya 147 | Réunion 173 | British 202 |
| Liechtenstein 147 | Romania 174 | Virgin Islands, United |
| Luxembourg 148 | Rwanda 174 | States 202 |
| | | |
| Macao 149 | St. Christopher and | Wake Island 203 |
| Madagascar 149 | Nevis 175 | Wallis and Futuna 203 |
| Madeira Islands 150 | St. Helena 176 | Western Sahara 203 |
| Malawi 150 | St. Lucia 176 | Western Samoa 203 |
| Malaysia 151 | St. Pierre and | |
| Maldives 151 | Miquelon 176 | Yemen 204 |
| Mali 152 | St. Vincent and the | Yemen, People's Democratic |
| Malta 152 | Grenadines 176 | Republic of 204 |
| Marshall Islands 153 | San Marino 177 | Yugoslavia 205 |
| Martinique 153 | Sao Tome and | |
| Mauritania 153 | Principe 177 | Zaire 205 |
| Mauritius 154 | Saudi Arabia 178 | Zambia 206 |
| Mayotte 154 | Senegal 179 | Zimbabwe 207 |

# HOT SPOTS: CURRENT EVENTS IN FOCUS

# Europe and the Soviet Union

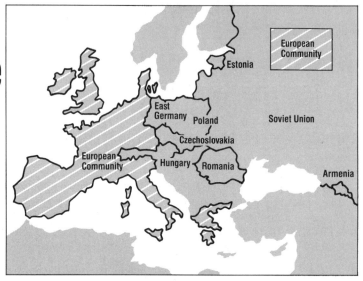

The end of the twentieth century will be remembered as a time when change came to Europe at a dizzying pace as new political and economic structures replaced the totalitarian Communist governments of Eastern Europe. These governments, as well as the partition of Europe, were legacies of the two World Wars that occurred in the first half of the 1900s.

These confrontations devastated much of the continent and ultimately divided Europe into East and West. While the Soviet Union controlled the countries of the East, the countries of Western Europe were allied to the United States, and Germany was partitioned between the two. The "cold war," an ideological and military standoff that saw massive military buildups and severe restrictions on communications, trade, and travel between the two sides, characterized European politics during this era. The nations of Eastern Europe evolved into Soviet-style, centralized Communist governments dominated by policies set by Moscow, while Western Europe maintained its capitalist systems; each bloc jealously guarded its sovereignty against outside influences.

By the late 1980s it became apparent that the cold war might be coming to an end as the nations of Europe shifted their priorities to the revitalization of their economies. Both the decentralized, capitalist countries and the centralized, socialist nations were suffering from maladies endemic to the world's developed nations—low growth rates, a decreasing standard of living, and an aging industrial base. While inflation, recession, and unemployment plagued the capitalist countries, the socialist countries suffered more from morale problems within the work force, which resulted in declining productivity and efficiency. Trade deficits became a major issue as light, high-technology industries developed in the United States, as well as in Japan and other Asian countries, and the world market was subsequently flooded with ingenious new electronic products which Europeans wanted to own but were not prepared to produce.

Ironically, each of the two opposing sides in the cold war looked to the other for a new direction in an attempt to dispel its economic woes. The West is moving towards centralization while the East is favoring decentralization; the West is experimenting with socialism while the East is opening the door to capitalism and democracy. Trade barriers are easing up, and it appears that the age of military buildup is coming to an end.

Western European centralization is taking shape as the European Community attempts to bridge centuries of national and economic rivalries to restore a common prosperity. By 1992, the twelve member nations of the European Community plan to remove all trade, enterprise, monetary, and mobility barriers and form a single economic unit, which will be governed by the European Council and European Parliament. Although the 1992 goal is to establish an economic unity, many European Community member nations endorse the concept of political union as well, while others, such as the United Kingdom, refuse to consider union in a supranational European state.

In an attempt to create a more equable society, Western European countries such as Sweden, France, and Greece have experimented with socialist programs with varying degrees of success. None of the countries of Western

Europe have used the Soviet model for development—a monolithic, centralized, single-party Communist state. Instead, socialists have risen up within the existing multi-party political framework and exerted their influence to enact socialist programs on an individual basis.

Following World War II, policies set by Moscow firmly governed the countries of Eastern Europe. They had learned the lessons of the Soviet military invasions of Hungary in 1956 and Czechoslovakia in 1968, following protests for reforms and increased personal freedoms. The Soviet Union, with its vast natural resources, supplied raw materials to the countries in Europe, which automatically returned manufactured goods to the Soviet Union. In turn, these countries were dependent on the Soviet Union and other Eastern European countries to satisfy the demand for consumer goods. This closed system, along with declining productivity, resulted in ever-increasing shortages in the entire Soviet bloc.

Like the countries of Eastern Europe, Soviet citizens learned to live with a repressive society that was plagued by shortages and poor quality goods. They were led to believe that a utopian socialist society could be achieved only through sacrifice and hard work. Hard work was exacted from the workers not by incentives as in capitalist systems, but rather through intimidation or group pressure.

A new age dawned when Mikhail Gorbachev rose to power in the Soviet Union. His program of restructuring, or "perestroika," was intended to decentralize some of the decision-making in the Soviet economy and encourage the development of privately-owned enterprise, or capitalism, particularly in the service sector. This revolutionary tactic was employed to stimulate growth, alleviate shortages, and provide individuals with more incentives to increase production and efficiency. In order to facilitate reform and perestroika, Gorbachev also implemented a policy of "glasnost," or openness, the purpose of which was to speed the reform process, stimulate creativity and personal initiative, and prepare the way for more decentralized decision-making. Glasnost has also resulted in greater personal freedoms, artistic expression, and access to information. Criticism of the economic system is not only tolerated but encouraged.

Within the Soviet Union, glasnost has had a profound effect, especially on the country's one hundred ethnic minorities who have for the first time been allowed to express their grievances about Soviet rule. New political parties founded along ethnic lines sprang up across the nation as various nationalities—such as the Estonians and Lithuanians—began to press for more autonomy and even independence. The glasnost policy has led to violence, however, as rising nationalism has renewed animosity between the Armenians and their Turkish rivals in neighboring Soviet Azerbaijan.

Another significant change in Soviet policy was the renunciation of the so-called "Brezhnev Doctrine," which asserted the Soviets' right to interfere in the affairs of other Communist countries. Accordingly, the Soviets began to withdraw their troops from many foreign countries, including the nations of Eastern Europe.

Cautiously at first, the countries of Eastern Europe began to test the limits of the new Soviet tolerance. Poland's Solidarity movement, led by Lech Walesa, prompted dire predictions of a Soviet invasion. When it became clear that the Soviet military was no longer a threat, reform movements and revolution began to spread across Eastern Europe like wildfire. In 1988 the Communists were firmly in control; by the end of 1989 all of the Communist governments had been either replaced or radically altered. Even the Soviet Union's powerful Communist party relinquished its strangle hold on the Soviet people by relinquishing its monopoly on power and establishing political pluralism.

Hungary's Communist government was the first to voluntarily enact reforms without pressure from a popular movement or leader. The government transformed itself from a centralized Communist regime to a Westernized socialist democracy in a little more than a year.

Perhaps the most dramatic event in 1989 was the demolition of the Berlin Wall after thousands of East Germans began a mass exodus to West Germany. Within two months after the destruction of the wall—perhaps the most potent symbol of Europe's partition—communism fell throughout the region. In Czechoslovakia, the change came relatively peacefully. In Romania, communism died only after thousands were killed. In Bulgaria, reform brought renewed ethnic tensions. By early 1990, all of the countries had restored basic personal freedoms and were moving toward establishing market economies and relations with the West.

Meanwhile, rumors continued to circulate about Gorbachev's possible political demise, even as he increased his power by assuming the powerful new role of executive president. While glasnost has changed the entire face of European politics, it has done little to bring peace and prosperity to his own country. Threatened with civil war and a stagnant economy, the man who changed the world in the 1980s continued to fight for his political survival.

# Soviet Union: Empire in Crisis

## Perspective

**1917**  Bolshevik Revolution brings Communists to power.

**1922**  Union of Soviet Socialist Republics is formed.

**1940**  Annexation of Baltic Republics and Moldavia ends territorial expansion.

**1985**  **March 11.** Mikhail Gorbachev is appointed general secretary of the Communist party.

**1988**  **February 28.** Armenians and Azerbaijanis clash, resulting in thirty-two deaths.
**November 16.** Estonians enact "Home Rule" legislation.

**1989**  **March 26.** New Parliament is elected.
**April 9.** Clash between police and demonstrators leaves twenty dead in Soviet Georgia.
**June 4.** Violence breaks out in Uzbekistan between rival ethnic groups.
**June 15.** Economic conditions prompt rioting in Kazakhstan.
**July 10.** Soviet miners' strike begins.
**September 8.** Ukrainian nationalist movement is formed.
**November 11.** In Moldavia, 140 are injured in riot.

**1990**  **January 15.** Renewed violence in Azerbaijan prompts Soviet invasion.
**February 7.** Communists give up monopoly on government.
**March 11.** Lithuania votes to secede from the Soviet Union.
**March 15.** Gorbachev assumes new post of executive president.

It could be a scene from Lebanon as opposing irregular militia—vigilantes, really—hurl insults and accusations across an enforced border zone. Sometimes their hatred bubbles over and rocks are thrown or shots are fired. Age-old religious and cultural differences have erupted into violence that has claimed the lives of more than 250 people. But it is not Beirut. It is the border region between the Soviet Socialist Republics of Armenia and Azerbaijan, just one of the many conflicts that threatens to tear apart the once-monolithic Soviet Union.

In Uzbekistan, mob violence has resulted in one hundred deaths and forced the evacuation of fifteen thousand Meskhetian Turks. In Kazakhstan, riots over food shortages have left several dead and scores injured. In Georgia, twenty were killed when soldiers wielding sharpened shovels and toxic gas attacked demonstrators, much to the chagrin of government officials. In Kazakhstan, food shortages and inflation prompted riots, which left several dead and many injured in the largest strike in the nation's history. The Baltic Republics continue to pass legislation to divorce themselves from Moscow's control. Independence movements in all of the republics continue to gain momentum.

All of this unrest resulted from a desperate attempt by Soviet leaders to breathe life into their moribund economy.

## Issues and Events

When Gorbachev came to power in 1985 he inherited a stagnating society. Decades of centralized planning had stifled creativity and inventiveness in the work force. Lack of incentives, inefficiency, and chronic alcoholism resulted in low productivity. An antiquated pricing system supported by massive subsidies contributed to a growing national debt. Consumers were plagued by chronic shortages while military expenditures soared.

To combat his society's many ills, Gorbachev has instituted radical changes that have shaken the very foundations of Soviet politics and society. While still firmly committed to a Leninist-Marxist socialist system, his program for "perestroika," or restructuring, has resulted in major changes in Soviet policy regarding industry, agriculture, and the role of government. Limited private enterprise has been introduced and centralized planning has given way to more individual decision-making. The Communist party has given up its monopoly on power and opened the door for political pluralism.

To facilitate restructuring, Gorbachev has also introduced a new policy of "glasnost," or openness, which has given Soviet citizens the opportunity to freely debate issues such as government policies and economic reforms. Constitutional changes provided for a new parliament, nominated and elected directly by the people as a forum for public discussion. In the spirit of glasnost, the government has eased up on foreign travel, religious worship, and freedom of the press.

Cautiously at first, people began to air their grievances and dissident groups began to spring up, each with its own agenda. Many of the Soviet Union's ethnic groups began to air their long-suppressed grievances against the Russians and other groups within the Union. Led by the Baltic states of Estonia and Lithuania, many republics demand the elevation of their national languages to official status.

Others want more economic or political autonomy, while the most radical agitate for complete independence. Groups who had suffered forced relocation by Stalin call for permission to return to their homelands. Ethnic rivalries and territorial disputes have erupted into violence. It is estimated that at least 450 people have died and many thousands have been wounded as a result of the new policy of openness.

Given that perestroika and glasnost were instituted to remedy the ailing Soviet economy, Gorbachev's programs have been less than successful. So far they have resulted in the worst of both Communism and capitalism—chronic shortages combined with inflation. Gorbachev claims that even more radical reform is needed, and that in his new role as executive president he will be able to force accelerated change.

Meanwhile the bonds of the Soviets' empire continue to weaken under the strain of the rising nationalism among the nation's one hundred or so different ethnic groups. The ruling Russians, who currently represent 51 percent of the population, are declining in numbers relative to most of the other groups. While they will remain the largest single group, the Russians will fall to 48 percent by the year 2000.

The challenge to Gorbachev is clear. He must somehow harness the energy released by glasnost and redirect it toward rebuilding the crippled economy. His policy so far of alternating stern warnings with the granting of concessions has met with limited success, and everyone agrees that if the economy does not soon show signs of improvement, Gorbachev may be in trouble. While the growing unrest may ultimately fracture the Union, a crackdown would mean a return to international isolation and further damage to the fragile economy.

## Background

The steady expansion of the Russian Empire began in earnest under Ivan the Terrible in the late 1500s. By the mid-1800s, expansion was essentially complete and the boundaries of the empire were similar to those recognized today. While most of the areas that comprised Russia were conquered militarily, others—such as Georgia and Armenia—voluntarily sought closer ties.

Due to the vast differences involved and the lack of modern communications, the Russians' influence in much of their empire was minimal until the Bolshevik Revolution in 1917 brought the Communists to power. Under the leadership of Vladimir Lenin, the state seized all private property, which resulted in a bitter civil war that lasted until 1922.

In 1922 the Union of Soviet Socialist Republics (USSR) consisted of six republics: Russia, Armenia, Azerbaijan, Byelorussia, Georgia, and the Ukraine. Turkmenia and Uzbekistan joined in 1924, followed by Tajikistan in 1929 and Kazakhstan and Kirgizia in 1936. Moldavia was integrated in 1940, along with the Baltic Republics. Each republic was formed to include people of similar ethnicity and language. The republics were then broken into smaller units in recognition of smaller ethnic groups.

Lenin advocated self-determination for all of the peoples of the old empire. After Lenin's death in 1924, Joseph Stalin put an end to this policy and extended the Union to its present size. Although the 1936 constitution guaranteed each republic the right to secede at any time, Stalin made it clear that this right would never be exercised. Stalin's purges in the 1930s and 1940s resulted in the deaths or forced relocation of those whose loyalty were questioned.

Under Stalin's policy, non-Russians were allowed to retain their language and folklore, but were expected to adopt Russian lifestyles. Russians have always occupied a disproportionate number of positions of power and have distributed themselves throughout the Soviet Union, while the other ethnic groups remain more confined to their homeland republics. The Russians have long inspired the resentment of minority ethnic groups, whom the Russians in turn regard with fear and suspicion.

Soviet founders believed that nationalism would disappear as the people became enlightened under Communist rule. The Stalinist system did not tolerate dissent, and the Soviets ruled their regime with an iron fist until Gorbachev came to power in 1985.

---

**Mikhail Sergeyevich Gorbachev** president of the Politburo and Communist party general secretary (1985- ). Born in 1931 in Stavropol province, son of a southern Russian peasant farmer ... attended Moscow University law school (1950-1955) ... worked in local politics (from 1952) before becoming first secretary of the Communist party in Stavropol (1970-1978) ... was admitted to full Central Committee membership (1971) ... was made secretary of agriculture (1978) by Leonid Brezhnev ... became a full member of the Politburo (1980) ... served as aide to Yuri Andropov (1982-1983) ... became the first executive president of the Soviet Union (1990).

# Estonia: The Flag Flies Again

## Perspective

|  |  |
|---|---|
| 1721 | Peter the Great captures the Baltic region. |
| 1920 | Soviet Union grants Estonia independence. |
| 1940 | **June.** Soviet Union invades Estonia. |
| 1987 | **August.** Estonians demonstrate against signing of secret Nazi-Soviet pact in 1939 that led to Russian invasion of Estonia. |
| 1988 | **January.** National Independence Party of Estonia is founded.<br>**March.** Leaders of National Independence Party are expelled to Sweden.<br>**July 6.** Flag of independent Estonia is restored.<br>**October 1.** Popular Front is formed.<br>**November 16.** Estonians enact "Home Rule" legislation. |
| 1989 | **January 18.** Estonia passes language law.<br>**July 27.** Soviet government authorizes economic independence in 1990.<br>**August 8.** Estonia passes voter residency requirements. |

Once again the blue, red, and white flag flown by Estonia during its brief period of independence is allowed to wave. Until glasnost came to Estonia, the flag was illegal. Its resurrection in 1988 has stirred up feelings of national pride among Estonians throughout the world. It has also brought renewed feelings of anger and bitterness toward the Soviet Union, which invaded Estonia in 1940 and has controlled it ever since.

## Issues and Events

Ethnic unrest is nothing new in Estonia. Estonians have long resented the Soviet occupation of their land. Even more important is the Estonian's fear of assimilation by the Russians, either through ever-increasing Soviet immigration to Estonia or through Soviet efforts to impose the Russian language and culture on Soviet minorities. Another source of friction between the two groups is what the Estonians refer to as their economic exploitation by the Russians. Food and high-quality goods produced in Estonia are sent to Moscow for distribution throughout the country, while low-quality goods are shipped back for sale in Estonia.

Since the introduction of glasnost, Estonian legislators have been busy enacting laws to create an autonomous, self-governing Estonia. In addition to legalizing the flag, they passed laws giving the Estonian language official status and establishing voter residency requirements. These nationalist laws have been bitterly protested by Russians living in Estonia who claim discrimination by the Estonians.

The most aggressive law was passed on November 16, 1988, which allows the Estonians to veto any laws that infringe on local jurisdiction. The Estonians have not yet tried to veto any Soviet laws, and Soviets have already declared the home rule and residency laws invalid.

Radical elements within the Popular Front have called for complete independence, and the Soviet government has hoped to defuse this movement by granting Estonia more autonomy. In 1990 Estonia was granted economic independence, including the freedom to establish a market economy and the right to control its own land and natural resources. Despite these efforts, it is probable that Estonia will follow the example of Lithuania by declaring its independence as a sovereign republic.

Gorbachev has made it clear that he is willing to compromise on any of the Estonians' current grievances regarding cultural and economic conditions. He is not, however, willing to discuss any past grievances about the Soviet invasion, nor will he consider any plan that would diminish the Soviet state.

## Background

Like its neighboring Soviet republics of Latvia and Lithuania, Estonia enjoyed only twenty years of independence during its long history. Danes conquered the territory in 1219 and sold it to the Teutonic Knights in 1346. The Swedes invaded in 1561 and held Estonia until its conquer by Peter the Great in 1721. Serfdom was practiced in the area until it was abolished in 1817. The 1800s also marked the growth of Estonian nationalism. Although the country gained its independence in 1920, freedom lasted only twenty years, until the Soviet invasion of 1940. After World War II, Estonia, Latvia, and Lithuania were made Soviet Socialist Republics.

Today there are approximately 1.1 million Estonians worldwide, one million of which live in the Soviet Union. Estonia's total population is 1,573,000.

The United States and other nations of the world do not recognize Soviet sovereignty in Estonia and the other Baltic states.

# Armenia: War with Azerbaijan

## Perspective

| | | |
|---|---|---|
| 1921 | **July.** | Nagorno-Karabakh region is awarded to Azerbaijan. |
| 1987 | **October.** | Street protests erupt in Nagorno-Karabakh. |
| 1988 | **February 20.** | Nagorno-Karabakh requests transfer to Armenian republic. |
| | **February 28.** | Soviet troops dispel anti-Armenian riot in Sumgait. |
| | **December 7.** | Twenty-five thousand are killed in Armenian earthquake. |
| 1989 | **January 8.** | Nagorno-Karabakh is placed under direct Soviet rule. |
| | **September.** | Azerbaijan blockades Armenia. |
| | **November 28.** | Nagorno-Karabakh is returned to Azerbaijan. |
| | **December 1.** | Armenia unilaterally annexes Nagorno-Karabakh. |
| 1990 | **January 16.** | Renewed violence prompts Soviet invasion. |

Throughout history the Armenian people have endured hardship and foreign rule. Numbering only 5.5 million, over 4.5 million now reside in the Soviet Union in the socialist republic of Armenia and the Armenian oblast of Nagorno-Karabakh in Azerbaijan. Despite seventy years of Soviet rule, they have retained a solid national identity and their own unique form of Christianity. The Soviets have served Armenian interests well by shielding them from their Turkic and Muslim neighbors to the south. In 1988, however, Soviet glasnost and growing nationalism contributed to the greatest civil unrest in the Soviet Union in recent history.

## Issues and Events

In October 1987, an Azerbaijani ruling banning Armenian history in the schools of Nagorno-Karabakh touched off massive demonstrations by Soviet Armenians. Glasnost allowed Armenians to air their many grievances regarding Azerbaijani policies to limit economic development and discourage the use of the Armenian language in the enclave. In February, the territory requested an administrative transfer to Armenia, but this move was quickly vetoed by the national government. Tensions continued to mount between the two groups and finally exploded on February 28 when Azerbaijanis killed 32 Armenians in Sumgait. Soviet troops were called in to stop the violence, which resulted in thirty-two deaths and 197 injuries. Continued violence resulted in more deaths, the imposition of emergency rule in the capitals of both republics, and a mass exodus of minority Armenians and Azerbaijanis to their homelands.

Gorbachev's efforts to defuse the growing hatred between the two groups were unsuccessful. In January 1989 the Soviet government placed Nagorno-Karabakh under direct rule, a move which angered both the Armenians and Azerbaijanis. In September Azerbaijan began a rail and road blockade of Armenia. Because 87 percent of Armenia's goods arrive through Azerbaijan, it wasn't long before vital supplies like fuel and food were in short supply. The blockade also effectively brought to a halt Armenia's efforts to rebuild areas devastated by the 1988 earthquake. The government returned Nagorno-Karabakh to Azerbaijan in November, and Armenia showed its outrage by unilaterally annexing the enclave a few days later. Enraged Azerbaijanis responded by killing more than sixty Armenians in renewed attacks in January 1990. Soviet troops were once again called in to restore the peace.

So far the growing violence has claimed more than 250 lives and there are reports that both sides are forming their own civilian militia. Gorbachev may be running out of time to negotiate peace before these ancient rivals launch a full-scale civil war.

## Background

Armenia emerged as a separate country in the first millennium B.C. It reached its greatest extent in the first century B.C. when it encompassed parts of present-day Turkey, Syria, Iraq, Iran, and the Soviet Union. In 301, Armenia became the first country to declare Christianity as its official state religion. After the late 300s, Armenia was successively conquered and divided by the Romans, Persians, Arabs, Mongols, and Turks. In 1828, the Russian Empire conquered the Persian-controlled section of Armenia. In 1915, the Turks began a systematic slaughter of Armenians in Turkish territory that resulted in one million deaths and mass emigration to Russian Armenia. After the Russian Revolution, Armenia formally became part of the Soviet Union, along with the Turkish republic of Azerbaijan.

The Armenian-dominated oblast of Nagorno-Karabakh was awarded to Azerbaijan in 1921 because existing transportation and other economic factors linked the territory to Azerbaijan rather than Armenia. Although the Soviets believed that nationalism would eventually disappear under Communist rule, the Armenians' hatred of the Turks and Azerbaijanis continues.

# Poland: Solidarity Takes Over

## Perspective

| | |
|---|---|
| *1944* | *Soviet forces drive out Germans.* |
| *1948* | *Stalinist regime is installed.* |
| *1956* | *Demonstrations lead to liberalized government under Wladyslaw Gomulka.* |
| *1970* | *Rioting topples Gomulka; Edward Gierek succeeds him.* |
| *1978* | *Pope John Paul II is elected the Vatican's first Polish pope.* |
| *1980* | *Strikes lead to formation of Solidarity.* |
| *1981* | *General Wojcieck Jaruzelski replaces Gierek as party leader; Solidarity is banned.* |
| *1983* | ***October.*** *Lech Walesa is awarded Nobel Peace Prize.* |
| *1988* | ***February.*** *Government's economic austerity program creates new wave of civil unrest.* |
| *1989* | ***April 5.*** *The government and Solidarity sign an agreement that outlines reforms.* <br> ***April 17.*** *Solidarity's legal status is restored.* <br> ***June.*** *Free elections result in sweeping victory for Solidarity.* <br> ***July 19.*** *Jaruzelski is elected president.* <br> ***August 24.*** *Solidarity's Tadeusz Mazowiecki is elected prime minister.* |

When Solidarity was banned in 1981, few could have imagined that in eight short years the renegade trade union would rise again to defeat the ruling Communists in free elections. Under the capable leadership of Lech Walesa, Solidarity managed to wrestle power away from the government, marking the first time that any Communist totalitarian government has peacefully relinquished control to democratic reformers. Remarkable as this feat may have been, a greater task lies ahead as Solidarity attempts to rebuild the shattered remains of an economy devastated by more than forty years of Communist rule.

## Issues and Events

Although the government managed to silence Solidarity in 1981, it could not combat the economic conditions that had prompted the union's formation. In 1988 austerity measures designed to reduce its $36 billion foreign debt aggravated the inflation and shortages already plaguing the Polish people. Demonstrations against the economic reforms began even before they went into effect and continued throughout the year.

By October it was obvious that the government's new plan was a dismal failure, as the economy continued to collapse. With the new era of "glasnost" in the Soviet Union, Polish leaders no longer feared intervention and decided to risk opening a dialogue with the still powerful Solidarity. On November 30, Lech Walesa was allowed to appear on television, uncensored, in a debate with the head of Poland's government-controlled, legal trade unions.

Leaders of the government, the party, the church, the trade unions, and Solidarity began a series of meetings in February 1989 to discuss Poland's future. Two months later they reached an agreement calling for sweeping changes, including new guarantees for freedom of the press and freedom to form unions. Political reforms included the creation of a bicameral legislature and a new office of the Presidency. The legal system was also revamped, allowing for a judicial branch independent of control by the Communist party.

June elections to the new legislature resulted in a sweeping victory for Solidarity. In the Sejm, or Parliament, Solidarity captured all of the seats it was allowed to contest, although the Communists were guaranteed 65 percent of the seats under the terms of the April agreement. In the Senate, where Solidarity was allowed to contest all of the seats, it won ninety-nine out of one hundred. Perhaps most embarrassing to the Communists was the defeat of their "national list" of thirty-five top candidates who ran unopposed for parliamentary seats. Only two of the thirty-five candidates received the required 50 percent of the vote to take office.

The new legislature then elected a president and prime minister. General Jaruzelski received a scant majority in his bid for the presidency, and was then able to push through the Communists' choice for prime minister. However, Jaruzelski's candidate was unable to form a cabinet and resigned less than a month later. On August 19, Tadeusz Mazowiecki, Lech Walesa's choice for the position, was elected to office and quickly formed a cabinet consisting of nine Solidarity members and four Communists.

Now firmly in power, Solidarity's task is to curb inflation of 100 percent, reduce the growing national debt, and ease the food and material shortages that plague consumers. Solidarity plans to implement a free market economy, but in the short term this will mean even higher prices, growing unemployment, and more shortages. Hoping to offset these problems, Solidarity will solicit foreign aid and investment and establish a system for unemployment compensation. Solidarity's long-term survival depends on its ability to bring about the change before the Polish people's patience wears thin. So far the food riots and strikes predicted by many have failed to materialize. It seems that the people are prepared to give Solidarity every chance to succeed.

## Background

Poland came under Communist control in 1944 after the Soviets drove the Germans back at the end of World War II. Under Soviet occupation, the government was Communist-dominated from the beginning, even though the party secretary, Wladyslaw Gomulka, advocated a "Polish road to socialism." For that, in fact, he was purged from the party in 1948, and Poland then became strictly Stalinist.

Following Stalin's death in 1953, the easing of various strictures led to greater demands from the populace, and massive demonstrations in 1956 led to a change in the government. Gomulka was recalled to the helm, and remained in charge for the next fourteen years, during which time things remained relatively calm. In 1970, as the economy slumped and the government imposed major price increases, workers in several cities took to the streets, holding demonstrations that led to rioting and a state of emergency. The disturbances were quelled, Gomulka was removed, and Edward Gierek became the party leader. The election of the Polish Karol Cardinal Ubjtyla to Pope in 1978 evoked a new spirit of nationalistic pride. In 1979, millions gathered to pay their respects to the new Pope John Paul II during his visit to his homeland.

When the government attempted to impose radical price increases during the following year, the citizens of Poland launched a series of protests—spearheaded by workers of the Lenin Shipyard in Gdansk under the leadership of electrician Lech Walesa. Striking and taking over the yard in the middle of August 1980, the workers of Gdansk were soon emulated by their comrades in other cities. Solidarity's quick success perhaps caught the government unaware. Within a year, the movement had attracted ten million members (out of a nation then of about thirty-six mil-

> **Lech Walesa** leader of the Polish Solidarity movement (1980- ). Born in 1943(?) in Popowo during World War II ... was fired from his job as an electrician in the Gdansk Shipyard after protesting rising food prices ... founded Solidarity (1980), an independent union to represent Polish workers, the only such organization in a Communist-bloc country ... received international acclaim as Solidarity gained power but was frequently imprisoned or under house arrest ... was arrested along with other union supporters when Solidarity was banned (1981) ... received the Nobel Peace Prize (1983) ... led Solidarity's rise to power (1989).

lion) and, unheard of in a Communist country, actually exercised the right of the workers to strike.

The birth of Solidarity soon brought down the government. Party leader Edward Gierek resigned in humiliation, and the party hierarchy floundered about in confusion and indecision. The Soviet Union leaned hard on the Polish United Workers' party to bring the situation under control. In 1981, General Wojcieck Jaruzelski, a career military man, gained leadership of the party as well as the government. When some impatient Solidarity leaders suggested a national referendum on the continued retention of communism itself, Jaruzelski immediately responded with a military crackdown in December 1981. Thousands of Solidarity members and supporters were arrested, the organization itself was banned and shut down, and Lech Walesa was arrested. After some eleven months of internment, Walesa was released and given back his job at the Lenin Shipyard in Gdansk. In 1986, all political prisoners were granted amnesty.

Martial law was suspended in December 1982, when most of the detainees still interned were released; martial law was formally lifted in July 1983. The government tried with limited success to build its own trade unions instead of those it had dissolved, but mass demonstrations continued on significant commemorative dates, and Solidarity lived underground. In October 1983, to the government's chagrin, Lech Walesa received the Nobel Peace Prize.

# Romania: Nowhere to Go But Up

## Perspective

| | |
|---|---|
| **1864** | *Serfs are emancipated.* |
| **1866** | *Romanian constitution is passed.* |
| **1878** | *Romania gains independence.* |
| **1907** | *Two hundred thousand are killed in a peasant uprising.* |
| **1916-1918** | *Romania enters World War I and doubles its territory.* |
| **1938** | *Royal dictatorship is established to combat growing fascism.* |
| **1939** | *Romania signs treaty with Germany.* |
| **1941** | *Romania invades Soviet Union.* |
| **1944** | *Soviet Union occupies Romania.* |
| **1947** | *Communist government is established.* |
| **1965** | *Nicolae Ceausescu rises to power.* |
| **1968** | *Romania denounces Soviet invasion of Czechoslovakia.* |
| **1980s** | *Severe austerity program results in serious shortages.* |
| **1987** | **November.** *Wave of strikes and protests is put down with mass arrests.* |
| **1988** | **March.** *Ceausescu announces plan to destroy eight thousand ethnic Hungarian villages in Romania.* |
| **1989** | **December 16.** *Demonstration is held in Timişoara in support of Hungarian rights activist.*<br>**December 17.** *Police open fire on demonstrators.*<br>**December 21.** *Riots spread to Bucharest.*<br>**December 23.** *Ceausescu is arrested after he attempts to flee.*<br>**December 25.** *Ceausescu and his wife are executed after a secret trial.*<br>**December 26.** *Ruling National Salvation Front names Ion Iliescu president.* |
| **1990** | **January.** *Demonstrations continue between pro- and antigovernment forces; elections are set for May; Communist party is banned.* |

The Romanian people have endured profound hardship since the early 1980s when their dictatorial leader, Nicolae Ceausescu, initiated an unbelievably severe austerity program to erase the country's foreign debt. Imports were reduced to next to nothing, while virtually everything the people produced was exported. For years the Romanians endured terrible shortages of food, fuel, electricity, and other necessities while Ceausescu lived a life of luxury.

During his twenty-two years in power, Ceausescu's regime became more and more repressive as he and his secret police increasingly intruded on every aspect of life. The media and travel were extremely restricted. Television was limited to a few hours a day. Permits were required to purchase typewriters. All foreign literature, including technical journals, was prohibited. Six and seven day work weeks were the norm. Birth control, sex education, and abortions were banned, and women were instructed to bear five children even though food was scarce. Ethnic groups such as Hungarians and Germans faced a growing threat from forced assimilation. Amnesty International continued to receive reports about torture in Romanian prisons. By the late 1980s, Romania was closed off from the world. For many years, fear of Ceausescu had kept the people under his control, but by 1989 their anger outweighed their fear. The Romanians had hit bottom and there was nowhere to go but up.

## Issues and Events

Despite its growing isolation, Romania hit the news in 1988 when Ceausescu announced a plan to destroy eight thousand villages in an effort to develop more agricultural land. The villagers, most of whom were of Hungarian descent, were to be reestablished in large, modern agri-industrial centers where they would supposedly enjoy a higher standard of living. Hungarians in Romania had long feared the government's continuing attempts to make them give up their language and lifestyle, and for many the plan was the final indignity. After more than thirteen thousand crossed into Hungary, word quickly spread about their plight. In 1989 the United Nations began an investigation of the program as international outrage grew. Anti-Romanian demonstrations began to take place in predominately Hungarian cities. Ultimately, one demonstration escalated into a revolution that overthrew the Ceausescu government.

Trouble began on December 16 when crowds gathered to prevent the arrest of the Reverend Laszlo Tokes, an outspoken advocate of human rights and Hungarian interests, in the city of Timişoara. By the next day the crowd had swelled to tens of thousands. Although the demonstration remained peaceful,

Ceausescu ordered his soldiers to open fire on the crowd. Hundreds—perhaps even thousands—were slain, but instead of stopping the protests, the government crackdown only ignited the people's passion. By December 21, the rioting had spread to the capital of Bucharest and the army was defecting to the side of the protestors. Ceausescu's security police continued to defend their leader even after his capture on December 23. The killing ended only after Ceausescu and his wife were tried, convicted, sentenced, and executed two days later. The entire revolution took only nine days, but resulted in the deaths of seven thousand people.

The country quickly established a new government consisting of a coalition of dissidents, intellectuals, and Communists. The ruling council appointed former Communist Ion Iliescu as president.

One of the new government's first acts was to unlock the warehouses of food and goods intended for export and deliver them to the nation's stores. It also turned up the heat and diverted more export-bound electricity to eager consumers. Television and print media restrictions were lifted and most of Ceausescu's repressive laws were quickly overturned.

Despite the immediate improvements, the political situation is far from stable. Elections originally scheduled for April were later postponed until May to allow new political parties more time to organize. The new government is still regarded with suspicion because many of its officials are former Communist party members. In mid-January Romania became the first Soviet bloc country to ban the Communist party, but passionate demonstrations both for and against the government continue.

Although Romanian industry and agriculture are backward by western standards, its economy is perhaps in better shape than its east European neighbors because Ceausescu's austerity program succeeded in eliminating Romania's foreign debt. Unfortunately, this economic stability was gained through tremendous sacrifice by the Romanian people. Nevertheless, it may be somewhat easier for Romania to attract foreign investment capital, provided that the political situation stabilizes.

## Background

The history of Romania has been marked by the continued repression of the peasant class. Neither the emancipation of the serfs nor a constitution enacted in the mid-1800s improved conditions for the peasants. Despite democratic laws, an aristocracy continued to rule the country and systematically excluded the peasants from the political process.

The first major peasant uprising occurred in 1907, when two thousand were killed for demanding better treatment by the landowners. Hungarian lands were brought under Romanian rule as a result of Romania's territorial conquests during World War I. Like the peasants, the new ethnic minorities were given little opportunity to participate in national affairs. Early attempts at land reform did not improve conditions in the countryside.

Growing fascism in the 1930s prompted the curtailment of democratic institutions in 1938. Romania sided with Germany against the Soviet Union in World War II and was ultimately defeated. The Soviets invaded Romania in August 1944 and established a Communist dictatorship in 1947. Again the peasants suffered when the Communists took their land during a drive for forced collectivization. Conditions improved somewhat after 1950 but Romania remained among the poorest nations in Europe.

By the early 1960s, the Romanian government had started a campaign to sever its economic and military ties with the Soviet Union. Nicolae Ceausescu rose to power during this period and established himself as a staunch nationalist. Romanian-Soviet relations were strained in 1968 when Romania refused to participate in the Warsaw Pact invasion of Czechoslovakia. During the 1970s, the Romanian government borrowed large amounts of money from the West to finance massive public works projects and monuments to Ceausescu's regime. By the early 1980s, Romania was having trouble meeting its loan payments. Ceausescu responded by implementing his notorious austerity program. Cold, hungry, and exhausted, the Romanians launched another major uprising in November 1986, and a wave of strikes and protests swept the country. Ceausescu responded with mass arrests.

Relations between the Romanians and their Hungarian minority have also been a source of tension in Romania. Hungarians, accounting for 8 percent of the total population, are Romania's second largest ethnic group. Rising Romanian nationalism in the 1960s and 1970s exacerbated preexisting tensions, so Ceausescu tried to force the Hungarians into the mainstream of Romanian society. Hungarian language educational programs and television were phased out, and Hungarian language literature was diminished. Hungarian names were not recognized, and christenings were banned for Hungarian children whose names had no Romanian equivalent. A 1988 plan to destroy eight thousand Hungarian villages was seen as yet another attempt to rob the Hungarians of their language and culture by immersing them in Romanian-dominated collectives.

# Czechoslovakia: Prague Spring Returns

## Perspective

| | |
|---|---|
| 1948 | Communists gain control of government. |
| 1968 | **January.** Reformer Alexander Dubcek is chosen as party chairman. **April.** "Prague Spring" reforms are enacted. **August.** Warsaw Pact invades Czechoslovakia. |
| 1969 | Dubcek is removed from office. |
| 1977 | Vaclav Havel and other dissidents draft Charter 77. |
| 1989 | **November 17.** Students protest for democracy and free elections; riot police injure hundreds. **November 19.** Thousands gather to protest police brutality; Civic Forum is formed. **November 24.** Alexander Dubcek addresses crowds in Prague; Communist leadership resigns. **November 29.** Communists relinquish one-party rule. **December 28.** Dubcek is elected chairman of parliament. **December 29.** Havel is elected president. |

When Soviet tanks rolled down the streets of Prague in 1968, the reform movement known as "Prague Spring" came to a dead halt. The reforms may have ended but the call for freedom was kept alive by dissidents like playwright Vaclav Havel, who spent the next twenty years in and out of jail protesting repressive government policies and Soviet domination. In 1989 a student protest sparked a revolt that eventually toppled the government and, in a dramatic reversal, brought Havel to power as the new president.

## Issues and Events

By 1989, student protests had become common in Czechoslovakia in the wake of the political changes that swept the Soviet Union and Eastern Europe. Riot police typically used tear gas and mass arrests to bring the growing crowds under control. The November 17 protest that sparked the revolution was not unusual until the police resorted to beatings, which resulted in hundreds of injuries.

On November 19, tens of thousands of outraged citizens gathered to protest the police brutality, and leaders of many anti-government groups converged to form the Civic Forum under the leadership of Havel. Mounting protests over the next few days spread across the country, and Alexander Dubcek returned from exile to address a half million people in Prague's Wenceslas Square. Some feared that the government might order martial law and open fire on the crowds. Instead, the heads of government yielded to the crowd's demands and resigned. Ultimately, the Communists were forced to give up one-party rule and agree to a new cabinet with a Communist minority. Dubcek was elected chairman of the parliament and Havel was named president.

Victory celebrations eventually gave way to the realities facing the new government. Elections were slated for early June and dozens of new political parties were legalized. Negotiations began with the Soviet Union concerning eventual Soviet troop withdrawal.

One of the biggest concerns is the future of the Communist party, which still maintains a majority in parliament. Many doubt that they will be able to adapt to the new demands of democracy and power sharing. The Communists fear persecution and reprisals as democracy takes root.

Ultimately, the reform movement will be a success only if the quality of life improves for the freedom-loving Czech people.

## Background

Czechoslovakia is the only nation in Eastern Europe that has firm democratic traditions. From its independence in 1918 until the German invasion in 1939, Czechoslovakia had an effective representative government.

After World War II, the Soviet Union set up a Stalinist Communist government. In April 1968, newly-appointed party chairman Alexander Dubcek initiated the Prague Spring reform plan. Prague Spring was remarkably similar to Soviet leader Mikhail Gorbachev's "perestroika," or restructuring, during the 1980s. It included more freedom of speech, multi-candidate elections, and economic reforms.

The reforms, as well as the enthusiastic response of the Czech people, frightened the Soviet Union. In August 1968, Warsaw Pact troops invaded Czechoslovakia and forced its leaders to sign a pact accepting Soviet occupation for an indefinite period. Dubcek was removed from office and banished to the countryside. In a sweeping purge, more than half a million people lost their jobs and Communist party membership. In 1977, several hundred dissidents organized Charter 77, a group whose manifesto called for improvements in civil rights. Vaclav Havel and other Charter 77 signatories were repeatedly the targets of government harassment and arrest.

# Hungary: Communism Bows Out

## Perspective

| | |
|---|---|
| 1947 | Communists seize power. |
| 1956 | Hungarians revolt against Stalinist repression; Soviets invade Hungary. |
| 1958 | Reform leader Imre Nagy is executed; Janos Kadar heads new conservative government. |
| 1988 | **May.** Communist party launches economic reform program; Kadar is replaced as head of party. |
| 1989 | **January.** Government agrees to enact more political and economic reforms.<br>**July 6.** Imre Nagy is officially vindicated.<br>**October 7.** Communist party disbands.<br>**October 17.** Modified constitution is unveiled. |

Throughout Eastern Europe, Communism has fallen in the wake of popular uprisings and economic decline. Hungary was a leader on the road to reform when the ruling Communist party introduced a Soviet-style program of economic restructuring in mid-1988. Later it became apparent to the Communists that reform could be achieved only by a complete break with the past. Rather than clinging to power until some opposition group grew strong enough to depose them, Hungary's pragmatic Communists chose to legislate themselves out of existence.

## Issues and Events

After the rebellion of 1956, the Hungarians learned to live with Soviet domination. When Soviet reforms seemed to indicate a changing political climate in Eastern Europe, the Hungarian government saw an opportunity to revitalize its beleaguered economy and improve its relations with the West. In May 1988, the ruling Communists announced plans to enact major economic reforms. When party chief Janos Kadar objected to the depth of the reforms, he was removed from office. In January 1989, plans to establish a multi-party political system were announced. The new system encouraged private enterprise and foreign investment, and the Communists sought out foreign business concerns to buy unprofitable state-owned enterprises.

For the Hungarian people, the most powerful sign of change came in the summer when Imre Nagy, the disgraced leader of the 1956 rebellion, was given a proper burial and restored as a national hero. More than two hundred thousand gathered to belatedly mourn his death and the deaths of all those who fought with him for freedom.

The Communist party, which numbered about eight hundred thousand, officially disbanded in October and then re-emerged as the Socialist party. The Socialists split into two factions, the ruling liberal group and another, more conservative group. Membership in both groups reached only 130,000, however, as most former Communists flocked to join one of fifty new political parties.

A modified constitution featuring basic human rights, separate branches of government, and free elections was unveiled in October. Parliamentary elections were scheduled for March 1990, and the country's first free referendum determined that presidential elections would be held sometime later.

Hungary's socialist leadership managed to remain in power only because it was able to adapt to the changing world. Unlike other Eastern European countries, Hungary has no organized opposition movement or charismatic leader to unite it. After the elections, the country will face the formidable task of merging its various factions to create a government that can lead the people into a new era of freedom and prosperity. Only tough austerity measures and popular support will bring the country out of its economic doldrums.

## Background

Communists seized power in Hungary following the Soviet invasion after World War II. The Soviets installed a dictator, Matyas Rakosi, who launched a program of Stalinist repression, forced collectivization, and purges. By 1953, the economy was a disaster, and the Soviets replaced Rakosi with Imre Nagy, a reformer. Nagy reversed Rakosi's agricultural and industrial policies until Rakosi again seized power in 1955. In July 1956, the Soviets exiled Rakosi but not before his repressive government sparked the ire of the Hungarian people. A student demonstration in October turned violent and led to a full-scale Soviet invasion. The Soviets reinstated Nagy in an attempt to pacify the people but the revolution continued. Ultimately, ten thousand people were killed and two hundred thousand fled the country before the Soviets crushed the insurrection. Nagy and hundreds of others were tried for treason and executed. Under the leadership of Janos Kadar, Stalinist collectivization and purges continued throughout the decade, but by the 1960s Kadar had evolved into one of Eastern Europe's more liberal leaders.

# East Germany: Reviving the German Question

## Perspective

| | |
|---|---|
| *1914* | Germany enters World War I. |
| *1919* | **June 28.** Treaty of Versailles inflicts severe hardship on Germany. |
| *1933* | Hitler establishes totalitarian dictatorship. |
| *1938* | **September.** Germany invades Poland; World War II begins. |
| *1945* | **May 8.** Germany surrenders; Allied forces divide Germany into occupation zones. |
| *1949* | German Democratic Republic (East Germany) and Federal Republic of Germany (West Germany) are formally established. |
| *1953* | **June 16.** East Berlin workers' uprising is suppressed by Soviets. |
| *1961* | **August.** Berlin Wall is built. |
| *1971* | Erich Honecker is named head of the Communist party. |
| *1972* | **November 8.** Basic Treaty provides for normalized relations between East and West Germany. |
| *1985* | **March 11.** Soviet Union's Mikhail Gorbachev rises to power and advocates reform in Eastern Europe. |
| *1989* | **September 10.** Hungary opens its borders to the West; three hundred thousand eventually escape.<br>**October 7.** Hundreds are injured by police during a demonstration in Leipzig.<br>**October 18.** Demonstrations continue; Egon Krenz replaces Honecker.<br>**November 7.** Protests continue; government leaders resign.<br>**November 9.** Berlin Wall and other borders are opened.<br>**December 1.** Communist party loses guarantee of power.<br>**December 3.** Egon Krenz resigns; leadership is eventually transferred to Prime Minister Hans Modrow.<br>**December 20.** Modrow and West Germany's Helmut Kohl meet to discuss reunification. |

November 9, 1989, will long be remembered by the German people. Many have said that on this day, the era marked by World War II officially came to an end when that most hated and tangible symbol of the cold war—the Berlin Wall—was finally opened. In the days immediately following the opening of the borders between East and West Germany, hundreds of thousands poured across the frontier and joined in a jubilant celebration.

As the rejoicing faded, Germans and the rest of the world turned to address the unresolved "German Question"—should the two Germanys once again join to form a single nation? Would a united Germany threaten European peace and stability?

## Issues and Events

Events in East Germany began to unfold in August 1989 when Germans vacationing in Hungary began escaping to West Germany through Hungary's more or less unguarded border with Austria. While Poland, Hungary, and Czechoslovakia were heeding the calls for reform issued by the Soviet Union's Mikhail Gorbachev, East Germany's Erich Honecker remained firmly committed to maintaining a Stalinist totalitarian government. On September 10, Hungary opened the border completely and thousands of Germans crossed to freedom. Because the West German government recognizes the unity of the German people, the refugees were welcomed and granted automatic citizenship.

Demonstrations began to take place throughout the country as East Germans called for free elections, freedom of the press, elimination of travel restrictions, and the dismantling of the hated secret police force. Hundreds were injured in Leipzig on October 7 when the police cracked down on ten thousand demonstrators. By November more than three hundred thousand had escaped to West Germany illegally and another two hundred thousand had crossed legally.

Ultimately the Communist government was forced to resign and give up its guarantee of power in East Germany. After the opening of the Berlin Wall, more than a million people crossed into the West, although all but a few returned to East Germany. Thousands of East Germans turned out to cheer West German Chancellor Helmut Kohl when he met with East Germany's new leader, Prime Minister Hans Modrow, to discuss the future of the two nations. High on the agenda was the issue of reunification.

West Germany has always favored reunification and this goal is specifically stated in its constitution. Kohl has presented a plan to the East Germans calling for a confederation leading to eventual reunification as early as the end of 1990. Kohl's proposal calls for the virtual abandonment of socialism before reunification could take place; East Germany would have to develop free markets, free elections, unrestricted foreign investment, and unlimited private enterprise.

In contrast, the East Germans abandoned their official goal of reunification when they rewrote their constitution in 1968. The protestors in East Germany sought an end to repression and the advancement of civil rights, but many remain firmly committed to socialism. Some fear that massive West German investment could turn them into a virtual colony of the West and that they would not benefit from the profits generated in their own country. Modrow reluctantly agreed to eventual reunification, although the details of the merger remain a serious concern.

The Soviet Union is especially sensitive about German reunification. The Russians suffered by far the worst casualties in the two world wars, which some argue were caused solely by German nationalism and expansionism. They lost almost six million in World War I and accounted for fifteen million of the forty million deaths during World War II. The Soviets argue that they have paid a high price for European peace and stability and would favor reunification only if Germany was completely demilitarized.

The United States position states that both sides would have to freely choose reunification, that the change would have to be gradual, and that Germany must relinquish all claims on Poland. The position of the European Community is similar to that of the United States, but they add their concern that West Germany must first meet its responsibilities concerning the establishment of a European common market in 1992.

It would seem that the world would have little to fear from a united Germany. With its powerhouse economy, West Germany has the most to gain from peace and stability, and the most to lose should war break out. In the meantime, almost eight hundred thousand NATO and Soviet troops are stationed in East and West Germany, with no plans for final withdrawal.

While the political partition of the two countries still remains, the separation of the German people has ended. For them, and for the world, it is the beginning of a new era as the cold war comes to an end.

## Background

Germany was not a single country until 1871 when the warring German states were united to form the German Empire. By 1890 Germany had become Europe's foremost industrial power.

In 1914, Germany joined with Austria against its rivals France and Britain during World War I. German forces overran France and Russia in a war that ultimately resulted in eight million deaths and twenty-one thousand injuries.

After Germany's defeat there was an attempt to establish a democratic government, but the country experienced economic collapse and political unrest due in part to the Treaty of Versailles. The treaty, signed in 1919, forced Germany to relinquish its African colonies, give up a substantial portion of its territory, disarm its military, pay for all war damages throughout Europe, and admit German guilt for starting the war.

Most historians agree that the harsh terms imposed by the Versailles Treaty were responsible for the conditions that led to Adolph Hitler's rise to power. Hitler's doctrine of nationalism and racism restored German pride and his increasing militarism improved the economy.

Hitler's plans to conquer Europe began with the annexation of Austria in March 1938. After taking over Czechoslovakia, Germany invaded Poland in September. Two days later France and Britain declared war and World War II was underway. Once again Germany invaded France and the Soviet Union and once again it was defeated only after enormous casualties had been inflicted.

After the war, Germany was divided into four zones; each was occupied by a different victorious Allied nation. The Russian zone, including East Berlin, eventually became the German Democratic Republic (East Germany). The Soviets established a Communist government based on the Soviet model. Meanwhile the American, British, and French portions and West Berlin were united to form the Federal Republic of Germany as a western-style democracy. The ensuing cold war, which began shortly after World War II, resulted in a break in relations between the two Germanys.

On June 16, 1953, thousands of East German workers demonstrated to protest high quotas and a deteriorating work environment. The Soviets quickly moved in to put down the disturbance, killing five hundred in the process. Disgruntled East Germans began migrating to West Germany in increasing numbers. By 1961, more than two thousand people per day were escaping to West Berlin and the estimated total number of emigrants approached two million. In an attempt to stem the tide, construction of the Berlin Wall began in August 1961. The Berlin Wall became a hated symbol of the cold war and almost two hundred East Germans were killed trying to overcome the almost impenetrable barrier. Relations between the two countries were nonexistent until 1972, when a treaty was signed to normalize them. In the late 1970s, improved relations between the United States and the Soviet Union resulted in increased travel, communications, and trade between East and West Germany.

# European Community: Establishing a Single Market Economy

## Perspective

| | |
|---|---|
| **1951** | Belgium, France, Italy, Luxembourg, Netherlands, and West Germany sign treaty in Paris, establishing European Coal and Steel Community (ECSC). |
| **1957** | ECSC countries sign treaties in Rome, creating European Economic Community (EEC), or Common Market, and European Atomic Energy Community (EURATOM). |
| **1961** | Denmark, Ireland, and United Kingdom begin negotiations for admittance to EEC. |
| **1967** | The EEC, ECSC, and EURATOM merge into the European Community (EC). |
| **1973** | Denmark, Ireland, and United Kingdom are admitted to EC. |
| **1981** | Greece becomes active member of European community. |
| **1985** | The European Council announces a deadline of 1992 for an internal market without frontiers. |
| **1986** | Spain and Portugal become the eleventh and twelfth members of the European Community. |
| **1987** | The Single European Act is ratified by all member nations. |

In 1985 the twelve member nations of the European Community approved a plan to bring to fruition the vision of the organization's founders in 1957. This plan, which was affirmed with the approval of the Single European Act in 1987, calls for the elimination of all barriers to free trade and enterprise among the member states. If the plan is successful, by the end of 1992 the European Community will emerge as a new economic superpower to rival the United States and Japan. As a result, trade relations with the United States in particular have become increasingly strained as the European nations begin to speak with one voice.

## Issues and Events

The 1985 White Paper on market reform that launched the unification effort called for the elimination of trade barriers and tariffs among member states; the free flow of manpower and capital from one country to another; the standardization of technical and academic qualifications; the harmonization of excise duties and value added tax (VAT) rates; and the development of a European monetary system. It is also hoped that by improving transportation and communications, as well as reducing business inefficiencies and monopolies within individual countries, new competition will result in increased efficiency, lower prices, and higher profits.

In order to accomplish these tasks, all of the twelve member nations were required to approve in principal more than three hundred legislative clauses that outlined the reform program in the Single European Act. This was accomplished by July 1987. Although there is agreement in theory, heated negotiations to hammer out specifics continue. One of the most controversial issues centers around standardizing the value added tax (VAT)—the European Community's main source of revenue, which is comprised of a percentage of the value of manufactured goods produced in each country. The rates currently vary widely among member states and severe protests from Ireland and Denmark allowed the passage of a standardization scheme only when a provision was made for member governments to opt for certain exemptions from the plan. Also at issue have been regional economic differences between the industrialized north and the agrarian south. The wealthier nations, such as France and West Germany, have agreed to pay billions of dollars to their southern neighbors, who may not benefit as much from reforms.

With the adoption of these reforms, the European Community's 325 million people will become the world's largest trading block. European Community business people are particularly excited about the new opportunities that lie ahead. The wave of mergers and takeovers that has swept the continent—a threefold increase between 1983 and 1987—shows a readiness to take advantage of the changes. It is expected that Europe will enjoy lower costs and prices, millions of new jobs, and an anticipated 4 to 6 percent increase in Gross Domestic Product (GDP).

Others are not as happy about European Community reforms. Over sixty-six former European colonies fear that preferential trade relationships established on the basis of historical ties will be jeopardized as a more unified trade policy is molded. The Italians, for example, protect Somali bananas while the British protect bananas from former Caribbean colonies. These developing countries also fear competition from within the European Community from its newest member states—Greece, Spain, and Portugal—where tropical agricultural products are grown.

Relations between the European Community and the United States have become increasingly strained since Spain's admission in January 1986. The United States claimed that European Community import quotas resulted in the loss of $600 million annually in grain sales to Spain, which formerly obtained half of its grain exports from the United States. In response, the United States imposed retaliatory duties on wine, beer, chocolate, cheese, and other products from the European Community. In January 1987, an agreement was reached that allowed for increased United States exports to Spain.

Another issue was the "pasta war" between 1986 and 1987, which involved a dispute over European pasta sales to the United States. The United States claimed that European Community subsidies to pasta exporters allowed the European Community products to undercut United States pasta on its wholesale markets. The United States originally demanded that the European Community reduce the pasta subsidy by 50 percent, but an agreement reached in August 1987 allowed for a reduction of only 27.5 percent.

The latest battle began in January 1989, when the European Community effectively banned all United States beef imports. The ban resulted from a new European Community regulation prohibiting importations of meat treated with growth hormones, affecting virtually all of the $130 million annual United States beef exports to the European Community. The United States responded by imposing a 100 percent tariff on European food exports, including Danish hams, French cheeses, and Italian tomatoes. While the Europeans argue that the ban is not protectionist (a measure to block United States beef imports to protect European Community beef producers), the United States fears that more such rules will discriminate against American exports as the European Community nears its 1992 deadline.

Not all of the resistance to economic integration comes from outside the European Community. Forces within the European Community fear that the resulting mobility and communications may have a homogenizing effect that could ultimately threaten Europe's long-established cultural and linguistic patterns. Great Britain's Margaret Thatcher continues to protest the more radical concepts of establishing a single currency or forming a political union. Others fear that East and West German economic reintegration will upset the European Community's delicate power balance and delay the merger.

Although only forty percent of the targeted three hundred decisions had been reached by mid-1989, it seems that a certain momentum has been achieved, making it likely that the 1992 deadline will be met and that Europe will then step to the forefront of the world's economic arena.

## Background

In the years following World War II, there developed in Western Europe a federalist movement of considerable strength, the members of which dreamed not only of economic cooperation but of a political union—a kind of United States of Europe.

On April 18, 1951, six nations—Belgium, France, Italy, Luxembourg, the Netherlands, and West Germany—signed a treaty establishing the European Coal and Steel Community (ECSC), the success of which led to further integration, such as the European Economic Community (EEC) and the European Atomic Energy Community (EURATOM) in 1958.

As the benefits of the EEC, or Common Market, to the six nations became apparent, other European nations wanted to join. Even the nationalist United Kingdom changed its mind and applied for membership in the EEC. As negotiations on the terms of entry were underway in January 1963, however, a veto by President Charles de Gaulle of France abruptly terminated the process. Although de Gaulle's action was directly aimed at the United Kingdom, which he saw as too servile to the United States, his veto effectively postponed any enlargement of the community, as it also blocked the entrance of Denmark, Ireland, and Norway.

In 1967, the EEC was formally consolidated with the ECSC and EURATOM; the collective name for all three groups became the European Community (EC).

After de Gaulle's retirement in 1969, the European Community began to expand. Great Britain, Ireland, and Denmark joined in 1973, Greece joined in 1981, and Spain and Portugal joined in 1986. Its purpose was to integrate the economies of Western Europe by gradually eliminating tariff barriers and by establishing common price levels and monetary union. Despite the at times acrimonious disputes in which the member nations have indulged, the Common Market is generally considered to be a resounding success, and much of the economic growth of Western Europe in the 1960s and 1970s can be attributed to the union.

The ruling body of the European Community is the European Council, which consists of the heads of government of the member nations and meets on a regular basis, usually three times a year. The European Parliament is the legislative branch. Although its members are popularly elected by the voters of the member nations, it has little actual power. The European Court of Justice renders judgments of disputes that arise among member nations.

# North America

Since the mid 1800s, the United States has played a dominant role in shaping the political and economic landscape of the North American continent. Although the nations of Central America are linked to their neighbors in the Southern Hemisphere by culture, language, and history, the United States has had a profound effect on their development, and has long considered Central America to be within its sphere of influence.

The policy of United States intervention in Central American affairs had its genesis with the Monroe Doctrine of 1823, when President James Monroe stated that no further European colonization or intervention in the New World would be tolerated. The statement was made primarily to warn Spain not to try to recapture any of its newly independent colonies and also to ward off further Russian expansion in Alaska.

The United States' first military action in Central America took place in 1846 during the Mexican-American War over the territory of Texas. Over twenty-one thousand were killed in the fighting, which resulted in an American victory and Mexico's loss of nearly half its territory. By 1860, the United States had entered a period of isolationism that lasted until 1889. During this year, the United States announced a new "good neighbor" policy, calling for political and military alliance among all of the nations in the Western Hemisphere. The year 1898 saw the beginning of the Spanish-American War and the transfer of Puerto Rico to American sovereignty. In 1899, an American entrepreneur founded the United Fruit Company, initiating an era of economic domination of Central America by United States interests. Within a short time, the company had acquired vast tracts of land for its banana plantations. Although the host countries initially benefited from the construction of new railroads and shipping facilities, the profits of these operations went to stockholders in the United States and proved to be a drain on the local economies.

In 1903, an agreement was reached to build the Panama Canal, which opened in 1914. Growing American interests in the area prompted the adoption of the Roosevelt Corollary of the Monroe Doctrine, stating United States intentions to exercise international police power in Latin America and effectively placing the entire region under United States military authority. Between 1904 and 1933, the United States repeatedly sent troops to the Dominican Republic, Cuba, Honduras, Nicaragua, and Haiti. Troops were sent to Mexico in 1914 after the Mexican Revolution and again in 1916 to try to capture Pancho Villa.

By the 1930s, the countries of Central America began to resent the United States intervention in their internal affairs, and America renounced the Roosevelt Corollary. After World War II, the "good neighbor" policy was reintroduced and prompted the founding of the Organization of American States (OAS), designed to establish cooperation and create a defensive alliance. Throughout the 1950s and 1960s, the United Fruit Company experienced decline as more and more of its land was nationalized by host governments. In 1959, Cuba nationalized American sugar interests, which led to an embargo and break in diplomatic relations in 1960. In 1961, Castro's communist government came to power, resulting in United States pressure on the OAS to expel Cuba. Cuba turned to the Soviet Union for economic assistance, a move that further infuriated the United States and led to the Cuban missile crisis of 1962. After the Cuban revolution, the United States generally tried to back right-wing or military governments in an effort to prevent any further Communist takeovers.

During the years of the Reagan administration, intervention in Central America increased as leftist factions in Nicaragua and El Salvador gained strength. Despite a massive outpouring of military and economic aid to the preferred right-wing factions, however, the United States had little effect in El Salvador, where the political situation remains unstable. In late 1989, President Bush authorized a military invasion of Panama. The country's dictator, Manuel Noriega, was arrested for his involvement in international drug smuggling. In Nicaragua, Daniel Ortega's leftist government was voted out in free elections in favor of United States-backed Violeta Chamorro.

Relations between Mexico and the United States have been strained repeatedly over the issues of drug traffic, the environment, and trade. Despite this, the two countries enjoy substantial foreign exchange, and tourists from the United States provide Mexico with additional revenues.

The biggest problem facing the United States and Mexico in the 1980s has been the issue of illegal immigration to the United States. In 1983, it was believed that between two and six million illegal aliens were living in the United States, and more than half of them were believed to be Mexicans. The United States steadily increased border patrols, stating that Mexican workers steal jobs from American workers and place a strain on social services, especially education. Agricultural organizations in Mexico and the United States argued that Mexican laborers perform a valuable function by taking low level jobs that Americans don't want. In 1986, the United States passed the Immigration Reform and Control Act, which threatened United States employers with fines for employing illegals and offered amnesty to three million illegals who could prove that they had been in the United States since 1981. The Mexican government denounced the passage of the act as racist and repressive although, in fact, Mexican leaders were probably more concerned that a crackdown on illegals would result in a loss of foreign exchange. Many illegals send back most of their wages to Mexico, and the country can ill afford to lose any of its revenues in this time of economic crisis. Enforcement of the law has been difficult, as illegals now arm themselves with forged papers to prove their legal status.

Mexican authorities are also angry about a new United States policy regarding immigrants from other Central American countries. During the 1980s, many refugees from war-torn El Salvador and Nicaragua fled to the United States to seek political asylum. In February 1989, the United States enacted legislation to tighten the standards for granting asylum. Many Nicaraguans and Salvadorans, fearing extradition under the new policy, are waiting in Mexico for an opportunity to enter illegally, or for the policy to change. Mexico is angry about its increased refugee burden and has also denounced President Bush's references to the possible employment of troops at the border to stem the drug traffic. Perhaps nothing will be able to stop the flow of people across the border as long as economic inequities between the two countries exist.

While the United States' relations with Canada have been more peaceful than those with nations to the south, the Canadians still are wary of their American neighbors. Canada has always enjoyed the protection of the United Kingdom and has not had to worry about United States hegemony. Despite a long and fruitful trade relationship, many Canadians regard Americans with suspicion, as illustrated during negotiations in the United States-Canada free-trade agreement, which took effect in January 1989. The agreement sought to formalize their trade relationship and reduce costs for both countries, increasing competitiveness and productivity. Although about 70 percent of the trade between Canada and the United Sates is already duty free, the trade pact called for the elimination of all remaining barriers by 1999. The bill prompted a nationalist movement among Canadians who feared United States economic and cultural domination. Many were also afraid that Canada's extensive social welfare system would suffer because higher minimum wages in Canada result in higher prices. Free trade, it is believed, might prompt government leaders to lower wages and standards to face the new competition from the United States. In addition, the Canadian government currently requires that all manufacturing firms that market in Canada must also build in Canada. As many as 40 percent of all factories in Canada are United States owned, and it is feared that most will return to the United States after this ruling is eliminated. There has also been discussion of the creation of a North American Common Market, including Mexico, to counteract adverse effects from the merging of the European Community market in 1992. Mexico has so far expressed little interest in such a union, as it fears further economic dependence on the United States.

# The United States: War on Drugs

## Perspective

| | |
|---|---|
| **1900** | Addiction to opium is recognized as a problem. |
| **1906** | Pure Food and Drug Act is passed. |
| **1914** | Harrison Anti-Narcotic Act makes unauthorized opium use a crime. |
| **1920** | 18th Amendment prohibits sale and manufacture of alcoholic beverages. |
| **1930** | Bureau of Narcotics is established; propaganda campaign is launched to combat growing use of cocaine and marijuana. |
| **1933** | Prohibition is repealed. |
| **1960s** | Increased use of marijuana ushers in a new era of drug abuse. |
| **1966** | Drug Abuse Control Amendment expands definition of illegal drugs. |
| **1970** | Comprehensive Drug Abuse Prevention and Control Act emphasizes penalties for drug sales and softens penalties for users. |
| **1972** | President Nixon declares war on drugs. |
| **1979** | Overall illegal drug use peaks. |
| **1983** | Crack cocaine makes its debut. |
| **1988** | **November.** Anti-Drug Use Bill increases penalties for users. |
| **1989** | **March.** William Bennett is appointed "drug czar." **September.** President Bush unveils National Drug Control Strategy. **December.** United States troops invade Panama to arrest dictator Manuel Noriega for drug smuggling. |
| **1990** | **February.** Presidents of Bolivia, Colombia, Peru, and the United States meet in Colombia to discuss cocaine trafficking. |

According to recent polls, more than half of all Americans consider drug abuse to be the most serious problem facing the United States today. More than twenty million people spent $100 billion on illegal drugs in 1988.

Unlike heroin, which was used mainly by the urban poor, the cocaine addiction of the 1980s penetrated all layers of society. This was underscored by the arrest of Washington, D.C. mayor Marion Barry on cocaine charges in January 1990. Drug abuse affects 6 to 15 percent of the labor force and costs businesses an additional $100 billion in absenteeism, medical expenses, and lost productivity. To facilitate the lucrative drug trade, violent new gangs have sprung up and staked out their territories. It is estimated that 50 to 80 percent of all crimes are drug-related. Medical facilities are filled with victims of drug-related violence and overdose, babies addicted from birth, and addicts who have contracted AIDS.

President Bush declared war on drugs soon after taking office in 1989. While some progress has been made, most believe that this is a war that cannot be won without tremendous sacrifices in terms of both money and precious civil liberties.

## Issues and Events

The president outlined his plans to combat drug abuse shortly after taking office. Like his predecessor Ronald Reagan, Bush endorsed expansion of treatment facilities and educational programs, stiffer penalties for drug users, and an emphasis on interdiction (curtailing the flow of illegal drugs). In addition, Bush favored increased use of the military and appointed William Bennett as the Director of the National Drug Control Policy. In his role as "drug czar," Bennett is responsible for coordinating the drug enforcement activities of more than thirty federal agencies. In January 1990, Bush requested $10.5 billion to fight drug abuse, 70 percent of which would go for enforcement and interdiction while 30 percent would be devoted to treatment and prevention.

Bennett asserts that he is winning his war against drugs because drug use is declining while arrests and seizures are rising. Critics argue that overall use has been dropping steadily since 1979 and that most of the decline has been among middle and upper class users, while addiction continues to spread among the poor and disadvantaged. Crime statistics remain high despite soaring arrests, which have created serious overcrowding in the prisons and courts. Civil liberties are jeopardized by drug testing, random searches, suspect profiles, and property seizures. While more drugs have been confiscated, it is believed that only 5 to 7 percent of the drugs smuggled into the country are intercepted by authorities.

Treatment facilities are sadly lacking. The cost of treatment is high—as much as $15,000 annually per person—and the success rate is less than 50 percent. Education has been a more effective tactic. While drug use was regarded as a "victimless crime" during the 1960s and 1970s, it is increasingly viewed as a crime against American culture. Even casual users are perceived as guilty of supporting a criminal network that thrives on murder and corruption.

The Bush administration has made the

eradication of illegal drug trafficking a major priority in foreign policy. Most notable was the invasion of Panama in 1989 to arrest dictator Manuel Noriega for his involvement in drug smuggling. The Bush administration has been working closely with the leaders of Bolivia, Colombia, and Peru to stop the flow of cocaine into the United States. At the February 1990 drug summit in Colombia, Bush promised billions of dollars in aid to the three countries over the next five years. He also promised to provide law enforcement training, control the export of chemicals needed to process cocaine, restrict the flow of weapons to guerrillas and drug dealers, and help Peru and Bolivia develop alternative crops.

In exchange, the three countries demanded that the United States double its efforts to reduce the demand for cocaine, which amounts to an estimated four hundred to seven hundred tons per year. The United States was also urged to consider the consequences if efforts to curtail the drug trade prove successful. The Americans' appetite for drugs has had an impact on the lives of millions of people throughout the world who grow, process, and distribute drugs. In Colombia, Bolivia, and Peru, the economic consequences would include mass unemployment, rural to urban migration, and general economic malaise. Politically, there is the threat of anti-democratic movements that would undoubtedly gain strength in the wake of economic instability. The United States, they argue, should be prepared to provide economic assistance to enable them to shift away from drug-based economics.

Some argue that the only way the drug war can be won is by legalizing and regulating drug usage. They contend that the money currently spent on enforcement could be diverted to treatment and prevention programs. Critics of this approach point to the rampant alcoholism that resulted after the Prohibition era as an indication of what would happen if drugs were legalized. There are about five times as many alcoholics as drug addicts, and a full 61 percent of the population are regular alcohol users, compared to less than 10 percent who use drugs. For every death from illegal drugs, one hundred die from the effects of alcohol and cigarettes. Until Americans decide to give up the drug habit, the war will not be won.

## Background

Drug abuse has been a problem in the United States since the mid-1800s, when an explosion of new chemicals revolutionized the field of medicine. Each new drug was heralded as a miracle cure for just about everything. Only after years of overuse were the drawbacks of unrestrained usage identified. Drugs were completely unregulated and could easily be obtained in patent medicine, candy, drinks, or cigars. Americans became dependent on drugs to cure their physical, emotional, and spiritual ills.

The opiates, or true narcotics, was the first class of drugs recognized as a problem in the United States. The earliest opium users were Chinese immigrants, who smoked the drug, and the upper classes, who received it from their physicians. Use expanded throughout society by the mid-1800s, when morphine was first derived from opium and the hypodermic needle was invented. By the turn of the century, addiction was identified as a problem—as many as two hundred thousand were addicted to opiates. Heroin, a more potent form of morphine, was also developed during this period but did not gain widespread legitimate use. Cocaine, introduced as one of many treatments for opium addiction, was also widely available in the 1800s.

The first effort by the United States to regulate the proliferation of drugs was the passage of the Pure Food and Drug Act in 1906. The first law prohibiting unauthorized drug use was the Harrison Anti-Narcotic Act of 1914, which forbade the use of opiates and cocaine except by prescription.

In 1920 alcohol was banned, and with the Prohibition era came sophisticated networks for the sale of illegal substances of all kinds. Crime rose as competing factions sought control over larger market shares. The government fought the illegal drug traffic by banning all use of heroin, establishing the Bureau of Narcotics to control smuggling, and launching a massive propaganda campaign to discourage drug use. It used another tactic to fight the illegal alcohol trade: Prohibition was abolished in 1933 and alcohol was again legalized.

Illegal drug use rose sharply in the 1960s, as young people began to smoke marijuana and take new drugs such as LSD, mescaline, stimulants, and depressants. In 1966 the Drug Abuse Control Amendment was passed to include the new drugs in existing anti-narcotics legislation, although penalties for marijuana use were set at the state level.

President Nixon began a war on drugs in the early 1970s that emphasized harsher penalties for drug traffickers. Drug use continued to rise throughout the decade, and use of heroin and hallucinogens peaked around 1975. Overall drug and alcohol use peaked around 1979.

President Carter tried to eliminate the marijuana problem by eradicating fields in Mexico with paraquat, a powerful herbicide. As a result, Colombia became the major United States source for marijuana. Colombian traffickers soon began to further exploit the United States appetite for illegal drugs by refining and smuggling cocaine. Once available only to the rich, cocaine became the poor people's drug choice after the 1983 invention of crack, a cheap and highly addictive form of the drug.

# Latin America

The Latin American republics have often been characterized by political instability. The military plays an important part in their political life, and civilian governments frequently rule only with military approval. Popularly elected democratic governments are often overthrown and replaced by military juntas. The imprisonment or exile of political leaders fallen from power, as well as assassination by political opponents, is commonplace, while citizens' civil liberties are often violated.

In many Latin American countries there is dramatic economic polarity: a political elite who enjoys luxury and privilege, contrasted with oppressed masses who survive in the most dire poverty. This large, underprivileged majority has often been systematically exploited by a succession of rulers interested only in personal wealth and power; ironically, many of the poor are nearly apolitical; their main concern is day-to-day survival for themselves and their families, rather than political organization.

The patterns of inequity in Latin America's wealth distribution were set down hundreds of years ago, during the region's colonial period, and the situation in modern Latin America is partly a result of European colonial influences upon an indigenous population.

The dominant colonial power in South America was Spain, although Portugal, the Netherlands, Britain, and France also acquired possessions in the area. Portugal's influence is evidenced in Brazil, where Portuguese is the predominant language.

Prior to the arrival of the Europeans around the sixteenth century, various Indian peoples inhabited the region. Among these were the Incas, whose sophisticated civilization flourished in the areas of present-day Ecuador, Peru, and Bolivia.

The first major wave of European settlement occurred in the 1500s with the arrival of the Spanish conquistadors. The resistance offered by most Indian groups was ineffectual and Indian lands quickly fell to the invaders.

Many of the early settlers were drawn to South America by the promise of wealth. As word of the continent's natural riches spread back to Europe, fortune-seeking colonists flocked to the region. Oftentimes the promise of gold and silver remained unfulfilled, but most settlers stayed on, establishing large plantations that laid the basis for much of South America's present economy. The colonists took the conquered Indians as slaves to work their farmlands, and soon a thriving agriculture was established.

Much of the indigenous population disappeared during the colonial period. Wars with the settlers, labor-intensive plantations, and exposure to European diseases claimed thousands of Indian lives. In addition, many of the Indians who managed to survive intermarried with the Europeans. Modern South America's large mestizo population, of mixed Spanish and Indian blood, is a result of these relationships.

As the Indians were decimated by colonial rule, blacks were brought from Africa to continue slave labor on the plantations. Development increased, and the descendants of the early settlers soon established a unique South American culture, combining influences of their ancestors into a life-style evolved from the plantation economy. Many of the remaining Indians continued their traditional way of life, however, and remained far from the centers of development, unaffected by the waves of change.

Prosperity continued, and in time the large-estate holders, many of them mestizos, found themselves wielding economic influence but enjoying few of the benefits of their profits. Native-born South Americans of Spanish descent were equally dissatisfied with colonial status. Political power remained in the hands of the mother country, whose people and government now had little in common with South American life. Resentment toward the ruling powers grew, along with the colonies' demands for a voice in their government.

Politically, the region was unstable following independence. It was a class that already possessed a certain amount of influence that won the fight for self-rule during the 1800s and the change in government only shifted power from the European rulers to South Americans of economic dominance. Thus the change in leadership did not bring beneficial reforms to the many people outside the small circle of those with economic influence. Dissent and upheaval often resulted; civilian governments alternated with military rule, power shifted from party to party, yet many remained impoverished.

Economically, however, the newly independent nations continued to develop, concentrating the wealth more solidly in the hands of the few. Foreign investment increased as well, and immigrants came from Europe and other parts of the world, though this made it difficult to institute significant reform and dismantle the oligarchic system of the past.

Great inequities in the distribution of wealth have led to the emergence of Marxist movements throughout the region. In Cuba, and more recently in Nicaragua, these leftist groups have taken over and attempted to establish more equitable economic systems with varying degrees of success. The struggle between leftist and right-wing elements in El Salvador is literally tearing the country apart as the moderate government attempts, without much success, to neutralize the two groups.

Political stability remains an important goal of the South American nations. Argentina has been governed by a series of military or civilian dictatorships over the years, the most stable of which was that of Juan Perón. Unlike most such governments, the influence of the Perón regime continued after the death of Perón himself. His widow, Isabel Perón, succeeded him to the presidency; and even after she was ousted, the strength of the Peronistas was such that their opponents thought it necessary to force her into exile. It was one of the series of post-Perón juntas that instigated the Falklands War in 1982. Argentina's defeat in that confrontation with Great Britain resulted in the fall of the junta and the eventual installation of a democratically elected government.

While Argentina has enjoyed a certain amount of political reform and stability since the demise of its military government, the country of Haiti has yet to experience democracy since the overthrow of the repressive Duvalier regime. In 1988, Haiti saw its newly elected government fall to a military coup, whose leader was in turn deposed by a rival military faction. Civilians regained control in 1990 after public outcry resulted in his resignation.

Colombia, the South American country with perhaps the strongest tradition of democracy, found itself in a new kind of war in the 1980s: a war against international drug traffickers. Pressure from the United States in particular has forced the Colombian government to use a strong hand against the international traffickers who process cocaine in Colombia and then sell it all over the world, primarily to the United States. The cocaine trade generates such huge profits, however, that corruption of government officials and law-enforcement personnel threatens government stability. Panama's Manuel Noriega has been accused of a wide range of illegal activities, including collusion with the Colombian drug lords. Noriega is currently awaiting trial in the United States for drug dealing. He surrendered only after a full-scale United States military invasion.

Most of the countries of Latin America enjoy an abundance of natural resources, and the wide exploitation of these resources is a concern throughout the region. Despite a lack of petroleum resources, Brazil is one of Latin America's most richly-endowed nations. The country enjoys vast amounts of arable land; a wealth of minerals, including gold and diamonds; and abundant forest resources. The last twenty years have seen a drive to convert the Amazonian rain forest to conventional agricultural use with disastrous results, as huge tracts of land have been rendered barren. Lack of funding, a result of the nation's huge foreign debt, has hampered recent efforts by the government to halt the devastation.

# Nicaragua: Defeat of the Sandinistas

## Perspective

| | |
|---|---|
| 1856-1857 | United States adventurer William Walker invades Nicaragua with a private army and sets up his own empire. |
| 1912-1925 | United States marines occupy Nicaragua to protect United States interests and to prop up Conservative party government. |
| 1927-1933 | Augusto César Sandino's popular rebellion against United States troops results in withdrawal of marines. |
| 1934 | Sandino is assassinated by the National Guard, led by Anastasio Somoza García. |
| 1936 | Samoza overthrows president and founds a political dynasty that lasts until 1979. |
| 1961 | Sandinista National Liberation Front (FSLN) is organized to fight Somozas. |
| 1979 | **July 19.** Series of popular uprisings throughout Nicaragua results in triumph of Sandinistas. |
| 1981 | Reagan administration fuels civil war by diverting aid to contras. |
| 1984 | **February-April.** The United States mines Nicaragua's harbors; Nicaragua sues in World Court. **November.** Sandinistas win 63 percent of vote in national elections. Daniel Ortega Saavedra is elected president. |
| 1985 | **April.** President Reagan imposes economic embargo against Nicaragua. |
| 1987 | **August.** Presidents of Nicaragua, El Salvador, Honduras, Costa Rica, and Guatemala meet in Guatemala City to sign Arias peace plan; Reagan gives cautious support. |
| 1989 | **January 30.** Ortega implements economic austerity program to combat rampant inflation. **February 14.** Nicaragua agrees to hold free elections in exchange for the disbanding of the contras. |
| 1990 | **February 25.** Violeta Barrios de Chamorro defeats Daniel Ortega in presidential elections. |

Violeta Chamorro's victory over Daniel Ortega in 1990 presidential elections stunned the nation and the world. Polls had predicted a sweeping victory for Ortega, and thousands participated in his massive campaign rallies. But discontent over deteriorating living conditions was more pervasive than anyone was willing to admit. Despite eleven years of civil war and foreign intervention, Ortega's defeat came not on the battlefield at the hands of his enemies, but in the polls at the hands of the people.

## Issues and Events

Ultimately it was the continuing civil war between the Sandinista government and the United States-backed contra rebels that cost Ortega the election. The war had resulted in thirty-thousand deaths and turned Nicaragua from one of Latin America's fastest-growing economies to one of it its poorest. The war required Ortega to maintain Central America's largest army and divert 60 percent of all government revenue into the military. It also necessitated an increasingly unpopular program of forced military service. The war was the biggest factor in Nicaragua's economic collapse, along with Ortega's economic mismanagement and a disastrous hurricane in 1988. By the end of that year, inflation had soared to a staggering 33,000 percent and annual personal income had plummeted to a mere $300 per person. Poverty and malnutrition were spreading at an alarming rate despite Ortega's attempt to stabilize the situation by implementing an economic austerity program in January 1990.

The 1990 presidential elections were part of the peace process outlined in the Arias plan, an agreement signed in August 1987 by the presidents of Nicaragua, Costa Rica, El Salvador, Guatemala, and Honduras in an effort to end violence in the region. In February 1989 the five nations convinced Ortega to hold free elections in early 1990 in exchange for the disbanding of the contras. Although the contras remained in Honduras, Ortega proceeded with the election under the assumption that his defeat was impossible.

The winner of the election was Violeta Chamorro, publisher and editor of La Prensa, a leading newspaper opposed to Ortega's repressive regime. Her party, the National Opposition Union, is an unlikely alliance of fourteen political parties with virtually nothing in common except their disapproval of the Sandinistas. The future remains uncertain as the inexperienced Chamorro begins to try to form a viable coalition government and take office. Even if she succeeds in forming a coalition among the various competing factions, there is still considerable speculation as to whether Ortega will indeed relinquish power. Regardless, the Sandinistas will still dominate the National Assembly, the army, and the state police.

Although it seems likely that the contras will support the Chamorro government and end the war, it will be a long road to economic recovery. How long will depend upon how much assistance the United States will provide and how much support the new president will get from her Sandinista-dominated legislature.

If and when Chamorro takes office it will represent the first peaceful transfer of power in Nicaragua's history. It will also mark the end of continued United States attempts to undermine the Nicaraguan government.

## Background

United States involvement in Nicaragua's affairs goes back more than a century, to William Walker's ill-fated attempt to set up a pro-slavery colony on the eve of the civil war. The United States marines were sent in 1912 to ensure control over a region that was being considered for a second canal between the Atlantic and Pacific oceans. Widespread rural poverty, coupled with the concentration of wealth in the hands of foreigners and their Nicaraguan agents, led to Augusto César Sandino's peasant revolt in 1927. Despite modern weaponry and superior forces, the United States marines were unable to dislodge Sandino and his supporters. In 1933 the marines withdrew, after a treaty made concessions to the peasants and gave Sandino a voice in the government. Yet one year later, Sandino was assassinated in a plot directed by Anastasio Somoza García, the head of the National Guard, widely thought to be backed by the United States.

Somoza took power soon afterward, exterminating Sandino's supporters, occupying their land, and silencing the middle-class opposition. For almost fifty years, the Somoza dynasty, with United States backing, ruled Nicaragua in a corrupt and brutal manner.

The Sandinista National Liberation Front (named in honor of the murdered Sandino) was founded in 1961 and within the decade began to gain support from the desperately poor landless peasants in the interior of the country. Peaceful protests in 1959 and 1967 were met with gunfire and mass arrests. After a 1972 earthquake, which leveled the center of Managua and took fifteen thousand lives, Somoza's son, Anastasio Somoza Debayle, diverted millions of dollars in relief money into his own companies.

In 1979, the dictatorship of the Samozas was overthrown by the Sandinistas, whose leadership included Daniel Ortega Saavedra. The United States government supported the new regime until 1981, when it became clear that Nicaragua was providing support for rebels in El Salvador and other insurgency groups throughout Latin America. As a result, the Reagan administration cut off all aid to Nicaragua and directed the CIA to divert funding to the Nicaraguan Resistance (contras) without Congressional approval.

The Sandinistas embarked on an ambitious program of social change. Two million acres of land belonging to the rich were confiscated and parceled out to sixty-eight thousand families as part of a vast agrarian reform program. A 1981 campaign to bring literacy, schools, and health care to rural areas improved the lives of the country's impoverished peasants. These reforms were frustrated, however, by the escalating civil war between the Soviet-backed Sandinistas and the United States-backed contras.

Relations between the United States and Nicaragua continued to deteriorate. In 1985, Reagan imposed an economic embargo against Nicaragua. His administration also defied a Congressional ban on further aid to the rebels by giving them profits from secret arms sales to Iran. Aid to the contras resumed in 1987, despite growing public indignation about the Iran-contra affair.

# El Salvador: War Games in Central America

## Perspective

| | |
|---|---|
| 1525 | Spanish conquistadors defeat Indians and establish sovereignty. |
| 1821 | Central America becomes independent from Spain. |
| 1838-1841 | As Federation of Central America collapses, member states become independent. |
| 1870-1900 | Economy based on coffee production develops. Coffee-producing land is taken over by a few wealthy landowners. |
| 1931-1932 | General Maximiliano Hernández overthrows popularly elected president. After failure of peasant rebellion led by Farabundo Martí, Hernández's troops massacre twenty thousand to thirty thousand peasants. |
| 1972 | Generals seize power after slate of moderates is elected. José Napoleón Duarte is exiled. |
| 1979 | Moderate generals come to power in coup and form military-civilian junta; guerrilla warfare breaks out. |
| 1980 | Leftist guerrillas and rightist death squads continue terrorist activities. **March.** Violence erupts at the funeral of assassinated pacifist Archbishop Oscar Romero; Duarte returns from exile to head junta. **December.** Bodies of four United States Catholic missionary workers are discovered. United States threatens to withdraw military aid until deaths are investigated. |
| 1984 | **May.** Moderate candidate José Napoleón Duarte is declared winner in the new elections; United States promises him the largest aid package to date. |
| 1987 | **August 7.** Heads of five Central American nations sign Arias peace plan. |
| 1989 | **March 19.** Alfredo Cristiani wins presidential election. **November 11.** Rebels launch major military offensive. **November 16.** Military personnel kill six Jesuit priests. |
| 1990 | **January 13.** Eight military officers and soldiers are arrested for Jesuit murders. |

The civil war in El Salvador reflects the decades-long struggle between the have nots—landless peasants demanding a more equitable distribution of wealth—and the haves—the landholding aristocracy and the military. During the past eleven years of civil war, billions of dollars in American aid has been spent in support of the Salvadoran government, about 10 percent of the Salvadoran population has been displaced and seventy thousand Salvadorans have been killed.

The adoption of the Arias peace plan in 1987 brought hope for an end to the fighting in war-torn Central America. The plan, adopted by all of the region's presidents and also by the United Nations, called for such measures as democratic elections, cease fires, suspension of outside military aid to insurgents, freedom of the press, and limits on armed forces. In 1989, peace in El Salvador remained elusive as left-wing guerrillas launched a major offensive and the right-wing military extremists were accused of killing six unarmed Jesuit priests in cold blood.

## Issues and Events

The conflict dates from late 1979, after the formation of a moderate-left, civilian-military junta, which followed nearly fifty years of right-wing military rule. Groups from both ends of the political spectrum launched attacks against the new government: right-wing groups resented the junta's limited attempts at land reform and income redistribution, while left-wing groups deemed the moderate government's reform attempts insufficient.

Right-winged vigilante groups known as death squads began to roam the countryside. Led in part by army Colonel Roberto D'Aubuisson, the death squads terrorized the population. Their violence was directed towards the government, the moderates, and the leftist groups. In March 1980 the death squads killed Archbishop Oscar Romero, an outspoken advocate for the rights of the poor. In December of that year, three North American nuns and a Catholic lay worker were found dead; they were also assumed to be death squad victims.

Several left-wing Marxist-Leninist guerrilla groups joined forces in 1980 to form the Democratic Revolutionary Front-Farabundo Martí National Liberation Front (FDR-FMLN). Reputedly reinforced with Soviet and Cuban aid channeled through Nicaragua, this group directed its offensive against the government and the moderates, although civilian casualties were common.

The 1984 victory of moderate politician José Duarte, who was openly supported by the

Reagan administration and most members of Congress, contributed to the administration's willingness to increase its commitment to the Salvadoran government. The American strategy was to combat the expansion of communism and right-wing extremists by supporting the moderate Duarte government. In 1986, with economic aid from the United States, the help of more than one hundred United States military advisors, and a large Central Intelligence Agency operation, the number of Salvadoran armed forces increased fourfold to some fifty-six thousand. In addition, they were also better equipped and trained than their opposition.

The Salvadoran government increased counterinsurgency offensives against the guerrillas' control zones; aerial assaults in 1984 took a heavy toll in terms of lives, livestock, and property. The purpose of the 1986 counterinsurgency plan was to involve military sweeps that would clear the way for the return of four hundred thousand displaced refugees, who were to be trained as anti-guerrilla forces.

The guerrillas accelerated their "war of attrition" in 1985 and 1986 through geographically widespread, low-level attacks on government troops, economic sabotage, attacks on United States targets, and kidnappings. In 1987, guerrillas seeking to overthrow the government raided a major military base, killing sixty-nine soldiers. Despite their efforts, the guerrillas have not been able to attract widespread support. FMLN numbers had been reduced to about seven thousand in 1989, down from twelve thousand in the early 1980s.

Peace talks in 1987 and 1988 resulted in a temporary lull in military action. In early 1989, Alfredo Cristiani, a moderate right-wing candidate, was elected president. The United States continued to support the new government with more than $4 million in military and economic aid.

The FMLN launched a major military offensive later in the year, attacking dozens of targets throughout the country. For the first time, war came to the capital city of San Salvador as the president's residence and fifty other sites were under siege. Hundreds were killed in the fighting, which culminated in the alleged murder of six Jesuit priests and their two servants by government troops. An outraged United States Congress threatened to withhold funds until those responsible were brought to justice. In early 1990, Cristiani reported that eight military personnel, including four officers, were being held in connection with the crime. If they are indeed convicted, it will end a decade of immunity from prosecution for the right-wing's military terrorists.

## Background

A Spanish colony since 1525, El Salvador achieved its independence in 1821 and in 1823 became part of the Federation of Central America, an unsuccessful attempt to unite Spain's former Central American colonies. The union was in a state of virtual collapse by 1838, and as the federation dissolved, its members became independent. In the late nineteenth century, the expanding world market for coffee accelerated the concentration of land into the hands of a few wealthy landowners. The Indians' communal landholdings were broken up, and a rural police force was established to quell the protests of the newly deprived peasants.

The support of the peasants contributed to the election of Arturo Araujo as president in 1931. Almost immediately, however, he was overthrown by General Maximiliano Hernández. The military coup sparked an armed revolt the following year. This revolt, led by the peasant hero Farabundo Martí, was crushed, and in the interval of several weeks, perhaps as many as thirty thousand Salvadorans were killed by Hernández's troops. For the next half century, a succession of military governments ruled El Salvador.

During this period, conditions continued to worsen for most Salvadorans. By 1970, the wealthiest 10 percent of landowners held almost 80 percent of the nation's arable land. Virtually half of those living in the countryside owned no land at all but worked as tenant farmers and migrant wage laborers. Industrialization, which brought little advantage to the ordinary Salvadoran, continued to concentrate wealth into the hands of the few. Infant mortality remained high, and the rate of unemployment hovered between 35 and 50 percent throughout the 1970s. Labor protests in San Salvador and sporadic guerrilla activity generated increasingly brutal repression by the government.

In 1972 a liberal coalition led by Duarte and Guillermo Ungo won the first election in El Salvador in many years. Charging massive vote fraud, the military stepped in once again. Ungo fled the country, but Duarte was captured, imprisoned, and tortured before being forced into exile. With United States support, the military government began a land-reform program that raised many expectations, but was rendered virtually ineffective by landowner opposition. A 1977 coup led by the right-wing general Carlos Humberto Romero ended the land-reform program. His widespread human-rights abuses also led the United States to halt aid temporarily. In 1979, a group of liberal military officers overthrew General Romero. Ungo returned from exile to take part in the civilian-military junta, and the land-reform program was again initiated. Progress toward peace and a more equal society turned out to be very short-lived, however.

# Haiti:
# Poverty and Repression

## Perspective

| | |
|---|---|
| 1492 | Columbus arrives at island of Hispaniola. |
| 1804 | Independence from France is won. |
| 1915-1934 | United States occupies Haiti under Monroe Doctrine. |
| 1957 | François "Papa Doc" Duvalier is elected president. |
| 1971 | Papa Doc dies; Jean-Claude "Baby Doc" Duvalier succeeds as president. |
| 1986 | **February 7.** Haitian President Jean-Claude Duvalier is overthrown and forced into exile; a junta, led by former Lt. General Henry Namphy, assumes power. |
| 1987 | **March 29.** Haitian voters approve new constitution. |
| 1988 | **June 20.** Leslie Manigat, newly-elected president, is overthrown by Namphy.<br>**September 18.** Namphy is overthrown in another coup. General Prosper Avril assumes power. |
| 1989 | **March 13.** Constitution is partially restored.<br>**April.** Two coup attempts fail. |
| 1990 | **March.** Growing civil unrest leads to Avril's resignation. |

Haiti is the most impoverished country in the Western Hemisphere, with a 1984 per capita GDP of $350, 30 percent of the population under 15, 49 percent of the work force unemployed, 79 percent of the population illiterate, and the highest infant mortality rate in the Caribbean region. Many hoped that the fall of the Duvalier regime in 1986 would mark the beginning of a new era of peace and prosperity, but most Haitians are still as poor as ever.

## Issues and Events

Despite continuing political unrest, the real struggle for most Haitians has been survival. A lack of natural resources, poor land management, and limited and overcrowded agricultural areas make for little opportunity. Although only 1 percent of its population owns half of the nation's wealth, this elite is determined to maintain political and economic control. Rampant corruption in the government and the military has traditionally reduced the effectiveness of foreign aid.

Widespread violence in 1987, allegedly caused by the Tontons Macoutes (a paramilitary group organized by the Duvalier regime), led to cancellation of elections and the suspension of about $60 million in United States economic aid.

The second leading source of income in Haiti has traditionally been tourism, but the island has lost appeal due to political unrest and widespread publicity of the acquired immune deficiency syndrome (AIDS) epidemic, which had cited Haitians as an abnormally high-risk people. Later, The United States Center for Disease Control took Haitians off its list of groups most at risk, but the damage to Haiti's tourist trade had already been done.

When presidential elections were finally held in 1988—the first in almost thirty years—the most popular presidential candidates boycotted the election, in which Manigat was named president. Soon afterwards, Manigat fired Lt. General Henry Namphy for insubordination; Namphy retaliated and put the military junta back in power.

Continued attacks by the Tontons Macoutes, who were blamed for attacks against churches, hospitals, and radio stations, led to a breakdown of public order. Namphy's apparent inability to stem the violence resulted in another military coup, which was led by Lieutenant General Prosper Avril.

Avril failed to deliver promised democratic reforms and was ultimately forced to resign amidst bitter anti-government protests. An interim civilian government was established under the leadership of Ertha Pascal-Trouillot, a Supreme Court justice.

## Background

Christopher Columbus landed on Hispaniola in 1492. In 1697 the western third, which was to become Haiti, was deeded to the French, while the eastern two-thirds would become the Dominican Republic. After a struggle for freedom by the slaves, who made up 90 percent of the population, Haiti gained its independence in 1804. A mulatto elite ruled the country for the next century. In 1957 François "Papa Doc" Duvalier was elected president and changed the constitution to extend the president's term to a lifetime.

Papa Doc's reign became synonymous with brutality and torture; dissenters were often murdered. His regime lasted until his death in 1971, when his 19-year-old son, Jean-Claude— known as "Baby Doc"—became president-for-life.

The military strength of the Duvalier government had been sufficient to control the Haitian people until 1986 when the Catholic church led thousands in demonstrations to protest the increasingly corrupt and repressive government.

# Panama: The Fall of a Despot

## Perspective

| | |
|---|---|
| 1903 | Panama declares its independence from Colombia. Canal treaty is signed with the United States. |
| 1914 | *August 15.* Panama Canal is opened. |
| 1977 | The Panama Canal Treaty abolishes the Canal Zone and provides for continued United States operation of the canal until 1999. |
| 1983 | Manuel Antonio Noriega becomes head of the National Guard. |
| 1986 | Noriega overthrows President Ardito Barletta. |
| 1988 | *February 4.* Noriega is indicted by Miami and Tampa grand juries on drug-trafficking and racketeering charges; refuses to be extradited. *February 25.* Noriega deposes President Eric Arturo Delvalle. *March.* United States imposes economic sanctions on Panama. |
| 1989 | *May 7.* Noriega's candidates are apparently defeated in national elections. *May 10.* Noriega voids elections. *December 15.* Noriega declares war against United States. *December 16.* Panamanian soldiers kill a United States marine. *December 20.* United States sends combat troops to Panama; Noriega takes refuge in Vatican embassy. |
| 1990 | *January 3.* Noriega surrenders. |

Known throughout the world as the site of the Panama Canal, this small country recently has become the channel for another kind of traffic— illegal drugs. In the mid-1980s, governmental corruption, monetary problems, and drug dealing created one of the worst political and economic crises in Panama's history and produced an embarrassing stalemate for the United States.

## Issues and Events

At the center of the storm was General Manuel Antonio Noriega, head of the Panama Defense Forces. Noriega reputedly had been helping Colombia's notorious drug cartel funnel drugs through Panama to the United States, a violation of United States law.

Ironically, his rise to power was backed in part by the United States, who had recruited Noriega in the 1960s to supply intelligence information about the Central American region. In the early 1970s, Noriega became head of the National Guard's G-2 intelligence and immigration section. Noriega used his position to establish close ties with drug dealers and gun runners.

In 1986, Noriega overthrew President Ardito Barletta and maintained control of the country by means of violence and intimidation. In 1988, the United States charged Noriega with conspiring with Colombian drug lords to smuggle drugs into the United States. The United States government demanded that he come to the United States to face charges. When Noriega refused, the United States retaliated by applying economic sanctions.

When elections in May 1989 resulted in an apparent 3:1 victory for his opposition, Noriega annulled the elections, sent out thugs to beat up the winners, and installed his own candidates in September. Despite continuing pressure by the United States for his resignation, crippling economic sanctions, growing diplomatic isolation, and two failed coup attempts, Noriega remained in power.

In his growing sense of invincibility, he declared war on the United States in December 1989. After a United States marine lieutenant was killed by Panamanian soldiers, President Bush ordered more than twenty thousand troops into Panama to capture Noriega. Noriega sought sanctuary in the Vatican embassy for fifteen days before surrendering to the United States, where he awaits trial.

The United States invasion left hundreds dead and $1 billion in property damage. Newly-installed President Guillermo Endara faces the massive task of rebuilding the country's crippled political and economic institutions.

## Background

The Spanish, who arrived in Panama in 1501, were the first to establish their rule over this strategically placed country. When Spain's power declined, Panama became a dependency of Colombia. In 1903, the United States helped Panama gain its independence in exchange for the right to build a canal across the isthmus and to intervene in Panama's domestic affairs.

Decades of political upheaval and anti-American protests followed. In the 1970s and early 1980s, Panama became a haven for financial investors but acquired heavy international debts to finance its economic development. With the signing of the 1977 Panama Canal Treaty, Panama is slowly emerging from under United States influence.

## Brazil: Saving the Rain Forest

### Perspective

| | |
|---|---|
| **1960** | Capital of Brazil is moved from Rio de Janeiro to Brasília. |
| **1964** | Military government assumes control. |
| **1973** | Trans-Amazon highway is completed. |
| **1979** | Gold mining at Serra Pelada draws peasants to Amazonia. |
| **1985** | The country returns to civilian government. |
| **1988** | **October 13.** Government freezes subsidies for cattle ranchers, miners, and lumber concerns.<br>**December 22.** Chico Mendes is murdered. |
| **1989** | **February 20.** Kaipo tribe stages protest against new reservoirs.<br>**April 6.** Our Nature program is launched. |

Chico Mendes was a gentle and thoughtful man who earned his living in the wilds of Brazil collecting latex from the giant rubber trees. Hardly the typical soldier, Mendes will go down in history as one of the great warriors in the battle to save the Amazon River basin, or Amazonia, from the ravages of unharnessed, wasteful development of one of the last of the world's major forests.

The great rain forests of the world cover only about 7 percent of the earth's surface, yet they contain about 80 percent of all vegetation. About one-third of the world's rain forests are in Brazil.

The exploitation of the Amazonian rain forest began in the early 1970s when the Trans-Amazon highway opened up the area to ranching, farming, forestry, and mining. Like the early pioneers in the United States, most Brazilians believe that the vastness of the wilderness will protect it from destruction. However, scientists believe that at the current rate of devastation, Brazil's rain forest may be consumed by the end of the century.

Among the principal culprits responsible for large-scale destruction are cattle ranchers, who burn huge tracts of forest to allow grasses to grow as range for livestock herds. Unfortunately, rain forest soils are very poor, and the heavy rains leach the valuable nutrients out of the soil. Without the protection of the forest canopy, what remains of the soil is washed away. Virtually all of the cattle ranches that existed in 1978 have been destroyed in this manner and subsequently abandoned.

The cattle ranchers, previously aided by government subsidies, ruthlessly defend their right to destroy the forest against anyone who stands in their way. It is estimated that cattle barons and other land owners in Amazonia have shot over one thousand people since 1980.

Like a half million others in Amazonia, Chico Mendes earned his living from the jungle. He was an "environmentalist" long before he had ever heard the word. His full name was Francisco Mendes Filho, and for ten years he led the 150,000-member National Council of Rubber Tappers. Perhaps his greatest achievement was the establishment of five million acres of "extractive reserves" to be protected and managed for ongoing forest industries such as rubber, nuts, and resins. His dream was to establish similar reserves in all areas where rubber workers had traditionally eked out a living.

Chico Mendes never lived to see his dream come to fruition. He was shot on December 22, 1988, allegedly by a family of cattle ranchers who claim ownership to some of the land designated as a reserve.

Mendes's dream lives on as Brazil and the rest of the world begin to realize that every wilderness—however vast—has its limits.

### Issues and Events

In an unprecedented move, the government of Brazil admitted in 1988 that development of the rain forest had perhaps gotten out of hand after more than six thousand man-made fires were reported in a single day in Rondonia along one of Brazil's new roads. These fires contributed a full 10 percent to the extra carbon dioxide injected into the atmosphere. Scientists believe this could cause a global warming trend called the "greenhouse effect" that could ultimately render the planet uninhabitable. The burning is also damaging because trees absorb carbon dioxide from the atmosphere, and thus their destruction doubles the potential for a world-wide ecological catastrophe.

The pressures for continued development are enormous. Although the government has long claimed that Amazonian development is necessary to support the country's huge, impoverished peasant class, in reality the poor people have not benefited from the program.

If development must continue, Brazil must find new and innovative means of using the forest without destroying it. Traditional farming and cattle ranching techniques are devastating, but native Brazilians have long practiced a type of slash and burn agriculture that has a very low environmental impact. Modern lumbering techniques such as selective cutting need to be employed instead of the cheaper clear-cutting approach. The country's many parks, Indian reserves, and extractive reserves need to be protected against illegal encroachment. The United States, Netherlands, France, West Germany, and Japan have offered to buy off a portion of Brazil's foreign debt to allow these funds to be used for environmental protection in so-called "debt for nature" swaps. However, the highly nationalistic Brazilians resent outside interference. They regard any plans that limit their use of the region as a threat to their sovereignty.

On October 13, 1988, the government ordered a freeze on subsidies for the cattle ranchers, miners, and lumbering concerns in the region. In April 1989, the first comprehensive Amazonian forest management program was launched. This plan, called "Our Nature," provided for forty-nine new environmental laws including zoning, national parks and reserves, and permits for burning. So far the plan has been fairly successful; fines totaling $10 million have been issued and burning has dropped substantially. However, continued success will depend on the availability of funding for equipment and personnel to enforce the laws.

Perhaps the best hope for Brazil's rain forest lies with its native population, who view themselves as the protectors of the rain forest. On February 20, 1989, the Kaipo Indian tribe invited other native people, environmentalists, and the foreign press to meet at the Altamira Conference to protest a new hydroelectric project that would flood a large area of their homeland. The Kaipo were successful in focusing the world's attention on their plight. Two months later, the World Bank scrapped plans to provide loans of $500 million for Amazonian hydroelectric projects. Japan also responded by calling off its plans to fund the construction of new highways in the region. In addition, the Indians know the secrets of Amazonia's plant kingdom, which may hold cures for many of the diseases that plague mankind. Botanists rely on the Indians' traditional cures to help identify plants with healing properties.

The world can only hope that Brazil will begin to value its rich forest resources and manage them in a more responsible manner.

## Background

Brazil was colonized during the early 1500s by Portuguese settlers, most of whom lived along the northeast coast and were involved in growing sugar. The discovery of gold in 1693 started a gold rush to the central highlands in the present-day state of Minas Gerais. By the mid-1800s, coffee had become the country's leading export as people flocked to the Sao Paulo region to work on the new plantations.

During the late 1800s, the rubber boom prompted limited migration to the Amazonian region. Each of these economic booms resulted in the establishment of large new plantations controlled by a few wealthy landowners. Land ownership patterns have changed very little over the years: over 43 percent of the arable land in Brazil is still owned by less than 1 percent of the population, and 70 percent of all rural families have no land at all.

After World War II the economy expanded rapidly as Brazil used its wealth of natural resources to create a thriving new manufacturing sector, which continued to expand until the early 1960s. In 1960, the nation officially moved its capital from Rio de Janeiro to the new futuristic city of Brasilia to serve as a base for the development of Amazonia.

Unrest in the early 1960s led to a military takeover in 1964. During this period Brazil experienced what is so often referred to as its "economic miracle" of high growth rates, declining inflation, and modest external debt. This period also marked the beginning of the drive to settle the Amazon region as the military sought to establish a greater presence in the country's hinterland. The Trans-Amazon highway, completed in 1973, was part of a great scheme to colonize the region. One hundred thousand families were to have been established along the road by 1974, but poor farming conditions and a lack of facilities hindered development. By 1977, only about seven thousand families had been established, and the unpaved highway is rendered impassable for six months of the year by seasonal rains.

In 1979, thousands of impoverished peasants flocked to Amazonia to find gold at Serra Pelada. In a few short years, over sixty thousand prospectors using crude hand tools dug a crater 250 feet deep in search of instant wealth. Tremendous quantities of gold, iron ore, bauxite, and manganese are all currently being mined at various locations in Amazonia, and violence between prospectors and mine companies is not uncommon.

Despite an economic downturn that began in the late 1970s, the government continued to borrow money for large-scale projects in Amazonia such as roads and reservoirs. Continued unrest, largely due to the rising foreign debt and land ownership inequities, led to a return to civilian rule in 1985. The change in leadership did little to improve the failing economic situation, however. Despite a trade surplus, the country's national debt now stands at $115 billion and inflation is rampant at 900 percent. Migration into the Amazon region continues at a rate of five hundred thousand per year.

# Colombia: Cocaine, Corruption, and Chaos

## Perspective

| | |
|---|---|
| 1899-1902 | Bloody civil war casts Colombia into series of bitter class struggles. |
| 1948-1966 | Era of terrorism and widespread street violence known as La Violencia rages for two decades. |
| 1970s | Marijuana becomes Colombia's first big illicit drug product. |
| 1979 | Colombia and United States sign extradition treaty. |
| 1982 | **August 7.** President Betancur is sworn into office. |
| 1984 | **March 10.** Colombian narcotics squads raid huge drug operation of Tranquilandia.<br>**April 30.** Assassination of Minister of Justice Lara leads to antidrug campaign by Betancur government.<br>**May 1.** Betancur declares national state of emergency; extradition of traffickers to United States begins. |
| 1985 | **November.** Guerrillas seize the Palace of Justice; 106 people die. |
| 1986 | **August.** President Virgilio Barco Vargas is sworn into office. |
| 1987 | **February 4.** Medellín cartel member Carlos Lehder is extradited to the United States.<br>**June.** Extradition treaty is declared unconstitutional.<br>**December.** Medellín cartel member Jorge Ochoa is freed from jail. |
| 1988 | **January.** Attorney General Carlos Mauro Hoyos is assassinated. |
| 1989 | **August 18.** Presidential front runner Luís Carlos Galán is assassinated.<br>**August 19.** President Barco launches offensive against narcos.<br>**December 15.** Gonzalo Gacha is killed in shootout with Colombian authorities. |

On February 4, 1987, Carlos Lehder received the surprise of his life when Colombian authorities stormed his palatial residence and arrested him along with fourteen of his bodyguards. Within hours he was extradited to the United States, where he faced charges of cocaine smuggling and racketeering. As a kingpin of the infamous Medellín cartel, Lehder had been engaged in the illegal production and sales of cocaine for over a decade with impunity. Colombian authorities were acting on a 1979 extradition treaty with the United States in which Colombia agreed to round up major drug smugglers and send them to the United States to be tried and punished. Although many minor "narcos" (drug dealers) had been arrested and extradited, never before had a member of the cartel been nabbed. Thirty-nine-year-old Lehder was sentenced to life plus a century and a half in prison. Gonzalo Gacha wasn't as lucky. When the authorities caught up with him in December 1989, Gacha was killed in a hail of gunfire. Gacha was widely believed to be responsible not only for drug trafficking, but also for the deaths of scores of people in connection with the latest battle between the cocaine barons and the forces of law and order.

Although United States authorities hailed these actions as major victories in the war on drugs, the events did not make a dent in the drug traffic between Colombia and the United States. Eighty percent of all of the cocaine in the United States comes from Colombia, whose narcos reap average profits of over $3 billion per year. With that kind of money at stake, others were more than ready to take over where Lehder and Gacha left off.

## Issues and Events

The Medellín cartel has a virtual stranglehold on the Colombian government. Cartel members like Pablo Excobar and the Ochoa family are among the most powerful men in the world. With their fabulous wealth and mafia-style tactics, they have been able to buy or intimidate Colombia's police, armed forces, politicians, and judges into doing whatever they want. After Lehder's arrest in February 1987, the Colombian Supreme Court suddenly declared the 1979 extradition treaty unconstitutional. In December of the same year, United States authorities were outraged when cartel member Jorge Ochoa was mysteriously freed from a Colombian prison. Ochoa reportedly distributed over $1 million in bribes to obtain his release. In January 1988, Attorney General Carlos Mauro Hoyos was kidnapped and assassinated after the Colombian government issued fresh warrants for the arrest of the Ochoa family.

Fearing the wrath of the dealers, most Colombians have been afraid to speak out against the drug trade. In August 1989 the cartel went too far when it assassinated presidential hopeful Luís Carlos Galán during a political rally. The people rose up and demanded justice. President Barco responded by launching a serious assault against the narcotics traffickers, including the reestablishment of the extradition treaty with the United States, the seizure of more than $200 million in property, over eleven thousand arrests, and special protection for judicial officials. The drug traffickers, referring to themselves as the "extraditables," issued a statement declaring war on the government, journalists, judges, and union leaders who opposed them. The declaration of war was punctuated by a series of bombings. The United States jumped to Barco's defense by committing $65 million to the Colombian government. Colombian leaders warn that it will be a long and bloody battle. Since August more than two hundred bombs have left eighty-nine dead, twelve hundred injured, and millions in property damage. Even with United States support, the Colombian government may not be a match for the powerful forces of the cocaine empire.

## Background

Ever since the constitutions of 1853 and 1858 were instituted, Colombia has been held up as a model republic—one of Latin America's few enduring democracies. It has, however, had more than its share of violence. Between 1899 and 1902, it underwent a horrendous civil war during which nearly 150,000 people were killed. Two more decades of unabated violence terrorized the country between 1948 and 1968, following the assassination of Jorge Eliécer Gaitán—hero of the underprivileged classes. During this era, known as La Violencia, three hundred thousand people were murdered as city streets became battlegrounds and the countryside was drowned in anarchy.

The greatest cause of so much unrest in Colombia's history has been the gross inequities of land and wealth distribution. The economy typically has had to rely on bonanza crops of one sort or another, rather than on steady growth.

Cocaine, the latest bonanza crop, is not native to Colombia. The Colombian drug lords made their money purchasing coca leaves and paste from Peru and Bolivia, refining the raw coca in Colombia, then overseeing its distribution in the United States. By handling all aspects of the cocaine's manufacture and sale, the narcos were able to reap fantastic profits. Most of the cocaine industry was based in and around Medellín, which features good air transport facilities, a large unemployed labor force, and a well developed chemical industry to provide substances required for processing. In addition, Medellín is surrounded by hills and forests that easily conceal jungle processing plants and air strips.

Medellín's most famous cartel member is Pablo Escobar Gaviria, known by many as "Don Pablo the Good" for his many philanthropic works. With an estimated fortune of more than $2 billion, he is also Medellín's richest cocaine baron. The city boasts a large zoo built by Escobar, as well as rows of housing for the poor. Fabio Ochoa and his sons Jorge, Juan, and Fabio Jr. run a family business that's reportedly worth at least $1 billion. Gonzalos Rodríguez Gacha rose to prominence during 1988 after Lehder's arrest. Known as "El Mexicano" for his love of Mexico, he once gave a sombrero to every resident of his home town.

Cocaine has had a tremendous effect on the Colombian economy. The profits are enormous. In 1989 a pound of cocaine could be purchased in Colombia for $700 and resold for as much as $5,000. It is believed that revenue from illegal exports of cocaine exceed those of coffee, Colombia's leading legitimate export crop. Thousands are employed as processors, pilots, distributors, lawyers, and killers. Billions of cocaine dollars are invested in Colombia each year. While the effect on the economy has been positive, Colombia has paid a high price for its prosperity. The country experiences an unparalleled level of peacetime violence, much of it drug-related. The homicide rate in Colombia is six times higher than in the United States, and paid assassins can be bought for as little as $10.

The judicial system has been hit the hardest. Judges must continually deal with threats of violence against themselves and their families. More than 220 judges and judicial employees have been assassinated by the drug dealers. In 1985 guerrillas seized the Palace of Justice, killed eleven Supreme Court justices, and destroyed extradition papers. Most drug-related crimes go unpunished because judges fear the wrath of the narcos. On several occasions, judiciary officials have gone on strike to protest the lack of protection afforded them by the government, and thousands have resigned in recent years.

In 1984, President Bentancur began Colombia's war against the narcos when government forces raided a major drug operation called Tranquilandia ("Land of Tranquility") near the Yari River. More than a billion dollars worth of cocaine was seized, while three hundred air force and police officers were discharged for their involvement in the drug trade and four hundred judges were placed under investigation. The narcos fought back by assassinating the country's Minister of Justice. Betancur redoubled the government's efforts by sanctioning arrests without warrant and enforcing extradition to the United States. During that year, twelve Colombians were successfully extradited to the United States, although none of the big drug dealers were arrested.

# Argentina: A Fragile Democracy

## Perspective

| | |
|---|---|
| **1816** | Argentina declares independence from Spain. |
| **1946** | Juan Perón comes to power, aided by his wife Eva Duarte. |
| **1955** | Perón is ousted from power. |
| **1973** | Perón returns from exile and is re-elected president. |
| **1974** | Perón dies; his second wife, Isabel, assumes presidency. |
| **1976-1983** | Violent struggles for leadership ensue among Peronistas; bloody "dirty war" is waged against Marxist guerrillas and political dissidents. |
| **1982** | **April 3.** Argentine junta announces takeover of South Georgia Island in Falklands.<br>**June 15.** Argentina forces surrender in Stanley to end Falklands War. |
| **1983** | **October.** Raúl Alfonsín and Radical Civic Union come to power and vow to establish constitutional democracy. |
| **1987** | **November 17.** Immunity from prosecution for human rights abuses during the "dirty war" is granted to most military personnel. |
| **1989** | **May 14.** Peronista candidate Carlos Menem is elected president.<br>**May 29.** Riots over economic conditions result in fifteen deaths.<br>**July 8.** Menem is sworn in five months early. |

Although Argentina is one of the most modern and industrialized, most culturally and educationally advanced nations in South America, it has been plagued by political and economic upheavals for a good part of the twentieth century. When Raúl Alfonsín and the Radical Civic Union (RCU) were elected in 1983, it was because the nation was worn out by the militarism, repression, and strong-arm leadership long associated with the Peronistas, or Judicialist Party. The RCU victory was short-lived. Although they made great strides in the area of human rights, they were unable to combat the deadly hyperinflation that was devastating the nation's economy. The RCU was forced to relinquish its leadership after a single term when 1989 elections showed a mandate for Carlos Menem, the Peronista candidate. The return of the Peronistas to power underscores the reality of Argentina's fragile new democracy.

## Issues and Events

The Radicals tried desperately to live with the Peronistas and bring to justice the former military leadership without destroying a working relationship with either group. All they were ever able to achieve was, at best, an uneasy truce. The Peronistas, who have traditionally enjoyed the support of Argentina's working class, did little to halt the general strikes that plagued Alfonsín's economic recovery programs. The military threatened to revolt when Alfonsín called for prosecution of those guilty of human rights abuses during the dirty war. In the end, the most serious threat to the Radicals was neither the Peronistas nor the military, but their inability to curb the inflation that had plagued the nation for more than three decades.

By 1989, the public had lost confidence in Alfonsín's economic policy and inflation reached record levels. On April 28, 1988, banks were forced to close because the government couldn't print enough money to satisfy demand. In May 1989, when the Peronistas claimed their presidential victory, prices were increasing 78 percent per month. Menem's election failed to stem the tide and by July the monthly inflation rate reached a staggering 197 percent. Riots and looting broke out, resulting in fifteen deaths and one hundred injuries. As always, the burden of inflation fell heaviest on those who are least able to afford it. Skyrocketing prices destroyed savings and shattered dreams. Tremendous shortages of almost everything resulted as producers held on to their goods in an effort to get the highest prices. Credit was no longer accepted, since the value of the charges when paid was so much less than at the time of purchase. While the rich have protected themselves by investing their money outside the country, the poor struggled to obtain food, medicine, and other basic necessities.

After intense negotiations the RCU gave up power to Menem on July 8, five months earlier than scheduled. In addition to inflation, Menem's fiscal problems also included a $60 million foreign debt, a bankrupt treasury, and a crushing load of state subsidies and unprofitable state-owned industries.

Ultimately, Menem's success or failure will rest on whether or not he can maintain the confidence of the Argentinean people. So far Menem has had more success than his predecessors in stabilizing the economy. Inflation dropped to 9 percent by September as a result of new wage and price controls. In December a new policy was initiated to end all government controls on the economy. The inflation rate quickly jumped again, underscoring Menem's warnings that complete economic recovery will require years, not months.

Of equal significance, Menem has not displayed his party's tendency toward repression and strong-arm tactics. The charismatic, sophisticated Menem enjoys a higher degree of support and cooperation from both the labor unions and the military than the Alfonsín government.

The fragility of Argentina's new constitutional democracy remains apparent, yet it has met with some startling successes. All of the personal freedoms established by the Radicals remain in place. Basic freedoms—such as those of speech, the press, and religion—have been granted to people who only a few years ago would not have dreamed of such privileges. It seems unlikely that, having had a taste of freedom, the Argentinean people will be willing to settle for anything else.

## Background

Argentina has never had a true democracy. The years following its attainment of independence from Spain in 1816 were filled with power struggles between the leaders of Buenos Aires and those of the outlying provinces. Dictatorship, terror, and reactionism marked the era between 1835 and 1852. The country received its first constitution in 1853 and finally became a united republic in 1862. Beginning in the 1880s, Argentina underwent enormous economic growth. During the first decades of the twentieth century, it gained cultural and educational prominence.

General Uriburu, a military tyrant, staged a successful coup d'etát in 1930, and various military regimes ruled ineptly until the 1943 revolution ushered in a period of absolute oppression, violence, and censorship. Meanwhile, Juan Perón had emerged as an outspoken champion of the working class. In 1946, he ascended to the presidency with strong support from the powerful labor unions. While his nine-year rule introduced widespread labor reform, he and his popular wife, Eva Duarte, proved to be brutal tyrants who completely curtailed personal freedoms, initiated strict censorship of the press, and suppressed political dissidence. A military coup finally ousted Perón in 1955.

Following nearly twenty years of revolving-door military regimes, Perón returned from exile to become president in 1973. A year later, following his death, his second wife, Isabel, took over the presidency until she was deposed in 1976. From that time until 1983, Argentina suffered through years of bloody power struggles, censorship, and political terror, which came to be known as the "dirty war." In 1980, a human-rights commission criticized the government for its exile, torture, and execution of political dissidents. The government excused itself on the grounds of self-defense against the intended intervention of Marxist guerrillas.

The rise to power of the Radicals in 1983 came on the heels of a great military blunder in 1982. In a bold move to take possession of the Falkland Islands, a British colony, Argentine troops seized control of South Georgia Island in the Falklands on April 3, 1982. The issue was settled in a matter of about three months, with Britain emerging victorious.

During the next twelve months, more than half the generals and two-thirds of the admirals were forced into retirement. Elections were forced, ushering the Radicals into power. The new president has sought to redirect Argentina and improve the country's international reputation.

In 1985, Argentina held a trial unprecedented in Latin American history. Five former military leaders who had ruled Argentina during the "dirty war" of the 1970s were found guilty in Civilian Court in connection with the kidnapping, torture, and murder of nine thousand citizens. Alfonsín was forced to impose a sixty-day state of siege to offset right-wing advocates of amnesty for the former military leaders. In 1987, army revolts flared because President Alfonsín refused to negotiate amnesty for former military leaders accused of human-rights abuses; one hundred thousand citizens demonstrated in support of his actions. Nonetheless, the government passed a new law on November 17, 1987, which granted immunity to all except the most senior officers accused of violating human rights.

Military leadership was once again challenged in 1986 when several were stripped of their rank and convicted for negligent handling of Argentine forces during the 1982 war with Great Britain over the Falkland Islands.

# East Asia and the Pacific

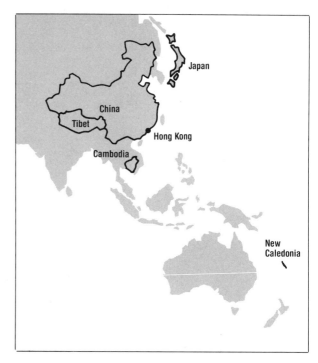

The next century is expected to be the Age of the Pacific. Japan—one of the world's most industrious nations—and the People's Republic of China—the most populous nation—will dominate the economic and political development of the region.

After suffering from almost complete devastation during World War II, Japan has risen to become one of the world's economic powerhouses. Although Japan is the largest economic power in the area, the influence of the "sleeping giant" of China pervades all planning in the Orient. Both China and Japan face similar challenges as they adjust to their new roles as world leaders. Intense nationalism bordering on xenophobia threatens to keep these countries from realizing the benefits of full integration into the world community. And yet, as they make more contacts with the outside world, their traditional cultural patterns and values are subsequently jeopardized. The need to strike a delicate balance between the old and the new has become critical to both countries.

While Japan has flourished under capitalism and democracy, China has lagged far behind as it struggles to modernize within the constraints of a Communist totalitarian government. Chinese attempts to launch an economic reform program were thwarted in 1989 by mass demonstrations as the people rallied for freedom and democracy. International outrage over the government's use of force to quell unrest in Tibet and Beijing resulted in increasing isolation at a time when foreign investment and tourism were critical to its economic growth.

The government crackdown had a devastating effect on Hong Kong, a British colony scheduled to revert to Chinese rule by the end of the decade. Although the Chinese have agreed to allow Hong Kong to retain its capitalist economy for fifty years, skepticism abounds. Both people and businesses have been leaving the territory at an alarming rate.

The Chinese also play a crucial role in the fate of Cambodia, a country devastated by decades of war and foreign intervention. Vietnam withdrew its military forces from Cambodia in 1989, but China continues to support the dreaded Khmer Rouge. Several million Cambodians died under the Khmer Rouge rule in the late 1970s, and it is feared the regime could once again gain power.

In the Pacific, New Caledonia's competing ethnic groups continue to struggle to create a common vision for the future of their island nation.

# New Caledonia: Rocky Road to Independence

## Perspective

| | |
|---|---|
| *1774* | Captain James Cook lands at New Caledonia. |
| *1853* | New Caledonia is annexed by France. |
| *1946* | New Caledonia becomes French overseas territory. |
| *1981* | **September.** *The assassination of pro-independence leader Pierre Declercq leads to unrest.* |
| *1988* | **June 26.** *Matignon Accord is signed.* |
| *1989* | **May 4.** *FLNKS president Jean-Marie Tjibaou is assassinated.*<br>**June 11.** *Elections to provincial assemblies are held.* |

The 1981 assassination of pro-independence leader Pierre Declercq sparked hostilities between the French and indigenous residents of this Pacific island paradise. Ironically, another assassination in 1989 may mark the end of the struggle by strengthening both groups' resolves to honor the terms of a new accord.

## Issues and Events

After Declercq's assassination, growing unrest led to the passage of a statute by France in 1984 that granted more autonomy to the territory and provided for a referendum for independence in five years. The islands' Europeans were angry that France gave into the Kanak's demands for a referendum; the Kanaks were also displeased because they felt five years was too long to wait. By November, Kanak separatists began setting up road blocks, raiding homes, and burning cars in an attempt to disrupt elections. Police responded with tear gas and stun grenades. Residents of Nouméa, the capital, were afraid to leave the city and travel in the Kanak-controlled countryside. On December 1, The Kanak Socialist National Liberation Front (FLNKS) established the independent state of Kanaky, or "Land of the People."

Over the next few years, France submitted various peace plans but FLNKS routinely rejected all proposals and boycotted elections. During a 1987 referendum on independence, FLNKS ignored an official ban on demonstrations, and France sent some seven thousand soldiers and riot police to subdue the inevitable violence that had come to characterize elections in the islands. When the FLNKS boycott resulted in 59 percent turnout, voters overwhelmingly chose to remain a French territory.

A breakthrough was reached in 1988 when FLNKS leader Jean-Marie Tjibaou agreed to sign the Matignon Accord. This agreement called for direct rule by France for one year, followed by ten years of limited self-government and an independence referendum in 1988. In addition, the plan called for revised provincial boundaries to give the Kanaks more political power.

While many new Caledonians supported the accord, some of the more radical Kanaks felt that ten years was too long to wait for independence. Tjibaou believed that the long transition period was needed to allow Kanaks to acquire the skills needed for effective self-government. He was quoted as saying, "There's no point in waving your flag at the front of the door (of the United Nations) if you have to crawl through the back door to beg for money."

Tjibaou's tragic assassination in May 1989 by a radical pro-independence Kanak was a great tragedy and the bonds between all New Caledonians were strengthened as they shared their grief. Provincial elections the following month remained peaceful, further nurturing hopes that the Matignon Accord will bring about an end to violence and the dawn of a new era.

## Background

New Caledonia became a French overseas territory in 1946 and its population received French citizenship. Of a population of more than 160,000, 43 percent are Kanaks, or indigenous Melanesians; 37 percent are French; and the remainder are other Pacific Islanders, Indonesians, and Vietnamese. Although the Kanaks are the largest single group, the French and all others tend to band together and thereby form a majority. The Europeans and others, who are concentrated in and around the capital city of Nouméa, want New Caledonia to remain a French territory. The Kanaks, who inhabit the country's underdeveloped rural area, demand independence and control of their native land.

# China: Reform and Repression

## Perspective

| | |
|---|---|
| **1949** | People's Republic of China is founded after four years of civil war. |
| **1950** | Land-reform law is adopted. |
| **1956** | Mao initiates "hundred flowers" campaign. |
| **1958** | Mao Zedong inaugurates Great Leap Forward. |
| **1966** | Cultural Revolution begins. |
| **1976** | Mao Zedong dies. |
| **1978** | Deng Xiaoping announces economic reforms. |
| **1986** | **December.** Student unrest leads to downfall of Hu Yaobang, head of the Communist party. |
| **1989** | **April 15.** Hu Yaobang's death prompts renewed student protests. **April 27.** Approximately 150,000 students gather in Beijing's Tiananmen Square. **May 13.** Hunger strikes begin. **May 20.** Martial law is imposed. **May 22.** Millions gather to deter military convoys. **June 4.** Chinese Army opens fire on demonstrators. |
| **1990** | **January 11.** Martial law is lifted. |

For the students of Beijing University, May 1989 was a time for rejoicing as they led a million people to the streets in their quest for democratic reforms. Intoxicated by their new found power, many felt invincible enough to call for the resignations of Deng Xiaoping and Li Peng, the most powerful men in China. Tragedy struck when the government retaliated by unleashing its troops against thousands of students and civilians, thus dashing any immediate hopes for reform in China.

## Issues and Events

Economic reform had been underway since 1978 when Deng Xiaoping launched a new program to modernize and expand China's economy. The new program represented a departure from the dogmatic conservatism of the 1960s and 1970s. For the first time, productivity was emphasized over politics. Workers were offered financial incentives for increased output, and decision-making by individuals rather than groups was encouraged. Intellectuals were elevated back to their pre-revolutionary status.

Chinese leaders were quick to deny that this was a return to capitalism, calling it a plan to "build socialism with Chinese characteristics." They tried to develop a unique and pragmatic program that would synthesize the benefits of capitalism into their socialist structure without suffering from its disadvantages.

By 1986 reform's negative effects began to cause concern. Limited government intervention resulted in a rising budget deficit, mounting inflation, and increased corruption in business. The country reported a $20 million trade deficit at the end of 1986. Many individuals felt they were unable to make the kinds of decisions expected of them after years of only group planning.

The reform program also manifested itself in growing student unrest. The first round of student demonstrations for more democracy and freedom of the press began in December 1986 in the city of Hefei and quickly spread to Shanghai and Beijing. Hu Yaobang, then leader of the Communist party, expressed sympathy for the students and was subsequently replaced by Zhao Ziyang. At this time, the arrests of about twenty students culminated the demonstrations. Renewed cries for democracy and an end to corruption began in April 1989, following Hu Yaobang's death. The government immediately issued a stern warning against further protests, but the students continued to gather in ever-increasing numbers. Tiananmen Square became the rallying point for students from Beijing University, where the protests were centered. Discussions between the government and the students began on April 29 in the form of a televised dialogue, an unusual event in China. Student marches and demonstrations continued, and a thousand students launched a hunger strike days before the arrival of the Soviet Union's reform-minded leader Mikhail Gorbachev. During Gorbachev's visits, the crowds calling for reform grew to more than a million and the Chinese premiere, Li Peng, met with students for a second televised debate. The following day Zhao Ziyang defied party directives and met with the students to beg them to end the hunger strike. Zhao was subsequently stripped of power by Peng Xiaoping, China's leading political figure and commander of the military forces. It was feared that Zhao might go on to organize a populist coup against Deng's government. On May 20 the government imposed martial law and threatened to use force to stop the unrest. Unmindful of the warnings, a million Beijing students and workers banded together to block incoming military convoys and urge the soldiers to defect to their side. For a while it seemed like the power of the people was invincible as the immense crowds marched through the streets calling for Li Peng's resignation. On May 30 a replica of the Statue of Liberty called the Goddess of Democracy was unveiled by students in Tiananmen Square. As troops continued to assemble in Beijing, it became clear that some kind of military action was imminent. Days later when the troops moved into the city center, only ten thousand people remained. Violence broke out as students attacked the soldiers, who fought back with tear gas and cattle prods. By June 4 the army was given permission to open fire on anyone still in the streets.

According to Chinese authorities, three hundred were killed, including twenty-three students. Western reporters claim the number was closer to two or three thousand.

Chinese propaganda efforts have since been hard at work trying to mend the wounds inflicted on the people; they refer to the unrest as the "Counterrevolutionary Rebellion," claim that it was organized by western forces plotting the overthrow of the Communist government, and assert that the students were merely pawns in the hands of the real saboteurs. Students are now subjected to mandatory military, government, or civil service before continuing their studies. The government has also been working to control inflation and fight corruption, two of the conditions the students were protesting.

Meanwhile, the economic reforms are on hold. International outcry following the crackdown was restrained, but both foreign investment in China and tourism fell off sharply. The action caused great harm to China's relationships with Taiwan and Hong Kong, both of which China hopes to annex.

The lifting of martial law in January 1990 marked the end of this particular episode in China's struggle for development and prosperity.

Home to a fifth of the world's population, China will continue to face both economic stagnation and periodic bouts of unrest and violence as long as the repressive government remains in place. There is no real mechanism for pluralism in Chinese politics; those who do not conform to the current policies are tossed out. In its continual struggle for stability, the government recognizes its obligation to protect not the rights of individuals, but the welfare of society as a whole. As totalitarian Communist governments around the world collapse, one can only wonder whether China will be next.

## Background

Change never seems to come to China without bloodshed. Between 1937 and 1950, the Chinese suffered five million casualties as the result of the Japanese invasion, World War II, and the Communist Revolution. When Mao took over in 1949, the economy was in a shambles. Wars, floods, and famines had brought agriculture and industry to a virtual standstill. In the years immediately following the war, China's quick recovery was hailed as an economic miracle. During this period China also began a land reform program. About half of the arable land was wrested from wealthy landowners and redistributed to landless peasants. The Socialist transformation also had a dark side—another one million people were killed in the process.

A period of liberalization began in 1956 with the slogan, "Let a hundred flowers bloom, let a hundred schools of thought contend." This program backfired, however, when dissidents used the campaign to denounce the new government, and was subsequently rescinded.

The Great Leap Forward was initiated by Mao in 1958 to raise agricultural and industrial output. The government encouraged the development of backyard factories, established huge agricultural communes, and stressed the merits of labor-intensive means of production. By 1960, the disillusioned and exhausted population suffered from food shortages and famine for the first time since the revolution. The country was flooded with industrial products of inferior quality. The program was a disaster that came close to toppling Mao from power.

By 1966, Mao again took control by launching the Cultural Revolution, an attempt to revive revolutionary zeal among the people and destroy all remaining capitalist forces within the society. During this period, students were taken from their homes and forced to perform hard manual labor. Intellectuals and professionals were persecuted, and the Red Guard, a radical-left "army" of teenagers mandated to eliminate enemies of the state, was formed. What ensued was a "witch hunt" in which fifty thousand people, many of whom were innocent, were killed in vigilante-like purges. The cultural revolution finally grounded to a halt in the early 1970s. After Mao's death in 1976, the government launched its new economic reform plan.

# China: Tibetan Nationalism

## Perspective

| | |
|---|---|
| 1950 | Chinese Communists invade Tibet. |
| 1959 | Popular uprising results in one hundred thousand deaths; Dalai Lama flees to India. |
| 1966 | Chinese destroy monasteries, ban religion, and impose forced labor during Cultural Revolution. |
| 1987 | **September.** Dalai Lama proposes peace plan.<br>**October.** Rioting breaks out in Lhasa. |
| 1988 | **December.** Police kill eighteen in Lhasa when riots begin on International Human Rights Day. |
| 1989 | **March.** Police open fire on pro-independence rioters; martial law is imposed; hundreds are killed.<br>**October 5.** Dalai Lama is awarded Nobel Peace Prize. |

When the Chinese People's Liberation Army swept across Tibet in 1950, it left behind a path of destruction and despair. The hatred that still burns in the young people of Tibet is a legacy of that time of violence and a testament to China's bungling mismanagement ever since.

## Issues and Events

The Tibetans have a lot to complain about. Of six thousand Buddhist temples in existence before the Chinese invaded in 1950, less than a dozen still stand. Billions of dollars in sacred religious artifacts were stolen by the Chinese. Several hundred thousand monks were forced to take secular jobs, and tens of thousands were arrested. Chinese agricultural policies resulted in widespread famine. During the Cultural Revolution in the 1960s, monasteries were closed and monks were taken to forced labor camps. The Chinese attempted to impose their culture on the Tibetans by forcing them to abandon their language and by prohibiting religious practices. It is estimated that more than one million Tibetans died as a direct result of Chinese rule.

Since 1980 the Chinese have made earnest efforts to try to correct their past mistakes in Tibet. The Chinese reversed agricultural policies and removed a ban on religious practices. In addition to allocating money to restore and renovate several temples, they reactivated more than one thousand monasteries. The Chinese claim they liberated Tibetans from a feudal society in which many were treated as slaves. They point to the hospitals, schools, and highways that they built.

Many reforms in Tibet have backfired or have been ineffective. Tourism was encouraged to bring in revenue but it was the Chinese merchants who benefitted the most. Similarly, preferential taxes in Tibet had the undesirable effect of attracting Chinese to the region. In fact, the Chinese have become so numerous that they now threaten to assimilate the Tibetans. Tibetan language laws have been passed, but the local Chinese ignore the regulations. Limits placed on the number of monks have restricted the spread of religion.

A period of serious unrest began in 1987 when the Tibetans began demonstrating for independence from China. Since that time there have been more than twenty serious riots resulting in more than six hundred deaths, thousands of arrests, and the imposition of martial law.

The Dalai Lama, who remains in India, continues to call for an end to the violence. For these efforts he was awarded the Nobel Peace Prize in 1989. Despite the fact that most still profess their devotion to the Dalai Lama, the new generation of Tibetans is becoming increasingly militant. China seems unable to heal the wounds it has inflicted on this ancient land, but it refuses to grant Tibet even limited self-government.

## Background

Chinese claims to Tibet date back to the 1200s when Mongolia conquered both China and Tibet. The Mongols adopted Tibetan Buddhism as their state religion and Tibet was ruled by monks for almost seven hundred years.

In 1904 the British invaded Tibet and tried to impose a treaty recognizing China's sovereignty over Tibet's defense and foreign affairs. The Chinese claimed full sovereignty over the area and therefore refused to sign the treaty. China lost control of Tibet in 1911 when a republican government replaced the Chinese imperial dynasty. Tibet declared its independence, expelled all Chinese residents; and functioned as a self-governing republic until 1951.

After the Communist Revolution in 1949, the People's Liberation Army invaded Tibet in 1950 and gained full control in 1951. For several years the region continued to be ruled by a committee headed by the fourteenth Dalai Lama, or spiritual leader of Tibet. All pretenses of Tibetan self-government were dropped after the 1959 uprising in which one hundred thousand Tibetans were killed. The Dalai Lama, fearing for his life, fled to India where he was granted political asylum.

# Hong Kong: Awaiting the Dragon

## Perspective

| | |
|---|---|
| 1842 | Hong Kong island is ceded to the British after the Opium War. |
| 1860 | British gain Kowloon through Treaty of Beijing. |
| 1898 | New Territories are leased to Britain for ninety-nine years. |
| 1949 | After World War II, rapid development turns Hong Kong into a major industrial and commercial center. |
| 1984 | **December 19.** The United Kingdom and China agree to return Hong Kong to Chinese sovereignty in 1997. |
| 1989 | **May.** Hong Kong Alliance in Support of the Patriotic Movement in China is formed.<br>**June.** Chinese crackdown on student protestors in Beijing creates loss of confidence in Hong Kong.<br>**December 20.** British grant right of abode to fifty thousand Hong Kong households to stop growing emigration. |
| 1990 | **January 8.** Ten thousand gather in Hong Kong to protest repression in China. |

British rule has been good for Hong Kong, a tiny enclave on China's southern coast. Only one-third the size of Rhode Island, Hong Kong is one of Asia's leading commercial and industrial powers. The people of Hong Kong enjoy a high standard of living as a result of their hard work and ingenuity. British rule of Hong Kong has also been good for China by providing it with a "window to the West." All this may end, however, when Hong Kong returns to Chinese rule in 1997. The people of Hong Kong are growing increasingly fearful that they will be swallowed by China, the great dragon to the north.

## Issues and Events

There are many reasons for Hong Kong's success, aside from its excellent deepwater harbor and cheap labor force. One is the stable government under British administration. Another is Hong Kong's status as a completely free port. A third is a virtual lack of government intervention in matters of manufacturing and commerce. In recent years, much of Hong Kong's growth can also be attributed to its special relationship with China. Through Hong Kong, China is able to trade freely with all of the nations of the world, even those with which it officially has no relations. Hong Kong also serves as an important funnel for foreign investment in China.

In 1984 the British government agreed to return Hong Kong to Chinese rule when its lease expires in 1997. Despite claims by the Chinese government that it will allow Hong Kong to operate unchanged for fifty years, growing distrust in the West has provoked rising hostility in China. The open fire by the Chinese on demonstrating students in Beijing in 1989 heightened fears about China's ability to govern Hong Kong without interference. During the student demonstrations, a coalition calling itself the Hong Kong Alliance in Support of the Patriotic Democratic Movement in China was formed and continues to agitate for reform in China. The Chinese claim that this group is subversive and warn that it will be banned after China takes over. The Chinese also have announced their People's Liberation Army will be stationed in Hong Kong, despite an initial agreement with the British to prevent this from happening.

This loss of confidence in Hong Kong's future has already had a grave impact on its economy. Economic growth is down by 50 percent, and both tourism and exports have significantly declined. The most immediate concern has been growing emigration by Hong Kong's largest companies and most skilled labor. In an attempt to stop the trend, the British government agreed to grant permanent British residence (or right of abode) to fifty thousand of Hong Kong's most skilled workers and entrepreneurs. The British hope that these people will choose to stay in Hong Kong, secure in the knowledge that they can escape to Britain if the situation becomes intolerable. The Chinese are less than pleased with this measure and claim that it violates the agreement.

## Background

British traders gained a foothold in China at the beginning of the eighteenth century. By 1841 they had gained complete control of the fine natural harbor at Hong Kong and declared it a free port. The following year, China lost the island of Hong Kong to the British after the Opium War, and the Arrow War resulted in British seizure of the Kowloon Peninsula. The Chinese leased the balance of the area now known as Hong Kong to the British in 1898 for a period of ninety-nine years.

Despite its relations to Britain, Hong Kong has always been inextricably tied to China. Of Hong Kong's six million people, 95 percent are of Chinese origin and 37 percent were born in China. China regards Hong Kong as an integral part of itself and has historically resented the presence of the British.

# Cambodia: Casualty of the Vietnam War

## Perspective

| | |
|---|---|
| **1863** | Cambodia becomes a French protectorate. |
| **1941** | Prince Norodom Sihanouk is made king of Cambodia. |
| **1953** | French grant Cambodian independence under Sihanouk. |
| **1969** | United States begins bombing North Vietnamese forces in Cambodia. |
| **1970** | United States-backed Lon Nol replaces Sihanouk; Khmer Republic is established. |
| **1975** | United States withdraws from Vietnam; Khmer Republic falls to Khmer Rouge. |
| **1976** | Democratic Kampuchea is established under Pol Pot, who initiates a genocidal program. |
| **1978** | Vietnamese troops invade Cambodia. |
| **1979** | Vietnam overthrows Pol Pot regime and installs Heng Samrin as head of People's Republic of Kampuchea (PRK). |
| **1982** | Coalition Government of Democratic Kampuchea (CGDK), headed by Sihanouk, is formed as a government in exile. |
| **1989** | **September 26.** Vietnamese troops leave Cambodia. |
| **1990** | **January.** Peace talks produce tentative agreement. |

May 20 in Cambodia is celebrated each year as the "Day of Hatred" for the Khmer Rouge regime, which ruled the country between 1975 and 1978. The Khmer Rouge sought to create a Communist Utopia, a classless society of peasants. Under the leadership of Pol Pot, a reform program was launched that ultimately resulted in the death of almost a third of the population and complete collapse of the country's economic and social structures.

For years Cambodia suffered from incursions from both sides during the Vietnam War. A United States-backed General—Lon Nol—came to power during the war by overthrowing Cambodia's hereditary ruler, Prince Norodom Sihanouk. When the Americans left Indochina in 1975, the Khmer Rouge quickly took over.

The Pol Pot regime was forced out of power in 1979—but not as a result of its barbarisms against the Cambodian people. Rather, it lost on the larger stage of the international competition between the two great Communist nations, the Soviet Union and China. China supported Pol Pot, while the newly unified Vietnam became a close ally of the Soviet Union. After a series of bitter border battles, an invasion by Vietnamese troops succeeded in installing a former lieutenant of Pol Pot, Heng Samrin, in power. Pol Pot and many of his Khmer Rouge supporters escaped to the hills, while two hundred thousand others became refugees in Thailand.

The Vietnamese-backed government, now led by Hun Sen, has maintained control of the country since 1979. With the reported withdrawal of Vietnamese troops in September 1990, the search for a solution to Cambodia's problems has become even more urgent as the Khmer Rouge once again threatens to take over.

## Issues and Events

The United Nations, as well as most of the countries of the world, has not formally recognized the Vietnamese-backed People's Republic of Kampuchea (PRK). Instead, the officially recognized government is an alliance of three of the country's resistance groups known as the Coalition Government of Democratic Kampuchea (CGDK). The CGDK is headed by Cambodia's former King Sihanouk and even includes the Khmer Rouge. With thirty thousand troops, the Khmer Rouge is the largest of the resistance groups in the CGDK. While the Khmer Rouge has been condemned for its three-year reign of terror, it continues to enjoy international recognition, as most countries have chosen not to recognize the government that resulted from Vietnam's act of aggression.

Since the withdrawal of Vietnamese troops, the Khmer Rouge has stepped up its guerrilla attacks. They have seized a number of cities in the northwest part of the country and have succeeded in disrupting transportation routes. More and more the people fear a Khmer Rouge military takeover. Rumors circulated concerning bombings in the capital of Phnom Penh, although no real damage was apparently done.

A breakthrough in ongoing negotiations concerning Cambodia's future was made in early 1990 when an agreement in principal was reached among the United Nations security council, the PRK, and the CGDK. The plan provides for United Nations rule for a period of about one year, followed by United Nations-supervised free elections. Despite general agreement regarding the overall framework, details of the plan must be hammered out. The CGDK claims that as many as seventy-five thousand Vietnamese troops may still be in Cambodia under the guise of the regular PRK army and militia. They also demand the expulsion of perhaps one million Vietnamese civilians who have moved to Cambodia since the invasion. The PRK demands that the CGDK give up its seat in the United Nations.

Crucial to any peace plan will be the curtailing of the flow of arms into the region. The Chinese continue to supply the Khmer Rouge. Both Vietnam and the Soviet Union support the ruling PRK. Even if the flow of arms can be stopped, it is unlikely that the Khmer Rouge will give up the fight. Although Pol Pot, the mastermind of Democratic Kampuchea's disastrous programs, supposedly retired in 1985, it is believed that he is still in control.

The ever-present Norodom Sihanouk continues to dominate all negotiations. Affable and tenacious, he has the support of most Cambodians and stands as a symbol of nationalism and unity. Sihanouk's alliance with the Khmer Rouge is a marriage of convenience. Although he recognizes that the Khmer Rouge are violent and dangerous, he has used their military prowess and association with the Chinese to his own advantage. Sihanouk believes that after elections are held in Cambodia, a United Nations peacekeeping force will be necessary to keep the Khmer Rouge in check. The Khmer Rouge continue to enjoy the support of many poor people living in rural areas whose hatred of the Vietnamese transcends their fear of the Khmer Rouge. It is hoped that as the Vietnamese presence fades, support for the Khmer Rouge will decline.

## Background

Cambodia broke away from French rule in 1953, when Prince Norodom Sihanouk, then king, who had ruled under French auspices since 1941, dissolved the parliamentary system and declared martial law, forcing the French to grant independence later that year. Sihanouk's reign was moderate, although he was largely ineffective at industrializing a country populated by subsistence farmers living in isolated villages. However, the growth of several small cities, as well as the emergence of rubber as a major export, were indications of Cambodia's economic improvement. Sihanouk's alignment with China was primarily a move to maintain neutrality in the Vietnam War. His efforts were doomed to failure, and in 1969 the United States began bombing North Vietnamese bases and supply routes within Cambodia. Sihanouk was exiled to China when Lon Nol came to power in 1970.

Sihanouk's government fell in 1970 to one of his generals, Lon Nol, who established the Khmer Republic. Lon Nol, who had United States support, was unable to unite the country. In fact, the Communist forces, known as the Khmer Rouge and led by Pol Pot, grew from a small force of four thousand to about seventy thousand in the five years Lon Nol was in office. Pol Pot waged guerrilla warfare against Lon Nol from the jungle. In the five years of Lon Nol's regime, hatred of the United States, due to the relentless bombing by the United States military, caused the Khmer Rouge forces to swell and a bloody civil war ensued. In 1975, as the Vietnam War was drawing to a close and the United States began withdrawing from Indochina, the Khmer Rouge became strong enough to overthrow the Khmer Republic.

The new government, known as Democratic Kampuchea, was formally led by the National United Front of Kampuchea and headed by Sihanouk, who was brought back from exile in China. The real ruler, however, was Pol Pot, who began a genocidal reign of terror. Determined to make Cambodia self-supporting in food production, the Pol Pot regime emptied the cities. Former urban residents, young and old, were placed in work camps in an attempt to create farmland out of the jungle. Currency was abolished and the economy suffered a complete collapse. All religious institutions, private property, and schools were also abolished. Determined to rid the country of its middle class, the regime systematically set about exterminating all those with college educations. Between the political exterminations and those who succumbed to the famine and rigors of the work camps, it has been estimated that at least three million of Cambodia's six million people died.

Traditional hostilities between Vietnam and Cambodia came to a head in December 1977, when relations were broken off. Some outsiders suspected that the Vietnamese used the atrocities of the Khmer Rouge merely as a public excuse, masking an ancient desire to control all of Indochina.

# Japan: Entering a New Era

## Perspective

| | |
|---|---|
| **600 B.C.** | Japan is founded by Emperor Jimmu. |
| **1542** | Portuguese land in Japan. |
| **1637** | All foreigners are expelled. |
| **1854** | United States Navy Commodore Matthew Perry forces Japan to trade. |
| **1868** | Meiji emperor implements Westernization program. |
| **1894** | Japanese militarism begins with war on China. |
| **1926** | Hirohito becomes Showa emperor. |
| **1941** | **December 7.** Japan attacks United States at Pearl Harbor. |
| **1945** | **August.** United States drops atomic bombs on Hiroshima and Nagasaki. **September 2.** Emperor Hirohito surrenders to United States. |
| **1946** | **January 1.** Emperor Hirohito renounces his divinity. |
| **1952** | Japan returns to self-rule. |
| **1989** | **January 7.** Emperor Hirohito dies and Heisei era begins under Emperor Akihito. |

With the death of emperor Hirohito on January 7, 1989, Japan entered a new era called *Heisei*, "achieving peace." The old era of *Showa*, or "enlightened peace," saw the rise of Japanese militarism in the 1930s, the defeat of the Japanese in World War II, the rebuilding of the economy, and the ultimate rise to become the world's second largest economic power. There is little doubt that the new era will bring continued success, and some believe that Japan will soon surpass the United States as the world's economic leader. The end of Showa also marks the end of the postwar era, which was dominated by the United States and its policies. In the age of Heisei, Japan must accept its role as a world leader and take greater responsibility for its trade policies and their impact on the rest of the world.

## Issues and Events

Perhaps the most controversial issue facing Japanese leaders is its enormous trade surplus. Japan has been under increasing pressure in the 1980s to "internationalize," or coordinate its economic policies with those of other countries. Japan's tendency to export more than it imports and produce far more than it can consume has created instability on the world market. This tension could possibly result in a political or economic backlash that would benefit no one. In the mid-1980s, Japan undertook several measures to help reduce its trade surplus, not the least of which was its move to increase the value of its currency, the yen, on the world market. Since 1985, the yen has risen 40 percent relative to the value of the dollar. The purpose of this increase was to increase the price of Japanese goods to make products from other countries more competitive. It was assumed that this action would result in decreased production, layoffs, and recession, but the Japanese quickly adapted to the new situation by developing their domestic markets. By moving their factories to Thailand, Malaysia, and other Asian countries, Japanese business was able to realize both lower production costs and an increase in exports of capital equipment to set up the new enterprises. The domestic market was then expanded in the financial sector and the leisure industries. To further stimulate Japanese consumers, several tax cuts have been enacted in the last few years.

In addition to devaluing the yen, the Japanese have also simplified their import procedures and allowed for greater foreign investment. Since these measures were taken, Japanese imports have risen 25 percent. Despite this increase, other problems remain such as the so-called "informal trade barriers," including the Japanese preference for goods made in their own country and the etiquette and formalities involved in successfully completing a business deal. Another barrier is Japan's lack of retail chain stores; most retail outlets are family businesses, a system which does not lend itself to mass marketing. Heavy protectionist policies regarding food, especially rice, have resulted in very high food costs in Japan. Japanese people spend about 20 percent of their income on food, compared to roughly 11 percent for United States citizens, and yet they are not allowed to import these foods even though it would be much cheaper to do so.

Japan's flexibility and willingness to help the United States overcome its mounting debt is of critical importance to both countries, whose fates seem to be inextricably tied. The United States imports a full 39 percent of all Japanese exports, and Japanese imports account for 23 percent of all United States exports. Japan depends on the United States for military support, while Japanese firms own about $30 billion worth of assets in the United States. The New York stock exchange crash in October 1987 underscored the interdependency of the world markets when the Tokyo and London markets immediately followed suit.

Japan also faces challenges on the domestic front. One of its problems is a lack of space, which translates into exorbitant land values and housing shortages. The average house in the United States is about 35 percent larger than the average Japanese home. Another problem is its school system, which has served Japan well in the past but does not foster the kind of creative thinking necessary to lead the country in the new age. Japan also faces a rapidly aging work force; by 2000, 16 percent of the population will be over 65, and Japan does not have a well developed social services program to deal with supporting, housing, and caring for the medical needs of its changing population. Finally, the role of corporation and the attitudes of the workers are continuing to evolve as affluence grows and economic growth slows. Companies are drifting away from paternal policies like guaranteeing workers jobs for life, and workers are placing their families ahead of their careers. How this will effect Japan's legendary productivity remains to be seen.

The role of the military is another source of debate as Japan takes its role as a world leader. The Japanese constitution prohibits the development of offensive military capabilities and Japan has generally relied on the United States for its defense. As Japan has gained more wealth, it has been under increased pressure to share the economic burden of that defense. With military spending amounting to only 1 percent of its GNP, Japan has risen to become the world's third largest military spender. Most of its money has gone toward high-technology defensive detection systems, aircraft, and ships. Japan currently has more destroyers in the Pacific than the United States. However, it has no aircraft carriers and no nuclear capabilities.

Political instability plagued Japan in 1989. Public resentment over misconduct by its leaders and the introduction of Japan's first sales tax resulted in the resignation of two prime ministers and stunning losses at the polls by the ruling Liberal Democratic Party. Japan's new prime minister, Toshiki Kaifu, has agreed to modify the sales tax to exclude certain basic necessities such as food.

Despite these continuing controversies, Japan can pride itself with one of the world's healthiest economies, negligible inflation and unemployment, a hefty 5 percent annual growth rate, high productivity, and a low crime rate.

## Background

According to legend, Japan was founded by Emperor Jimmu, a descendant of the Sun Goddess, in 600 B.C. Jimmu was a direct ancestor of the current dynasty. The Chinese writing system was introduced in A.D. 405 and Buddhism arrived in 552. From 710 until 1867, shoguns, nobles, and regents ruled the country. The role of the emperor has always been—as it is today—largely ceremonial. Europeans landed in Japan in 1542, but were expelled in 1637. The United States forced Japan to reopen its doors in 1854, and in 1868 the country embarked on a Westernization program under the Meiji emperor. By the late 1800s, the Japanese military had made territorial gains in Asia and the Pacific. In 1941, Japan attacked the United States base at Pearl Harbor, but was forced to surrender in 1945 after the United States destroyed Hiroshima and Nagasaki with atomic bombs. From the ashes of war and destruction, Japan quickly rebuilt its devastated economy by establishing small factories to produce basic necessities. These factories were more like communes, and the workers were generally paid with food. By the 1950s, the economic boom had begun, and workers were paid wages instead of food. The Japanese put their wages in savings, which provided the banks with money to lend to the companies. The companies expanded, but remained somewhat communal in nature. Workers were allowed to share in a group decision-making process that solidified worker commitment to the firm. Group harmony and a strong work ethic resulted in amazing efficiency and productivity. Today, about one quarter of the Japanese work for these large firms, which have been wildly successful and have inspired imitators throughout the world. Japanese companies have been particularly successful at improving on existing technologies, but have been weak at developing new products.

The Japanese equate a trade surplus with success. They have been trained to believe that because they live on a small, mountainous island chain with very little arable land, they must export manufactured goods to provide trade credit for food. Without this security, they believe their country would face collapse and starvation.

# South Asia

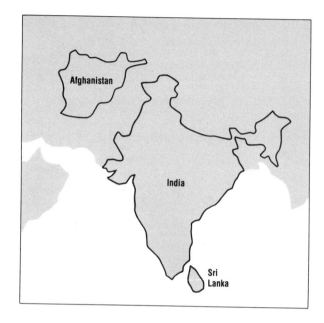

The major sources of conflict in South Asia are modern examples of ancient problems. In India, the Sikhs have been fighting for their own nation since Sikhism was founded in the fifteenth century. In Sri Lanka, the tribal wars between the majority Sinhalese and the minority Tamils can be traced as far back as the early centuries A.D., when the ancestors of the modern Tamils began migrating south from India. Afghanistan, strategically located between such great powers as the Soviet Union, Iran, and India, has historically been viewed as a buffer state by its powerful neighbors and fought over on that account. The modern-day invasion of Afghanistan by the Soviet Union in order to aid the local Communist party is only the modern equivalent of the traditional desire of Russia to extend its power to the south—with the goal of Russian access to the Indian Ocean.

Since the withdrawal of Soviet troops in February 1989, the situation in Afghanistan is volatile. Afghanistan is left to confront the civil war between the fiercely independent guerrillas—known as mujahidin—and the government. Guerrilla opposition to the Soviet-backed central government is steeped in history and tradition: the Afghan tribes have always resisted any central government, whatever the nominal leadership.

Religious and tribal antagonisms and rivalries continue to abound throughout South Asia. The seemingly irreconcilable differences between the Hindus and Muslims in India have cost the lives of millions of Indians in the twentieth century. The separation of the former British colony of India into three nations (India, Pakistan, and Bangladesh) dramatically illustrates the area's religious strife.

Another religious minority, the Sikhs, is now urging the formation of an independent state in India's Punjab. The violence between the Sikhs and the Indian government, which led to Indira Gandhi's assassination, continues as the Indian government attempts to meet some of the Sikh demands.

The desire of the minority Tamils for independence from the majority Sinhalese on Sri Lanka has led to violence on that island. While the Tamils complain of increasingly harsh government reprisals, the government charges that the Tamils are being aided by the large minority of Tamils in India, who are suspected of mounting guerrilla attacks. The Indian government's attempts to mediate the conflict failed, and Indian troops were launched to keep the peace. India's persistent military presence has led to strain between normally friendly India and Sri Lanka.

India is plagued by boundary disputes with many of the nations of South Asia. India has argued—and occasionally fought—with Pakistan over the Kashmir region ever since Indian independence.

Armed conflict between India and Pakistan, or even between India and China, is always a possibility in the Indian subcontinent, a possibility that becomes even more serious upon consideration of India's and China's nuclear capabilities.

# Sri Lanka:
# Ethnic Rivalry Explodes

## Perspective

| | |
|---|---|
| 1796 | *British seize control of Ceylon.* |
| 1948 | *February 4. Ceylon becomes independent dominion.* |
| 1972 | *May 22. Ceylon adopts new constitution, becomes Republic of Sri Lanka.* |
| 1978 | *January. Junius Jayawardene assumes office.* |
| 1983 | *July. Rioting between majority Sinhalese and minority Tamils sparks the beginning of civil war.* |
| 1987 | *July 29. Indo-Sri Lankan Agreement is signed. Indian troops are sent to Sri Lanka.* |
| 1988 | *December. Ranasinghe Premadasa is elected president despite JVP efforts to sabotage elections.* |

Sri Lanka, formerly Ceylon, a teardrop-shaped island off the southern tip of India, has in recent months been plagued by a rapidly escalating climate of violence between radical factions of the majority Sinhalese and the minority Tamils. The Sinhalese, who compose three-quarters of the population, are primarily Buddhist, while the Tamils are primarily Hindu and speak the language of the fifty million Tamils in India. The Tamils live mainly in northern Sri Lanka, which is generally less prosperous than the south.

## Issues and Events

While these two rival groups have a centuries-old history of disputes, the last few years have seen the level of violence increase dramatically, due in part to the emergence of two opposing radical groups. The "Tamil Tigers" are a guerrilla group which protests Sinhalese discrimination against Tamils and advocates the establishment of an independent Tamil nation in northern Sri Lanka. The People's Liberation Front (JVP) is a left-wing Sinhalese nationalist group whose objective is the subjugation and repression of the Tamil people.

Rising violence by both groups resulted in military reprisals by the government and repeated accusations of torture and other abuses against the Tamils. In an effort to protect Sri Lanka's Tamils, India entered into negotiations with Sri Lanka.

On July 29, 1987, Indian Prime Minister Rajiv Gandhi and the Sri Lankan government signed an accord which included several concessions to the Tamils, including increased political autonomy, citizenship for the Tamils who emigrated from India in the nineteenth century, and acceptance of Tamil as an official language. In return, the Tamils were to abandon their campaign for an independent homeland. Three thousand Indian troops were sent to Sri Lanka to monitor the negotiated settlement and enforce a declared cease-fire.

Both the Tamil Tigers and the JVP resented the agreement and the presence of the Indian troops and retaliated by resuming their attacks on various military and civilian targets. By the end of 1988, more than ten thousand people were killed in the six years since the outbreak of the war, and the number of Indian troops swelled to fifty thousand.

On September 18, 1989, President Premadasa and India's Prime Minister Gandhi signed an agreement calling for the withdrawal of all Indian troops by December 31. Ghandi was later defeated by V.P. Singh, and his successor failed to endorse the agreement. As a result, troop withdrawal has been postponed indefinitely.

In a further attempt to stem the rising tide of violence and anarchy, twenty-one groups (including the Tamil Tigers) also began negotiations in late September, although the extremist JVP boycotted the meeting. In addition to civil war, the country also faces overpopulation, lagging economic development, and rising unemployment.

## Background

The Sinhalese have been established on the island of Sri Lanka since the sixth century B.C., although the Tamils did not appear in substantial numbers in Ceylon until the tenth century. Controlled first by India, then by the Portuguese, the Dutch, and finally, the British, Ceylon achieved independence on February 4, 1948. The country adopted a new constitution on May 22, 1972, which changed the island's name from Ceylon to the Republic of Sri Lanka.

Traditional rivalries exploded into violence in 1983 when Tamil Tigers killed thirteen Sinhalese soldiers. The ensuing riots resulted in over 350 fatalities and seventy-nine thousand homeless. Since then, the unrest between the two groups has grown geometrically.

Attempts by president Junius Jayawardene to stem the violence were fruitless during his ten-year reign, despite continued military pressure and repeated attempts at negotiation.

# Afghanistan: Civil War and Turmoil

## Perspective

| | |
|---|---|
| 1919 | **August 19.** *Afghanistan gains independence from Britian.* |
| 1973 | **July 17.** *Mohammad Daoud seizes power and abolishes constitution.* |
| 1978 | **April.** *People's Democratic Party of Afghanistan (PDPA) stages Marxist coup and establishes Taraki as president.*<br>**December.** *Soviet Union and Afghanistan sign Treaty of Friendship, Good Neighborliness, and Cooperation.* |
| 1979 | **September.** *Internal rivalry splits PDPA; Amin kills Taraki and seizes power.*<br>**December.** *Soviet Union invades. Soviet troops kill Amin and establish Babrak Karmal as head of new government.* |
| 1986 | **May 4.** *Karmal resigns and is replaced by former secret police chief Najibullah.* |
| 1989 | **February 15.** *Soviets withdraw remaining troops.*<br>**February 23.** *Mujahidin establish government-in-exile.*<br>**July 7.** *Seige of Jālālābād fails.* |

When the Soviet Union withdrew its 115,000 troops from Afghanistan in 1989, western analysts predicted that the Marxist government in Kabul, lacking popular support, would collapse within a few months. A year later, Najibullah's government is still clinging tenaciously to power. Meanwhile, the disastrous civil war, which has claimed more than a million lives and created five million refugees, rages on.

## Issues and Events

After the Soviet troop withdrawal, rebel mujahidin leaders met in Pakistan to create a government-in-exile and seek international recognition. The United States stated that before it could recognize the new government, it must establish a base on Afghan territory. This led to the battle of Jālālābād, the bloodiest in the ten-year history of the war. Located midway between the Pakistan border and Kabul, Jālālābād was an ideal military target. Despite alleged tactical assistance from United States and Pakistani advisors, the mujahidin were able to hold the city for only five months, during which five thousand soldiers and civilians were killed. The mujahidin's seige of Jālālābād failed because the rebels could not coordinate their efforts. Skilled in guerrilla tactics, they lacked the discipline and strategy to capture and secure their target.

The mujahidin have also been plagued by dwindling popularity and strength, while Najibullah has been hard at work improving his image and expanding his power base. For example, the mujahidin have not been able to form an effective coalition. The rebels' interim government was created by eight Sunni Muslim factions, but it excluded both the former king Zahir Shah and the Shiite groups based in Iran. Najibullah, in contrast, has managed to defuse potentially explosive divisions within his government. The mujahidin's *jihad*, or holy war, has lost its support now that the foreign invaders have been expelled and the government is embracing Islam. Real authority on the countryside is vested in scores of minor mujahidin commanders. While the mujahidin leaders often fail to consult with their commanders, Najibullah has effectively negotiated several cease-fires with individual commanders in the Kabul area. The mujahidin's ruthless tactics, applauded when they were directed against the Russians, are now publicly denounced as their fury is directed at fellow Afghans. Their tactic of employing long-range shelling and rocket attacks on both Kabul and Jālālābād has resulted in thousands of civilian casualties since the Russian pullout. Mujahidin leaders are also accused of killing or torturing those who surrender to them or offer to defect to their side. Finally, Najibullah began divesting himself of any connection to the Russians as soon as the pullout was accomplished. He denies that his government is—or ever was—Marxist, and embraces free markets, democracy, and religious freedom. He continues to call for negotiations and cultivate an image as a moderate, reasonable, competent leader while the mujahidin, who refuse to negotiate, are portrayed as fanatical extremists who are concerned only with their own narrow self-interests.

Critical to the balance of power in Afghanistan is the continuing influx of money and weapons from foreign powers. While Iran and China have been cutting off their aid to the mujahidin, the United States, Saudi Arabia, and Pakistan continue to support the rebels. This aid, however, is minor compared to that which the Soviet Union continues to provide to Kabul to the tune of $300 million each month. Between twenty-five and forty planes arrive daily from the Soviet Union carrying food and military supplies. It is inevitable that the winds of war will continue to blow over

Afghanistan as long as they are fanned by foreign support.

## Background

Turbulence has been the only constant in the region now called Afghanistan, located in the path of major trade and invasion routes from central Asia into the Middle East and India. Starting in 328 B.C. with the invasion by Alexander the Great, a succession of conquerors swept across Afghanistan. One result of the numerous invasions was great ethnic diversity, and society developed as a complex network of tribal interrelationships based on ancestry, ethnicity, and language. The arrival of Islam in A.D. 642 provided a common bond among people of various ethnic groups. Afghanistan's many tribes united to form an independent nation in 1747, when Ahmad Shah Durrani was elected king by tribal leaders.

Another result of Afghanistan's history as a major crossroads is a decided hatred of foreign intervention in its affairs. The British experienced the brunt of this animosity when they sought to halt Russian expansionism by establishing a presence in Afghanistan in 1839. This ignited the first of three wars between Great Britain and Afghanistan. By the third war in 1919, an exhausted Great Britain, which had maintained control over Afghanistan's foreign affairs, gave in to King Amanullah's demands for total independence. Even after independence, real power was in many cases still vested in tribal leaders.

The throne continued to change hands until 1964, when parliamentary rule was put into effect with a new constitution. Extremists on both sides, however, grew increasingly vocal. Amid charges of corruption and the problems of a drought-ridden economy, former prime minister Mohammad Daoud staged a bloodless coup on July 17, 1973. Daoud declared Afghanistan a republic, which it remained until the People's Democratic Party of Afghanistan (PDPA), a newly formed coalition of two rival Marxist parties, killed Daoud and his family in 1978. Nur Mohammad Taraki took control of the new government.

The Marxists attempted rapid social change by enacting radical decrees, including land reform, the emancipation of women, and programs to fight illiteracy.

Violent opposition, mostly based on Islamic beliefs conflicting with the PDPA's policies, developed immediately and grew into countrywide insurgency. After the original Marxist coup in April 1978, the Soviet Union signed a treaty with the new regime. As the insurgency movement grew, Russian advisers and equipment became critical to the survival of Marxism and the government.

A succession of bloody coups resulted in the eventual installation of Babrak Karmal, whom the Soviets immediately supported with an invasion of fifty thousand troops. The Soviet invasion prompted the rise of the mujahidin, or "holy warriors," who vowed to fight to the death to expel the invaders and protect their Islamic way of life.

When Mikhail Gorbachev came to power in 1985, the Afghanistan war had become one of the Soviet Union's most pressing problems. Gorbachev replaced Karmal with the ruthless former secret police chief Najibullah in an attempt to gain a military victory. But still the rebellious mujahidin could not be subdued and the war continued to escalate. By 1988, the Soviets disclosed that thirteen thousand of their soldiers had been killed, thirty-five thousand were wounded, and three hundred were missing. The war cost the Soviets over $1 billion a year and severely damaged the Soviet Union's relations with most of the Islamic world, as well as the United States. The Soviets finally withdrew their troops in February 1989.

Throughout their war against the Soviets, the mujahidin enjoyed overwhelming national and international support for their cause. Substantial amounts of money and arms from all over the world were funneled to the mujahidin through Pakistan.

The Soviets, on the other hand, experienced nothing but condemnation for the invasion. The oil rich Islamic countries of the Middle East joined China and the United States in their unyielding denouncements of the Soviets' expansionist tactics. The United Nations annually passed resolutions calling for Soviet troop withdrawal. The Soviets' futile involvement in the war has been likened to the United States' intervention in Vietnam.

# India: Conflict over Sikh Nationalism

## Perspective

| | |
|---|---|
| 1469 | Nanak, founder of Sikhism, is born. |
| 1801 | Ranjit Singh establishes a Sikh empire in the Punjab. |
| 1849 | British conquer Punjab, ending Sikh independence. |
| 1947 | Partition of India and Pakistan creates independent nations with Hindu and Muslim majorities. Sikhs demand the creation of an independent state. |
| 1966 | Indian government creates new Punjab state with Sikh majority. |
| 1983 | **October.** Emergency rule is invoked in Punjab to suppress terrorist violence by Sikh militants. |
| 1984 | **June 6.** Indian troops storm Golden Temple and kill one thousand Sikhs. **October 31.** Indian prime minister Indira Gandhi is assassinated by two Sikh members of her security guard; in ensuing violence, Hindu mobs kill almost two thousand Sikhs. |
| 1985 | **September.** Emergency rule is lifted. |
| 1987 | **May 11.** Emergency rule is reestablished in Punjab as a result of increased terrorist attacks. |
| 1988 | **May 30.** Sikh high priests are evicted from the Golden Temple Management Committee. |
| 1989 | **March 3.** Sikh prisoners held since the 1984 invasion of the Golden Temple are released. **November.** V.P. Singh replaces Rajiv Gandhi as Prime Minister. |

The assassination on October 31, 1984, of Indian prime minister Indira Gandhi by two Sikh members of her personal bodyguard focused world attention on the problems and demands of India's Sikh minority. Indira Gandhi's son and successor, Rajiv Gandhi, stated that the Sikh problem had the highest priority of his new administration. Concentrated in the strategically important and economically prosperous state of Punjab, the Sikhs have had increasingly tense relations with India's central government in the 1980s. The Sikhs' holy city of Amritsar and their shrine, the Golden Temple, were the center of conflict.

## Issues and Events

Violence has escalated since late 1983 in the Sikhs' northwestern border state of Punjab, which separates the predominantly Hindu sections of India from Muslim Pakistan. While some radical nationalist factions advocated an independent Sikh nation, to be called Khalistan, others supported the transformation of the Punjab into an autonomous Sikh homeland. Growing violence caused hundreds of deaths and led to the imposition in October 1983 of direct rule in the Punjab by India's central government.

By the spring of 1984, Sikh militants, led by Jarnail Singh Bhindranwale, were stockpiling arms and supplies in the Golden Temple. Terrorist attacks on prominent Hindus and on Sikh leaders who disagreed with extremist tactics were followed by increased government security measures. After Sikh extremists declared on May 31 that they would block the transfer of grain, water, and power from the Punjab to other areas of India, eleven people died in a police-Sikh clash at the Golden Temple.

On June 2, the federal government declared the Punjab "restricted," which put it off limits to journalists and foreigners. About fifty thousand police and federal militia were put under the control of the army, followed on June 3 by a curfew, a halt in transportation, and a military presence at other Sikh shrines.

Machine guns, mortars, and antitank rockets supported the June 6 assault on the Golden Temple by Indian army troops. The Sikh militants were finally defeated with one thousand dead, including Jarnail.

The assassination of Prime Minister Gandhi in her residential compound in New Delhi was interpreted in India as a reprisal for the storming of the Golden Temple. Despite initial assurances by new Prime Minister Rajiv Gandhi that the assassination was an act by individuals, not a conspiracy, violence against Sikhs and their property erupted throughout the country, resulting in almost two thousand Sikh deaths by mid-November. Reactions to the assassination in overseas Sikh communities ranged from joy over the death of Gandhi—seen as an oppressor—to sorrow that the extremist faction had precipitated a crisis.

As violence continued through 1985, Prime Minister Gandhi made several gestures toward resolving the conflict. The Sikhs, however, continued to press their other demands, including demands for the government to dissolve the special court formed to try purported terrorists; for Sikh army deserters to no longer be court-martialed; for the Indian army to be withdrawn from the Punjab; for detainees held without charge to be released; and for the government to make restitution for losses suffered in the November 1984 riots. Meanwhile, four Sikhs (one of whom died before capture) were charged with conspiracy in the assassination of Indira Gandhi. Of the three remaining suspects, one was acquitted and the other two were executed in 1989. On the other hand, those responsible for the slaughter of the two thousand Sikhs were never brought to justice.

Violence continued throughout the 1980s as Sikh militants and Hindu nationalists perpetuated their cycle of revenge, while government troops continued their crackdown on Sikh terrorists. Hundreds have been slain each year in the continuing struggle. Fatalities in 1988 rose to three thousand, the highest level since 1984.

The major obstacle to a peaceful settlement between the Sikhs and the Indian government is the lack of unified Sikh leadership. There are six main Sikh factions and over twenty terrorist groups. The aim of the Sikh terrorists is to gain complete control of the Punjab not only by driving out the Hindus, but also by intimidating their moderate Sikh counterparts by means of bombings and assassinations. Moderate Sikhs who could take part in a negotiated settlement would face the risk of death at the hands of their terrorist rivals.

Sikh extremists maintained their control of the Golden Temple and continued to use it as an arsenal. The Indian army invaded the sacred shrine each year since 1986. Moderate Sikhs scored a victory in 1988 when the powerful Sikh Temple Management Committee evicted the five Sikh high priests who had supported the terrorists in an attempt to restore the sanctity of the temple.

In 1989 the government released all 188 Sikh prisoners held since the 1984 invasion of the Golden Temple, but this initiative did little to placate militant Sikh groups.

Gandhi lost in his bid for reelection in November 1989. Many Sikhs are hopeful that India's new leader will be able to heal the nation's wounds. Meanwhile, emergency rule continues, terrorism is rampant, and negotiations remain at a standstill.

## Background

The Sikh religion is a relative newcomer, and the development of the Sikhs as a distinct people is even more recent. Sikhism took form during the fifteenth and sixteenth centuries in the Punjab, the northwestern region of the Indian subcontinent spanning the present Punjab states in India and Pakistan.

The first guru, or spiritual leader, of Sikhism was Nanak, born in 1469 about 40 miles (65 km) from Lahore, in present-day Pakistan. Nanak proclaimed that he was neither a Hindu nor a Muslim but instead was the bearer of a new teaching that superseded both Hinduism and Islam.

Nanak drew on both religions in framing his beliefs. He took the idea of the unity of God and an absolute prohibition of images and idols from Islam. From the Hindus came the belief in an eternal cycle of death and rebirth, and the word *sikh* derives from the Hindi word for *disciple*.

After Nanak died in 1539, he was followed by nine gurus. During this period, the Sikhs were forced to take up arms against Muslim persecution. It was also during this period that the holy city of Amritsar was founded and the Golden Temple was built. In 1699 the last of the gurus, Gobind Singh, established the brotherhood of the Khalsa, "Pure Ones." When the succession of gurus came to an end with Gobind Singh's assassination in 1708, military and spiritual leadership of the Sikhs fell to the members of the Khalsa brotherhood. During the eighteenth century, the Khalsa successfully harassed the Muslim rulers of the Punjab. By the beginning of the nineteenth century, the Khalsa leader Ranjit Singh had taken possession of the Punjab's capital city of Lahore and had proclaimed himself maharajah of the Punjab.

Inevitably, the Sikhs clashed with the British in India. By 1849, the Sikhs were defeated, and the Punjab was annexed to British India. Thereafter, the Sikhs served the British loyally. Sikh troops played an important part in suppressing the Indian mutiny of 1857 and made up more than 20 percent of the British Indian Army in World War I. After the war, relations between British and Sikhs deteriorated.

In the sectarian upheaval that preceded the partition of India and Pakistan in August 1947, no riots were more violent than those in the Punjab between the Sikhs and their traditional foes, the Muslims. Thus, when Pakistan and India became independent, more than two million Sikhs fled into India from Islamic Pakistan.

Bitterly disappointed that they had failed to secure their own independence and reestablish a Sikh nation, the Sikhs of the Indian Punjab began agitating for greater political autonomy, and a new era of Sikh nationalism began. In 1966, in an effort to mollify the Sikhs, the Indian government redrew the boundaries of Punjab State so that it contained a majority of Punjabi-speaking Sikhs.

Despite the fact that they represent only 2 percent of the country's population, minority communities of Sikhs can be found throughout much of India. Sikhs still play an important role in India's security forces, and there are Sikhs in civilian occupations from cab driver to cabinet minister. In 1982, at the urging of Prime Minister Indira Gandhi, Zail Singh was elected by the Indian parliament as president of India—the first Sikh ever to hold that office.

# The Middle East and North Africa

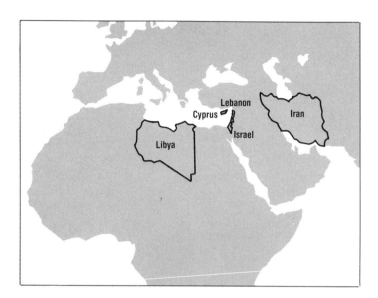

Although the description of the Middle East as a "powder keg" was already a cliché in the nineteenth century, twentieth century events have rendered that description just as accurate. The end of World War II saw the termination of the artificial peace that had been imposed by the great powers since the nineteenth century. Great Britain and France in particular had carved out their individual spheres of influence, and each had respected and supported the other in maintaining a truce among the various religious and ethnic groups that were forced to live together in the Middle East. Britain and France pulled out of the Middle East at the end of World War II, leaving the newly independent nations to fend for themselves. The region has been torn by sporadic conflict ever since.

The support and protection of Israel was the focus of United States policy in the Middle East in the years immediately following World War II. In the 1970s, protecting American petroleum interests in Arab nations became a second objective of the United States government. These two interests, a free Israel and a free-flowing oil supply, tend to pull American diplomacy in two directions. Policies aimed at bolstering Israel are opposed by the Arab oil-producing nations, and pro-Arab policies are deemed unacceptable by Israel.

The area known as the Middle East generally includes the countries of the Arabian peninsula and Iraq, Iran, Israel, Jordan, Lebanon, and Syria, and its influence extends to encompass the countries of North Africa in the same general region. The island of Cyprus shares the region's history as an important historical crossroads. Islam is the majority religion of the area, and many share the Arabic language and culture.

Because of the region's mineral riches and strategic value, internal conflicts quickly take on international significance. The Middle East and North Africa contain vast oil deposits upon which the industrialized world depends. The area's waterways, including the Strait of Hormuz and the Suez Canal, are of commercial and military importance. In a less influential part of the world, a border such as that between Iraq and Iran would most likely remain a regional concern. But when the flow of oil to the west is threatened, a conflict such as this quickly gains international attention.

Many of the historic troubles of the Middle East are indigenous. It is the birthplace of three of the world's great religions: Judaism, Christianity, and Islam, all of which have become intertwined with the political and economic problems of the region. Islam, the religion of the overwhelming majority, is mainly composed of two sects: the majority Sunnis and the rapidly-growing Shiite minority. The Shiite fundamentalist movement in Iran, led by the Ayatollah Khomeini, underscored the rivalry between these two groups and threatened the stability of the entire region. A third Muslim group, especially prominent in Syria and Lebanon, is the Druze. Although the Druze regard their religion as a branch of Islam, other Muslim sects view it as heretical. Much of the unrest and violence of the Middle East is the result of the long-standing enmity that each of these groups feels toward the other two. There is also considerable tension in Israel between the Orthodox and the other branches of Judaism.

The site of some of the world's most ancient civilizations, the Middle East was host to people of many different cultures. The great civilization of ancient Egypt developed on the banks of the Nile, and the area of the Tigris and Euphrates rivers saw the society of Mesopotamia flourish. Invaders and immigrants were diverse, and the many peoples coming to the region included Assyrians, Hebrews, Phoenicians, Chaldeans, Medes, and Persians. Islam was founded in the A.D. seventh century. As the Arabs expanded their empire, their religion and culture spread throughout the Middle East and North Africa.

The Arab Empire came to an end about the tenth century and was followed some centuries later by the empire of the Ottoman Turks, who were also Muslim. The Ottoman Empire dominated until Turkey was defeated in World War I. Many of the Arab states remained under foreign rule as British or French mandates of the League of Nations.

Much of the tension in the Middle East has resulted from this diversity of religion and culture. In both Cyprus and Lebanon, attempts by the colonial powers to design governmental systems to ensure the rights of various ethnic groups proved to be dismal failures. No more successful was the effort to establish both Arab and Jewish states in the former British mandate of Palestine.

The area of Palestine, comprising present-day Israel, was mandated to the British in 1920. As Jewish immigration to the region increased, so did Arab-Jewish hostility. In an attempt to quell the growing discontent, Britain placed restrictions on Jewish immigration.

Following World War II, many Jews directed their energies to establishing the nation of Israel, though at the same time postwar sentiment for the Jews was widespread. Although immigration restrictions had not been rescinded, Jewish immigration to Palestine increased, which heightened Arab-Jewish hostility. In 1947, Britain turned to the United Nations for help in solving the problem.

The result was the division of Palestine into a state with specified Arab and Jewish zones, plus the neutral city of Jerusalem. In 1948, the independent state of Israel was proclaimed, and fighting broke out between Arabs and Jews. The Arab state envisioned by the United Nations never materialized, and Palestinian Arabs became refugees.

Hostilities between Israel and the surrounding Arab states have continued. Major conflicts included a 1956 war focused on the Suez Canal, the Six-Day War of 1967, and a war in October 1973. A milestone in Arab-Israeli relations came in 1979 with the signing of a peace treaty between Egypt and Israel. However, the Arabs as an ethnic group are not nearly so united as their combined opposition to Israel would imply, and the Arab world denounced Egypt's peace initiative. The Palestinians continue in their quest for a homeland. Following several years of increasing unrest, they unilaterally declared their independence in Israel's occupied territories in 1988.

Although part of the African continent, North Africa is linked by religion and culture to the Middle East. The region of North Africa generally includes Egypt, Algeria, Morocco, Tunisia, and Libya. Three of these nations—Algeria, Morocco, and Tunisia—are former French colonies. In the past, Italy governed Libya, while Britain oversaw Egypt.

Despite North Africa's cultural link with the Middle East, its colonial past ties it to the rest of the African continent. The period of European expansion in Africa saw colonists drawn by the profits of slavery and other trades, and they settled in enclaves that had little regard for the natural boundaries that had arisen from ethnicity or tribal allegiance. The colonies thus came to be demarcated by artificial borders created by treaties and agreements among the colonial powers. The land of the region had fostered a nomadic life-style, and the foreign-imposed boundaries prevented the people from following their traditional way of life. When independence was finally achieved, the artificial boundaries remained, sometimes uniting diverse peoples into a single nation, and sometimes separating a single people by an international border. Dissension was often the result; many borders were finalized only recently, and many remain in dispute. Libya's Bedouin tribes, for example, long presented a unified resistance to the imposition of what they viewed as artificial borders.

Libya is also an example of the nationalistic determination that sometimes arose as a result of foreign intervention and control. Colonel Mu'ammar al-Qadhafi, the unofficial leader of the Libyan state, is of Bedouin descent and is not part of the traditional Libyan elite. Thus, he is well acquainted with the widespread poverty often resulting from autocratic rule and foreign influence. Motivated by anti-imperialistic beliefs, Qadhafi came to power in 1969, promoting the removal of foreign interests from his country and establishing a government based on Islam. Although most of Libya is desert, the country benefits from its large oil deposits, and in this oil Qadhafi has found a weapon of international significance. Qadhafi's political goal is unification of the Arab world.

# Lebanon: Politics, Religion, and Demographics

## Perspective

| | |
|---|---|
| 1943 | **November 22.** Independent Lebanese state is established by the French. |
| 1948 | Israel is founded. One hundred thousand displaced Palestinians settle in Lebanon. |
| 1975 | **April.** Fighting between Christians and Palestinian guerrillas erupts in Beirut. |
| 1976 | **April.** Syrian-dominated Arab Defense Force (ADF) enters Lebanon. |
| 1978 | **March 15.** Palestinian attacks prompt Israeli invasion of southern Lebanon.<br>**April.** United Nations peace-keeping forces (UNIFIL) arrive.<br>**June.** Israeli troops withdraw. |
| 1982 | **June 6.** Israel invades Lebanon in retaliation for Palestinian terrorist attacks.<br>**August.** Evacuation of Palestinian Liberation Organization (PLO) is carried out by UNIFIL.<br>**September 14.** President Gemayel is assassinated.<br>**September 15.** Israel invades West Beirut; Palestinian refugees are massacred by Lebanese Forces; UNIFIL returns to evacuate foreign forces. |
| 1983 | **April 18.** United States embassy is bombed.<br>**October.** United States marine headquarters is bombed. |
| 1984 | **March.** United States marines withdraw. |
| 1985 | **June 6.** Israeli troops withdraw. |
| 1986 | **April 7.** Israelis bomb Palestinian refugee camps. |
| 1987 | **June 1.** Prime Minister Karami is assassinated. |
| 1988 | **September 22.** General Aoun is appointed interim Prime Minister. |
| 1989 | **March 14.** General Aoun announces campaign to evict Syrians.<br>**September 23.** Arab League-sponsored cease fire goes into effect.<br>**October 22.** Taif Accord is reached.<br>**November 5.** René Moawad is elected president.<br>**November 22.** Moawad is assassinated.<br>**November 24.** Elias Hrawi is elected president. |

Today, with Lebanon in physical, economic, and political ruin, it is difficult to believe that for most of the period following World War II, the country was viewed as the one area of the Middle East that seemed to be solving its political and religious problems. Its capital, Beirut, was the financial center of the Middle East, with a cultural life that was the envy of other cities in the area.

The government established by the French in 1943 provided for proportional representation of the various religious groups in civil service, the cabinet, and the legislature. These proportions were fixed according to the demographics of the 1932 census. Christians, who comprised 51 percent at that time, were provided a dominant role in government. By the 1970s, the Muslim population outnumbered the Christians, but Muslims were unable to gain a more dominant role commensurate with their numbers. Today the Muslims account for 75 percent of the country's population, but the Christians are loathe to relinquish any power. This rivalry, as well as religious and ethnic animosities, upsets the delicate balance in Lebanon.

## Issues and Events

General Michael Aoun, commander of the Christian Lebanese Army, continues to dominate the political scene in Lebanon. Aoun was appointed interim prime minister in 1988 when the government failed to agree on a new leader.

As General Aoun vowed to drive the Syrians out of Lebanon, 1989 became one of the most violent years in the history of the war. Unremitting artillery fire resulted in nine hundred deaths, four thousand wounded, fifteen thousand homes destroyed, and the physical destruction of much of Beirut. Over three quarters of a million civilians, or half of Beirut, fled their homes. One hundred thousand gave up and left the country before a cease-fire engineered by the Arab league went into effect on September 23. Although the shelling stopped, the violence and conflict did not. A peace accord drafted in Taif, Saudi Arabia, in October was followed by the election of a new president in November. Lebanese Christians opposed the plan because it did not call for an immediate Syrian troop withdrawal. President

René Moawad was in office only seventeen days before he was killed by a car bomb. His replacement, Elias Hrawi, called for General Aoun to resign his post and vacate the Presidential Palace. When Aoun refused, Syrian troops moved in, only to find Aoun shielded not only by his troops, but by thousands of civilian Maronite Christian supporters.

Some experts fear that the situation in Lebanon is so hopeless that the only possible outcome is "partition." In this case Lebanon would be broken down into two or more smaller countries. Others are hopeful that a unified Lebanon can still become a reality. For this to be achieved, a complete overhaul of the political system is imperative. Christians generally favor a system of semi-autonomous regions. Moslems usually advocate a unified Lebanon, but seek more representation in government. A unified Lebanon will remain a mere dream until the country's many warring factions put away their weapons and fight instead to rebuild their devastated country.

## Background

Sectarian tensions erupted into civil war in 1975, when a bus load of Palestinians was ambushed by gunmen in Christian East Beirut. Since that time, life in Lebanon has meant living amid exploding bombs, artillery fire, and snipers.

Today, Lebanon has a vast number of factions, each with its own small army. The shifting alliances and locations of these militia have created an ever changing political landscape. What started as a struggle between Christian Phalangists and Palestinians has ultimately developed into dozens of conflicts between and among virtually every special interest group imaginable. Christians have made war against other Christians, and Muslims against other Muslims. New groups rise up seemingly overnight to attack some other group.

Lebanon has always looked to the rest of the world to solve its problems. The Syrians entered the war in 1976 at the request of the Lebanese government. Israeli and United Nations forces invaded Lebanon in 1978, and again in 1982 to drive the unwanted Palestinian Liberation Organization (PLO) out of Beirut. The presence of these invading armies has been welcomed by some and abhorred by others.

Most Christians, who make up about 25 percent of the population, belong to the Phalange party, and the Phalangists support independent militia known collectively as the "Lebanese Forces." Supported by Israel, the Lebanese Forces are often in conflict with the Palestinians; one faction is also vehemently anti-Syrian while another is not. Christian militia, which number about six thousand, are currently in control of an area north of Beirut extending halfway to Tripoli, west of the Lebanon Mountains.

The regular Lebanese Army is also comprised of a majority of Christians, although there is a significant number of Sunni Muslims. The twenty-thousand-strong Lebanese Army is commanded by General Aoun and defends the Christian areas of Beirut. General Aoun is vehemently anti-Syrian and his army is supplied by Iraq.

The Muslim community comprises about 75 percent of the population of Lebanon and are mainly Sunni or Shiite. Like the Christians, the Muslims are also organized into independent militia. Two of the most prominent groups are the Amal and the Hizbullah, both of which are Shiite Muslim. The Amal, who number about six thousand, are closely allied to Syria. Their current targets are the Palestinians and the Hizbullah, or Party of God. The Hizbullah, which are closely tied to Iran and number about three thousand, have fought ferociously against the Amal, and are allegedly holding several United States and European hostages. Collectively, all of the Muslim militia control the southwestern part of the country.

The Palestinians, who are also Muslim, live mainly in refugee camps near Beirut and have been attacked repeatedly by various factions such as the Lebanese Forces and the Amal. Some of the Palestinians belong to the Palestinian Liberation Organization (PLO), which has been involved in terrorist activities throughout the world. In 1970 the Palestinians established their headquarters in Beirut and used Lebanon as a base from which to attack Israel. They have also fought against the Lebanese Forces and the Amal. Today Lebanon has about four hundred thousand Palestinians of whom ten thousand are involved in the PLO. Their chief allies are the Syrians and other Arab countries.

The Druze, whose religion is separate from Islam but based on its tenets, have formed a militia within their Progressive Socialist Party. The Druze militiamen number about five thousand and are allied with Syria. The Druze have clashed with the Lebanese Forces and the Lebanese Army, and currently control an area from southeast of Beirut to the Syrian border.

The Syrians, who entered the war in 1976, currently number about forty thousand and control about 70 percent of the country. They are dominant in the north and east parts of the country. Syrians are allied to the Soviet Union and opposed to Israel, the Lebanese Forces, and the Lebanese Army.

About one thousand Israeli troops are stationed in a six-mile strip along Lebanon's southern border. The Israelis are supported by six thousand UNIFIL troops, as well as the United States and many Western European countries. Their main enemies are the Syrians and the PLO.

# Cyprus: An Island Divided

## Perspective

| | |
|---|---|
| 1571 | Ottoman Turks conquer Cyprus. |
| 1878 | Cyprus administration is transferred to Britain. |
| 1925 | Cyprus is made British crown colony. |
| 1931 | Greek Cypriots riot for enosis, or union with Greece. |
| 1950 | **October 15.** Michael Christodoulos becomes Archbishop Makarios III. |
| 1955 | National Organization of Cypriot Fighters, favoring enosis, initiates campaign of terror against British. |
| 1959 | Agreement is reached among Greece, Turkey, and United Kingdom on constitution for independent Cyprus. |
| 1960 | **August.** Cyprus is declared independent republic with Archbishop Makarios III as president. |
| 1963 | Greek and Turkish Cypriots clash over proposals by President Makarios for changes in constitution. |
| 1964 | Turkish vice-president resigns; Greek-Turkish corule suffers de facto breakdown. United Nations peacekeeping force is introduced. |
| 1974 | **July 15.** Greek-led National Guard ousts Makarios. Turkey invades Cyprus and occupies northern third of island.<br>**December.** Makarios returns to the presidency. |
| 1975 | Turkish Cypriot federated state is proclaimed in Turkish-held territory. |
| 1977 | Makarios dies and is succeeded by Spyros Kyprianou. |
| 1983 | Turkish Republic of Northern Cyprus (TRNC) issues unilateral declaration of independence after talks between the two sides break down. |
| 1985 | **January.** Greek and Turkish Cypriot leaders meet unsuccessfully under United Nations auspices to discuss federation of their states.<br>**May 5.** TRNC approves its first constitution.<br>**June 9.** Rauf Denktash is elected president of TRNC. |
| 1988 | **February 21.** Georgios Vassiliou defeats Kyprianou in presidential elections.<br>**June.** Prime Minister Turgut Ozal becomes the first Turkish leader in thirty years to visit Greece. |
| 1989 | **July 19.** Demonstrations by Greek Cypriots result in postponement of September summit. |

When the former British crown colony of Cyprus became an independent republic in 1960, it came equipped with a constitution that took into account the ethnic makeup of the island: 78 percent Greek and 18 percent Turkish. The Turkish population, for example, was guaranteed the office of vice-president, three out of ten cabinet posts, and the power to veto acts of the legislature. That constitution failed to improve the long-festering hostility between the Cypriot Greeks and Turks; in fact, relations deteriorated. The Greek majority, led by Archbishop Makarios III, was intent on *enosis*, or union with Greece. The Turkish minority, on the other hand, was determined to form a separate federated Turkish republic in the northern part of the island, where most of the Turkish population lived.

For twenty-five years, the situation worsened: British troops had to intervene, the United Nations sent in a peacekeeping force, the Greek government in Athens engineered a coup, and a force from Turkey invaded the island and set up what was in effect a separate government in the Turkish enclave. Thus when the leader of the Turkish Cypriots and the president of the Greek part of Cyprus met in January 1985, the international community hoped that an agreement could be reached that would finally bring peace to the island republic. After four days, the talks broke down with no agreement of any kind but plenty of recriminations. Subsequent negotiations have been equally fruitless.

## Issues and Events

The unilateral declaration of independence by Turkish Cypriots on November 15, 1983, established the Turkish Republic of Northern Cyprus in the Turkish-occupied part of the island. This step was only a logical culmination of developments since Turkey's invasion of the country nine years before, although it seemed to distance the prospects of unification under a central government.

Most Greek Cypriots had always considered their ultimate destiny to be enosis with the Greek motherland. Soon after Archbishop Makarios III was installed as the republic's first president, he began to prepare the groundwork for modifications intended to upset the delicate balance of power between the Turkish and Greek factions.

In 1963, when Makarios proposed changes in the constitution that quite decisively would diminish the power of the Turkish minority, serious clashes occurred between the two ethnic groups. With the hostilities spreading over the island, the Turkish contingent of the legislature ceased to attend, the Turkish ministers withdrew from the cabinet, and in January 1964 the Turkish vice-president resigned. Full-scale civil war was averted only by the intervention of British troops. The United Nations later arranged for a peacekeeping force, which has remained there ever since.

Increased tensions on the island in the early 1970s, partly created by the military junta then in power in Athens, culminated in July 1974 in a junta-backed coup d'état by the Greek Cypriot National Guard, which temporarily ousted Makarios. The coup brought on an invasion by Turkish forces, which quickly occupied the northern third of the island, effectively dividing it along ethnic lines. Some 165,000 Greek Cypriots fled the Turkish-held territory, while sixty-five thousand Turkish Cypriots from other parts of the island sought refuge there. In February 1975, a Turkish Cypriot state was proclaimed, which later declared its independence in 1983. Turkey has been the only country to recognize the Turkish Republic of Northern Cyprus as an independent nation and has sent an estimated thirty thousand troops to support its status.

All parties have strong incentives for reconciliation. Relations between Greece and Turkey have improved considerably over the last few years, though Greece would like to see Turkey withdraw its thirty-six thousand troops from the island and Turkey would like to avoid a Greek veto should it decide to enter the European Community (EC). North Cyprus has suffered economically since it was estranged from the South, and Greek Cypriot refugees would like to get their land back. In addition, the United Nations would like to resolve the issue so it can withdraw its twenty-three hundred member peacekeeping force, which currently is suffering a $160 million deficit.

Both Cypriot factions are ultimately seeking reunification. The main problem is that the Turks want more autonomy than the Greeks are willing to accept. For a lasting peace to be achieved, both factions will have to put aside their political, cultural, and religious differences and allow a new Cypriot national identity to evolve. Only then will there be a solid foundation for a unified Cyprus.

## Background

Greeks began to colonize the island in the 1400s B.C., and during the following millennia, while ruled successively by the Assyrians, Persians, Macedonians, Egyptians, Romans, and Byzantines, its character remained predominantly Greek.

The island was later captured by the French Venetians, and finally the Ottoman Turks in 1571, who ruled there for over three hundred years.

Much of the pattern that has characterized Cypriot life to this day was established under Turkish rule. Although the Turks allowed the Greek islanders to restore their own Orthodox church and hierarchy, which previously had been subjugated to Roman Catholicism, they also introduced, by immigration from Anatolia, the problem of a second ethnic community—the Muslim Turks—which today divides the island into antagonistic camps.

After his 1878 defeat by Russia in the Russo-Turkish War, Sultan Abdul Hamid II, in an attempt to check further Russian advances into the area, persuaded the British to assume the administration of Cyprus while retaining nominal title to it. Petitions by the populace for enosis with Greece were ignored. When the Turks sided with the Central Powers in World War I, the administrators annexed the island to the British crown. Turkey consented to this arrangement by the Treaty of Lausanne in 1923, and two years later Cyprus was made a crown colony.

In 1931, serious riots broke out on the island as a result of continued agitation for enosis. The British answered by abolishing the legislative council they had introduced in 1882. In 1943, however, they established municipal government based on adult suffrage in preparation for self-government after World War II. But the post-war plans they proposed were resisted by Greek and Turkish Cypriots alike, and in 1955 the National Organization of Cypriot Fighters, known by its Greek acronym EOKA, initiated a campaign of terror in its fight for enosis. The following year, the British deported Archbishop Makarios III, an outspoken advocate of enosis, exiling him to the Seychelles in the Indian Ocean. The violent reaction to this move forced them to declare an island-wide state of emergency.

International attempts to find a solution to the crisis finally resulted in an accord among Greece, Turkey, and the United Kingdom for the establishment of an independent republic whose constitution would be jointly guaranteed by all three countries. As the history of that republic demonstrates, however, the search for solutions must continue.

# Libya:
# The Enigmatic Qadhafi

## Perspective

| | |
|---|---|
| 1912 | Italy gains control of Libya from Turkey. |
| 1943 | Italy loses Libya to the British during World War II. |
| 1951 | **December 24.** Mohamed Idris al-Sanusi is named king of newly-independent Libya. |
| 1959 | Oil is discovered. |
| 1969 | **September 1.** King Idris is overthrown. Revolutionary Command Council, led by Qadhafi, proclaims republic. |
| 1970 | **June.** United States withdraws from Wheelus Air Base. |
| 1973 | **August.** Qadhafi successfully takes control of foreign-held oil interests. |
| 1975 | Libya invades Chad's Aouzou Strip. |
| 1977 | Short war is fought with Egypt. Association with Palestine Liberation Organization (PLO) is evident. Relations with West begin to cool. |
| 1979 | Qadhafi gives up public office. |
| 1981 | **May.** United States expels all Libyan diplomats. **August.** United States and Libyan planes engage in dogfight over Gulf of Sidra; one Libyan jet is shot down. |
| 1986 | **January.** United States freezes Libyan assets in retaliation for Libya's role in promoting terrorism. **April 15.** United States planes bomb five sites in Libya. |
| 1988 | **October.** War with Chad ends. |
| 1989 | **January 4.** United States planes shoot down two Libyan jets. |

Colonel Mu'ammar al-Qadhafi, the charismatic leader of the Socialist People's Libyan Arab Jamahiriya, or Libya, is a favorite villain in the Western press and is even at times characterized as a "madman." Relations between Libya and the West, notably the United States, have been especially bitter. The United States, and most of the other Western powers, have objected in particular to Qadhafi's support, financial and otherwise, of international terrorist organizations. He has been the chief supporter of the Palestine Liberation Organization (PLO), and his denunciations of Israel have been particularly virulent. He has also angered other African leaders by his territorial ambitions, notably in Chad and Sudan, which have had a disruptive influence on African political affairs. Qadhafi's power is a direct result of the petroleum revenues that have been at his disposal since the mid-1970s, when the Arab oil boycotts caused the world price of oil to escalate dramatically.

## Issues and Events

Relations between the United States and Libya reached an all-time low on April 15, 1986, when the United States Air Force hit five military targets in Libya in retaliation for the April 5 bombing of a West Berlin discotheque frequented by United States military personnel. It is believed that over one hundred Libyans died during the bombings, including Qadhafi's own adopted infant daughter.

Before this event, United States and Libyan military forces had clashed repeatedly in the Mediterranean Sea, where Qadhafi tried to extend Libya's territorial waters beyond that which was internationally acceptable. In January 1986, tensions escalated when President Reagan imposed severe economic sanctions against Libya. International reaction to the United States-Libyan confrontation was generally negative although a few countries, such as the United Kingdom and Israel, applauded the United States military raid. Since 1986, there have been no United States bombings or other attacks on Libyan territory.

On September 1, 1988, during celebrations of the nineteenth anniversary of Libya's revolution, Qadhafi announced several policy changes. He outlined a new economic program which decreased centralized state ownership of property; indicated a new concern for human rights; opened the door for exiles to return; and announced a possible decrease in the country's military forces.

Relations between United States and Libya were again strained in late 1988 when the United States accused Libya of building a chemical weapons plant, while Libya claimed the facility was built to produce pharmaceuticals.

Renewed tensions resulted in an air clash in which United States planes shot down two Libyan military aircraft over the Mediterranean. Relations took a turn for the better two weeks later when the United States allowed its Libyan oil companies to resume production, which had been curtailed as part of the sanctions imposed in 1986.

During 1989 Qadhafi continued his policy of moderation and liberalization. He lifted travel restrictions, reined in the fanatical Revolutionary Committees, and freed thousands of political prisoners. He also sought to improve relations with his north African neighbors by joining the newly-formed Arab Maghreb Union and beginning negotiations with Egypt.

Oil-rich Libya will undoubtedly remain an important force in the Arab world. Many Western countries see in Libya vast economic opportunities. Many poor African countries have received large sums of aid and therefore see Libya as a great benefactor, while others fear Qadhafi's territorial ambitions. Most Arab leaders regard Qadhafi with suspicion, despite his continual diplomatic overtures and professed dedication to all Arab people.

## Background

Following Libya's independence from Italian colonial rule after World War II, the country was ruled by Mohamed Idris al-Sanusi, or Idris, beginning in 1951.

The Libyan monarch granted access to the United States, Great Britain, and France to construct military bases in the country. Many segments of the Libyan population viewed these bases with hostility, regarding them as staging areas for the West's support of Israel, to which Libya's Arab population was totally opposed.

The resources of Libya were funneled into the pockets of foreigners and the elite Libyan minority, while the general population became increasingly poor. While in school, Qadhafi became convinced that his country was being exploited by imperialists. He became an earnest and dedicated revolutionary and joined the Libyan army, where he gathered a cadre of young revolutionaries who were convinced that a military context was the only means to change Libya. Axiomatic was the belief that the ruling elite would resist any form of social or political reform; and Qadhafi had seen early on that the vital resource of oil was finite—its use as an economic tool to force political change was clearly imperative.

The Free Officers' Union of the Libyan army staged a military coup on September 1, 1969, under 27-year-old Lieutenant Mu'ammar al-Qadhafi. Within four hours the Revolutionary Command Council (RCC) had control of the country

As chairman of the council, Qadhafi quickly moved to institute massive economic and religious reforms. He promoted public works, granted major wage increases, and laid the foundations for a working welfare system. In 1975 he launched an expanded development plant to provide for agricultural development, low-cost housing, education, free medical care, and personal loans to Libyan citizens. Strict respect for Islamic law was imposed. Qadhafi launched a cultural revolution to free Libya from foreign influences. In 1970 he succeeded in getting the United States to abandon its Wheelus Air Base, an event which Libyans celebrate as a national holiday. He threatened to nationalize the oil industry unless the companies agreed to increase Libya's share of the profits. When the oil companies acquiesced, Qadhafi was spurred to try for wider Arab unity, using oil as a political weapon. The Libyan navy is an important presence in the Mediterranean and a large fraction of its personnel have been trained by the Soviet Union.

In 1979, Qadhafi resigned as secretary-general of the General People's Congress, the governing organization that succeeded the

**Mu'ammar Muhammad al-Qadhafi** Libyan leader and head of government. Born in the desert near Tripoli in 1942 ... graduated from the University of Libya (1963) and Libyan Military College (1965) ... led a military coup overthrowing King Idris (1969) ... became president of the Revolutionary Command Council (1969-1977) and secretary of the General People's Congress (1977-1979) then continued rule with no formal title ... was known as a devout Muslim and Arab nationalist ... was influential in the world oil market and encouraged international terrorism.

RCC in 1977, to "further the revolution. "He remained the ideological voice and leader of the Revolutionary Committees. These committees originated the liquidation orders aimed at several "enemies of the revolution" in the late 1970s and early 1980s.

The form of socialism that Qadhafi's regime introduced into Libya undermines the traditional power of tribal leaders and restricts private ownership of business and real estate. Qadhafi characterizes this socialism as the *jamahiriya*, or "state of the masses." He draws inspiration from a personal interpretation of Islam not always congruent with the views held by Muslim clergy, emphasizing a direct relationship between believers and God.

Central to Qadhafi's political philosophy is the unity of all Arab people, regardless of nationality. He believes that the Arab people will be secure only when they are united under one government. Qadhafi's diplomatic efforts to establish an Arab nation have been less than successful. Other Arab leaders are suspicious of Qadhafi's motives, unsure of his methods, and otherwise occupied with their own internal problems. An attempted merger with Egypt and Syria in 1972 resulted in deteriorating relations which culminated in a brief war with Egypt in 1977. Libya's unsuccessful war with Chad, which ended in 1988, was attributed to Qadhafi's expansionist policies.

Another cornerstone of Qadhafi's political beliefs is that the world's "imperialistic forces" seek to destroy the Arab world. Qadhafi has been an outspoken critic of both the United States and the Soviet Union. He believes that the state of Israel is an attempt by the Western imperialists to establish a stronghold in traditional Arab lands. Qadhafi denies Israel's right to exist, and firmly supports the Palestinians in their quest for a homeland. He has been accused of helping train and shelter radical terrorists such as Abu Nidal, although he denounces acts of violence against innocent civilians. The United States has stated that Libya must end its support for terrorism before normal diplomatic ties can be reestablished.

# Iran: The Tide Turns

## Perspective

| | |
|---|---|
| 610 | Muhammad begins his ministry. |
| 650 | Islam is introduced to Iran. |
| 1906 | Iran passes its first constitution. |
| 1908 | Oil is discovered. |
| 1921 | Pahlavi dynasty begins. |
| 1941 | Mohammad Reza Pahlavi becomes shah. |
| 1961 | Shah initiates White Revolution. |
| 1963 | Ruhollah Khomeini is exiled for protesting White Revolution policies. |
| 1979 | **January 6.** Shah flees Iran as domestic turmoil grows.<br>**February 1.** Khomeini returns from exile to take charge of the government.<br>**March 30.** Islamic Republic of Iran is established with Khomeini as leader for life.<br>**November 4.** Iranian students seize United States embassy and hold sixty-six hostages. |
| 1980 | **September 22.** War with Iraq begins. |
| 1981 | **January 20.** United States hostages are released. |
| 1987 | **July 31.** More than four hundred Iranians are killed in riots during pilgrimage to Mecca. |
| 1988 | **July 3.** United States accidentally destroys Iranian commercial airliner; 290 passengers are killed.<br>**August 20.** Iran reaches a cease-fire agreement with Iraq. |
| 1989 | **February 14.** Khomeini offers $5 million reward for the death of author Salman Rushdie.<br>**June 3.** Khomeini dies.<br>**July 28.** Hashemi Rafsanjani is elected president. |

The Islamic fundamentalist revolution that swept through Iran was likened to a tidal wave that threatened to engulf the Middle East and plunge the region into a new Dark Age. The death of the Ayatollah Khomeini in 1989 marked the beginning of a more moderate regime in Iran, but it will take a long time for the nation to recover from the death and destruction left in the wake of Khomeini's fanatical movement.

## Issues and Events

When the Ayatollah Khomeini returned to Iran in 1979 after a sixteen-year exile, he was hailed as a conquering hero. The shah fled the country as antigovernment protests threatened to topple his thirty-eight-year monarchy. Khomeini quickly established a new, theocratic republic based on the tenets of Islam. Traditional Islamic law—which prescribes controversial punishments such as flogging, amputations, and stoning—was reinstated. Alcohol, frozen meat, foreign cars, and broadcast music were banned. Women were relegated to their former status and forced to wear the *chador*, or full-length black veil. Religion permeated every aspect of life. A new constitution appointed Khomeini to be the *fagih*, or supreme spiritual and political leader for life.

Although he enjoyed widespread support, Khomeini faced serious opposition from left-wing groups and ethnic minorities, particularly the Kurds and Bahais. He lost no time eliminating his opposition, and by the end of 1979 more than seven hundred people were tried and executed. By 1987 the number killed had risen to seven thousand and the United Nations Human Rights Commission continued to receive complaints about torture and unfair trials.

When the shah was permitted to enter the United States in October 1979 to receive medical treatment, a great furor arose and Iranians demanded that he be returned to Iran to face trial. The United States chose to protect their former ally and, in an act of revenge, the American embassy was seized in a mob action by Iranian students. Most of the sixty-six hostages were held for more than a year before their release in early 1981. The United States retaliated by freezing billions of dollars of Iranian assets and banning oil imports.

An important goal of Khomeini's regime was to spread the new Islamic revolution throughout the world. The revolution also underscored the traditional rivalry between Sunni and Shiite Muslims, the two major factions of Islam. Iranians are Shiites, and while most other nations have Sunni majorities, they also have significant numbers of Shiites. When war broke out between Iran and Iraq in 1980, moderate Arab nations feared an Iranian victory could strengthen the appeal of the fundamentalist movement. Like Iran, most Arab nations had for years maintained a tenuous balance between modern, western ways and traditional religious life. Khomeini vowed to conquer Iraq, then Israel and Lebanon. He was widely believed to be plotting the downfall of every government in the Persian Gulf region, while Iran was accused of aiding Shiite terrorists around the world. Consequently, Iraq enjoyed the support of all oil-rich Arab nations while Iran drifted deeper into economic and diplomatic isolation. The war was one of the worst in the world's history. More than one million people, including many civilians, were slain. Iraq was accused of using chemical weapons that were internationally banned after World War I. The United States' involvement in the war ultimately resulted in the death of 250 civilians when an Iranian airliner was mistaken for an F-14 fighter jet. No settlement to the dispute between Iran and Iraq was reached even though the two finally agreed to a cease-fire in 1988. It remains questionable whether the uneasy peace will hold.

Relations with the Arab world reached an all-time low when Iranians apparently created a riot during the 1987 *hajj*, an annual pilgrimage to Mecca in Saudi Arabia. Saudi police killed 402 Iranians and Iran has subsequently boycotted the hajj, which is central to the Islamic faith. In 1989 relations with Europe worsened when Khomeini offered a $5 million reward for the death of author Salman Rushdie for his *Satanic Verses*, a book offensive to Muslims and consequently banned throughout the Islamic world.

Khomeini's death later in the year may have ultimately marked the end of the revolution in Iran. Power now rests with the new President Hashemi Rafsanjani, a skilled politician who is cautiously seeking to end Iran's diplomatic isolation and repair its war-torn economy. Unemployment stands at 30 percent, inflation at 70 percent, and industry is operating at only 30 percent of capacity. Oil revenues are half of the pre-revolutionary level, and the United States continues to hold billions of dollars in Iranian assets. Rebuilding will not be an easy task. Most of the educated work force have long since left the country, and the gap between the rich and the poor continues to widen.

Rafsanjani's task is to promote economic progress without threatening the cultural identity and nationalism of the fiercely independent and fervently religious Iranian people.

## Background

The ancient Persian Empire came to an end in A.D. 650 when it was defeated by the Arab armies of Islam. Until the late twentieth century, various foreign powers or dynasties ruled Iran. The rulers, which were called shahs, wielded absolute power in 1906, when the country adopted its first constitution. In 1908, the country discovered oil in the Persian Gulf area. The Pahlavi dynasty began in 1925 when Reza Khan, an army officer, seized the throne. In 1941 he was forced to abdicate and his son, Mohammad Reza Pahlavi, became the last shah of Iran.

The shah initiated a massive modernization program in 1961 called the "White Revolution," which involved radical economic, social, and administrative reforms. The growing petroleum industry enhanced development. In addition to land reform, the shah's program called for controversial changes such as the emancipation of women. A conservative backlash, led in part by the religious leader Ayatollah Ruhollah Khomeini, was characterized by widespread rioting and strikes. By 1963 the shah's regime was more or less stabilized and Khomeini was exiled to Iraq. Foreign workers continued to flood Iran as rapid development continued. By 1974 the country was earning $21 billion annually from its oil exports. Many clergy feared that the country was becoming too westernized, and in 1977 a nationalist uprising began to develop. Although he was still in exile, the Ayatollah Khomeini led the growing rebellion by means of taped sermons that were distributed throughout the country. By January 1979 the situation was so serious that the shah left the country and opened the door for Khomeini's new, Islamic government.

---

**Khomeini, Ayatollah Ruhollah** Iranian head of government (1979-1989) and spiritual leader of Iran's Shiite Muslims. Born in Khomeyn in central Iran in 1900 ... became prominent Islamic scholar and teacher ... was exiled (1964-1979) because of his severe criticism of Shah Mohammad Reza Pahlavi ... returned to Iran to lead a revolution that ousted the shah and placed Khomeini in control of the government (1979) ... instituted an Islamic fundamentalist regime that faced civil war, conflict with Iraq, and international isolation ... died June 4, 1989, at age 89.

## Legacies of the Six-Day War: Jerusalem, Gaza Strip, Golan Heights, West Bank

The Six-Day War of 1967 was Israel's most spectacular victory in the series of Arab-Israeli wars that began with the country's independence in 1948. On June 5, 1967, Israel responded to Arab provocations by launching an air attack that effectively destroyed enemy air capabilities. With domination of the air assured, Israel quickly moved its ground troops into Arab territory on several fronts. By the time the war ended on June 10, Israel had occupied the Sinai Peninsula, the Gaza Strip, all of Jerusalem, the Golan Heights bordering Syria, and the Jordan-controlled West Bank of the Jordan River. Israel announced that, except for Jerusalem, it would give back the occupied territories only after substantial progress had been made in Arab-Israeli relations. Jerusalem, according to the Israelis, would never be returned and would become the capital of the Jewish state.

Conflict between Jews and Arabs had erupted sporadically since the British received a League of Nations mandate for Palestine in 1920. The mandate, which included a provision for the creation of a Jewish homeland, marked the beginning of massive Jewish migration to the area.

In November 1947, the United Nations approved a plan that provided for the partition of Palestine into roughly equal Jewish and Arab states. The first full-scale war between the Jews and Arabs was triggered when Israel declared its independence on May 14, 1948. The armies of Egypt, Lebanon, Syria, Jordan, and Iraq were held off by the Israelis, and by the time a cease-fire was reached in 1949, Israel had considerably increased its territory. The 1948 war also resulted in massive emigration of local Arabs from Israeli-controlled territories to adjacent Arab-held lands. The Arab state envisioned by the United Nations partition plan never materialized, and the Palestinian Arabs became permanent refugees.

Fighting broke out again in 1956, and again Israel made substantial territorial gains. Israel later traded this territory back to Egypt in exchange for access to the Gulf of Aqaba. The 1967 war was in part triggered when Egypt shut off this access. In 1973, Egypt, Syria, and Jordan attacked Israel but they were driven back by 1974.

The Camp David accords of 1979 (in which Israel and Egypt agreed to a peace treaty) provided for the return of the Sinai Peninsula to Egypt in 1982, but all of the other occupied territories remain under Israeli rule.

Palestinian refugees living in the occupied areas have also been a legacy of the 1967 war. The Palestinian Liberation Organization (PLO) was founded in 1964 to represent and unite the Palestinians, but became notorious for terrorist acts against Israel and its allies. The PLO, under the leadership of Yasser Arafat, vehemently denied Israel's right to exist.

Between December 1987 and January 1990, more than six hundred Palestinians were killed, fifteen thousand wounded, and fifty thousand arrested in a prolonged uprising known as the intifadah. In 1988, the PLO declared the independence of the occupied areas, as the state of Palestine and Arafat has for the first time accepted the existence of Israel and expressed a willingness to negotiate. Increasingly regarded as the oppressor rather than the oppressed, Israel continues to struggle with its territorial legacies of the Six-Day War.

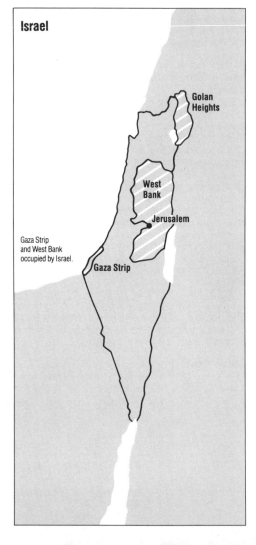

# Jerusalem

## Perspective

| | |
|---|---|
| **1920** | Jerusalem becomes part of British mandate for Palestine. |
| **1947** | United Nations votes to partition Palestine into Jewish and Arab states with autonomous Jerusalem under international supervision. |
| **1948** | Jerusalem is divided between Jordan and Israel during Arab-Israeli War. |
| **1950** | Israel designates Jerusalem as its capital. |
| **1967** | Following Six-Day War, East Jerusalem is overrun by Israel and annexed. Partition of Jerusalem ends and Jewish families begin to move into Arabian East Jerusalem. |
| **1987** | **December.** Palestinian intifada, or uprising, spreads to Jerusalem. |
| **1988** | **January.** Arab neighborhoods are placed under curfew after Israelis and Palestinians clash at Temple Mount.<br>**November.** Palestinians declare an independent state, including East Jerusalem. |

Of all the Israeli conquests of the Six-Day War, probably none struck a more responsive chord in the hearts of Jews everywhere than the occupation of Jerusalem. The ancient city, while also sacred to Christians and Muslims, occupies a special place in the tradition of Judaism and the Jewish people. As Rome is the focus of the Roman Catholic church and Mecca is that of Islam, so Jerusalem occupies a central position in Judaism. It was inevitable that the Israeli occupation of Jerusalem would take on a symbolic significance far in excess of its political and military importance.

In 1947, as British influence in the Holy Land waned, the United Nations evolved a plan to make Jerusalem an autonomous city under international supervision. Instead, Jordan seized Jerusalem's Old City during the Arab-Israeli conflict of 1948 and divided the city. The Wailing Wall, one of the most sacred sites in the Jewish faith, was closed to Jewish worship. The city's sections were separated by concrete barriers, barbed wire, and land mines. It remained a divided city until the Six-Day War, when the Israelis triumphantly captured the Old City. The army blew up the walls that separated Israeli and Jordanian sectors of the city. In 1950 the Israeli government announced that henceforth Jerusalem would be the capital city of Israel. Most foreign countries continued to maintain their embassies in Tel Aviv-Yafo, however, as a way of staying out of the conflict between Israel and the Arabs over sovereignty of the Old City.

## Issues and Events

Before 1967, Jerusalem's importance had suffered considerable decline. However, under the administration of Mayor Teddy Kollek, it has rebounded into a richly diverse city vibrant with prosperity and change. Within twenty years of its reunification, the population grew from 266,300 to 468,900 in 1987. More than a million visitors pour in every year. Huge strides have been made in improving the roads, the sewage system, and many other services.

In order to preserve the beauty and historic appearance of the city, these changes have been made with great care. To maintain the city's historical character, Kollek organized the Jerusalem Committee, an international group of prominent city planners and architects. With the committee's help, all superhighways have been banned from the city, and a limit of eight stories was set for new buildings, which had to be faced with the distinctively colored Jerusalem stone. Flower gardens were planted throughout the area, particularly in the Old City.

Israeli dominance over Jerusalem has created a potential problem for the large Arab population. Before 1967, there were no Jews in the 28 square-mile (73 square km) area of East Jerusalem. The Israeli government decided to establish Jewish settlements there. In 1969, the new suburb of Ramat Eshkol was founded, and by the 1980s, there were more than seventy thousand Jews in East Jerusalem.

Compared to other occupied areas, there has been relatively little actual violence in the city, but its potential is great. Arabs for the most part are concentrated in the lower economic classes; they are the menial workers, domestic workers, waiters, and construction workers. Integration has proved difficult, and most Arab and Israeli children attend separate schools. Although Arabs may vote in Israeli elections, only about 10 percent exercise the right.

Arab resentment has been fanned by the actions of the Israeli army, whose target has been Temple Mount, where three religions intersect and clash. Muslims believe Temple Mount is where Muhammad ascended through the seven heavens into the presence of God. It is administered by a Muslim political-religious trust; members of the Christian and Jewish religions are allowed only limited access to the area. But Temple Mount is also the site of Solomon's Temple; it is where Abraham came to sacrifice his son, Isaac, and it is where Jesus taught and threw the moneychangers out of the temple.

In January 1988, Palestinians raised their banned flag at Temple Mount while burning

American and Israeli banners. The Israeli police fired tear gas into the Al-Aqsa mosque on Temple Mount, but were driven back by rock-throwing crowds. At least seventy Palestinians were injured as a result of gassing and beatings by police.

Jerusalem will undoubtedly be the most difficult issue to face Palestinians and Israelis should negotiations take place regarding a new Arab state in Israel's occupied territories. It is highly unlikely that either side would be willing to abandon its claim to the sacred city. One possible solution might be joint administration of the city by both parties. Until a settlement is reached, Muslims and Jews will continue to battle for control of the most revered city in the Holy Land.

# Gaza Strip

## Perspective

|  |  |
|---|---|
| 1920 | Gaza becomes part of British mandate for Palestine. |
| 1948 | Palestinians flee to Gaza when Israel declares its independence. |
| 1949 | Gaza becomes Egyptian possession. |
| 1967 | During Six-Day War, Gaza is occupied by Israeli troops. |
| 1987 | **December.** Palestinian uprising begins in Gaza and spreads to West Bank. |
| 1988 | **November.** Palestinians declare an independent state, including Gaza Strip. |

A small strip of land only 140 square miles (360 square km) along the Mediterranean Sea, the Gaza Strip is one of the poorest, most densely populated areas on the face of the Earth. Many of the territory's half million residents live in squalor in refugee camps, although about forty thousand have managed to get enough money together to purchase Israeli-provided homes outside the camps. Over sixty thousand Gaza residents commute daily to Israel, where they are employed as construction workers and menial laborers in exchange for subsistence wages. The Gaza Strip has been the site of Jewish-Arab problems since 1947. Originally part of the British mandate for Palestine, it became the sanctuary of thousands of Palestinians as Jews occupied the areas that now make up Israel. Refugee camps under United Nations auspices were set up, and the region came under Egyptian rule.

In the Six-Day War of 1967, Israel occupied the Gaza Strip and set up administrative control. It announced that the area, along with the other Arab territories it conquered in the war, would be returned only after substantive progress was made in Israeli-Arab relations. In the Camp David accords of 1979, Israel agreed to negotiate with Egypt over the eventual conversion of Gaza to "autonomous control." Little progress has been made in that direction, however, and Gaza remains under Israeli military occupation.

## Issues and Events

Israel has occupied the Gaza Strip and the West Bank for two decades amidst increasing Palestinian hostility and international pressure sympathetic to the Palestinian cause. Gaza continues to be the site of violence from both Israelis and Arabs. On April 13, 1984, Israeli troops stormed a bus that had been hijacked by four armed Arabs. Although one passenger was killed, thirty-four other Israeli hostages were released. Two of the Arab terrorists were killed in the gunfire, but the fate of the other two caused a storm of controversy. A commission of inquiry concluded that the Israeli security men had taken the offenders into a field and beaten them to death.

The growth of Israeli settler vigilante groups committed to reprisals against Arabs and the growth of Arab terrorists committed to violence against Jews have disturbed many Israelis, who see the vigilantes as a sign that the quality of Israeli society and morality has deteriorated. There is increasing concern about the price Israel must pay for the continued occupation and administration of Gaza.

The most recent Palestinian uprising in Israel's occupied territories began in Gaza on December 8, 1987, and spread quickly to other areas. Violence erupted when an Israeli taxi struck and killed four Palestinian laborers while they waited at a bus stop for a ride to their jobs in Israel. Palestinians claimed that the action was deliberate and responded by attacking Israeli patrols with stones and Molotov cocktails. Several Palestinians were killed by Israeli gunfire.

Officials of the United Nations in the Gaza Strip expressed concern that Israeli forces continued to use live ammunition against the Palestinian demonstrators, many of whom were young, unarmed children and teenagers. Curfews were imposed, and food shortages resulted when Israelis blockaded areas around the refugee camps. Defense Minister Itzhak Rabin instituted an "iron fist" policy against the demonstrators, which involved the use of beatings and plastic bullets.

Yasser Arafat's November 1988 Palestinian declaration of independence had little effect on the uprising, which continued into 1990. There is little doubt that Israel would like to rid itself of the Gaza Strip, but it will not do so until it is certain that a lasting peace with its Arab neighbors is assured.

# Golan Heights

## Perspective

| | |
|---|---|
| 1946 | Syria becomes fully independent from French League of Nations mandate. Historically, Golan Heights is part of Syria. |
| 1948-1967 | With establishment of the state of Israel, Syrian gunmen use Golan Heights to harass Israeli settlements. |
| 1966 | Coup d'état brings extremist regime into power. Attacks on Israel from Golan Heights escalate. |
| 1967 | During Six-Day War, Israelis capture Golan Heights. Syrian occupants evacuate. |
| 1974 | Following another conflict, Syria and Israel agree to "area of separation" between their forces patrolled by United Nations. |
| 1981 | Menachem Begin announces that Israel has annexed Golan Heights. |
| 1985 | United States State Department holds that peace-for-territory bargain in Middle East applies to all Israeli fronts, including Golan Heights. |

The Golan Heights is a strategic, hilly region on the border separating Syria and Israel. Traditionally a part of Syria, the region remained a part of the new nation in 1946 when Syria gained its independence from France. The hills were fortified by Arab forces during the Arab-Israeli war from 1947 to 1948. After the Jewish state of Israel was founded in 1948, Arab artillery embedded in the Heights heavily damaged new Israeli settlements across the border.

In the Six-Day War of 1967, Israel attacked and occupied the Golan Heights. Israel announced that, along with other Arab-conquered lands, the Golan Heights would be returned to Syria only after substantive progress was made in improving Israeli-Arab relations.

After the 1973 Arab-Israeli war, Israel and Syria agreed to an "area of separation" between their forces; this demilitarized zone ranges from about 1,000 yards to 3 miles (1 to 5 km) in width and stretches for 48 miles (77 km). An international force under the auspices of the United Nations patrols the buffer zone; it is regarded as one of the more successful United Nations peacekeeping missions. United States and Soviet officers work together in truce-supervision offices in Cairo and Damascus. The truce held even during Israel's invasion of Lebanon in 1982.

## Issues and Events

A near crisis occurred in 1981 when Israeli prime minister Menachem Begin announced that Israel was annexing the Golan Heights. The Israeli legislature, or Knesset, promptly approved the annexation by a wide margin.

It was a highly popular move in Israeli quarters, particularly among the seven thousand Israeli settlers in the Golan Heights.

The Israeli action, however, was denounced in most of the rest of the world. The United Nations Security Council voted unanimously to declare the annexation null and void, while the United States protested the action by suspending $300 million in special aid to Israel. Syria led the denunciations that came from the Arab world; but Syrian president Hafez Assad, with large numbers of troops bogged down in Lebanon, was unable to counter the action. Begin was adamant on the action; it was an important step in the fulfillment of a cherished dream: an Israel that encompassed all its biblical territories.

Meanwhile, this ruggedly beautiful plateau has become a tourist attraction.

The Druze who live on the Golan Heights are divided on the subject of Israeli annexation. An important minority sect in Syria and Lebanon, the Druze number about 12,500 in the Golan, and are generally more friendly toward Israel than are the traditional Muslims. Although a small minority accepted Israeli citizenship, sentiments appeared to shift after some members of the Druze community, who were demanding the return of the Golan to Syria, clashed with Israeli police in 1988. The majority of the Muslims are opposed to the annexation and support the Syrians, who consider recovery of the Golan a sacred cause.

The Syrians are not in a position to reopen hostilities with Israel, and instead have been forced to rely on diplomacy and international public opinion. Syria has claimed itself to be the victim of unprovoked Israeli aggression, and has used the Israeli occupation and annexation of the Golan as a further reason for refusing to recognize Israel's existence.

At one time it seemed likely that Israel's annexation of the Golan Heights foreshadowed the fate of the other occupied territories, but the recent Palestinian uprisings in the Gaza Strip and West Bank make this less than likely. The Golan Heights was the most desirable candidate for annexation because the local population did not include any Palestinians who would protest the action.

In 1987, members of the Arab League agreed that no Arab state can make a separate agreement with Israel, so the entire matter of all the occupied areas must be dealt with simultaneously. No agreement about the future of the Gaza Strip or West Bank can be considered final until Israel and Syria can reach a settlement about the Golan Heights.

# West Bank

## Perspective

| | |
|---|---|
| *1920* | Palestine west of Jordan River becomes part of a "British mandate for Palestine"; eastern part becomes Transjordan and later Jordan. |
| *1948-1949* | During Arab-Israeli War, Jordan seizes and occupies West Bank. |
| *1950* | Jordan annexes West Bank. |
| *1967* | In Six-Day War, Israel seizes and occupies West Bank; Israeli settlement begins. |
| *1977* | Under Prime Minister Menachem Begin, Israel increases settlements. |
| *1981* | Begin declares that Israel will never leave Judea or Samaria, ancient names for West Bank. |
| *1987* | **December.** Palestinian uprising, or intifada, begins. |
| *1988* | **July.** Jordan renounces its claim to the West Bank.<br>**November.** Palestinians declare an independent state, including the West Bank. |

Of all the issues that separate Israel from its Arab neighbors, nothing so inflames emotions as Israel's occupation and settlement of the West Bank. International criticism of Israel's settlement policy of the territory notwithstanding, Israel has consistently carried out a policy of planting such a large Jewish population in the West Bank that its return to Jordan would never be feasible.

The seeds of the modern dilemma go back to the years following World War I, when the British mandate for Palestine was established. That mandate included land west of the Jordan River. The land immediately east of the river became known as Transjordan, and later Jordan. During the first Arab-Israeli war, from 1948 to 1949, the Hashemite Kingdom of Jordan seized and occupied a portion of the former mandate on the west bank of the river. Known as the West Bank, in 1950 Jordan annexed and continued to govern the area until the Six-Day War of 1967. At that time, Israel quickly overran the West Bank, forced out the Jordanian army, and occupied the territory. Jewish settlement of the West Bank began almost immediately, and in 1981 Israel announced that it had no intention of giving up the territory, that it in fact represented the biblical Judea and Samaria, and that it traditionally belonged to the Jewish people.

## Issues and Events

In 1986, there were fifty thousand Jewish settlers living in over one hundred communities in the West Bank. Despite this sizable population, the Israelis still constitute less than 10 percent of the West Bank population.

The immediate problem of the large Arab population is its opposition to Jewish occupation of the territory. Despite a tough military program to root out all support for the Palestine Liberation Organization (PLO), there is no question of the PLO's popularity there. Violence has been the inevitable result. By the 1980s, Arab violence was endangering travel in the West Bank, and Jewish vigilante groups sprang up to impose law and order in the territory. In 1984, about twenty-five settlers were accused of organized terrorist activities.

Terrorism—both Arab and Jewish—in the West Bank has had a polarizing effect on Israel's population. Most politicians condemned acts of Jewish terrorism; and both of the nation's major political parties, Labor Alignment and Likud, called for prosecution of the Jewish underground responsible for the acts. A few right-wing groups, however, including the militant settlers' organization Gush Emunim, "bloc of the faithful," blamed the government for failing to protect Jewish settlers in the West Bank and forcing the settlers to take the law into their own hands.

The problem of the West Bank was complicated in 1988 when Jordan's King Hussein renounced his country's claim to the West Bank. This meant that Israel would be forced to negotiate directly with the Palestinians, rather than with the Jordanians, about the future of the territory. Israel, which does not recognize the PLO, has tried to directly negotiate with West Bank residents in a less then successful effort to quell the *intifadah* uprisings that began in December 1987.

Violence has become commonplace in the West Bank as the intifadah drags on. While Palestinians continue to suffer death, persecution, and a drastically reduced standard of living in their quest for freedom, the United States, Egypt, and other countries increasingly press for a negotiated resolution to the conflict.

# Sub-Saharan Africa

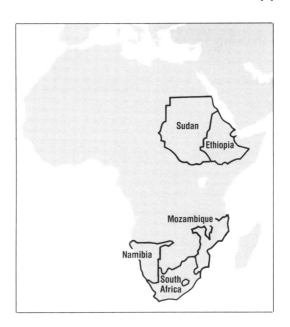

As the twentieth century draws to a close, Africa—especially that part south of the Sahara—is beset by problems already solved or alleviated to a large degree in the rest of the world. Widespread famine is the most serious issue, and it is accompanied by the related problem of an out-of-control population explosion. Southern Africa is still torn by conflicts arising from colonial policies of the past, including land distribution, racial and ethnic rivalries, and religious divisions.

During the early 1980s, a widespread and long-lasting drought struck Africa. Its effects were felt most by the already poverty-stricken nomadic and seminomadic peoples of the area. Accustomed to living just above the starvation level in even the best years, these peoples died by the hundreds of thousands. Worldwide efforts to rush relief to the famine victims resulted in vast amounts of food finding its way to Africa, but it is believed that ongoing civil wars and inefficient government agencies have slowed food distribution. Despite those relief efforts, experts agree that the real cure for the famine is peace. In Sudan and Ethiopia, the civil wars that contributed so heavily to famine and suffering are based on longstanding ethnic rivalries. In the Mozambique conflict, ethnicity and race play little or no role in a war that is strictly political in origin.

In South Africa, racial tensions continue to plague the nation as the blacks fight for political representation and the dismantling of apartheid laws that enforce racial segregation. Since the 1970s, the black majority has become increasingly angry. Acts of civil disobedience eventually led to the government's declaration of a state of emergency in 1985. Bowing to increasing international pressure, South Africa's government began to offer major concessions, but the unrest will continue until voting rights for blacks become a reality.

Namibia and Mozambique also continue to suffer from problems left over from colonial days. Mozambique, long a Portuguese colony, is finding difficulty achieving economic viability after centuries of subjugation, while Namibia has been trying to free itself of imperialism since World War I. After the war, Namibia, a former German colony, was in effect the colony of another colony, the Union (now Republic) of South Africa. After World War II, South Africa refused to relinquish its control over Namibia, despite orders to do so by the United Nations. Under South African rule, Namibia's ruling whites prospered at the expense of the majority black population. Namibia finally gained independence in 1990, but it still faces the task of creating peace and prosperity for all of its citizens.

# South Africa: Apartheid and the Homelands

## Perspective

|  |  |
|---|---|
| 1833 | Slavery is abolished in South Africa. |
| 1899-1902 | Boer War is fought between British and Boers. |
| 1910 | Union of South Africa is created. |
| 1913 | Native Lands Act is passed. |
| 1936 | Native Representation Act is passed. |
| 1950s | National party institutes apartheid policies. |
| 1951 | Black homelands are created. |
| 1960 | Uprising is held in Sharpesville. |
| 1961 | *May 10.* Republic of South Africa is established. |
| 1976 | Riots occur at Soweto. |
| 1984 | New constitution with limited political rights for coloreds and Asians is put into force. |
| 1985 | *July.* Continued unrest prompts government to declare state of emergency, detaining blacks without charges. |
| 1986 | *April.* Government announces the end of the pass laws. *May.* Crossroads riots result in sixty-nine deaths and sixty thousand homeless. |
| 1989 | *August 14.* F.W. de Klerk replaces P.W. Botha as president. |
| 1990 | *February 2.* 30-year ban on African National Congress is lifted. *February 11.* Nelson Mandela is freed after 27 years in prison. |

South Africa is like a time bomb. No one knows if or when the explosion will occur. The white minority, which makes up only 18 percent of the population, continues to maintain its complete political, economic, and social domination of the majority black Africans. The African majority, after years of subjugation by whites, is asserting its right to full participation in government and the abolition of a white supremacist society.

## Issues and Events

Student protests erupted into full-scale rioting in 1976 in Soweto, a black section of Johannesburg, resulting in hundreds of deaths and thousands of injuries. The riots marked the awakening of black consciousness in South Africa and the beginning of a protest movement that continues today.

Apartheid, which is Afrikaans for "apartness," has been used to separate the races in all aspects of life. Pressures from within and without to abolish apartheid are becoming increasingly undeniable even to the leaders of South Africa's ruling and normally intransigent National party. This reassessment of total apartheid has a number of causes, including increasing resistance by blacks, the growing dependency on black labor, and mounting pressure from the international community.

An important part of apartheid has been the creation of "homelands" for the native black population. The homelands were to be organized along ethnic lines and given what the South African government called "full independence." Homelands residents were forced to renounce South African citizenship, a ploy by the government to create a white majority of South African citizens. Black African leaders, and most foreign observers, opposed the creation of these homelands and denied that they would have true independence, as their governments would be puppets of the South African government. Neither the United Nations nor any foreign government has recognized Transkei (the first of the homelands to be granted "independence" in 1976), Bophuthatswana, Venda, or Ciskei as sovereign countries. Much of the population of the homelands is made up of blacks who have been forcibly displaced. The South African government has agreed in principle to halt the forced resettlements.

The constitution that came into force in 1984 and the events that followed its passage provide an example of the ruling party's attempt to adapt to realities and at the same time maintain racial dominance. It provides for a system in which whites (18 percent of the population), coloreds (10 percent; persons of mixed racial parentage), and Asians (3 percent; Indians) hold parliamentary sessions on separate "affairs" in three different languages in three different chambers. Blacks, who make up 69 percent of the population, continue to be excluded from any national power. Their dissatisfaction has led to numerous demonstrations and protests. In response to continued unrest, the government declared a state of emergency in July 1985, thus assuming the right to arrest blacks and hold them without charges or explanation.

In 1986, the government announced an end to the hated "pass laws" that forced blacks to carry passport identification. A backlash by whites led to the "Crossroads riots," which resulted in sixty-nine deaths and sixty thousand homeless. In May 1987, more than three million black workers joined in the largest strike in the nation's history. Fearing that the tenth anniversary of the Soweto Township uprisings would trigger antiapartheid violence, the government imposed another state of emergency in June 1986, which has extended into 1990. It is estimated that as many as four thousand people have been killed since the state of emergency was imposed in 1986.

South Africa gained a new president for the first time in ten years when F.W. de Klerk replaced P.W. Botha in August 1989. De Klerk began 1990 by lifting a 30-year ban on the powerful African National Congress and releasing political activist Nelson Mandela from prison. De Klerk still faces the awesome task of bringing full equality and sufferage to South African blacks while defusing the racial tensions that threaten to erupt into civil war.

## Background

Race has been the central cause of problems in South Africa since the arrival of the first Dutch settlers, also called Boers, in the 1650s. When the British took over the Cape Colony in 1803, four major groups inhabited the territory, including the Boers, or Afrikaners; slaves of African-Malay descent, who would be the basis of the country's colored population; the nomadic Hottentots, who were badly treated by the Boers; and the black Bantu peoples, who lived beyond the frontiers and were in constant conflict with the expanding settlements. Under the influence of reform movements originating in Britain, Hottentots were put on an equal racial footing with whites in 1828, and slavery was abolished in the Cape Colony in 1834.

These acts, combined with British restriction settlement, the establishment of English as the sole official language, and the abolition of the old Dutch administrative system, led to the Great Trek, which began in 1836. Over twelve thousand Boers left the southern Cape for Natal and the Transvaal to the northeast, where they created their own states and laws. In the Boer states, laws were passed whose object was to prevent vagrancy and establish the "proper relation between master and servant," and strict lines of demarcation between Boer and Bantu areas were established.

After the discovery of diamonds and gold in the Transvaal, the assertion of British rule in the area led to the Boer War from 1899 to 1902. Under British auspices, the Union of South Africa was created by 1910. The status of blacks did not improve under the Act of Union.

The country passed the Native Lands Act in 1913, establishing Bantu areas and forbidding black ownership of land within designated white areas, which comprised over 87 percent of the total area. The Mines and Works act in 1926 laid down the principle of the color bar, in which blacks were excluded from skilled jobs. In 1936, the Native Representation Act put blacks, who in some areas had the right to vote, on separate voting rolls from whites and circumscribed other political rights. When the predominantly Afrikaner National party came to power in 1948, the concept of "separate development," or apartheid, came to fruition.

In 1949, the Mixed Marriages Act made interracial marriage a crime. In 1950, the Population Registration Act required that all citizens must be registered by race, while the Group Areas Act of 1950 allocated specific residential areas in cities and towns to various racial groups. The Reservation of Separate Amenities Act and Black Education Act resembled segregation laws of the American South before the 1950s.

After Soweto there was a sharp upsurge in black political and union activities on one hand, and a commitment to armed struggle on the other. The African National Congress led the armed struggle from military bases in neighboring states. The ANC has United Nations recognition and observer status.

More moderate forces operating within South Africa come under the umbrella of the United Democratic Front (UDF) and are led by prominent figures such as the Nobel Peace Prize winner Bishop Desmond Tutu. A third force on the black political scene is Inkatha, a Zulu-based national movement led by Chief Gatsha Buthelezi.

Both the ANC and the UDF seek the establishment of universal majority rule in a democratic, unified South Africa and the elimination of apartheid.

The ruling National party, which has held power since 1948, has sought a united white South Africa, establishment of independent black homelands, and social and economic reforms to improve the status of blacks without endangering white control of the government. The National party argues that white rule is justified because whites have transformed the country into Africa's richest and most powerful nation, while surrounding, black-controlled countries suffer from poverty and economic stagnation.

In recent years, the thrust of South African policy has been to destroy armed opposition and to put into place sufficient minor reforms to defuse growing black militancy without threatening white rule. Efforts have also been made to induce neighboring black states to deny bases to guerrillas.

# Namibia: The Struggle for Independence

## Perspective

| | |
|---|---|
| *1884* | Germany extends its protection over South West Africa. |
| *1915* | South African troops conquer German South West Africa. |
| *1920* | League of Nations mandates South West Africa to South Africa. |
| *1966* | United Nations adopts resolution terminating League of Nations mandate. South West Africa People's Organization (SWAPO) begins guerrilla war against South African administration. |
| *1971* | International Court of Justice rules that South Africa's presence in Namibia is illegal. |
| *1973* | United Nations recognizes SWAPO as "authentic" representative of Namibia. |
| *1975* | SWAPO establishes military bases in Angola. Cuban troops are sent to Angola to protect its new Marxist government. |
| *1978* | United Nations adopts resolution calling for free elections leading to Namibian independence. South African-sponsored elections are boycotted by SWAPO and declared invalid by United Nations. |
| *1983* | **December.** South Africa invades Angola to destroy SWAPO bases. |
| *1985* | **June.** South Africa sets up an interim government that excludes SWAPO. United Nations condemns the action. |
| *1988* | **August 22.** South Africa, Angola, and Cuba sign a cease-fire.<br>**December 22.** South Africa, Angola, and Cuba sign a series of accords providing for Cuban troop withdrawal from Angola and independence for Namibia. |
| *1989* | **April.** SWAPO and South African forces clash at Angola border.<br>**June 12.** SWAPO exiles are allowed to return to Namibia.<br>**September 14.** SWAPO leader Sam Nujoma returns to Namibia.<br>**November 7.** SWAPO wins first free elections. |
| *1990* | **March 21.** Namibia achieves independence. |

On March 21, 1990, Africa's last colony gained its independence. And while there may be reason for rejoicing among Namibia's long-oppressed black population, the road ahead is filled with challenges for the new government.

## Issues and Events

The government's first task is to heal the ethnic and racial tensions that divide the country. It must improve the living conditions for the blacks while protecting the rights of the white minority. A land of many ethnic groups, SWAPO is dominated by the largest black group, the Ovambo. Other black ethnic groups view the party with distrust, claiming that SWAPO was responsible for torture and other human rights abuses while it was exiled in Angola. Whites in Namibia, although they account for only 7 percent of the population, still control Namibia's industry and economy. If Namibia is to grow and prosper, it must prevent a mass exodus of whites. However, it must also enact land reform and other policies to improve the living conditions for the nation's blacks. White supremacist groups continue to roam the country and impose their will by means of force and intimidation.

The new government must also deal with the reality that the country is still intimately tied to South Africa. Its main port, Walvis Bay, remains in the hands of South Africans and most of the industry is owned by firms based in South Africa. If unrest continues in neighboring Angola, South African military occupation remains a very real possibility.

Finally, the stability of the new government is questionable. While SWAPO leader Sam Nujoma has abandoned his former preference for a one-party government, some doubt that the former guerrilla organization will be capable of power-sharing on a long term basis. SWAPO's ability to honor agreements was questioned when its incursions into Namibia in early 1989 violated the 1988 accord and almost sabotaged the independence process.

What happens in Namibia may well have a profound impact on politics in the entire region. If Namibia is able to overcome the obstacles that lie ahead, it will provide a model for moderate forces in South Africa who are working for a coalition government in their own racially-divided nation, where similar problems exist. On the other hand, if Namibia fails it will be a victory for South Africa's conservative white supremacists and make political reform that much harder to achieve.

## Background

The earliest known inhabitants of southern and central Namibia were Bushmen and nomadic Hottentots who periodically crossed the Orange River, which constitutes the territory's southern border. Sometime before the eighteenth century, the Herero, a Bantu-speaking, cattle-raising people, occupied much of central Namibia and reduced the Bushmen to serfdom. Later the Ovambo, another Bantu group, crossed the Nunene River from the north and occupied the more fertile areas of northern Namibia. Major conflicts over grazing lands arose in the mid-1800s between white-influenced Nama (largely descendants of white and Hottentot liaisons) and the Herero, and continued until 1892.

The British government of the Cape Colony, in what is now South Africa, first took advantage of the native wars and calls for help by annexing about 400 square miles (1,000 square km) around Walvis Bay in 1878. In 1883, Adolph Luderitz established a trading post at Angra Pequena on the southern coast, and Germany soon extended its protection to almost all of what is now Namibia. The Germans brutally imposed their rule on South West Africa, first routing the Nama and, in response to a native revolt, virtually annihilating the Herero. As a result of the revolt, the remaining Herero and Nama were forced to carry passes and to labor for whites. Their cattle were confiscated. Most importantly, the majority of people in Namibia were now Ovambo rather than Herero.

During World War I, South African troops conquered German South West Africa and ruled the eighty thousand native inhabitants. South Africa wished to incorporate South West Africa into the Union, but the League of Nations declared it a mandate. In contravention of the intent of the 1920 mandate, South Africa began to administer the area as if it had been annexed. It also seized land from the majority blacks and gave it to minority whites and instituted a strict policy of apartheid. Many blacks were dispossessed and turned into contract laborers. Revolts by blacks in 1922 and 1925 were brutally suppressed.

During the 1930s, the South African government continued along a path of incorporation of Namibia into the Union. World War II and the creation of the United Nations, which took over the administration of the old mandates, interrupted this path. In 1946, South Africa called upon the United Nations to allow the formal incorporation of South West Africa into South Africa. The United Nations, committed to a policy of turning mandates into self-governing countries, denied the request. Nevertheless, South Africa continued its policy of gradual incorporation. In 1966, a United Nations General Assembly resolution terminated the mandate and in 1968 resolved that the country should be called Namibia, after the Nama, one of the historic tribes of the area. In 1971 the International Court of Justice ordered South Africa to end its administration of the country. South Africa refused to recognize the jurisdiction of the court, however, and continued its rule over what it insisted on calling South West Africa. It also began to carry out a "homelands" policy in South West Africa that forced people into racially segregated black communities that were puppet creations of Pretoria.

The 1960s also saw the emergence and growth of SWAPO, a liberation organization made up primarily of Ovambo dissidents who had decided that the preparations for independence were taking too long. In 1966, they began guerrilla raids into Namibia from Zambia and in 1973 the United Nations recognized SWAPO as the "authentic" representatives of the Namibian people.

In 1975, when Angola, Namibia's northern neighbor, gained its independence from Portugal, a power struggle developed between the Popular Movement for the Liberation of Angola (MPLA) and the UNITA forces. South Africa, anxious to ensure a non-Communist and friendly government so close to its borders, gave logistical support to UNITA. When the MPLA, with Cuban help, triumphed in 1976, SWAPO was allowed to move its bases from Zambia to Angola. The South Africans continued to support the UNITA guerrillas who remained in the field, and the South African army made repeated incursions into Angolan territory to destroy SWAPO bases.

Namibia's status has always been an especially emotional issue. Black African republics objected to the area's government by the white-supremacists of South Africa. One reason South Africa was unwilling to surrender sovereignty over the country is that it viewed Namibia as a strategic buffer state between it and the black African nations surrounding it. In addition, South Africa wished to retain control of Namibia's valuable mineral resources, particularly diamonds and uranium.

In the early 1980s, international pressures on South Africa to grant independence increased. South African military incursions grew both in number and size. After eight years of United Nations-sponsored negotiations, South Africa, Angola, and Cuba finally reached an agreement on December 22, 1988. The plan was hailed as a triumph in east-west cooperation—the United States used its influence on South Africa while the Soviet Union encouraged Angola and Cuba. The accord provided for the orderly return of the SWAPO exiles, United Nations-supervised elections, the withdrawal of South African troops from Angola and Namibia, and the removal of Cuban troops from Angola by 1991.

# Mozambique: Renamo's Reign of Terror

## Perspective

| | |
|---|---|
| 1498 | Portuguese navigator Vasco da Gama lands on the coast en route to India. |
| 1505 | Portuguese establish a foothold in Mozambique to support spice trade. |
| 1629 | Prazos are established. |
| 1837 | Portuguese authority is vested in a governor general. |
| 1878 | Native Labor Code is enacted. |
| 1891 | Chartered companies are organized. |
| 1930 | Colonial Statute of 1930 places Mozambique under the direct control of Portuguese government. |
| 1961 | Portuguese government institutes reforms. |
| 1962 | Front for the Liberation of Mozambique (Fremilo) is founded. |
| 1964 | War for independence begins. |
| 1975 | **June 25.** Mozambique gains its independence with Somora Machel as president; Portuguese flee the country. |
| 1977 | Mozambican National Resistance (Renamo) is formed. |
| 1984 | **March 16.** Nkomati Accord to end support for each other's rebels is signed by Mozambique and South Africa. |
| 1986 | **October 19.** President Machel dies in a plane crash. Joaquim Chissano assumes power. |
| 1987 | **July 18.** In Homoine, 386 civilians are massacred. |
| 1989 | **August 8.** Peace talks begin. |

As the people of Homoine, a village in southern Mozambique, went to sleep on July 17, 1987, they had no indication that their lives would be forever changed. Armed with guns and machetes, about forty soldiers stormed the town before dawn and systematically massacred 386 of the town's citizens while they slept in their beds. More than three thousand people fled the village in terror, fearing the gunmen would return.

This incident was but one of thousands of acts of terrorism and destruction blamed on the Mozambique National Resistance, or "Renamo," as they are known. Since 1977 Renamo has roamed the countryside attacking everything from government installations to innocent children in an apparent attempt to destabilize the Marxist government led by Joaquim Chissano.

## Issues and Events

Very little is known about Renamo and its shadowy leader, Alfonso Dhlakama. Unlike most guerrilla groups, Renamo seems uninterested in territorial acquisition and stages its attacks across the entire country rather than trying to gain complete control over a particular area. Also unlike most rebel groups, Renamo, which numbers about fifteen thousand, does not try to convert the common people to a particular political philosophy. More than anything, Renamo is bent on destroying the existing government.

Renamo was formed in 1976 as a backlash to the newly-independent Machel government's attempts to impose land reform, eliminate tribal leaders, and curtail religious activity. Initially supported by the white Zimbabwe (then Rhodesian) government, Renamo served to protect that country from rebel armies that sought to set up bases on neighboring Mozambique. After Zimbabwe's conversion to socialism in 1980, South Africa took over sponsorship of the group, hoping to keep Mozambique's roads and railways closed and thereby perpetuate the dependence of inland Africa and South African port facilities. After the signing of the Nkomati Accord in 1984, South Africa supposedly withdrew its support for Renamo in return for Mozambique's pledge to end its support for South African rebels. Despite the lack of any apparent foreign assistance, Renamo violence has continued to increase. All of this has had a devastating effect on the country's already troubled economy, but the real disaster is the war's effect on human lives. People throughout Mozambique live in constant fear of attack. Children are kidnapped and forced to fight with Renamo's troops. In addition to one hundred thousand dead, more than five million people have been forced from their homes. Renamo has repeatedly destroyed crops and shipments of food aid throughout the country. According to the United Nations, almost three million people are dependent on foreign aid for survival.

The Mozambique government enjoys aid and assistance from the Soviet Union, most of Europe, Canada, Japan, Brazil, Botswana, India, and Nigeria. Mozambique is the only case in which the United States backs a Marxist government rather than the "freedom fighters" that seek its demise. Neighboring Zimbabwe, Tanzania, and Malawi have offered additional troops to protect their lines of transportation. Even South Africa has offered Mozambique's President Chissano non-lethal military assistance.

Perhaps the greatest single factor contributing to Renamo's success is the inept and ill-equipped Mozambican army. The rebels seem to be able to capture enough weapons and provisions to continue their reign of terror without outside support. In its own defense,

Renamo claims the atrocities committed against civilians were perpetrated by other groups. It also claims that it has gained popular support in the rural areas where it has supposedly set up successful small farms, schools, and other facilities. Relief workers established in the countryside testify that there is no evidence to support this claim.

Despite the continuing turmoil and hardship, Mozambique's Marxist government is surprisingly stable and seems to enjoy the support of the people. Even after the tragic death of the government's founder, President Machel, the transfer of power to Joaquim Chissano was smooth and orderly.

The year 1989 was a landmark year for Mozambique. For the first time, both the government and Renamo expressed interest in reaching a negotiated settlement. On August 8, Mozambican church leaders met with Renamo and presented them with a Fremilo peace plan calling for Renamo to renounce violence and participate in the existing political structure. Renamo countered with its own proposal, which included constitutional reforms, the withdrawal of Zimbabwean troops, and multi-party elections. The government has also softened up its Marxist rhetoric and offered a general amnesty to all who cease fighting and pledge to support the government.

## Background

Under Portuguese rule, Mozambique developed neither the infrastructure nor the cultural identity that would have been necessary to prepare it for independence. The country continues to suffer from Portugal's lack of investment and excessive exploitation.

Mozambique's first contacts with the outside world began during the eighth century when Arab merchants established trading posts where cloth, ceramics, salt, and weapons were exchanged for Mozambique's ivory, gold, and palm oil.

In 1948, Portuguese explorer Vasco de Gama landed at Mozambique during his first voyage to India. By 1505, Portugal gained dominance over the Arabs in the region and established trading posts on Mozambique's coast as part of a plan to dominate the Eastern spice trade. Gold was the prize that lured early explorers to venture inland along the Zambezi River in 1531. For the next hundred years, Portuguese influence was confined primarily to the coast and along the river until the "prazos," or large land grants, were issued. The "prazeros," or lease holders, were given complete control over all of the people and resources within their territory. The prazos enabled the Portuguese to maintain control of the region with a minimum of effort, while the prazeros had their own armies and defended the land from encroaching African chiefs. The late 1800s were marked by the discovery of gold in South Africa and Mozambicans flocked to the region to work in the mines. The Native Labor Code was enacted in 1878 shortly after the abolition of slavery. This law was intended to end the 300-year-old institution of forced labor by allowing the indigenous Africans to decide whether or not to work for Europeans. However, this law was often circumvented by the chartered companies established in the 1890s to grow sugar and cotton for export. The human abuses by these companies were greater than the prazeros and more than 100,000 Africans were forced to flee to neighboring countries.

In 1930, Mozambique was once again placed directly under Portuguese rule from Lisbon. During this period the companies were dissolved and Portuguese settlement and development of Mozambique were encouraged. Africans were encouraged to give up their language and culture and become "civilized." Those who did not comply were subject to severe discrimination.

By the early 1960s, rising African nationalism forced Portugal to institute reforms allowing for greater participation by Africans in government, improved living conditions, and an end to legal discrimination. These measures were not enough to stem the growing independence movement. Led by the Front for the Liberation of Mozambique, the pro-independence forces and Portuguese troops clashed for eleven years before independence was achieved in June 1975. Samora Machel, the charismatic leader of the Fremilo movement, became president.

President Machel set up a Marxist government whose main priority was agricultural development. Almost immediately, the whites, who ran the commercial sector of the economy, fled the country. In the first three years after independence, agricultural and industrial production dropped by 50 percent, and Portugal refused to import Mozambican goods.

In 1977, Machel tried to establish a Soviet-style bureaucracy, but inefficiency and inertia continued. By 1980, Machel's socialist policies were softened somewhat and small businesses were returned to private hands. Throughout the 1980s, the economy continued to falter as a result of recurrent drought and the continuing war with Renamo. Mozambique remains one of the world's poorest countries.

# Ethiopia: The Politics of Famine

## Perspective

| | |
|---|---|
| **1930** | Haile Selassie becomes emperor of Ethiopia and gives Ethiopia its first constitution. |
| **1952** | United Nations establishes Eritrea as an autonomous unit within Ethiopia. |
| **1958** | Separatist movements form in Eritrea and Tigray provinces. |
| **1962** | Ethiopia incorporates Eritrea. Eritrean guerrillas launch a civil war that still continues. |
| **1971** | Drought begins in northern provinces; Selassie endeavors to cover up seriousness of situation. |
| **1974** | **September.** Haile Selassie is overthrown in military coup. Mengistu Haile Mariam eventually takes over as leader of government. |
| **1982** | Serious drought arises in most of the country. |
| **1984** | **August.** World attention begins to focus on relief-agency reports, stating that famine in Africa has grown to overwhelming proportions.<br>**October.** Mengistu allows press coverage of drought-stricken area. |
| **1987** | **Summer.** Drought recurs; foreign aid averts disaster. |
| **1988** | **April.** Relief agencies are evicted by Ethiopian government. |
| **1989** | **February 27.** Tigrean People's Liberation Front (TPLF) captures all of Tigray province.<br>**May 16.** Coup attempt fails.<br>**September 7.** Eritrean People's Liberation Front (EPLF) begins peace talks with government.<br>**October 28.** Government requests international food donations to avoid another famine.<br>**December.** TPLF troops close in on Ethiopia's capital, Addis Ababa. |

Since 1984, world attention has focused on Ethiopia, where the combined effects of civil war and drought have created a continuing famine. Between 1984 and 1985, at least a million people died in Ethiopia alone, at least seven million people were believed to be starving, and perhaps a total of twenty million were thought to be affected on the entire African continent. More than $2 billion in foreign aid was required to alleviate the affects of Ethiopia's famine.

In 1987, the specter of famine loomed again as the vital rains failed to come, but catastrophe was averted, thanks to foreign aid. The situation in 1990 appeared grim once again. Summer rains never came in 1989, and the political situation began to deteriorate. As many as four million people again faced the possibility of starvation, while the government continued to divert its power and resources into a war that has drained the life from Ethiopia for almost three decades.

## Issues and Events

When famine threatened in 1982, Mengistu, like his predecessor Haile Selassie, was reluctant to admit that a serious food shortage existed because it might weaken support for his regime. By the time he allowed press coverage of the drought-stricken area in late 1984, the famine had reached monumental proportions. Shocking images of the dead and dying were shown around the world and resulted in a massive outpouring of foreign aid.

The causes of famine in Ethiopia are many. Like other African countries, Ethiopia is highly susceptible to drought. It is also plagued by soil erosion, deforestation, and overpopulation. But the main causes of Ethiopia's suffering have nothing to do with the environment. Traditional agricultural patterns in Ethiopia were disrupted when the Marxist government forced the creation of collectivized farms, which proved highly inefficient and unproductive. Money that should have been spent on agricultural development has gone into military expenditures. It is believed that Ethiopia's military expenditures exceed 60 percent of its annual budget. Mengistu's army of more than three hundred thousand—one of Africa's largest—has been necessary to defeat the Eritrean and Tigrean rebels in their protracted civil war.

The war has severely disrupted food distribution systems in the country. Both the rebels and government forces are guilty of bombing food shipments or blocking roads. Government forces have been accused of using food as a weapon in an attempt to starve the people of the northern provinces into submission; rebel forces have been accused of blocking incoming aid because they fear the shipments might also contain military equipment. In 1988 Mengistu evicted the Red Cross and other relief agencies because they were interfering with the war effort. One of the government's most controversial programs involved the forced relocation of 1.5 million people from the dry, northern part of the country to the more fertile productive plains of the south. Another program, "villagization," is a plan to move three million people from remote hillside farms to villages, where services such as medical care and an adequate water supply are available.

Critics of these programs claim that people are forced to relocate against their will. Many escaped to Somalia after resettlement to avoid having to adjust to strange, new lifestyles. Others, weakened by malnutrition, perished en route. Families were often separated, and the new habitats were sometimes worse than those the people had been forced to evacuate. Eritrean rebels protest the political implications of both the resettlement and villagization programs. The resettlement program is claimed to be a means of depopulating the troublesome Eritrean region and destroying hopes for a separate Eritrean state, while villagization is decried as forced collectivization.

Serious setbacks in 1989 prompted Mengistu to begin negotiations to end the civil war. The year began with a stunning series of military defeats by the Tigrean People's Liberation Front, which captured the entire province of Tigray in February. Tens of thousands of government soldiers were killed during this campaign.

The increasingly restless and demoralized military attempted a coup in May that resulted in the deaths of fourteen of Mengistu's top generals. Mengistu's future was further threatened when the Soviet Union, Ethiopia's main source of weapons, announced that it may not renew an arms treaty scheduled to expire in 1991.

Jimmy Carter mediated peace talks between the Eritrean People's Liberation Front (EPLF) and the Mengistu government. The talks—the first in twenty-eight years of warfare—failed to produce results. By the end of 1989, Tigrean rebel forces had launched a major offensive and were positioned less than one hundred miles from the capital of Addis Ababa. The city braced itself for war under the greatest threat ever imposed by the rebel insurgency.

Mengistu can stay in power and keep Ethiopia intact only by maintaining a huge army and therefore incurring tremendous military expenditures. There is no doubt that Ethiopia will continue to suffer as long as Mengistu remains in charge, but it is likely that his downfall will be as slow and painful as the starvation of the Ethiopian people.

## Background

Haile Selassie gave Ethiopia its first constitution shortly after taking the throne in 1930. A descendant of Ethiopia's ruling family, Selassie could trace his ancestry back over twenty-four hundred years, legend has it, to King Solomon and the Queen of Sheba. Selassie's forty-four-year reign was notable for its enduring and autocratic nature: the constitution stated that "the person of the Emperor is sacred, his dignity is inviolable, and his power indisputable."

Selassie revised the constitution in 1955 and offered to reform Ethiopia's system of government in 1974, largely because his powerful image was being tarnished by an inability to control increasing poverty. Growing popular awareness of the weakness of the feudalistic landholding system led to conflict over the need for land reform and modern agricultural methods. A group composed of the country's own military overthrew Salassie's government in September 1974. Speculation at the time was that Selassie's failure to control food shortages, soaring prices, and poor living conditions had brought the revolution. Even with a per capita income of about eighty-five dollars a year, a population that was 90 percent illiterate, and drought conditions from 1971 to 1974 that killed a hundred thousand people, Selassie refused to ask for international aid, preferring to keep the country's troubled condition a secret.

The military junta, known as the Dergue, initially moved with irresolution and a lack of clear planning. It installed two prime ministers and then ousted them before appointing General Aman Mikael Andom as head of government. A radical faction came to the forefront and its members in the Dergue shot Aman. Ultimately a leader of the radical faction emerged: Mengistu Haile Mariam, who was only thirty-two years old at the time, became Ethiopia's head of state.

When Mengistu's Marxist policies met with opposition, he responded by launching a program of mass arrests and executions between 1977 and 1978, referred to as the "red terror." More than ten thousand were killed during this purge.

Mengistu also faced resistance in the form of an escalating civil war inherited from Haile Selassie. The war began shortly after the United Nations decided to give the former Italian colony of Eritrea to Ethiopia in 1952. The region was to be governed separately as an autonomous area within Ethiopia. Ethiopia violated the terms of the agreement ten years later by annexing the territory. At this point, separatist movements in Eritrea and the neighboring province of Tigray launched a full-scale war against the Ethiopian government. The Mengistu government has never had full control of Eritrea and Tigray. Primarily, it has held the major cities while the rebels controlled the countryside. The Tigrean and Eritrean armies each command about thirty thousand soldiers. The Eritreans demand a referendum to determine the future of their territory, while the Tigreans seek political reform and the resignation of the Mengistu regime.

# Sudan: A Country Divided

## Perspective

| | |
|---|---|
| **1898** | British and Egyptian forces conquer Sudan and administer it as two territories. |
| **1946** | Northern and southern territories are united. |
| **1955** | Fighting breaks out between north and south. |
| **1956** | Sudan gains independence. |
| **1962** | Fighting escalates to civil war. |
| **1969** | Military coup places Gaafar Nimeiry in power. |
| **1972** | Government and rebels sign Addis Ababa peace accord. |
| **1983** | Sharia (Islamic law) is imposed, causing renewed fighting. |
| **1985** | African drought affects five million people. **April 6.** Nimeiry is overthrown by military coup. |
| **1986** | **April 11.** Elections are held in the North only. Sadiq Mahdi becomes prime minister. |
| **1989** | **April 1.** Operation Lifeline-Sudan begins. **June 30.** Military coup ousts Mahdi. **December.** Peace talks break down. Government launches renewed attacks against southern villagers. |

Sudan is the largest country in Africa—too large, perhaps, to accommodate the diversity of its peoples. Nine years after the country was united in 1946, fighting erupted between the northern Arabs and the southern blacks. Differences in their religions, languages, and cultures have polarized the two groups, and tensions have remained high ever since. The latest round of violence began in 1983 when the Moslem north attempted to impose the severe code of traditional Islamic law on the south, which is predominately Christian or Animist.

## Issues and Events

The coup that overthrew the government of Sadiq Mahdi in June 1989 sparked hopes for an end to the seven-year conflict that has claimed more than ten thousand lives. The military had overthrown Mahdi because of his inability to bring peace to Sudan.

In December, representatives of the new government met with the rebels under the mediation of Jimmy Carter, but once again the talks broke down over the Islamic law issue. Instead of seeking a compromise, the government hinted that perhaps the only solution was for the south to secede and form its own country. The rebel leaders rejected this option and continued to press for increased autonomy within a federal structure.

Meanwhile, southern Sudan continues to suffer from the consequences of drought, floods, and the relentless war. More than three million people have been displaced from their homes, resulting in a disastrous disruption in agricultural production and widespread famine. The war resulted in the starvation of more than 250,000 people in 1988 when relief efforts were blocked by the North. The United Nations averted a similar disaster in 1989 by implementing a herculean relief effort called Operation Lifeline-Sudan. The agency convinced both sides to respect "corridors of tranquility" through which unescorted planes, trains, and trucks were able to deliver more than one hundred thousand tons of food.

## Background

In 1898, British and Egyptian forces under the future Lord Kitchener conquered Sudan. The region was administered as two territories until 1946. In 1952, preparations began for Sudanese independence. The southern Sudanese feared domination by the northern Muslims and started a revolt that still continues. Despite this, Sudan attained its independence in 1956.

In 1957, Christian mission schools in the south were forced to close, and all foreign missionaries were expelled in 1964. The southern Sudanese refused to allow the north to impose their religion and culture upon them and responded with military resistance.

In 1969, Colonel Gaafar Nimeiry seized control of the government in a military coup. In 1972, he signed the Addis Ababa pact with the southern Sudanese, granting them some autonomy and temporarily halting the civil war. Renewed fighting resulted in 1983 when Nimeiry imposed Islamic law, a controversial legal code which prescribes punishments such as flogging, amputations, and stoning, and is used throughout the Arab world.

Widespread famine, economic instability, and the ongoing war led to Nimeiry's downfall in a 1985 military coup. In 1986, Sudan held its first democratic election in eighteen years, but the south refused to participate when the new government failed to repeal the sharia laws.

# WORLD GAZETTEER: PROFILES OF NATIONS & PLACES

The following World Gazetteer presents an up-to-date overview of the world's independent countries and their possessions. Geographic, political, and population-related information is derived from the most current Rand McNally data available. Ethnic groups, religions, trade partners, exports, and imports are listed in order of decreasing size and/or importance. Languages are similarly organized, with official language(s) listed first. Political parties are cited alphabetically, as are membership entries, which represent member nations of the following organizations:

Arab League (AL)
Association of South East Asian Nations (ASEAN)
Commonwealth of Nations (CW)
Council for Mutual Economic Assistance (CEMA)
European Community (EC)
North Atlantic Treaty Organization (NATO)
Organization for Economic Cooperation and Development (OECD)
Organization of African Unity (OAU)
Organization of American States (OAS)
Organization of Petroleum Exporting Countries (OPEC)
United Nations (UN)
Warsaw Pact

# AFGHANISTAN

**Official name** Republic of Afghanistan
**PEOPLE**
**Population** 15,210,000. **Density** 60/mi² (23/km²). **Urban** 19%. **Capital** Kabul, 972,836. **Ethnic groups** Pathan 50%, Tajik 25%, Uzbek 9%, Hazara 9%. **Languages** Dari, Pashto, Uzbek, Turkmen. **Religions** Sunni Muslim 74%, Shiite Muslim 15%. **Life expectancy** 37 female, 37 male. **Literacy** 20%.
**POLITICS**
**Government** Socialist republic. **Parties** People's Democratic. **Suffrage** Universal, over 18. **Memberships** UN. **Subdivisions** 29 provinces.
**ECONOMY**
**GNP** $3,520,000,000 **Per capita** $240. **Monetary unit** Afghani. **Trade partners** Exports: U.S.S.R., Pakistan, India. Imports: U.S.S.R., Japan. **Exports** Natural gas, dried fruit, carpets. **Imports** Automobiles, petroleum, textiles, sugar.
**LAND**
**Description** Southern Asia, landlocked. **Area** 251,826 mi² (652,225 km²). **Highest point** Nowshāk, 24,557 ft (7,485 m). **Lowest point** Amu Darya River valley, 850 ft (259 m).

**People.** Afghanistan shares borders with the Soviet Union, China, India, Pakistan, and Iran. This crossroads position has created a population that is ethnically and linguistically diverse. Religion, however, plays a strong unifying role. Most Afghans are Muslim, and Islamic laws and customs determine lifestyles and beliefs, both religious and secular. The population is mainly rural, consisting primarily of farmers, and a small nomadic group.

**Economy and the Land.** The main force of Afghanistan's underdevelopment is agriculture and the recent civil war. Subsistence farming and animal husbandry account for much of the agricultural activity. Crop production has been aided by irrigation systems. A terrain of mountains and valleys, including the Hindu Kush, separates the desert region of the southwest from the more fertile north, an area of higher population density and the site of natural gas deposits. Increased development has made natural gas an important export. Winters are generally cold, and summers are hot and dry.

**History and Politics.** Once part of the Persian Empire, the area of present-day Afghanistan saw invasions by Persians, Macedonians, Greeks, Turks, Arabs, Mongols, and other peoples. An Arab invasion in A.D. 652 introduced Islam. In 1747 Afghan tribes led by Ahmad Shah Durrani united the area and established today's Afghanistan. Power remained with the Durrani tribe for more than two centuries. In the nineteenth and early twentieth centuries, Britain controlled Afghanistan's foreign affairs. A Durrani tribe member and former prime minister led a military coup in 1973 and set up a republic, ending the country's monarchal tradition. The new government's failure to improve economic and social conditions led to a 1978 revolution that established a Marxist government and brought Soviet aid. Intraparty differences and citizenry dissent resulted in a Soviet invasion in 1979. Fighting between government forces and the *mujahidin* (holy warrior) guerrillas continued. In 1988 the Soviets agreed to remove their military forces. Internal strife between factions, which has resulted in the deaths of many citizens, continues to plague the country. ■

# ALBANIA

**Official name** People's Socialist Republic of Albania
**PEOPLE**
**Population** 3,233,000. **Density** 291/mi² (112/km²). **Urban** 34%. **Capital** Tiranë, 210,800. **Ethnic groups** Albanian (Illyrian) 96%. **Languages** Albanian, Greek. **Religions** Muslim 20%, Christian 5%. **Life expectancy** 73 female, 69 male. **Literacy** 75%.
**POLITICS**
**Government** Socialist republic. **Parties** Labor. **Suffrage** Universal, over 18. **Memberships** UN. **Subdivisions** 26 districts.
**ECONOMY**
**GNP** $2,800,000,000 **Per capita** $936. **Monetary unit** Lek. **Trade partners** Exports: Yugoslavia, Czechoslovakia, Romania. Imports: Yugoslavia, Czechoslovakia, W. Germany. **Exports** Asphalt, bitumen,

petroleum products, metals and minerals. **Imports** Machinery, tools, iron and steel products.
**LAND**
**Description** Southeastern Europe. **Area** 11,100 mi$^2$ (28,748 km$^2$). **Highest Point** Korab, 9,026 ft (2,751 m). **Lowest point** Sea level.

**People.** A homogeneous native population characterizes Albania, where Greeks are the main minority. Five centuries of Turkish rule shaped much of the culture and led many Albanians to adopt Islam. Since 1944, when the current Communist regime was established, an increased emphasis on education has more than tripled the literacy rate. In 1967 religious institutions were banned. Albania claims to be the world's first atheist state.

**Economy and the Land.** Reputedly one of the poorest countries in Europe, Albania has tried to shift its economy from agriculture to industry. Farms employed about 60 percent of the work force in 1970, a significant decrease from more than 80 percent before 1944. Mineral resources make mining the chief industrial activity. The terrain consists of forested hills and mountains, and the climate is mild.

**History and Politics.** Early invaders and rulers included Greeks, Romans, Goths, and others. In 1468, the Ottoman Turks conquered the area and it remained part of their empire until the First Balkan War in 1912. Invaded by Italy and occupied by Germany during World War II, Albania set up a Communist government in 1944, following the German retreat. A strict approach to communism caused the country to sever ties with its one-time allies—the Soviet Union, and most recently China. ■

# ALGERIA

**Official name** Democratic and Popular Republic of Algeria
**PEOPLE**
**Population** 24,880,000. **Density** 27/mi$^2$ (10/km$^2$). **Urban** 43%. **Capital** Algiers, 1,507,241. **Ethnic groups** Arab-Berber 99%. **Languages** Arabic, Berber dialects, French. **Religions** Sunni Muslim 99%, Christian and Jewish. **Life expectancy** 62 female, 59 male. **Literacy** 45%.
**POLITICS**
**Government** Socialist republic. **Parties** National Liberation Front, others. **Suffrage** Universal, over 18. **Memberships** AL, OAU, OPEC, UN. **Subdivisions** 48 departments.
**ECONOMY**
**GDP** $45,234,000,000 **Per capita** $2,125. **Monetary unit** Dinar. **Trade partners** Exports: France, U.S., Italy. Imports: France, W. Germany, Italy. **Exports** Petroleum, natural gas. **Imports** Building materials and other manufactures, machinery, food.
**LAND**
**Description** Northern Africa. **Area** 919,595 mi$^2$ (2,381,741 km$^2$). **Highest point** Tahat, 9,541 ft (2,908 m). **Lowest point** Chott Melrhir, -131 ft (-40 m).

**People.** Indigenous Berbers and invading Arabs shaped modern Algeria's culture, and today most of the population is Muslim and of Arab-Berber, Arab, or Berber descent. European cultural influences, evidence of over a century of French control, exist in urban areas. Since independence in 1962, free medical care has been instituted and the educational system has been greatly improved.

**Economy and the Land.** A member of the Organization of Petroleum Exporting Countries (OPEC), Algeria produces oil and natural gas. Agriculture is divided between state and privately-owned farms. The government continues to emphasize gas production and exportation, while it maintains a socialistic economy and promotes development of private business. Algeria's terrain is varied. The Tell, Arabic for hill, is a narrow Mediterranean coastal region that contains the country's most fertile land and highest population. South of this lie high plateaus and the Atlas Mountains, which give way to the Sahara Desert. The climate is temperate along the coast and dry and cool in the plateau region.

**History and Politics.** In the eighth and eleventh centuries, invading Arabs brought their language and religion to the native Berbers. The Berbers and Arabs together became known as Moors, and conflicts between Moors, Turks, and Spaniards erupted periodically over several centuries. France began conquering Algeria in 1830, and by 1902 the entire country was under French control. The revolution against French rule began in 1954, but it was not until 1962 that the country was declared independent. Since a bloodless coup in 1965, the political situation has been relatively stable. A 1989 referendum approved a new constitution allowing multiparty elections. Algeria remains aligned with other Arab countries against Israel. ■

## AMERICAN SAMOA
See UNITED STATES.

## ANDORRA

**Official name** Principality of Andorra
### PEOPLE
**Population** 51,000. **Density** 291/mi² (113/km²). **Capital** Andorra, 14,928. **Ethnic groups** Spanish 61%, Andorran 30%, French 6%. **Languages** Spanish, French. **Religions** Roman Catholic. **Life expectancy** 81 female, 75 male. **Literacy** 100%.
### POLITICS
**Government** Coprincipality (Spanish and French protection). **Parties** None. **Suffrage** Limited adult, over 21. **Memberships** None. **Subdivisions** 7 parishes. **Monetary unit** French franc, Spanish peseta. **Trade partners** Spain, France.
### LAND
**Description** Southwestern Europe, landlocked. **Area** 175 mi² (453 km²). **Highest point** Pic de Coma Pedrosa, 9,665 ft (2,946 m). **Lowest point** Valira River valley, 2,756 ft (840 m).

**People.** Much of Andorran life and culture has been shaped by its mountainous terrain and governing countries, France and Spain. Population is concentrated in the valleys, and despite a tourism boom in past decades, the peaks and valleys of the Pyrenees have isolated the small country from many twentieth-century changes. Spanish is the official language, and cultural and historic ties exist with the Catalonian region of northern Spain. The majority of the population is Spanish; Andorran citizens are a minority.

**Economy and the Land.** The terrain has established Andorra's economy as well as its lifestyle. Improved transportation routes together with other factors have resulted in a thriving tourist industry—a dramatic shift from traditional sheepherding and tobacco growing. In addition, duty-free status has made the country a European shopping mecca. Tobacco is still the main agricultural product, though only about 4 percent of the land is arable. Climate varies with altitude; winters are cold and summers are cool and pleasant.

**History and Politics.** Tradition indicates that Charlemagne freed the area from the Moors in A.D. 806. A French count and the Spanish bishop of Seo de Urgel signed an agreement in the 1200s to act as coprinces of the country, establishing the political status and boundaries that exist today. The coprincipality is governed by the president of France and the bishop of Seo de Urgel. The country has no formal constitution, no armed forces other than a small police force, and no political parties.

■

## ANGOLA

**Official name** People's Republic of Angola
### PEOPLE
**Population** 8,668,000. **Density** 18/mi² (7.0/km²). **Urban** 25%. **Capital** Luanda, 1,200,000. **Ethnic groups** Ovimbundu 37%, Mbundu 25%, Kongo 13%, mulatto 2%, European 1%. **Languages** Portuguese, indigenous. **Religions** Animist 47%, Roman Catholic 38%, other Christian 15%. **Life expectancy** 44 female, 40 male. **Literacy** 20%.
### POLITICS
**Government** Socialist republic. **Parties** Popular Movement for Liberation-Labor. **Suffrage** Universal adult. **Memberships** OAU, UN. **Subdivisions** 18 provinces.
### ECONOMY
**GDP** $2,541,000,000 **Per capita** $346. **Monetary unit** Kwanza. **Trade partners** U.S., U.S.S.R., Cuba, Portugal, Brazil. **Exports** Petroleum, coffee, diamonds. **Imports** Machinery, food, transportation equipment.
### LAND
**Description** Southern Africa. **Area** 481,354 mi² (1,246,700 km²). **Highest point** Serra do Môco, 8,596 ft (2,620 m). **Lowest point** Sea level.

**People.** Angola today is made up mostly of various Bantu peoples—mainly Ovimbundu, Mbundu, Kongo, and others. Despite influences from a half-century of Portuguese rule, Angolan traditions remain strong, especially in rural areas. Each group has its own language, and although Portuguese is the official language, it is spoken by a minority. Many Angolans, retaining traditional indigenous beliefs, worship ancestral spirits.

**Economy and the Land.** A 1975 civil war, the resultant departure of skilled European labor, and continuing guerrilla activity have taken their toll on Angola's economy. The country has been working toward recovery, however, encouraging development of private industries and foreign trade. Although not a member of the Organization of Petroleum Exporting Countries (OPEC), Angola is a large oil producer. Cabinda, an enclave separated from the rest of the country by Zaire and the Zaire River, is the main site of oil production. Diamond mining remains an important activity, as does agriculture. Much of the land is forested, however, and is therefore not suited for commercial farming. The flat coastal area gives way to inland plateaus and uplands. The climate varies from tropical to subtropical.

**History and Politics.** Bantu groups settled in the area prior to the first century A.D. In 1483 a Portuguese explorer became the first European to arrive in Angola, and slave trade soon became a major activity. Portuguese control expanded and continued almost uninterrupted for several centuries. In the 1960s, ignored demands for popular rule led to two wars for independence. Three nationalist groups emerged, each with its own ideology and supporters. In 1974 a coup in Portugal resulted in independence for all Portuguese territories in Africa, and Angola became independent in 1975. A civil war ensued, with the three liberation groups fighting for power. By 1976, with the assistance of Cuban military personnel, the Popular Movement for the Liberation of Angola (PMLA) had established control. Angola, Cuba, and South Africa signed an accord in 1988 providing for Cuban troop withdrawals by July 1991. Rival parties of the PMLA struggle for a share in the government. ∎

## ANGUILLA See UNITED KINGDOM.

## ANTARCTICA

**Official name** Antarctica **Capital** None. **Memberships** None.
**LAND**
**Description** Continent in Southern Hemisphere. **Area** 5,400,000 mi² (14,000,000 km²). **Highest point** Vinson Massif, 16,066 ft (4,897 m). **Lowest point** Sea level.

**People.** Antarctica, which surrounds the South Pole, is the southernmost continent, the coldest place on earth, and one of the last frontiers. There are no native inhabitants, and its temporary population is made up mainly of scientists from various countries operating research stations.

**Economy and the Land.** Harsh climate and terrain have inhibited resource exploration and development. Antarctica's natural resources include coal, various ores, iron, offshore oil and natural gas. Fishing for krill, a marine protein source, is another activity. Crossed by several ranges collectively known as the Transantarctic Mountains, Antarctica can be roughly divided into a mountainous western region and a larger eastern sector consisting of an icy plain rimmed by mountains. With its tip about 700 miles (1,127 km) from southern South America, the mountainous Antarctic Peninsula and its offshore islands jut northward. Nearly all Antarctica is ice covered, precipitation is minimal, and the continent is actually a desert.

**History and Politics.** In the 1770s, Captain James Cook of Britain set out in search of the southernmost continent and sailed completely around Antarctica without sighting land. Explorations beginning in 1820 resulted in sightings of the mainland or offshore islands by the British, Russians, and Americans. British explorer Sir James C. Ross conducted the first extensive explorations. After a lull of several decades, interest in Antarctica was renewed in the late nineteenth and early twentieth centuries. Captain Robert F. Scott and Ernest Shackleton of Britain and Roald Amundsen of Norway led the renewed interest. Amundsen won the race to the South Pole in 1911. An Antarctic Treaty signed in 1959 permitted only peaceful scientific research to be conducted in the region. It also delayed settlement until 1989 of overlapping claims to the territory held by Norway, Australia, France, New Zealand, Chile, Britain, and Argentina. In 1988 several countries signed agreements to allow exploitation of Antarctica's natural resources. ∎

## ANTIGUA AND BARBUDA

**Official name** Antigua and Barbuda
**PEOPLE**
**Population** 79,000.
**Density** 462/mi² (178/km²). **Urban** 31%.
**Capital** St. John's, Antigua I., 24,359. **Ethnic groups** Black. **Languages** English, local dialects.
**Religions** Anglican, Protestant, Roman Catholic. **Life expectancy** 72 female, 68 male.
**Literacy** 90%.
**POLITICS**
**Government** Parliamentary state.
**Parties** Labor, United National Democratic.
**Suffrage** Universal, over 18. **Memberships** CW, OAS, UN. **Subdivisions** 7 parishes.

**ECONOMY**
**GDP** $161,000,000 **Per capita** $2,013. **Monetary unit** East Caribbean dollar. **Trade partners** U.S., U.K.. **Exports** Manufactures, machinery and transportation equipment, mineral fuel. **Imports** Petroleum, manufactures, food, machinery.

86  ANTIGUA AND BARBUDA • ARGENTINA • ARUBA • ASCENSION ISLAND

## LAND
**Description** Caribbean islands. **Area** 171 mi$^2$ (443 km$^2$).
**Highest point** Boggy Pk., Antigua I., 1,319 ft (402 m).
**Lowest point** Sea level.

**People.** Most Antiguans are descendants of black African slaves brought by the British to work sugarcane plantations. The largest urban area is St. John's, but most Antiguans live in rural areas. British rule has left its imprint; most people are Protestant and speak English.

**Economy and the Land.** The dry, tropical climate and white-sand beaches attract many visitors, making tourism the economic mainstay. Once dependent on sugar cultivation, the nation has shifted to a multicrop agriculture. The country is composed of three islands: Antigua, Barbuda, and uninhabited Redondo. Formed by volcanos, the low-lying islands are flat.

**History and Politics.** The original inhabitants of Antigua and Barbuda were the Carib Indians. Columbus arrived at Antigua in 1493, and after unsuccessful Spanish and French attempts at colonization, the British began settlement in the 1600s. The country remained a British colony until 1967, when it became an associated state of the United Kingdom. Antigua gained independence in 1981. ∎

# ARGENTINA

**Official name** Argentine Republic

## PEOPLE
**Population** 32,680,000
**Density** 30/mi$^2$ (12/km$^2$).
**Urban** 85%. **Capital** Buenos Aires, 2,922,829.
**Ethnic groups** White 85%, mestizo, Amerindian, and others 15%.
**Languages** Spanish, English, Italian, German, French. **Religions** Roman Catholic 90%, Jewish 2%, Protestant 2%. **Life expectancy** 73 female, 66 male. **Literacy** 94%.

## POLITICS
**Government** Republic.
**Parties** Justicialist (Peronista), Radical Civic Union, Union of the Democratic Center.
**Suffrage** Universal, over 18. **Memberships** OAS, UN. **Subdivisions** 22 provinces, 1 district, 1 national territory.

## ECONOMY
**GDP** $64,829,000,000 **Per capita** $2,263. **Monetary unit** Austral. **Trade partners** Exports: U.S.S.R., U.S., Netherlands. Imports: U.S., Brazil, W. Germany. **Exports** Grains and other food, vegetable oils, soybeans, animal feed. **Imports** Machinery, chemicals, iron and steel and other manufactures, crude materials.

## LAND
**Description** Southern South America. **Area** 1,073,400 mi$^2$ (2,780,092 km$^2$). **Highest point** Cerro Aconcagua, 22,831 ft (6,959 m). **Lowest point** Salinas Chicas, -138 ft (-42 m).

**People.** An indigenous Indian population, Spanish settlement, and a turn-of-the-century influx of immigrants have made Argentina an ethnically diverse nation. Today, most Argentines are descendants of Spanish and Italian immigrants. Other Europeans, mestizos of mixed Indian-Spanish blood, Indians, Middle Easterners, and Latin American immigrants diversify the population further. Spanish influence is evident in the major religion, Roman Catholicism; the official language, Spanish; and many aspects of cultural life.

**Economy and the Land.** Political difficulties beginning in the 1930s have resulted in economic problems and have kept this one-time economic giant from realizing its potential. The most valuable natural resource is the rich soil of the pampas, fertile plains in the east-central region. The greatest contributors to the economy, however, are manufacturing and services. The second largest country in South America, Argentina has a varied terrain, with northern lowlands, the east-central pampas, the Andes Mountains in the west, and the southern Patagonian steppe. The climate likewise varies, from subtropical in the north to subarctic in the south.

**History and Politics.** The earliest inhabitants of the area were Indians. In the 1500s silver-seeking Spaniards arrived, and by 1580 they had established a colony on the site of present-day Buenos Aires. In 1816 Argentina officially announced its independence from Spain. A successful struggle for independence ensued, and in 1853 a constitution was adopted and a president elected. Prosperity continued through the 1920s, and immigration and foreign investment increased. Unsatisfactory power distribution and concern over foreign investment resulted in a military coup in 1930. Thus began a series of civil and military governments; coups; the election, overthrow, and reelection of Juan Perón; and controversial human-rights violations. In 1982 Argentina lost a war with Britain over the Falkland Islands. Years of struggling with human rights transgressions followed. Since winning the election in 1989, the Peronistas are attempting to deal with severe economic problems. ∎

# ARUBA See NETHERLANDS.

# ASCENSION ISLAND
See UNITED KINGDOM.

## Places and Possessions of AUSTRALIA

| Entity | Status | Area | Population | Capital/Population |
| --- | --- | --- | --- | --- |
| **Ashmore and Cartier Islands** (Indian Ocean; north of Australia) | External territory | 61 mi$^2$ (159 km$^2$) | None | None |
| **Christmas Island** (Indian Ocean) | External territory | 52 mi$^2$ (135 km$^2$) | 2,000 | None |
| **Cocos (Keeling) Islands** (Indian Ocean) | Part of Australia | 5.4 mi$^2$ (14 km$^2$) | 600 | None |
| **Coral Sea Islands** (South Pacific) | External territory | 1.0 mi$^2$ (2.6 km$^2$) | None | None |
| **Heard and McDonald Islands** (Indian Ocean) | External territory | 154 mi$^2$ (400 km$^2$) | None | None |
| **Norfolk Island** (South Pacific) | External territory | 14 mi$^2$ (36 km$^2$) | 1,900 | Kingston |
| **Tasmania** (South Pacific island; south of Australia) | State | 26,178 mi$^2$ (67,800 km$^2$) | 456,000 | Hobart, 47,921 |

# AUSTRALIA

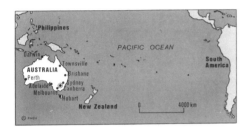

**Official name** Commonwealth of Australia
**PEOPLE**
**Population** 16,950,000. **Density** 5.7/mi$^2$ (2.2/km$^2$). **Urban** 86%. **Capital** Canberra, 247,194. **Ethnic groups** European 95%, Asian 4%, Aboriginal and other 1%. **Languages** English, indigenous. **Religions** Anglican 26%, Roman Catholic 26%, other Protestant 24%. **Life expectancy** 79 female, 72 male. **Literacy** 100%.
**POLITICS**
**Government** Parliamentary state. **Parties** Democrats, Labor, Liberal, National. **Suffrage** Universal, over 18. **Memberships** CW, OECD, UN. **Subdivisions** 6 states, 2 territories.
**ECONOMY**
**GDP** $167,441,000,000 **Per capita** $10,758. **Monetary unit** Dollar. **Trade partners** Japan, U.S.. **Exports** Grain and other food, coal, minerals, metals and other manufactures, wool. **Imports** Manufactures, machinery, transportation equipment, chemicals, petroleum.
**LAND**
**Description** Continent between South Pacific and Indian oceans. **Area** 2,966,155 mi$^2$ (7,682,300 km$^2$). **Highest point** Mt. Kosciusko, 7,310 ft (2,228 m). **Lowest point** Lake Eyre (North), -52 ft (-16 m).

**People.** Australia's culture reflects a unique combination of British, other European, and aboriginal influences. Settlement and rule by the United Kingdom gave the country a distinctly British flavor, and many Australians trace their roots to early British settlers. Planned immigration also played a major role in Australia's development, bringing more than three million Europeans since World War II. Refugees, most recently from Southeast Asia, make up another group of incoming peoples. The country is home to a small number of aborigines. The nation's size and a relatively dry terrain have resulted in uneven settlement patterns, with people concentrated in the rainier southeastern coastal area. The population is mainly urban, though overall population density remains low.

**Economy and the Land.** Australia's economy is similar to economies in other developed nations, and is characterized by a postwar shift from agriculture to industry and services, as well as inflation and unemployment. Wool is a major export, and livestock raising takes place on relatively flat, wide grazing lands surrounding an arid central region. Commercial crop raising is concentrated on a fertile southeastern plain. Plentiful mineral resources provide for a strong mining industry. Australia is the world's smallest continent but one of its largest countries. The climate is varied, and part of the country lies within the tropics. Because it is south of the equator, Australia has seasons the reverse of those in the Northern Hemisphere.

**History and Politics.** Aboriginal peoples probably arrived about forty thousand years ago and established a hunter-gatherer society. The Dutch explored the area in the seventeenth century, but no claims were made until the eighteenth century, when British Captain James Cook found his way to the fertile east and annexed the land to Britain. The first colony, New South Wales, was founded in 1788, and many of the early settlers were British convicts. During the 1800s, a squatter movement spread the population to other parts of the island, and the discovery of gold led to a population boom. Demands for self-government soon began, and by the 1890s all the colonies were self-governing, with Britain maintaining control of foreign affairs and defense. Nationalism continued to increase, and a new nation, the Commonwealth of Australia, was created in 1901. Australia fought on the side of the British during both world wars, and postwar years saw increased attention paid to the rights of the dwindling aboriginal population. Since World War II, participation in international affairs has expanded, with attention turned particularly to Asian countries.

■

# AUSTRIA

**Official name** Republic of Austria
### PEOPLE
**Population** 7,644,000. **Density** 236/mi² (91/km²). **Urban** 56%. **Capital** Vienna, 1,489,153. **Ethnic groups** German 99%. **Languages** German. **Religions** Roman Catholic 85%, Protestant 6%. **Life expectancy** 77 female, 70 male. **Literacy** 99%.
### POLITICS
**Government** Republic. **Parties** Freedom, People's, Socialist, others. **Suffrage** Universal, over 19. **Memberships** OECD, UN. **Subdivisions** 9 states.
### ECONOMY
**GDP** $66,053,000,000 **Per capita** $8,714. **Monetary unit** Schilling. **Trade partners** W. Germany, Italy, Switzerland. **Exports** Iron and steel and other manufactured goods, machinery, chemicals. **Imports** Manufactures, machinery, petroleum, chemicals.
### LAND
**Description** Central Europe, landlocked. **Area** 32,377 mi² (83,855 km²). **Highest point** Grossglockner, 12,457 ft (3,797 m). **Lowest point** Neusiedler See, 377 ft (115 m).

**People.** The majority of Austrians are native born, German speaking, and Roman Catholic, a homogeneity belying a history of invasions by diverse peoples. With a long cultural tradition, the country has contributed greatly to music and the arts—Vienna, the capital, is one of the great cultural centers of Europe.

**Economy and the Land.** Austria's economy is a blend of state and privately-owned industry. After World War II the government began nationalizing industries, returning many to the private sector as the economy stabilized. Unemployment is low, and the economy remains relatively strong. The economic mainstays are services and manufacturing. Agriculture is limited because of the overall mountainous terrain, with the Danube River basin in the east containing the most productive soils. In addition to the country's cultural heritage, the alpine landscape also attracts many tourists. The climate is generally moderate.

**History and Politics.** Early in its history, Austria was settled by Celts, ruled by Romans, and invaded by Germans, Slavs, Magyars, and others. Long rule by the Hapsburg family began in the thirteenth century, and in time Austria became the center of a vast empire. In 1867 Hungarian pressure resulted in the formation of the dual monarchy of Austria-Hungary. Nationalist movements against Austria culminated in the 1914 assassination of the heir to the throne, Archduke Francis Ferdinand, and set off the conflict that became World War I. In 1918 the war ended, the Hapsburg emperor was overthrown, Austria became a republic, and present-day boundaries were established. Political unrest and instability followed. In 1938 Adolf Hitler incorporated Austria into the German Reich. A period of occupation after World War II was followed by Austria's declaration of neutrality and ongoing political stability. Today Austria enjoys economic prosperity with strong ties to the western European community. ■

# AZORES See PORTUGAL.

# BAHAMAS

**Official name** The Commonwealth of the Bahamas
### PEOPLE
**Population** 251,000. **Density** 47/mi² (18/km²). **Urban** 58%. **Capital** Nassau, New Providence I., 135,000. **Ethnic groups** Black 85%, white 15%. **Languages** English, Creole. **Religions** Baptist 29%, Anglican 23%, Roman Catholic 22%. **Life expectancy** 69 female, 64 male. **Literacy** 89%.
### POLITICS
**Government** Parliamentary state. **Parties** Free National Movement, Progressive Liberal. **Suffrage** Universal, over 18. **Memberships** CW, OAS, UN. **Subdivisions** 21 districts.
### ECONOMY
**GDP** $2,258,000,000 **Per capita** $9,817. **Monetary unit** Dollar. **Trade partners** Exports: U.S. Imports: Libya, Mexico, Nigeria. **Exports** Petroleum, chemicals. **Imports** Crude petroleum.

## LAND
**Description** Caribbean islands. **Area** 5,380 mi$^2$ (13,934 km$^2$). **Highest point** Mt. Alvernia, Cat I., 206 ft (63 m). **Lowest point** Sea level.

**People.** Only about 29 of the 700 Bahamian islands are inhabited, and most of the people live on Grand Bahama and New Providence. The majority blacks are mainly descendants of slaves routed through the area or brought by British Loyalists fleeing the American colonies during the revolutionary war.

**Economy and the Land.** Because the thin soils of these flat coral islands are not suited for agriculture, for years the country struggled to develop a strong economic base. The solution was tourism, which capitalizes on the islands' most valuable resource—a semitropical climate. Because it is a tax haven, the country is also an international finance center.

**History and Politics.** Christopher Columbus's first stop on his way to America in 1492, the Bahamas were originally the home of the Lucayo Indians, whom the Spaniards took for slave trade. The British arrived in the 1600s, and the islands became a British colony in 1717. Independence was achieved in 1973.
■

# BAHRAIN

**Official name** State of Bahrain
## PEOPLE
**Population** 478,000. **Density** 1,790/mi$^2$ (692/km$^2$). **Urban** 82%. **Capital** Manama, Bahrain I., 108,684. **Ethnic groups** Bahraini 68%, Asian 25%, other Arab 4%, European 3%. **Languages** Arabic, English, Farsi, Urdu. **Religions** Muslim 85%, Christian 7%. **Life expectancy** 71 female, 67 male. **Literacy** 63%.
## POLITICS
**Government** Monarchy. **Parties** None. **Suffrage** None. **Memberships** AL, UN. **Subdivisions** 12 regions.
## ECONOMY
**GDP** $5,133,000,000 **Per capita** $12,369. **Monetary unit** Dinar. **Trade partners** Exports: United Arab Emirates, Singapore, Japan. Imports: U.S., Japan, U.K.. **Exports** Refined petroleum, chemicals, aluminum. **Imports** Crude petroleum, machinery, manufactured goods, transportation equipment.
## LAND
**Description** Southwestern Asian islands (in Persian Gulf). **Area** 267 mi$^2$ (691 km$^2$). **Highest point** Mt. Dukhan, Bahrain I., 440 ft (134 m). **Lowest point** Sea level.

**People.** Most residents of Bahrain are native-born Muslims, with the Sunni sect predominating in urban areas and Shiites in the countryside. Many of the country's thirty-three islands are barren, and population is concentrated in the capital city—Manama, on Bahrain Island—and on the smaller island of Muharraq. The oil economy has resulted in an influx of foreign workers and considerable westernization, and Bahrain is a Persian Gulf leader in free health care and education.

**Economy and the Land.** The one-time pearl-and-fish economy was reshaped by exploitation of oil and natural gas, careful management, and diversification. A major refinery processes crude oil piped from Saudi Arabia as well as the country's own oil, and Bahrain's aluminum industry is the Gulf's largest non-oil activity. Because of its location, Bahrain is able to provide Gulf countries with services such as dry docking, and the country has become a Middle Eastern banking center. Agriculture exists on northern Bahrain Island, where natural springs provide an irrigation source. Much of the state is desert. Summers are hot and dry and winters are mild.

**History and Politics.** From about 2000 to 1800 B.C. the area of Bahrain flourished as a center for trade. After early periods of Portuguese and Iranian rule, the al-Khalifa family came to power in the eighteenth century, and it has governed ever since. Bahrain became a British protectorate in the nineteenth century, and independence was gained in 1971. Friendly international relations and political allegiance to the Arab League characterize the current government.
■

# BALEARIC ISLANDS See SPAIN.

# BANGLADESH

**Official name** People's Republic of Bangladesh
## PEOPLE
**Population** 107,510,000. **Density** 1,934/mi$^2$ (747/km$^2$). **Urban** 12%. **Capital** Dhaka, 1,850,000. **Ethnic groups** Bengali 98%. **Languages** Bangla, English. **Religions** Muslim 84%, Hindu 15%. **Life expectancy** 47 female, 48 male. **Literacy** 29%.
## POLITICS
**Government** Islamic Republic. **Parties** Awami League, Jamaat-e-Islami, Jatiya, others. **Suffrage** Universal, over 18. **Memberships** CW, UN. **Subdivisions** 4 divisions.
## ECONOMY
**GDP** $17,204,000,000 **Per capita** $170. **Monetary unit** Taka. **Trade partners** Exports: U.S., Japan. Imports: Japan, U.S., Singapore. **Exports** Textiles, shellfish and other food, clothing, jute, leather. **Imports** Iron and steel and other manufactures, petroleum, machinery, food, chemicals.
## LAND
**Description** Southern Asia. **Area** 55,598 mi$^2$

# BANGLADESH • BARBADOS

(143,998 km²). **Highest point** Reng Mtn., 3,141 ft (957 m). **Lowest point** Sea level.

**People.** Bangladesh's population is characterized by extremes. The people, mostly peasant farmers, are among Asia's poorest and most rural. With a relatively small area and a high birthrate, the country is also one of the world's most densely populated. Many Bangladeshis are victims of disease, floods, and ongoing medical and food shortages. Islam, the major religion, has influenced almost every aspect of life. Bangla is the official language.

**Economy and the Land.** Fertile flood plain soil is the chief resource of this mostly flat, river-crossed country, and farming is the main activity. Rice and jute are among the major crops. Farm output fluctuates greatly, however, subject to the frequent monsoons, floods, and droughts of a semitropical climate. Because of this and other factors, foreign aid, imports, and an emphasis on agriculture have not assuaged the continuing food shortages. Floods, which put 75 percent of the country under water, left twenty-five million people in dire straits.

**History and Politics.** Most of Bangladesh lies in eastern Bengal, an Asian region whose western sector encompasses India's Bengal province. Early religious influences in Bengal included Buddhist rulers in the eighth century and Hindus in the eleventh. In 1200 Muslim rule introduced the religion to which the majority of eastern Bengalis eventually converted, while most western Bengalis retained their Hindu beliefs. British control in India, beginning in the seventeenth century, expanded until all Bengal was part of British India by the 1850s. When British India gained independence in 1947, Muslim population centers were united into the single nation of Pakistan in an attempt to end Hindu-Muslim hostilities. More than 1,000 miles (1,600 km) separated West Pakistan, formed from northwest India, from East Pakistan, comprised mostly of eastern Bengal. The bulk of Pakistan's population resided in the eastern province and felt the west wielded political and economic power at its expense. A civil war began in 1971, and the eastern province declared itself an independent nation called Bangladesh, or

"Bengal nation." That same year, West Pakistan surrendered to eastern guerrillas joined with Indian troops. The state has seen political crises since independence, including two leader assassinations and several coups. In 1982 General Ershad took control in a bloodless coup, assuming the office of president in 1983. Buddhist tribal groups, which claim religious persecution, are agitating for autonomy. ■

# BARBADOS

**Official name** Barbados

## PEOPLE
**Population** 255,000. **Density** 1,536/mi² (593/km²). **Urban** 42%. **Capital** Bridgetown, 7,466. **Ethnic groups** Black 92%, white 3%, mixed 3%, East Indian 1%. **Languages** English. **Religions** Anglican 40%, Pentecostal 8%, Methodist 7%, Roman Catholic 4%. **Life expectancy** 75 female, 70 male. **Literacy** 99%.

## POLITICS
**Government** Parliamentary state. **Parties** Democratic Labor, Labor. **Suffrage** Universal, over 18. **Memberships** CW, OAS, UN. **Subdivisions** 11 parishes.

## ECONOMY
**GDP** $1,230,000,000 **Per capita** $4,920. **Monetary unit** Dollar. **Trade partners** U.S., Trinidad and Tobago, U.K.. **Exports** Electrical equipment, sugar, clothing. **Imports** Machinery, manufactures, petroleum, food, chemicals.

## LAND
**Description** Caribbean island. **Area** 166 mi² (430 km²). **Highest point** Mt. Hillaby, 1,115 ft (340 m). **Lowest point** Sea level.

**People.** A history of British rule is reflected in the Anglican religion and English language of this easternmost West Indian island. It is one of the world's most densely populated countries, and most citizens are black descendants of African slaves.

**Economy and the Land.** Barbados's pleasant tropical climate and its land have determined its economic mainstays: tourism and sugar. Sunshine and year-round warmth attract thousands of visitors and, in conjunction with the soil, provide an excellent environment for sugar cane cultivation. Manufacturing consists mainly of sugar processing. The coral island's terrain is mostly flat, rising to a central ridge.

**History and Politics.** Originally settled by South American Arawak Indians, followed by Carib Indians, Barbados was uninhabited when the first British settlers arrived in the 1600s. More colonists followed, developing sugar plantations and bringing slaves from Africa to work them. The country remained under British control until it became independent in 1966. ■

# BELGIUM

**Official name** Kingdom of Belgium
**PEOPLE**
**Population** 9,877,000. **Density** 838/mi$^2$ (324/km$^2$). **Urban** 96%. **Capital** Brussels, 136,920. **Ethnic groups** Fleming 55%, Walloon 33%, mixed and others 12%. **Languages** Dutch (Flemish), French, German. **Religions** Roman Catholic 75%. **Life expectancy** 77 female, 70 male. **Literacy** 99%.
**POLITICS**
**Government** Constitutional monarchy. **Parties** Flemish: Freedom and Progress, Social Christian, Socialist. Walloon: Liberal Reform, Socialist. **Suffrage** Universal, over 18. **Memberships** EC, NATO, OECD, UN. **Subdivisions** 9 provinces.
**ECONOMY**
**GDP** $79,076,000,000 **Per capita** $8,008. **Monetary unit** Franc. **Trade partners** Exports: France, W. Germany, Netherlands. Imports: W. Germany, Netherlands, France. **Exports** Diamonds and other manufactures, chemicals, transportation equipment. **Imports** Diamonds and other manufactures, fuel, machinery, transportation equipment.
**LAND**
**Description** Western Europe. **Area** 11,783 mi$^2$ (30,518 km$^2$). **Highest point** Botrange, 2,277 ft (694 m). **Lowest point** Sea level.

**People.** Language separates Belgium into two main regions. Northern Belgium, known as Flanders, is dominated by Flemings, Flemish-speaking descendants of Germanic Franks. French-speaking Walloons, descendants of the Celts, inhabit southern Belgium, or Wallonia. Both groups are found in centrally located Brussels. In addition, a small German-speaking population is concentrated in the east. Flemish and French divisions often result in discord, but diversity has also been a source of cultural richness. Belgium has often been at the hub of European cultural movements.

**Economy and the Land.** The economy, as well as the population, was affected by Belgium's location at the center of European activity. Industry was early established as the economic base, and today the country is heavily industrialized. Although agriculture plays a minor economic role, Belgium is nearly self-sufficient in food production. The north and west are dominated by a flat fertile plain, the central region by rolling hills, and the south by the Ardennes Forest, often a tourist destination. The climate is cool and temperate.

**History and Politics.** Belgium's history began with the settlement of the Belgae tribe in the second century B.C. The Romans invaded the area around 50 B.C. and were overthrown by Germanic Franks in the A.D. 400s. Trade, manufacturing, and art prospered as various peoples invaded, passed through, and ruled the area. In 1794 Napoleon annexed Belgium to France. He was defeated at Waterloo in Belgium in 1815, and the country passed into Dutch hands. Dissatisfaction under Netherlands rule led to revolt and, in 1830, the formation of the independent country of Belgium. Germans overthrew the country during both world wars. Linguistic divisions mark nearly all political activity, from parties split by language to government decisions based on linguistic rivalries. ■

# BELIZE

**Official name** Belize
**PEOPLE**
**Population** 189,000. **Density** 21/mi$^2$ (8.2/km$^2$). **Urban** 50%. **Capital** Belmopan, 2,935. **Ethnic groups** Creole 40%, mestizo 33%, Amerindian 16%. **Languages** English, Spanish, Garifuna, Mayan. **Religions** Roman Catholic 62%, Anglican 12%, Methodist 6%, Mennonite 4%. **Literacy** 91%.
**POLITICS**
**Government** Parliamentary state. **Parties** People's United, United Democratic. **Suffrage** Universal, over 18. **Memberships** CW, UN. **Subdivisions** 6 districts.

## ECONOMY

**GDP** $195,000,000 **Per capita** $1,219. **Monetary unit** Dollar. **Trade partners** Exports: U.S., Mexico, U.K. Imports: U.S., Netherlands Antilles, U.K.. **Exports** Fruit and vegetables, shellfish, manufactures, machinery. **Imports** Clothing and other manufactures, food, petroleum, machinery.

## LAND

**Description** Central America. **Area** 8,866 mi$^2$ (22,963 km$^2$). **Highest point** Victoria Pk., 3,680 ft (1,122 m). **Lowest point** Sea level.

**People.** With the lowest population of any Central American country, Belize has a mixed populace, including descendants of black Africans, mestizos of Spanish-Indian ancestry, and Indians. Population is concentrated in six urban areas along the coast. Most people are poor, but participation in the educational system has led to a high literacy rate.

**Economy and the Land.** An abundance of timberland resulted in an economy based on forestry until woodlands began to be depleted in the twentieth century. Today the economy focuses on agriculture, with sugar the major crop and export. Arable land is the primary resource, but only a small portion has been cultivated. Industrial activity is limited. The recipient of much foreign aid, Belize hopes to expand export of agricultural surpluses and to develop a tourist industry based on its climate and sandy beaches. The coastal region consists of swampy lowlands rising to the Maya Mountains inland. The hot, humid climate is offset by sea breezes.

**History and Politics.** Until about the eleventh century A.D., Belize was the site of a flourishing Mayan civilization. Spain claimed the region in the sixteenth century. A British shipwreck in 1638 resulted in the first European settlement and began a process of British colonization, accompanied by extensive logging, piracy, and occasional Spanish and Indian attacks. In 1862 the area officially became the crown colony of British Honduras. Its name was changed to Belize in 1973, and independence was achieved in 1981. To assist economic and political development, Belize seeks closer relations with Spanish-speaking Central American countries and English-speaking Caribbean states. ■

# BENIN

**Official name** People's Republic of Benin
## PEOPLE
**Population** 4,667,000. **Density** 107/mi$^2$ (41/km$^2$). **Urban** 35%. **Capital** Porto-Novo (designated), 123,000; Cotonou (de facto), 215,000. **Ethnic groups** Fon, Adja, Yoruba, Bariba, others. **Languages** French, Fon, Adja, indigenous. **Religions** Fetishism 70%, Muslim 15%, Christian 15%. **Life expectancy** 46 female, 42 male. **Literacy** 17%.
## POLITICS
**Government** Socialist republic. **Parties** People's Revolutionary. **Suffrage** Universal adult. **Memberships** OAU, UN. **Subdivisions** 6 provinces.
## ECONOMY
**GDP** $1,153,000,000 **Per capita** $307. **Monetary unit** CFA franc. **Trade partners** Exports: Nigeria, Netherlands, France. Imports: France, U.K., Netherlands. **Exports** Shoes, food, textile fibers, palm oil. **Imports** Textiles and other manufactures, machinery, food, cigarettes.
## LAND
**Description** Western Africa. **Area** 43,475 mi$^2$ (112,600 km$^2$). **Highest point** 2,235 ft (681 m). **Lowest point** Sea level.

**People.** The mostly black population of Benin is composed of numerous peoples. The main groups are the Fon, the Adja, the Yoruba, and the Bariba. The nation's linguistic diversity reflects its ethnic variety; French is the official language, a result of former French rule. Most Beninese are farmers, although urban migration is increasing. Indigenous beliefs predominate, but there are also Christians, especially in the south, and Muslims in the north.

**Economy and the Land.** Political instability has been both the cause and effect of Benin's economic problems. The agricultural economy is largely undeveloped, and palm trees and their by-products provide the chief source of income and activity for both farming and industry. Some economic relief may be found in the exploitation of offshore oil. The predominately flat terrain features coastal lagoons and dense forests, with mountains in the northwest. Heat and humidity characterize the coast, with less humidity and varied temperatures in the north.

**History and Politics.** In the 1500s, Dahomey, a Fon kingdom, became the power center of the Benin area. European slave traders came to the coast in the seventeenth and eighteenth centuries, establishing posts and bartering with Dahomey royalty for slaves. As the slave trade prospered, the area became known as the Slave Coast. In the 1890s France defeated Dahomey's army and subsequently made the area a territory of French West Africa. In 1960, the country gained independence, followed by political turmoil, various coups, and a military overthrow which installed the current socialist government in 1972. In 1975 the nation changed its name from Dahomey to Benin. A nonaligned country, Benin's foreign policy emphasizes friendly relations with neighboring Nigeria. ■

# BERMUDA

**Official name** Bermuda
### PEOPLE
**Population** 57,000. **Density** 2,714/mi² (1,056/km²). **Urban** 100%. **Capital** Hamilton, Bermuda I., 1,676. **Ethnic groups** Black 61%, white 37%. **Languages** English. **Religions** Anglican 37%, Roman Catholic 14%, African Methodist Episcopal 10%. **Life expectancy** 76 female, 69 male. **Literacy** 98%.
### POLITICS
**Government** Dependent territory (U.K.). **Parties** Progressive Labor, United. **Suffrage** Universal, over 21. **Memberships** None. **Subdivisions** 9 parishes, 2 municipalities.
### ECONOMY
**GDP** $1,148,000,000 **Per capita** $16,400. **Monetary unit** Dollar. **Trade partners** Exports: Italy, U.S., U.K. Imports: U.S., Netherlands Antilles, U.K.. **Exports** Pharmaceuticals, electrical machinery. **Imports** Textiles and other manufactures, food, machinery, petroleum.
### LAND
**Description** North Atlantic islands (east of North Carolina). **Area** 21 mi² (54 km²). **Highest point** Town Hill, Bermuda I., 259 ft (79 m). **Lowest point** Sea level.

**People.** The population of this British colony is mainly black descendants of African slaves, but also includes Portuguese, British, Canadian, Caribbean peoples, and some United States military staff.

**Economy and the Land.** A mild climate, beautiful beaches, and a scenic, hilly terrain make tourism Bermuda's economic mainstay. Foreign businesses, attracted by tax exemptions, provide additional economic contributions. There is limited light manufacturing, agriculture, and fishing, and no heavy industry. Situated about 650 miles (1,046 km) east of North Carolina in the United States, the archipelago consists of many small islands and islets. About twenty are inhabited, several of which are connected by bridges and collectively known as the Island of Bermuda.

**History and Politics.** The colony received its name from Juan de Bermudez, a Spanish explorer who sailed past the islands in 1503, not landing because of the dangerous coral reefs. Colonization began following a British shipwreck in 1609. Racial inequality resulted in unrest in the late 1960s and 1970s. As a British colony, Bermuda recognizes Great Britain's queen as the head of state. ∎

# BHUTAN

**Official name** Kingdom of Bhutan
### PEOPLE
**Population** 1,550,000. **Density** 86/mi² (33/km²). **Urban** 5%. **Capital** Thimphu, 12,000. **Ethnic groups** Bhotia 60%, Nepalese 25%, indigenous 15%. **Languages** Dzongkha, Tibetan and Nepalese dialects. **Religions** Buddhist 75%, Hindu 25%. **Life expectancy** 49 female, 46 male. **Literacy** 5%.
### POLITICS
**Government** Monarchy (Indian protection). **Parties** None. **Suffrage** One vote per family. **Memberships** UN. **Subdivisions** 18 districts.

### ECONOMY
**GDP** $187,000,000 **Per capita** $130. **Monetary unit** Ngultrum, Indian rupee. **Trade partners** India. **Exports** Cement, forestry products, food. **Imports** Fuel, rice, tires, machinery and manufactures.
### LAND
**Description** Southern Asia, landlocked. **Area** 17,954 mi² (46,500 km²). **Highest point** Kula Kangri, 24,784 ft (7,554 m). **Lowest point** Manās River valley, 318 ft (97 m).

**People.** A mountainous terrain long isolated Bhutan from the outside world and limited internal mingling of its peoples. The population is ethnically divided into the Bhotia, Nepalese, and various tribes. Of Tibetan ancestry, the Bhotes are a majority and as such have determined the major religion, Buddhism, and language, Dzongkha, a Tibetan dialect. The Nepalese are mostly Hindu and speak Nepalese; tribal dialects diversify language further. A largely rural population, many villages grew up around *dzongs*, monastery fortresses built in strategic valley locations during Bhutan's past. Training programs have been instituted to improve the country's low literacy rate and skilled labor shortage.

**Economy and the Land.** Partially due to physical isolation, Bhutan has one of the world's least developed economies and remains dependent on foreign aid. There is potential for success, however. Forests cover much of the land, limiting agricultural area but offering opportunity for the expansion of forestry. Farming is concentrated in the more densely populated, fertile valleys of the Himalayas, and the country is self-sufficient in food production. The climate varies with altitude; the icy Himalayas in the north give way to temperate central valleys and a subtropical south.

**History and Politics.** Bhutan's early history remains mostly unknown, but it is thought that by the early sixteenth century, descendants of Tibetan invaders were ruling their lands from strategically located dzongs. In the 1600s a Tibetan lama consolidated the area and became political and religious leader. Proximity to and interaction with British India resulted in British control of Bhutan's foreign affairs in the nineteenth and early twentieth centuries. In 1907 the current hereditary monarchy was established. India gained independence from Britain in 1947 and soon assumed the role of adviser in Bhutan's foreign affairs. Indian ties were strengthened in the late 1950s to counter Chinese influence. At the same time, modernization programs were instituted, improving primitive transportation and communication systems, and bringing Bhutan further into the twentieth-century mainstream. ■

# BOLIVIA

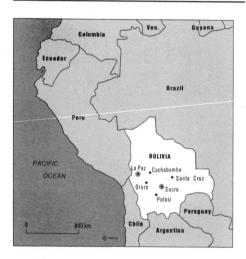

**Official name** Republic of Bolivia
**PEOPLE**
**Population** 7,298,000. **Density** 17/mi$^2$ (6.6/km$^2$). **Urban** 48%. **Capital** La Paz (seat of government), 992,592; Sucre (seat of judiciary), 86,609. **Ethnic groups** Quechua 30%, Aymara 25%, mixed 25-30%, European 5-15%. **Languages** Spanish, Quechua, Aymara. **Religions** Roman Catholic 95%, Methodist and other Protestant. **Life expectancy** 53 female, 49 male. **Literacy** 63%.
**POLITICS**
**Government** Republic. **Parties** Movement of the Revolutionary Left, Nationalist Democratic Action, Nationalist Revolutionary Movemen. **Suffrage** Universal adult (married, 18; single, 21). **Memberships** OAS, UN. **Subdivisions** 9 departments.
**ECONOMY**
**GDP** $6,266,000,000 **Per capita** $1,025. **Monetary unit** Boliviano. **Trade partners** Exports: Argentina, U.S. Imports: U.S., Argentina, Japan, Brazil. **Exports** Natural gas, tin alloys, minerals, food. **Imports** Machinery, manufactures, wheat and other food, chemicals.
**LAND**
**Description** Central South America, landlocked. **Area** 424,165 mi$^2$ (1,098,581 km$^2$). **Highest point** Nevado Illimani, 22,579 ft (6,882 m). **Lowest point** Paraguay River valley, 325 ft (100 m).

**People.** Indians compose the majority of Bolivia's population, while minorities include mestizos, of Spanish-Indian descent, and Europeans. Although most people are poor, Bolivia has a rich cultural heritage, evidenced by early Aymaran and Quechuan artifacts; Spanish-influenced Indian and mestizo art; and twentieth-century achievements. Roman Catholicism is the major religion, and is frequently combined with Indian beliefs.

**Economy and the Land.** Although the underdeveloped Bolivia is among South America's poorest nations, it is rich in natural resources. While farming is the main activity, mining makes the largest contribution to the gross national product. Population, industry, and major cities are concentrated on the western altiplano, an Andean high plateau where many continue to practice agriculture according to ancestral methods. The eastern llano, or lowland plain, contains fuel deposits and is the site of commercial farming. The yungas, hills, and valleys between the antiplano and the llano form the most developed agricultural region. Successful development of Bolivia's rich resources is partially dependent upon political stability. The climate varies from tropical to semiarid and cool, depending on altitude.

**History and Politics.** The Aymara Indian culture flourished in the area that is now Bolivia between the seventh and tenth centuries. In the mid-1400s the area was absorbed into the expanding empire of the Incas, who controlled the region until ousted by the Spanish in 1535. Simón Bolívar, the Venezuelan organizer of the South American movement to free Spanish colonies, helped lead the way to independence, which was gained in 1825. As Bolivia developed economically, the Indian population remained ensconced in poverty and enjoyed few rights. After years of turmoil, a 1952 revolution installed a government that introduced suffrage, land and educational reforms. Several military coups followed, and civilian control was re-established in 1982. Although economic instability and high inflation rates have long troubled Bolivia, the economy has shown signs of growth since 1987. ■

# BOTSWANA

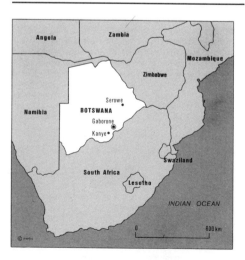

**Official name** Republic of Botswana

## PEOPLE
**Population** 1,280,000. **Density** 5.7/mi$^2$ (2.2/km$^2$). **Urban** 19%. **Capital** Gaborone, 95,163. **Ethnic groups** Tswana 95%; Kalanga, Baswara, and Kgalagadi 4%; white 1%. **Languages** English, Tswana. **Religions** Tribal religionist 50%, Roman Catholic and other Christian 50%. **Life expectancy** 56 female, 53 male. **Literacy** 41%.
## POLITICS
**Government** Republic. **Parties** Democratic, National Front, People's. **Suffrage** Universal, over 21. **Memberships** CW, OAU, UN. **Subdivisions** 11 districts.
## ECONOMY
**GDP** $1,165,000,000 **Per capita** $1,104. **Monetary unit** Pula. **Trade partners** Switzerland, U.S., U.K., Southern African countries. **Exports** Diamonds, cattle, animal products, copper, nickel. **Imports** Food, motor vehicles, textiles, petroleum.
## LAND
**Description** Southern Africa, landlocked. **Area** 224,711 mi$^2$ (582,000 km$^2$). **Highest point** 4,969 ft (1,515 m). **Lowest point** Confluence of Shashi and Limpopo rivers, 1,684 ft (513 m).

**People.** The population of this sparsely-populated country is composed mostly of Tswana, Bantu peoples of various groups. Following settlement patterns laid down centuries ago, Tswana predominate in the more fertile eastern region, and the minority Bushmen are concentrated in the Kalahari Desert. There is also a white minority population. English is the official language, reflecting years of British rule, but the majority speak Tswana. Half of the people follow traditional beliefs, while the rest are Christian.

**Economy and the Land.** Agriculture and livestock raising are the primary activities, although they are limited by the southwestern Kalahari Desert. The most productive farmland lies in the east and north, where rainfall is higher and grazing lands are plentiful. Since the early seventies, when increased exploitation of natural resources began, the economy has developed rapidly. Diamond mining is the main focus of this growth, together with development of copper, nickel, and coal. The climate is mostly subtropical.

**History and Politics.** In Botswana's early history, Bushmen, the original inhabitants, retreated into the Kalahari region when the Tswana invaded and established their settlements in the more fertile east. Intertribal wars in the early nineteenth century were followed by conflicts with the Boers, settlers of Dutch or Huguenot descent. These conflicts led the Tswana to seek British assistance, and the area of present-day Botswana became part of the British protectorate of Bechuanaland. When the Union of South Africa was created in 1910, those living in Bechuanaland (later Botswana), Basutoland (later Lesotho), and Swaziland requested and were granted exclusion from the Union. British rule continued until 1966, when the protectorate of Bechuanaland became the Republic of Botswana. The country maintains a policy of nonalignment in foreign affairs and seeks to expand relations with other nations. In addition, Botswana would like to reduce its economic dependence on South Africa, whose apartheid policy it opposes. ∎

# BRAZIL

**Official name** Federative Republic of Brazil
## PEOPLE
**Population** 148,980,000. **Density** 45/mi$^2$ (18/km$^2$). **Urban** 73%. **Capital** Brasília, 1,567,709. **Ethnic groups** White 54%, mixed 39%, black 6%. **Languages** Portuguese, Spanish, English, French. **Religions** Roman Catholic 89%, Protestant 6%. **Life expectancy** 66 female, 61 male. **Literacy** 74%.
## POLITICS
**Government** Republic. **Parties** Democratic Movement, Liberal Front, Social Democratic, others. **Suffrage** Universal, over 16. **Memberships** OAS, UN. **Subdivisions** 23 states, 3 territories, 1 federal district.
## ECONOMY
**GDP** $226,787,000,000 **Per capita** $1,688. **Monetary unit** Cruzado. **Trade partners** Exports: U.S., Japan, Netherlands. Imports: U.S., Iraq, Saudi Arabia. **Exports** Coffee and other food, manufactures, machinery, iron ore. **Imports** Petroleum, machinery, chemicals, wheat and other food.
## LAND
**Description** Eastern South America. **Area** 3,286,488 mi$^2$ (8,511,965 km$^2$). **Highest point** Pico da Neblina, 9,888 ft (3,014 m). **Lowest point** Sea level.

**People.** The largest South American nation, Brazil is also the most populous. Indigenous Indians, Portuguese colonists, black African slaves, and European and Japanese immigrants shaped the mixed population. Today, native Indians compose less than 1 percent of the population, and the group is disappearing rapidly due to contact with modern cultures and other factors. Brazil is the only Portuguese-speaking nation in the Americas, and Roman Catholicism is the major religion.

**Economy and the Land.** Brazil's prosperous economy stems from a diversified base of agriculture, mining, and industry. Most commercial farms and ranches lie in the southern plateau region, and coffee, cocoa, soybeans, and beef are important products. Mineral resources include iron-ore deposits, many found in the central and southern plateau regions. Additional mineral deposits have recently been discovered in the Amazon area. During and after World War II, the country focused on industrial expansion in the southeast, and in 1960 it moved the capital from Rio de Janeiro to Brasília to redistribute activity. Undeveloped states have been targeted for development, but such programs may require displacement of the Indian population. Forests cover about half the country, and the Amazon River basin is the site of the world's largest rain forest. The northeast consists of semiarid grasslands, and the central-west and south are marked by hills, mountains, and rolling plains. Overall the climate is semitropical to tropical, with heavy rains.

**History and Politics.** Portugal obtained rights to the region in a 1494 treaty with Spain and claimed Brazil in 1500. As the native Indian population died out, blacks were brought from Africa to work the plantations. In the 1800s, during the Napoleonic Wars, the Portuguese royal family fled to Rio de Janeiro, and in 1815 the colony became a kingdom. In 1821 the Portuguese king departed for Portugal, leaving Brazil's rule to his son, who declared Brazil an independent country and himself emperor in 1822. Economic development in the mid-1800s brought an influx of Europeans. Following a military takeover in 1889, Brazil became a republic. Economic problems resulted in a 1930 military coup, a dictatorship that lasted until 1945, and military takeovers in 1954 and 1964. The country returned to civilian rule in 1985. Key political issues have been the massive foreign debt and worldwide concern over the destruction of the rain forest. ∎

# BRITISH INDIAN OCEAN TERRITORY See UNITED KINGDOM.

# BRUNEI

**Official name** Negara Brunei Darussalam
**PEOPLE**
**Population** 253,000. **Density** 114/mi² (44/km²). **Urban** 58%. **Capital** Bandar Seri Begawan, 63,868. **Ethnic groups** Malay 65%, Chinese 20%, indigenous 8%, Tamil 3%. **Languages** Malay, English, Chinese. **Religions** Muslim 63%, Buddhist 14%, Roman Catholic and other Christian 10%. **Life expectancy** 73 female, 70 male. **Literacy** 78%.
**POLITICS**
**Government** Monarchy. **Parties** National United. **Suffrage** None. **Memberships** ASEAN, CW, UN. **Subdivisions** 4 districts.
**ECONOMY**
**GDP** $3,032,000,000 **Per capita** $13,782. **Monetary unit** Dollar. **Trade partners** Exports: Japan, Singapore, Thailand. Imports: Singapore, Japan, U.S.. **Exports** Petroleum, natural gas. **Imports** Manufactures, machinery, food, transportation equipment, chemicals.
**LAND**
**Description** Southeastern Asia (island of Borneo). **Area** 2,226 mi² (5,765 km²). **Highest point** Mt. Pagon, 6,070 ft (1,850 m). **Lowest point** Sea level.

**People.** The majority of Brunei's population is Malay, with minorities of Chinese and indigenous peoples. Most Malays are Muslim, and the Chinese are mainly Christian or Buddhist. Many Chinese, although wealthy, are unable to become citizens due to language-proficiency exams and strict residency requirements. The standard of living is high because of Brunei's oil-based economy, yet wealth is not equally distributed.

**Economy and the Land.** Oil and natural gas are the economic mainstays, giving Brunei a high per capita gross domestic product. Much food is imported, however, and diversification is a current goal. Situated on northeastern Borneo, Brunei is generally flat and covered with dense rain forests. The climate is tropical.

**History and Politics.** Historical records of Brunei date back to the seventh century. The country was an important trading center, and by the sixteenth century the sultan of Brunei ruled Borneo and parts of nearby islands. In 1888 Brunei became a British protectorate, and in 1984, it gained independence from Great Britain. The nation is ruled by a sultan. ∎

# BULGARIA

**Official name** People's Republic of Bulgaria
**PEOPLE**
**Population** 9,015,000. **Density** 211/mi² (81/km²). **Urban** 67%. **Capital** Sofia, 1,119,152. **Ethnic groups** Bulgarian (Slavic) 85%, Turkish 9%, Gypsy 3%, Macedonian 3%. **Languages** Bulgarian. **Religions** Bulgarian Orthodox, Muslim. **Life expectancy** 74 female, 69 male. **Literacy** 93%.
**POLITICS**
**Government** Socialist republic. **Parties** Communist, National Agrarian Union. **Suffrage** Universal, over 18. **Memberships** CEMA, UN, Warsaw Pact. **Subdivisions** 9 regions.
**ECONOMY**
**GNP** $57,800,000,000 **Per capita** $6,437. **Monetary unit** Lev. **Trade partners** U.S.S.R.. **Exports** Machinery and equipment, agricultural products, fuel and minerals. **Imports** Fuel and minerals, machinery and equipment, chemicals, consumer goods.
**LAND**
**Description** Eastern Europe. **Area** 42,823 mi² (110,912 km²). **Highest point** Musala, 9,596 ft (2,925 m). **Lowest point** Sea level.

five years. The rights of Bulgaria's ethnic Turks have become a major political issue. ■

# BURKINA FASO

**Official name** Burkina Faso
**PEOPLE**
**Population** 9,019,000. **Density** 85/mi$^2$ (33/km$^2$). **Urban** 8%. **Capital** Ouagadougou, 442,223. **Ethnic groups** Mossi 30%, Fulani, Lobi, Malinke, Bobo, Senufo, Gurunsi, others. **Languages** French, indigenous. **Religions** Animist 65%, Muslim 25%, Roman Catholic and other Christian. **Life expectancy** 47 female, 44 male. **Literacy** 9%.
**POLITICS**
**Government** Provisional military government. **Parties** None. **Suffrage** None. **Memberships** OAU, UN. **Subdivisions** 30 provinces.
**ECONOMY**
**GDP** $833,000,000 **Per capita** $128. **Monetary unit** CFA franc. **Trade partners** Exports: France, China, Ivory Coast. Imports: France, Ivory Coast, U.S.. **Exports** Grain and other food, cotton, oil seeds. **Imports** Grain and other food, petroleum, manufactures, machinery.
**LAND**
**Description** Western Africa, landlocked. **Area** 105,869 mi$^2$ (274,200 km$^2$). **Highest point** Téna Kourou, 2,451 ft (747 m). **Lowest point** Volta Noire River valley, 650 ft (200 m).

**People.** Bulgaria's ethnic composition was determined early in its history when Bulgar tribes conquered the area's Slavic inhabitants. Bulgarians, descendants of these peoples, are a majority today, while Turks, Gypsies, and Macedonians compose the main minority groups. Postwar development is reflected in an agriculture-to-industry shift in employment and a resultant rural-to-urban population movement.

**Economy and the Land.** Following World War II, the Bulgarian government began a program of expansion, turning the undeveloped agricultural nation into an industrial state modeled after the Soviet Union. Today the industrial sector is the greatest economic contributor and employer. Farming, however, continues to play an economic role. Rich soils in river valleys, as well as a climate similar to that of the American Midwest, make the area well suited for raising livestock, growing grain and other crops. The overall terrain is mountainous.

**History and Politics.** The area of modern Bulgaria was absorbed by the Roman Empire by A.D. 15 and was subsequently invaded by the Slavs. In the seventh century Bulgars conquered the region and settled alongside Slavic inhabitants. Rule by the Ottoman Turks began in the late fourteenth century and lasted until 1878, when the Bulgarians defeated the Turks with the aid of Russia and Romania. The Principality of Bulgaria emerged in 1885, with boundaries approximating those of today, and in 1908 Bulgaria was declared an independent kingdom. Increased territory and a desire for access to the Aegean Sea were partially responsible for Bulgaria's involvement in the Balkan Wars of 1912 and 1913 and alliances with Germany during both world wars. Following Bulgaria's declaration of war on the United States and Britain in World War II, the Soviet Union declared war on Bulgaria. Defeat came in 1944, when the monarchy was overthrown and a Communist government established shortly thereafter. Pressure from the people for more participation in the government resulted in the resignation of General Zhivkov, Bulgaria's leader for thirty-

**People.** The agricultural Mossi, descendants of warrior migrants, are Burkina Faso's majority population. Other groups include the Fulani, Lobi, Malinke, Bobo, Sehufo, and Gurunsi. Ethnic languages vary, although French is the official language.

**Economy and the Land.** Burkina Faso's agricultural economy suffers from frequent droughts and an underdeveloped transportation system. Most people engage in subsistence farming or livestock raising, and industrialization is minimal. Resources are limited but include gold and manganese. The country remains dependent on foreign aid, much of it from France. The land is marked by northern desert, central savanna, and southern forests, while the climate is generally tropical.

**History and Politics.** The Mossi arrived from central or eastern Africa during the eleventh century and established their kingdom in the area of Burkina Faso. The French came in the late nineteenth century. In 1919 France united various provinces and created the colony of Upper Volta. The colony was divided among other French colonies in 1932, reinstituted in 1937 as an administrative unit called the Upper Coast, and returned to territorial status as Upper Volta in 1947. It gained independence in 1960. Economic problems and accusations of government corruption led to leadership changes and military rule, including numerous coups. In 1984, the country changed its name from Upper Volta to Burkina Faso. ■

# BURMA

**Official name** Socialist Republic of the Union of Burma
## PEOPLE
**Population** 40,865,000. **Density** 156/mi$^2$ (60/km$^2$). **Urban** 24%. **Capital** Rangoon, 2,458,712. **Ethnic groups** Bamar (Burmese) 69%, Shan 9%, Kayin 6%, Rakhine 5%. **Languages** Burmese, indigenous. **Religions** Buddhist 89%, Muslim 4%, Christian 5%. **Life expectancy** 59 female, 56 male. **Literacy** 67%.
## POLITICS
**Government** Provisional military government. **Parties** National League for Democracy, National Unity Party, others. **Suffrage** Universal, over 18. **Memberships** UN. **Subdivisions** 7 divisions, 7 states.
## ECONOMY
**GDP** $6,812,000,000 **Per capita** $185. **Monetary unit** Kyat. **Trade partners** Exports: Singapore, Western European countries, China. Imports: Japan, Western European countries, Singapore. **Exports** Teak and hardwoods, rice and other grains, metals, minerals. **Imports** Machinery and transportation equipment, building materials.
## LAND
**Description** Southeastern Asia. **Area** 261,228 mi$^2$ (676,577 km$^2$). **Highest point** Hkakabo Razi, 19,296 ft (5,881 m). **Lowest point** Sea level.

**People.** The population of Burma is highly diverse, with many ethnic groups including Tibetan-related Bamar, who compose the majority; Kayin, who inhabit mainly the south and east; and Thai-related Shan, found on the eastern plateaus. Diversity results in many languages, although Burmese predominates. Buddhist monasteries and pagodas dot the landscape, and minority religions include Christianity, indigenous beliefs, and Islam. The primarily rural population is concentrated in the fertile valleys and on the delta of the Irrawaddy River.

**Economy and the Land.** Fertile soils, dense woodlands, and mineral deposits provide a resource base for agriculture, forestry, and mining. Burma has been beset with economic problems, however, caused mainly by the destruction of World War II, as well as postindependence instability. Today agriculture continues as the economic mainstay. The hot, wet climate is ideal for rice production. In addition, dense forests provide for a timber industry, and resource deposits include petroleum and various minerals. Burma's economic future most likely depends on exploitation of natural resources and political stability. The terrain is marked by mountains, rivers, and forests, and the climate is tropical.

**History and Politics.** Burma's Chinese and Tibetan settlers were first united in the eleventh century. Independence ended with the invasion of Mongols led by Kublai Khan, followed by national unification in the fifteenth and eighteenth centuries. Annexation to British India in the nineteenth century ended Burma's monarchy. During World War II, Japanese occupation and subsequent Allied-Japanese conflicts caused much economic and physical damage. Burma officially became independent in 1948. After initial stability, the government was unable to withstand separatist and political revolts, and military rule alternated with civilian governments. In 1974, a new government was installed and a new constitution adopted. Yet another military coup in 1988 was widely protested, forcing concessions and the promise of elections from the military, which are scheduled for 1990. ■

# BURUNDI

**Official name** Republic of Burundi
## PEOPLE
**Population** 5,380,000. **Density** 501/mi$^2$ (193/km$^2$). **Urban** 6%. **Capital** Bujumbura, 229,980. **Ethnic groups** Hutu 85%, Tutsi 14%, Twa 1%. **Languages** French, Kirundi, Swahili. **Religions** Roman Catholic 62%, Animist 32%, Protestant 5%, Muslim 1%. **Life expectancy** 48 female, 45 male. **Literacy** 23%.
## POLITICS
**Government** Provisional military government. **Parties** Unity and Progess. **Suffrage** Universal adult. **Memberships** OAU, UN. **Subdivisions** 15 provinces.

Army in 1987. The Constitution was suspended and thousands of Burundians have since died in ethnic clashes between the Tutsi and the Hutu. ■

## CAMBODIA

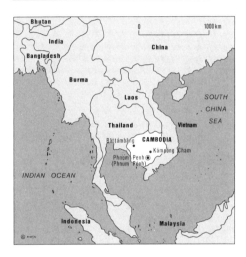

### ECONOMY
**GDP** $1,032,000,000 **Per capita** $219. **Monetary unit** Franc. **Trade partners** Exports: W. Germany, Finland. Imports: Belgium, Iran, France. **Exports** Coffee, tea, textiles. **Imports** Manufactures, machinery, petroleum, food, chemicals, automobiles.
### LAND
**Description** Eastern Africa, landlocked. **Area** 10,745 mi$^2$ (27,830 km$^2$). **Highest point** 9,055 ft (2,760 m). **Lowest point** Lake Tanganyika, 2,534 ft (772 m).

**People.** One of Africa's most densely populated nations, Burundi has a populace composed mainly of three Bantu groups. The Hutu are a majority, while the Tutsi, descendants of invaders from Ethiopia, wield most of the power. The Twa are Pygmy hunters, probably descended from the area's inhabitants prior to the influx of the Hutu. Most Burundians are subsistence farmers and Roman Catholic, evidence of foreign influence and rule.

**Economy and the Land.** An undeveloped country, Burundi relies mainly on agriculture, although undependable rainfall, depleted soil, and erosion occasionally combine for famine. Coffee is a major export. Exploitation of nickel deposits, industrial development through foreign investment, and expansion of tourism offer potential for growth. Although the country is situated near the equator, its high altitude and hilly terrain result in a pleasant climate.

**History and Politics.** In the fourteenth century, invading pastoral Tutsi warriors conquered the Hutu and Pygmy Twa and established themselves as the region's power base. The areas of modern Burundi and Rwanda were absorbed into German East Africa in the 1890s. Following Belgian occupation during World War I, in 1919 the League of Nations placed present-day Burundi and Rwanda under Belgian rule as part of Ruanda-Urundi. After World War II Ruanda-Urundi was made a United Nations trust territory under Belgian administration. In 1962 Urundi became Burundi, an independent monarchy, and political turmoil soon followed. A Tutsi-dominated government replaced the monarchy in 1966. A 1976 coup installed a government that sought a redistribution of power, but was overthrown by the

**Official name** State of Cambodia
### PEOPLE
**Population** 8,153,000. **Density** 117/mi$^2$ (45/km$^2$). **Urban** 11%. **Capital** Phnom Penh, 700,000. **Ethnic groups** Khmer 90%, Chinese 5%. **Languages** Khmer, French. **Religions** Buddhist 95%, Animist, Muslim. **Life expectancy** 45 female, 42 male. **Literacy** 48%.
### POLITICS
**Government** Socialist republic. **Parties** People's Revolutionary. **Suffrage** None. **Memberships** UN. **Subdivisions** 20 provinces. **Monetary unit** Riel. **Trade partners** Vietnam, U.S.S.R., Eastern European countries, Japan, India. **Exports** Rubber, rice, pepper, wood. **Imports** Food.
### LAND
**Description** Southeastern Asia. **Area** 69,898 mi$^2$ (181,035 km$^2$). **Highest point** Mt. Aoral, 5,948 ft (1,813 m). **Lowest point** Sea level.

**People.** The Khmer, one of the oldest peoples in Southeast Asia, constitute the major ethnic group in Cambodia. The population has declined significantly since the mid-1970s due to war, famine, human-rights abuses, and emigration. Because of an urban-evacuation campaign initiated by the Khmer Rouge, Cambodia's previous regime, most Cambodians live in rural areas, working as farmers or laborers. Although the new government does not encourage religion (an activity often punished by death during the Khmer Rouge era), the practice of Buddhism, the main religion, is on the rise.

**Economy and the Land.** Cambodia's flat central region and wet climate make it well suited for rice production. Along with rubber, rice was the mainstay of the economy before the seventies, but the Vietnam and civil wars all but destroyed agriculture. This sector of the economy has begun to recover recently, but a shortage of skilled labor, combined with the effects of war, have held back industry. The terrain is marked by the central plain, forests, and mountains in the south, west, and along the Thai border. The climate is tropical, with high rainfall and humidity.

**History and Politics.** Cambodia traces its roots to the Hindu kingdoms of Funan and Chenla, which reigned in the early centuries A.D. The Angkor Empire dominated until the fifteenth century, incorporating much of present-day Laos, Thailand, and Vietnam and constructing the stone temples of Angkor Wat, considered one of Southeast Asia's greatest architectural achievements. By 1431 the Siamese had overrun the region, and subsequent years saw the rise of the Siamese, Vietnamese, and Lao. By the mid-1700s Cambodia's boundaries approximated those of today. During the 1800s, as French control in Indochina expanded, the area became a French protectorate. Cambodia gained independence in 1953 under King Sihanouk, who, after changing his title to "prince," became prime minister in 1955 and head of state in 1960. In 1970, after Sihanouk was ousted, Lon Nol was installed as prime minister, and the monarchy of Cambodia changed to the Khmer Republic. During this time the Vietnam War spilled over the Khmer Republic's borders, as United States forces made bombing raids against what they claimed were North Vietnamese bases. Resulting anti-American sentiment gave rise to discontent with Lon Nol's pro-United States regime. The Khmer Communists, or Khmer Rouge, seized power in 1975 and, led by Pol Pot, exiled most Cambodians to the countryside. An estimated three million died under the Khmer Rouge, many were executed because they were educated or had links to the former government. Vietnamese troops supported by some Cambodian Communists invaded Cambodia in late 1978, and by early 1979 they had overthrown the Khmer Rouge. Withdrawal of Vietnam in 1989 has renewed fears that the Khmer Rouge may regain power. ■

# CAMEROON

**Official name** Republic of Cameroon
## PEOPLE
**Population** 11,580,000. **Density** 63/mi² (24/km²). **Urban** 42%. **Capital** Yaoundé, 583,000. **Ethnic groups** Cameroon Highlander 31%, Equatorial Bantu 19%, Kirdi 11%, Fulani 10%. **Languages** English, French, indigenous. **Religions** Animist 51%, Christian 33%, Muslim 16%. **Life expectancy** 53 female, 50 male. **Literacy** 41%.
## POLITICS
**Government** Republic. **Parties** People's Democratic Union. **Suffrage** Universal, over 21. **Memberships** OAU, UN. **Subdivisions** 10 provinces.
## ECONOMY
**GDP** $8,385,000,000 **Per capita** $941. **Monetary unit** CFA franc. **Trade partners** Exports: France, Netherlands, U.S. Imports: France, U.S. Japan. **Exports** Petroleum, coffee, cocoa, aluminum, cotton, wood. **Imports** Machinery, manufactures, transportation equipment, pharmaceuticals, alumina.
## LAND
**Description** Central Africa. **Area** 183,569 mi² (475,442 km²). **Highest point** Cameroon Mtn., 13,451 ft (4,100 m). **Lowest point** Sea level.

**People.** Immigration and foreign rule shaped Cameroon's diverse population, composed of some two hundred groups speaking twenty-four major African languages. Both English and French are official languages, resulting from the merging of former French-ruled eastern and British-ruled western territories. Population is concentrated in the French-speaking eastern region. The majority of people practice indigenous beliefs that often influence Islamic and Christian practices as well.

**Economy and the Land.** Recent economic plans have focused on agriculture, industry, and the development of oil deposits. Agriculture is still the country's economic base, but oil is a major export. A varied terrain features southern coastal plains and rain forests, central plateaus, mountainous western forests, and northern savanna and marshes. Although this has hindered transportation development and thus slowed economic growth, improvements are being made. Climate varies from a hot, humid coastal region to fluctuating temperatures and less humidity northward.

**History and Politics.** The Sao people reached the Cameroon area in the tenth century. The Portuguese arrived in the 1500s, and the following three centuries saw an influx of European and African peoples and an active slave trade along the coast. In 1884 Germany set up a protectorate that included modern Cameroon by 1914. During World War I British and French troops occupied the area, and in 1919, following the war, the League of Nations divided Cameroon into eastern French and western British mandates. The Cameroons became trust territories in 1946, and French Cameroon became an independent republic in 1960. In 1961 the northern region of British Cameroon elected to join Nigeria, and the southern area chose to unite with the eastern Republic of Cameroon. This resulted in a two-state Federal Republic of Cameroon. A 1972 referendum combined the states into the United Republic of Cameroon, and in 1984, the official name became the Republic of Cameroon. The government has a foreign policy of nonalignment. ■

# CANADA

**Official name** Canada
## PEOPLE
**Population** 26,415,000. **Density** 6.9/mi² (2.6/km²). **Urban** 76%. **Capital** Ottawa, 300,763. **Ethnic groups** British origin 40%, French origin 27%, other European 23%, native Canadian 2%. **Languages** English, French, indigenous. **Religions** Roman Catholic 47%, United Church 16%, Anglican 10%, other Christian. **Life expectancy** 79 female, 72 male. **Literacy** 93%.
## POLITICS
**Government** Parliamentary state. **Parties** Liberal, New Democratic, Progressive Conservative. **Suffrage** Universal, over 18. **Memberships** CW, NATO, OAS, OECD, UN. **Subdivisions** 10 provinces, 2 territories.
## ECONOMY
**GDP** $348,291,000,000 **Per capita** $13,783. **Monetary unit** Dollar. **Trade partners** U.S., Japan. **Exports** Motor vehicles, paper and other manufactures, wood and other crude materials. **Imports** Motor vehicles, machinery, manufactures, food, petroleum.
## LAND
**Description** Northern North America. **Area** 3,849,674 mi² (9,970,610 km²). **Highest point** Mt. Logan, 19,524 ft (5,951 m). **Lowest point** Sea level.

**People.** Canada was greatly influenced by French and British rule, and its culture reflects this dual nature. Descendants of British and French settlers compose the two main population groups, and languages include both English and French. French-speaking inhabitants, called Québecois, are concentrated in the Province of Québec. Minorities include descendants of various European groups, indigenous Indians, and Inuit. Because of the rugged terrain and harsh climate of northern Canada, population is concentrated near the United States border.

**Economy and the Land.** Rich natural resources—including extensive mineral deposits, fertile land, forests, and lakes—helped shape Canada's diversified economy, which ranks among the world's most prosperous. Economic problems are those common to most modern industrial nations. Agriculture, mining, and industry are highly developed. Canada is a major wheat producer; mineral output includes asbestos, zinc, silver, and nickel; and crude petroleum is an important export. The service sector is also active. Second only to the Soviet Union in land area, Canada has a terrain that varies from eastern rolling hills and plains to mountains in the west. The Canadian Shield consists of ancient rock and extends from Labrador to the Arctic Islands. It is covered by thick forests in the south and tundra in the north. Overall, summers are moderate and winters long and cold.

**History and Politics.** Canada's first inhabitants were Asian Indians and Inuit, an Arctic people. Around the year 1000, Vikings were the first Europeans to reach North America, and in 1497 John Cabot claimed the Newfoundland coastal area for Britain. Jacques Cartier established French claim when he landed at the Gaspé Peninsula in the 1500s. Subsequent French and British rivalry culminated in several wars during the late seventeenth and eighteenth centuries. The wars ended with the 1763 Treaty of Paris, by which France lost Canada and other North American territory to Britain. To aid in resolving the continued conflict between French and English residents, the British North America Act of 1867 united the colonies into the Dominion of Canada. Canada fought on the side of the British during World War I. In 1926, along with other dominions, Canada declared itself an independent member of the British Commonwealth, and in 1931 Britain recognized the declaration through the Statute of Westminster. Canada once again allied itself with Britain during World War II. In 1988, Canada saw vigorous debate over a free trade pact with the United States, which narrowly won approval. The Québec separatist movement is striving for independent status for French-speaking Québec. ■

# CANARY ISLANDS See SPAIN.

# CAPE VERDE

**Official name** Republic of Cape Verde

## PEOPLE
**Population** 370,000. **Density** 238/mi² (92/km²). **Urban** 5%. **Capital** Praia, São Tiago I., 37,480. **Ethnic groups** Creole (mulatto) 71%, African 28%, European 1%. **Languages** Portuguese, Crioulo. **Religions** Roman Catholic 80%, Nazarene and other Protestant 10%. **Life expectancy** 61 female, 57 male. **Literacy** 37%.
## POLITICS
**Government** Republic. **Parties** African Party for Independence. **Suffrage** Universal, over 15. **Memberships** OAU, UN. **Subdivisions** 12 districts.

## ECONOMY
**GNP** $135,100,000 **Per capita** $450. **Monetary unit** Escudo. **Trade partners** Exports: Algeria, Italy, Ivory Coast. Imports: Portugal, Netherlands, France. **Exports** Fish, bananas, vegetables, salt. **Imports** Grain and other food, manufactures, machinery, petroleum, chemicals.
## LAND
**Description** Western African islands. **Area** 1,557 mi$^2$ (4,033 km$^2$). **Highest point** Pico, Fogo I., 9,281 ft (2,829 m). **Lowest point** Sea level.

**People.** The Portuguese-African heritage of Cape Verde's population is a result of Portuguese rule and the forced transmigration of Africans for slavery. Although Portuguese is the official language, the majority speaks Crioulo, a creole dialect. Most people are Roman Catholic, but indigenous practices exist, sometimes in combination with Catholicism. The mainly poor population is largely undernourished and plagued by unemployment. The country consists of five islets and ten main islands, and all but one are inhabited.

**Economy and the Land.** The volcanic, mountainous islands have few natural resources and low rainfall; thus the country's economy remains underdeveloped. Fishing and agriculture are important for both subsistence and commercial purposes. Much of the land is too dry for farming, and drought is a frequent problem. Cape Verde's location on air and sea routes and its tropical climate offer potential for expansion into services and tourism. However, Cape Verde will most likely continue to rely on foreign aid for some time.

**History and Politics.** The islands that make up Cape Verde were uninhabited when the Portuguese arrived around 1460. Settlement began in 1462, and by the sixteenth century Cape Verde had become a shipping center for the African slave trade. Until 1879 Portugal ruled Cape Verde and present-day Guinea-Bissau as a single colony. A movement for the independence of Cape Verde and Guinea-Bissau began in the 1950s, and a 1974 coup in Portugal ultimately resulted in autonomy for both countries, with Cape Verde proclaiming independence in 1975. Plans to unify Cape Verde and Guinea-Bissau were abandoned following a 1980 coup in Guinea-Bissau. Cape Verde follows a foreign policy of nonalignment and takes a special interest in African affairs. ■

# CAYMAN ISLANDS
See UNITED KINGDOM.

# CENTRAL AFRICAN REPUBLIC

**Official name** Central African Republic
## PEOPLE
**Population** 2,843,000. **Density** 12/mi$^2$ (4.6/km$^2$). **Urban** 42%. **Capital** Bangui, 473,800. **Ethnic groups** Baya 34%, Banda 27%, Mandja 21%, Sara 10%. **Languages** French, Sango, Arabic, indigenous. **Religions** Protestant 25%, Roman Catholic 25%, Animist 24%, Muslim 15%. **Life expectancy** 45 female, 41 male. **Literacy** 18%.

## POLITICS
**Government** Republic. **Parties** Democratic Rally. **Suffrage** Universal, over 21. **Memberships** OAU, UN. **Subdivisions** 14 prefectures.
## ECONOMY
**GDP** $641,000,000 **Per capita** $245. **Monetary unit** CFA franc. **Trade partners** Exports: France, Belguim, Israel. Imports: France, Zaire, Japan. **Exports** Wood, coffee, diamonds, cotton. **Imports** Manufactures, machinery, transportation equipment, food, chemicals.
## LAND
**Description** Central Africa, landlocked. **Area** 240,535 mi$^2$ (622,984 km$^2$). **Highest point** Mont Ngaoui, 4,626 ft (1,410 m). **Lowest point** Ubangi River valley, 1,100 ft (335 m).

**People.** Lying near Africa's geographical center, the Central African Republic was the stopping point for many precolonial nomadic groups. The resultant multiethnic populace was further diversified by migrations during the slave-trade era. Of the country's many languages, Sango is most widely used. Overall, the population is rural and suffers from poverty and a low literacy rate.

**Economy and the Land.** Fertile land, extensive forests, and mineral deposits provide adequate bases for agriculture, forestry, and mining. Economic development remains minimal, however, impeded by poor transportation routes, a landlocked location, lack of skilled labor, and political instability. Subsistence farming continues as the major activity, and agriculture is the chief contributor to the economy. The country consists of a plateau region with southern rain forests and a northeastern semidesert. The climate is temperate, and ample rainfall sometimes results in impassable roads.

**History and Politics.** Little is known of the area's early history except that it was the site of many migrations. European slave trade in the nineteenth century led to the 1894 creation of a French territory called the Ubangi-Chari. This in turn combined with the areas of the present-day Congo, Chad, and Gabon in 1910 to form French Equatorial Africa. The Central African Republic gained independence in 1960. A 1966 military coup installed military chief Jean-Bedel Bokassa, who in 1976 assumed the title of emperor, changed the republic to a monarchy, and renamed the nation the Central African Empire. A 1979 coup ended the monarchy and reinstated the name Central African Republic. The country enacted a new constitution in 1986. ∎

# CHAD

**Official name** Republic of Chad
**PEOPLE**
**Population** 4,984,000. **Density** 10/mi$^2$ (3.9/km$^2$). **Urban** 27%. **Capital** N'Djamena, 303,000. **Ethnic groups** Sara and other African, Arab. **Languages** Arabic, French, indigenous. **Religions** Muslim 44%, Christian 33%, Animist 23%. **Life expectancy** 45 female, 41 male. **Literacy** 17%.
**POLITICS**
**Government** Republic. **Parties** National Union for Independence and Revolution. **Suffrage** Universal, over 18. **Memberships** OAU, UN. **Subdivisions** 14 prefectures.
**ECONOMY**
**GDP** $630,000,000 **Per capita** $135. **Monetary unit** CFA franc. **Trade partners** France, Nigeria and other African countries. **Exports** Cotton, meat, fish, crude animal products. **Imports** Cement, petroleum, flour, sugar, tea, machinery, textiles.
**LAND**
**Description** Central Africa, landlocked. **Area** 495,755 mi$^2$ (1,284,000 km$^2$). **Highest point** Mt. Koussi, 11,204 ft (3,415 m). **Lowest point** Bodélé Depression, 525 ft (160 m).

**People.** Centuries ago Islamic Arabs mixed with indigenous black Africans and established Chad's diverse population. This variety has led to a rich but often troubled culture. Descendants of Arab invaders mainly inhabit the north, where Islam predominates and nomadic farming is the major activity. In the south—traditionally the economic and political center—the black Sara predominate, operating small farms and practicing indigenous or Christian beliefs. Chad's many languages also reflect its ethnic variety.

**Economy and the Land.** Natural features and in-

stability arising from ethnic and regional conflict have combined to prevent Chad from prospering. Agriculture and fishing are economic mainstays and are often conducted at subsistence levels. The Sahara extends into Chad's northern region, and the southern grasslands with their heavy rains compose the primary agricultural area. The relative prosperity of the region, in conjunction with its predominantly Sara population, has fueled much of the political conflict. Future growth is greatly dependent on political equilibrium. Climate varies from the hot, dry northern desert to the semiarid central region and rainier south.

**History and Politics.** African and Arab societies began prospering in the Lake Chad region around the eighth century A.D. Subsequent centuries saw the landlocked area become an ethnic crossroads for Muslim nomads and African groups. European traders arrived in the late 1800s, and by 1900 France had gained control. When created in 1910, French Equatorial Africa's boundaries included modern Chad, Gabon, the Congo, and the Central African Republic. Following Chad's independence in 1960, the southern Sara gained dominance over the government. A northern rebel group has emerged and government-rebel conflict has continued. Libyan troops entered Chad in 1980, and conflict continued until they were finally expelled in 1987. Libya and Chad formally ended their war in October 1988. ∎

# CHANNEL ISLANDS
See UNITED KINGDOM.

# CHILE

**Official name** Republic of Chile
**PEOPLE**
**Population** 13,140,000. **Density** 45/mi$^2$ (17/km$^2$). **Urban** 84%. **Capital** Santiago, 425,924. **Ethnic groups** White and mestizo 95%, Amerindian 3%. **Languages** Spanish. **Religions** Roman Catholic 89%, Pentecostal and other Protestant 11%. **Life expectancy** 73 female, 67 male. **Literacy** 91%.
**POLITICS**
**Government** Republic. **Parties** Humanist, National Renovation, Radical, Social Democratic, others. **Suffrage** Universal, over 18. **Memberships** OAS, UN. **Subdivisions** 12 regions, 1 metropolitan region.
**ECONOMY**
**GDP** $15,996,000,000 **Per capita** $1,363. **Monetary unit** Peso. **Trade partners** Exports: U.S., Japan, W. Germany. Imports: U.S., Japan, Brazil. **Exports** Copper,

fruits and vegetables, animal feed, minerals. **Imports** Manufactures, machinery, transportation equipment, petroleum, food.

**LAND**
**Description** Southern South America. **Area** 292,135 mi$^2$ (756,626 km$^2$). **Highest point** Nevado Ojos del Salado, 22,615 ft (6,893 m). **Lowest point** Sea level.

**People.** Chile's land barriers—the eastern Andes, western coastal range, and northern desert—have resulted in a mostly urban population concentrated in a central valley. Mestizos, of Spanish-Indian heritage, and descendants of Spanish immigrants predominate. In addition to an Indian minority, the population includes those who trace their roots to Irish and English colonists or nineteenth-century German immigrants. The country enjoys a relatively high literacy rate, but poverty remains a problem.

**Economy and the Land.** Chile's land provides the natural resources necessary for a successful economy, but longtime instability has taken its toll. The northern desert region is the site of mineral deposits, and mining is a major component of trade, making Chile vulnerable to outside market forces. An agricultural zone lies in the central valley, while the south offers forests, grazing land, and some petroleum deposits. The climate varies from region to region but is generally mild.

**History and Politics.** Upon their arrival in the 1500s, the Spanish defeated the northern Inca Indians, although many years were spent in conflict with Araucanian Indians of the central and southern regions. From the sixteenth through nineteenth centuries, Chile received little attention from ruling Spain, and colonists established a successful agriculture. In 1818 Bernardo O'Higgins led the way to victory over the Spanish and became ruler of independent Chile. By the 1920s, dissent arising from unequal power and land distribution united the middle and working classes but social-welfare, education, and economic programs were unable to eliminate inequalities rooted in the past. A 1960 earthquake and tidal wave added to the country's problems. Leftist Salvador Allende Gossens was elected to power in 1970, governing until his death in 1973 in a military coup which installed Augusto Pinochet. Civil disturbances and grave human-rights abuses marked his right-wing government. This dictatorship ended with the election of a new leader in December 1989. ∎

# CHINA

**Official name** People's Republic of China
**PEOPLE**
**Population** 1,092,100,000. **Density** 296/mi$^2$ (114/km$^2$). **Urban** 21%. **Capital** Beijing (Peking), 5,970,000. **Ethnic groups** Han Chinese 93%, Zhuang, Hui, Uygur, Yi, Miao, Manchu, Tibetan, others. **Languages** Chinese dialects. **Religions** Confucian, Taoist, Buddhist, Muslim. **Life expectancy** 69 female, 67 male. **Literacy** 66%.
**POLITICS**
**Government** Socialist republic. **Parties** Communist. **Suffrage** Universal, over 18. **Memberships** UN. **Subdivisions** 22 provinces, 5 autonomous regions, 3 municipalities,.

**ECONOMY**
**GNP** $262,000,000,000 **Per capita** $251. **Monetary unit** Yuan. **Trade partners** Exports: Hong Kong, Japan, U.S. Imports: Japan, U.S., Hong Kong. **Exports** Textiles and other manufactures, petroleum, food, crude materials. **Imports** Manufactures, machinery, chemicals, wood and other crude materials.
**LAND**
**Description** Eastern Asia. **Area** 3,689,631 mi$^2$ (9,556,100 km$^2$). **Highest point** Mt. Everest, 29,028 ft (8,848 m). **Lowest point** Turfan Depression, -505 ft (-154 m).
*The above information excludes Taiwan.*

**People.** Population is concentrated in the east, and Han Chinese are the majority group. Zhuang, Hui, Uygur, Yi, Miao, Manchu, and Tibetan peoples compose minorities. Many Chinese languages are spoken, but the national language is Modern Standard Chinese, or Mandarin—based on a northern dialect. Following a Communist revolution in 1949, religious activity was discouraged. It is now on the increase, and religions include Confucianism, Taoism, and Buddhism, plus Islam and Christianity. China ranks first in the world in population, and family-planning programs have been implemented to aid population control. With a recorded civilization going back about 3,500 years, China has contributed much to world culture.

**Economy and the Land.** Most economic progress dates from 1949, when the new People's Republic of China faced a starving, war-torn, and unemployed population. Industry is expanding, but agriculture continues as the major activity. Natural resources include coal, oil, natural gas, and minerals, many of which remain to be explored. A current economic plan focuses on growth in agriculture, industry, science and technology, and national defense. China's terrain is varied: two-thirds consists of mountainous or semiarid land, with fertile plains and deltas in the east. The climate is marked by hot, humid summers, while the dry winters are often cold.

**History and Politics.** China's civilization ranks among the world's oldest. The first dynasty, the Shang, began sometime during the second millennium B.C. Kublai Khan's thirteenth-century invasion brought China the first of its various foreign rulers. In the nineteenth century, despite government efforts to the contrary, foreign influence and intervention grew. The government was weakened by the Opium War with Britain in the 1840s; the Taiping Rebellion, a civil war; and a war with Japan from 1894 to 1895. Opposition to foreign influences erupted in the anti-foreign and anti-Christian Boxer Rebellion of 1900. After China became a republic in 1912, the death of the president in 1916 triggered the warlord period, in which conflicts were widespread and power was concentrated among military leaders. Attempts to unite the nation began in the 1920s with Sun Yat-sen's Nationalist party, initially allied with the Communist party. Under the leadership of Chiang Kai-shek, the Nationalist party overcame the warlords, captured Beijing, and executed many Communists. Remaining Communists reorganized under Mao Zedong, and the Communist-Nationalist conflict continued, along with Japanese invasion and occupation. By 1949 the Communists controlled most of the country, and the People's Republic of China was proclaimed. Chiang Kai-shek fled to Taiwan, proclaiming T'aipei as China's provisional capital. After Mao's death in 1976, foreign trade and contact expanded. In 1979 the United States recognized Beijing, rather than T'aipei, as China's capital. When a retrenchment of the government from liberalization erupted violently in student demonstrations in 1989, many people were killed or arrested. See also TAIWAN. ■

## CHRISTMAS ISLAND
See AUSTRALIA.

## COCOS ISLANDS See AUSTRALIA.

## COLOMBIA

**Official name** Republic of Colombia

### PEOPLE
**Population** 30,860,000. **Density** 70/mi$^2$ (27/km$^2$). **Urban** 67%. **Capital** Bogotá, 3,967,988. **Ethnic groups** Mestizo 58%, white 20%, mulatto 14%, black 4%. **Languages** Spanish. **Religions** Roman Catholic 95%. **Life expectancy** 66 female, 61 male. **Literacy** 88%.

### POLITICS
**Government** Republic. **Parties** Conservative, Liberal, others. **Suffrage** Universal, over 18. **Memberships** OAS, UN. **Subdivisions** 23 departments, 5 commissariats, 4 intendencies, 1 federal district.

### ECONOMY
**GDP** $34,187,000,000 **Per capita** $1,198. **Monetary unit** Peso. **Trade partners** Exports: U.S., W. Germany, Netherlands. Imports: U.S., Japan, Venezuela. **Exports** Coffee, petroleum, bananas and other food, manufactures. **Imports** Machinery, chemicals, manufactures, petroleum, vehicles.

### LAND
**Description** Northern South America. **Area** 440,831 mi$^2$ (1,141,748 km$^2$). **Highest point** Pico Cristóbal Colón, 19,029 ft (5,800 m). **Lowest point** Sea level.

**People.** Colombia's mixed population traces its roots to indigenous Indians, Spanish colonists, and black African slaves. Most numerous today are mestizos, those of Spanish-Indian descent. Roman Catholicism, the Spanish language, and Colombia's overall culture evidence the long-lasting effect of Spanish rule. Over the past decades the population has shifted from mainly rural to urban as the economy has expanded into industry.

**Economy and the Land.** Industry now keeps pace with traditional agriculture in economic contributions, and mining is also important. Natural resources include oil, coal, natural gas, most of the world's emeralds, plus fertile soils. The traditional coffee crop also remains important for Colombia, a leading coffee producer. The terrain is characterized by a flat coastal region, central highlands, and wide eastern llanos, or plains. The climate is tropical on the coast and in the west, with cooler temperatures in the highlands.

**History and Politics.** In the 1500s Spaniards conquered the native Indian groups and established the area as a Spanish colony. In the early 1700s, Bogotá became the capital of the viceroyalty of New Granada, which included modern Colombia, Venezuela, Ecuador, and Panama. Rebellion in Venezuela in 1796 sparked revolts elsewhere in New Granada, including Colombia, and in 1813 independence was declared. In 1819 the Republic of Greater Colombia was formed and included all the former members of the Spanish viceroyalty. Independence leader Simón Bolívar became president. By 1830 Venezuela and Ecuador had seceded from the republic, followed by Panama in 1903. The Conservative and Liberal parties, dominating forces in Colombia's political history, arose from differences between supporters of Bolívar and Santander. Conservative-Liberal conflict led to a violent civil war from 1899 to 1902, as well as to *La Violencia*, The Violence, a civil disorder that continued from the 1940s to the 1960s and resulted in about three hundred thousand deaths. From the late fifties through the seventies, the government alternated between conservative and liberal rule. Political unrest reduced the effectiveness of both parties. By the 1980s, growing drug traffic presented Colombia with new problems. In 1989 the government declared war on the drug cartels after antigovernment terrorism increased. ∎

## COMOROS

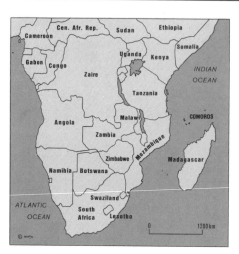

**Official name** Federal Islamic Republic of the Comoros
**PEOPLE**
**Population** 452,000. **Density** 524/mi$^2$ (202/km$^2$). **Urban** 25%. **Capital** Moroni, Njazidja I., 20,112. **Ethnic groups** African-Arab descent (Antalote, Cafre, Makua, Oimatsaha, Sakalava). **Languages** Arabic, French, Swahili, Malagasy. **Religions** Sunni Muslim 86%, Roman Catholic 14%. **Life expectancy** 52 female, 48 male. **Literacy** 15%.
**POLITICS**
**Government** Islamic republic. **Parties** Union for Progress. **Suffrage** Universal adult. **Memberships** OAU, UN. **Subdivisions** 3 islands.
**ECONOMY**
**GNP** $114,000,000 **Per capita** $248. **Monetary unit** Franc. **Trade partners** Exports: France, U.S., W. Germany. Imports: France, Madagascar, Somalia. **Exports** Cinnamon, essential oils, vanilla. **Imports** Petroleum, rice, meat, sugar and honey.
**LAND**
**Description** Southeastern African islands. **Area** 863 mi$^2$ (2,235 km$^2$). **Highest point** Kartala, Njazidja I., 7,746 ft (2,361 m). **Lowest point** Sea level.
*The above information excludes Mayotte.*

**People.** The ethnic groups of Comoros' Njazidja, Nzwani, and Mwali islands are mainly of Arab-African descent, practice the Muslim religion, and speak a Swahili dialect. Roman Catholic descendants of Malagasy immigrants compose the majority on French-ruled Mayotte Island. Arab culture, however, predominates throughout the island group. Poverty, disease, a shortage of medical care, and low literacy continue to plague the nation.

**Economy and the Land.** The economic mainstay of Comoros is agriculture, and most Comorans practice subsistence farming and fishing. Plantations employ workers to produce the main cash crops. Of volcanic origin, the islands have soils of varying quality, and some are unsuited for farming. Terrain varies from the mountains of Njazidja to the hills and valleys of Mayotte. The climate is cool and dry, with a winter rainy season.

**History and Politics.** The Comoro Islands saw invasions by coastal African, Persian Gulf, Indonesian, and Malagasy peoples. Portuguese explorers landed in the 1500s, around the same time Arab Shirazis, most likely from Persia, introduced Islam. The French took Mayotte in 1843 and had established colonial rule over the four main islands by 1912. Comoros declared unilateral independence in 1975. Mayotte, however, voted to remain under French administration. ∎

## CONGO

**Official name** People's Republic of the Congo
**PEOPLE**
**Population** 2,267,000. **Density** 17/mi$^2$ (6.6/km$^2$). **Urban** 40%. **Capital** Brazzaville, 595,102. **Ethnic groups** Kongo 48%, Sangha 20%, Mbochi 12%, Teke 17%. **Languages** French, indigenous. **Religions** Christian 50%, Animist 42%, Muslim 2%. **Life expectancy** 48 female, 45 male. **Literacy** 80%.
**POLITICS**
**Government** Socialist republic. **Parties** Workers'. **Suffrage** Universal, over 18. **Memberships** OAU, UN. **Subdivisions** 9 regions, 1 federal district.
**ECONOMY**
**GDP** $2,194,000,000 **Per capita** $1,276. **Monetary unit** CFA franc. **Trade partners** Exports: U.S., Italy, Spain, France. Imports: France, Brazil. **Exports** Petroleum, diamonds, wood products. **Imports** Machinery, grain and other food, petroleum, chemicals.
**LAND**
**Description** Central Africa. **Area** 132,047 mi$^2$ (342,000 km$^2$). **Highest point** 2,963 ft (903 m). **Lowest point** Sea level.

**People.** The Congo's four main groups, the Kongo, Sangha, Mbochi, and Teke, create an ethnically and linguistically diverse populace. The official language, French, reflects former colonial rule. Population is concentrated in the south, away from the dense forests, heavy rainfall, and hot climate of the north. Educational programs have improved, although rural inhabitants remain relatively isolated.

**Economy and the Land.** Brazzaville was the commercial center of the former colony called French Equatorial Africa. The Congo now benefits from the early groundwork laid for service and transport industries. Subsistence farming occupies most Congolese, however, and takes most of the cultivated land. Low productivity and a growing populace create a need for foreign aid, much of it from France. Offshore petroleum is the most valuable mineral resource and a major economic contributor. The land is marked by coastal plains, a south-central valley, a central plateau, and the Congo River basin in the north. The climate is tropical.

**History and Politics.** Several tribal kingdoms existed in the area during its early history. The Portuguese arrived on the coast in the 1400s, and slave trade flourished until it was banned in the 1800s. A Teke king then signed a treaty placing the area, known as Middle Congo, under French protection. In 1910 Middle Congo, the present-day Central African Republic, Gabon, and Chad were joined to form French Equatorial Africa. The Republic of the Congo became independent in 1960. Subsequent years saw unrest, including coups, a presidential assassination, and accusations of corruption and human-rights violations. In 1979 a newly-elected president granted amnesty to political prisoners, and the country has remained relatively stable. The nation maintains a policy of nonalignment with both Communist and Western countries. ∎

# COOK ISLANDS
See NEW ZEALAND.

# CORSICA See FRANCE.

# COSTA RICA

**Official name** Republic of Costa Rica
**PEOPLE**
**Population** 2,958,000. **Density** 150/mi² (58/km²). **Urban** 50%. **Capital** San José, 241,464. **Ethnic groups** White and mestizo 96%, black 3%, Amerindian 1%. **Languages** Spanish. **Religions** Roman Catholic 93%. **Life expectancy** 76 female, 71 male. **Literacy** 88%.
**POLITICS**
**Government** Republic. **Parties** National Liberation, Social Christian Unity, others. **Suffrage** Universal, over 18. **Memberships** OAS, UN. **Subdivisions** 7 provinces.
**ECONOMY**
**GDP** $3,814,000,000 **Per capita** $1,400. **Monetary unit** Colon. **Trade partners** Exports: U.S., W. Germany, Guatemala. Imports: U.S., Venezuela, Mexico. **Exports** Coffee, bananas, food, manufactures. **Imports** Chemicals, paper and other manufactures, petroleum, machinery, food.
**LAND**
**Description** Central America. **Area** 19,730 mi² (51,100 km²). **Highest point** Cerro Chirripó, 12,530 ft (3,819 m). **Lowest point** Sea level.

**People.** Compared with most other Central American countries, Costa Rica has a relatively large population of European descent, mostly Spanish with minorities of German, Dutch, and Swiss ancestry. Together with mestizos, people of Spanish-Indian heritage, they compose the bulk of the population. Descendants of black Jamaican immigrants inhabit mainly the Caribbean coastal region. Indigenous Indians in scattered enclaves continue traditional lifestyles; some, however, have been assimilated into the country's majority culture.

**Economy and the Land.** Costa Rica's economy, one of the most prosperous in Central America, has not been without problems, some resulting from falling coffee prices and rising oil costs. Agriculture remains important, producing traditional coffee and banana crops, while the country attempts to expand industry. Population and agriculture are concentrated in the central highlands. Much of the country is forested, and the mountainous central area is bordered by coastal plains on the east and west. The climate is semitropical to tropical.

**History and Politics.** In 1502 Christopher Columbus arrived and claimed the area for Spain. Spaniards named the region Rich Coast, and settlers soon flocked to the new land to seek their fortune. Rather than riches, they found an Indian population unwilling to surrender its land. But many Spaniards remained, establishing farms in the central area. In 1821 the Central American provinces of Costa Rica, Guatemala, El Salvador, Honduras, and Nicaragua declared themselves independent from Spain, and by 1823 they had formed the Federation of Central America. Despite efforts to sustain it, the federation was in a state of virtual collapse by 1838, and Costa Rica became an independent republic. Since the first free elections in 1889, Costa Rica has experienced a presidential overthrow in 1919 and a civil war in 1948, which arose over a disputed election. In the 1980s the country worked to promote peaceful solutions to armed conflicts in the region. ∎

# CUBA

**Official name** Republic of Cuba
**PEOPLE**
**Population** 10,640,000. **Density** 249/mi² (96/km²). **Urban** 72%. **Capital** Havana, 1,914,466. **Ethnic groups** White 66%, mixed 22%, black 12%. **Languages** Spanish. **Religions** Roman Catholic, Pentecostal, Baptist. **Life expectancy** 75 female, 72 male. **Literacy** 98%.
**POLITICS**
**Government** Socialist republic. **Parties** Communist. **Suffrage** Universal, over 16. **Memberships** CEMA, UN. **Subdivisions** 13 provinces, 1 city, 1 municipality.
**ECONOMY**
**GNP** $18,000,000,000 **Per capita** $1,767. **Monetary unit** Peso. **Trade partners** U.S.S.R.. **Exports** Sugar, petroleum, minerals. **Imports** Petroleum, machinery, manufactures, grain and other food, chemicals.
**LAND**
**Description** Caribbean island. **Area** 42,804 mi² (110,861 km²). **Highest point** Pico Turquino, 6,470 (1,972 m). **Lowest point** Sea level.

**People.** Most Cubans are descendants of Spanish colonists, African slaves, or a blend of the two. The government provides free education and health care, and although religious practices are discouraged, most people belong to the Roman Catholic church. Personal income, health, education, and housing have improved since the 1959 revolution, but most food products and consumer goods remain in short supply.

**Economy and the Land.** Cuba's economy is largely dependent on sugar, although other forms of agriculture are also important. The most fertile soils lie in the central region between mountain ranges, while mineral deposits, including oil and nickel, are found in the northeast. In addition to agriculture and mining, industry is an economic contributor. Most economic activity is nationalized, and Cuba remains dependent on aid from the Soviet Union. Mountains, plains, and a scenic coastline make Cuba one of the most beautiful islands in the West Indies. The climate is tropical.

**History and Politics.** Christopher Columbus claimed Cuba for Spain in 1492, and Spanish settlement began in 1511. When the native Indian population died out, African slaves were brought to work plantations. The United States joined with Cuba against Spain in the Spanish-American War in 1898. Cuba gained full independence in 1902. Unrest continued, however, and the United States again intervened from 1906 to 1909 and in 1917. A 1933 coup ousted a nine-year dictatorship, and a subsequent government overthrow in 1934 ushered in an era dominated by Sergeant Fulgencio Batista. After ruling through other presidents and serving an elected term himself, Batista seized power in a 1952 coup that established an unpopular and oppressive regime. Led by lawyer Fidel Castro, a revolutionary group opposed to Batista gained quick support, and Batista fled the country on January 1, 1959, leaving the government to Castro. Early United States support of Castro soured when nationalization of American businesses began. American aid soon ceased, and Cuba looked to the Soviet Union for assistance. The United States ended diplomatic relations with Cuba in 1961. In 1962 the United States and the Soviet Union became embroiled in a dispute over Soviet missile bases in Cuba that ended with removal of the missiles. In the early 1980s more than one hundred thousand Cubans were allowed to emigrate to the United States. The nation maintains ties with the Soviet Union and has sent aid to several Third World countries. ∎

# CURAÇAO See NETHERLANDS.

# CYPRUS

**Official name** Republic of Cyprus
**PEOPLE**
**Population** 524,000. **Density** 230/mi² (89/km²). **Urban** 50%. **Capital** Nicosia, 48,221. **Ethnic groups** Greek. **Languages** Greek, English. **Religions** Greek Orthodox. **Life expectancy** 76 female, 72 male. **Literacy** 89%.
**POLITICS**
**Government** Republic. **Parties** Democratic, Democratic Rally, Progressive Party of the Working People. **Suffrage** Universal, over 18. **Memberships** CW, UN. **Subdivisions** 6 districts.
**ECONOMY**
**GDP** $2,337,000,000 **Per capita** $3,462. **Monetary unit** Pound. **Trade partners** Exports: U.K., Lebanon, Libya. Imports: U.K., Italy, Japan. **Exports** Clothing and shoes, fruit and vegetables, machinery, petroleum, manufactures. **Imports** Textiles and other manufactures, machinery, petroleum, food, motor vehicles.

## LAND
**Description** Southern part of the island of Cyprus. **Area** 2,276 mi² (5,896 km²). **Highest point** Ólimbos, 6,401 ft (1,951 m). **Lowest point** Sea level.

**People.** Most Cypriots occupying the southern two thirds of the island are of Greek ancestry, and their religion, language, and general culture reflect this heritage. Family and religion are a dominant influence in the community. Decades of British rule had little impact.

**Economy and the Land.** Conflict between the Greek and Turkish Cypriots has severely disrupted the economy of the island. With foreign assistance, Greek Cypriots have made considerable progress, expanding traditional southern agriculture to light manufacturing and tourism. Known for its scenic beauty and tourist appeal, southern Cyprus is marked by a fertile southern plain bordered by the rugged Troodos Mountains to the southwest. Sandy beaches dot the coastline. The Mediterranean climate brings hot, dry summers and damp, cool winters.

**History and Politics.** History of Cyprus and North Cyprus follows NORTH CYPRUS. ∎

# CYPRUS, NORTH

**Official name** Turkish Republic of Northern Cyprus
## PEOPLE
**Population** 173,000. **Density** 134/mi² (52/km²). **Capital** Nicosia (Lefkoşa). **Ethnic groups** Turkish 99%, Greek, Maronite, and others 1%. **Languages** Turkish. **Religions** Sunni Muslim.
## POLITICS
**Government** Republic. **Parties** Communal Liberation, National Unity, Republican Turkish, Revival. **Memberships** None.
## ECONOMY
**GDP** $185,000,000 **Per capita** $1,156. **Monetary unit** Turkish lira. **Trade partners** Turkey, U.K., W. Germany. **Exports** Food and livestock, manufactured goods, crude materials. **Imports** Manufactured goods, machinery and transportation equipment, mineral fuels.
## LAND
**Description** Northern part of the island of Cyprus. **Area** 1,295 mi² (3,355 km²). **Highest point** 3,360 ft (1,024 m). **Lowest point** Sea level.

**People.** The northern part of the island is occupied by Cypriots of Turkish ancestry who speak Turkish and are Sunni Muslims. The 1974 Turkish invasion resulted in a formal segregation of this settlement pattern. The Turkish Cypriot ancestors arrived on the island during the three centuries of Ottoman rule.

**Economy and the Land.** Since the partition of the island, North Cyprus has become somewhat isolated. Lacking in capital, experience, foreign aid, and official recognition, it remains agriculturally based and dependent upon Turkey for tourism, trade, and assistance. North Cyprus is dominated by the mostly barren Kyrenia Range.

**History and Politics.** In the Late Bronze Age—from 1600 to 1050 B.C.—a Greek culture flourished in Cyprus. Rule by various peoples followed, including Assyrians, Egyptians, Persians, Romans, Byzantines, French, and Venetians. The Ottoman Turks invaded in 1571. In the nineteenth century, Turkey ceded the island to the British as security for a loan. Although many Turks remained on Cyprus, the British declared it a crown colony in 1925. A growing desire for *enosis*, or union, with Greece led to rioting and guerrilla activity by Greek Cypriots. The Turkish government, opposed to absorption by Greece, desired separation into Greek and Turkish sectors. The present Greek government is committed to absolute separation between Greece and Cyprus. Cyprus became independent in 1960, with treaties forbidding either enosis or partition, but Greek-Turkish conflicts continued. A 1974 coup by pro-enosis forces led to an invasion by Turkey. The resulting partition runs east-west across the island dividing Nicosia, which serves as a capital for both countries. North Cyprus, which is not recognized internationally, maintains a separate government with a prime minister and a president. ∎

# CZECHOSLOVAKIA

**Official name** Czechoslovak Socialist Republic
## PEOPLE
**Population** 15,670,000. **Density** 317/mi² (123/km²). **Urban** 65%. **Capital** Prague, 1,193,513. **Ethnic groups** Czech 64%, Slovak 31%, Hungarian 4%. **Languages** Czech, Slovak, Hungarian. **Religions** Roman Catholic 77%, Protestant 20%, Orthodox 2%. **Life expectancy** 75 female, 68 male. **Literacy** 99%.
## POLITICS
**Government** Socialist republic. **Parties** Civic Forum, Communist, others. **Suffrage** Universal, over 18. **Memberships** CEMA, UN, Warsaw Pact. **Subdivisions** 2 socialist republics.
## ECONOMY
**GNP** $135,600,000,000 **Per capita** $8,754. **Monetary unit** Koruna (Crown). **Trade partners** U.S.S.R., E. Germany, Poland. **Exports** Machinery, iron and steel and other manufactures, railway vehicles. **Imports** Machinery, petroleum, manufactures, crude materials, chemicals, food.
## LAND
**Description** Eastern Europe, landlocked. **Area** 49,382 mi² (127,900 km²). **Highest point** Gerlachovka, 8,711 ft (2,655 m). **Lowest point** Bodrog River, 308 ft (94 m).

**People.** Czechs and Slovaks, descendants of Slavic tribes, predominate in Czechoslovakia. Characterized by a German-influenced culture, Czechs are concentrated in the regions of Bohemia and Moravia. Slovaks, whose culture was influenced by Hungarian Magyars, reside mainly in Slovakia. Czech and Slovak are official languages. Minorities include Hungarians, or Magyars; Ukrainians; Germans; Poles; and Gypsies, a rapidly growing group concentrated in Slovakia. Most people are Roman Catholic; the government licenses and pays clergy.

**Economy and the Land.** An industrial nation, Czechoslovakia has a centralized economy and one of the highest standards of living in Eastern-bloc countries. Coal deposits in Bohemia and Moravia form the base for industrial development, and Bohemia remains an economically important region. Nearly all agriculture is collectivized; despite high farm outputs, some food must be imported. Farming areas are found in the river valleys of north-central Bohemia and central Moravia, and Slovakia remains largely agricultural. A rolling western area, central hills, low mountains in the north and south, and the Carpathian Mountains in the east characterize Czechoslovakia's terrain. The climate is temperate.

**History and Politics.** Slavic tribes were established in the region by the sixth century. By the tenth century Hungarian Magyars had conquered the Slovaks in the region of Slovakia. Bohemia and Moravia became part of the Holy Roman Empire, and by the twelfth century Bohemia had become a strong kingdom that included Moravia and parts of Austria and Poland. Austria gained control of the area in 1620, and later became part of Austria-Hungary. With the collapse of Austria-Hungary at the end of World War I, an independent Czechoslovakia, consisting of Bohemia, Moravia, and Slovakia, was formed. Nazi Germany invaded Czechoslovakia in 1939, and the Soviet Union liberated the nation from German occupation in the winter and spring of 1944 to 1945. By 1948 Communists controlled the government, and political purges continued from 1949 to 1952. A 1968 invasion by the Soviet Union and Bulgaria, Hungary, Poland, and East Germany resulted when the Czechoslovakian Communist party leader introduced liberal reforms. Demonstrations forced the Communist party to agree to a coalition government in 1989. Vaclav Havel, a longtime opposition leader, was elected interim president until elections, which are planned for 1990. ■

# DENMARK

**Official name** Kingdom of Denmark
## PEOPLE
**Population** 5,135,000. **Density** 309/mi² (119/km²). **Urban** 86%. **Capital** Copenhagen, 473,000. **Ethnic groups** Danish (Scandinavian), German. **Languages** Danish. **Religions** Lutheran 91%. **Life expectancy** 78 female, 72 male. **Literacy** 99%.
## POLITICS
**Government** Constitutional monarchy. **Parties** Conservative, Liberal, Social Democratic, Socialist People's, others. **Suffrage** Universal, over 18. **Memberships** EC, NATO, OECD, UN. **Subdivisions** 14 counties, 2 independent cities.

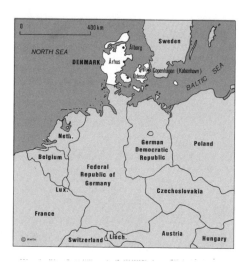

## ECONOMY
**GDP** $58,062,000,000 **Per capita** $11,589. **Monetary unit** Krone. **Trade partners** W. Germany, Sweden, U.K.. **Exports** Manufactures, machinery, meat, chemicals, furskins and other crude materials. **Imports** Manufactures, machinery, petroleum, chemicals, transportation equipment, food.
## LAND
**Description** Northern Europe. **Area** 16,638 mi² (43,092 km²). **Highest point** Yding Skovhøj, 568 ft (173 m). **Lowest point** Lammefjord, -23 ft (-7 m).
*The above information excludes Greenland and the Faeroe Is.*

**People.** Denmark is made up of the Jutland Peninsula and more than four hundred islands, about one hundred of which are inhabited. Greenland, which is situated northeast of Canada, and the Faeroe Islands, which are located between Scotland and Iceland in the North Atlantic, are also part of Denmark. Lutheran, Danish-speaking Scandinavians constitute the homogenous population of the peninsula and surrounding islands, although a German minority is concentrated near the West German border. The government provides extensive social services and programs. The literacy rate is high, and Denmark has made significant contributions to science, literature, and the arts.

**Economy and the Land.** Despite limited natural resources, Denmark has a diversified economy. Agriculture contributes to trade, and pork and bacon are important products. Postwar expansion focused on industry, and the country now imports the raw materials it lacks and exports finished products. The North Sea is the site of oil and natural gas deposits. On the Faeroe Islands, traditional fishing continues as the economic mainstay. Most of Denmark's terrain is rolling, with hills covering much of the peninsula and the nearby islands. Coastal regions are marked by fjords and sandy beaches, especially in the west. The climate is temperate, with North Sea winds moderating temperatures. The rugged Faeroe Islands are damp, cloudy, and windy.

**History and Politics.** By the first century, access to the sea had brought contact with other civilizations. This led to the Viking area, which lasted from the ninth to eleventh centuries and resulted in temporary Danish rule of England. In the fourteenth century, Sweden, Norway, Finland, Iceland, the Faeroe Islands, and Greenland were united under Danish rule. Sweden and Finland withdrew from the union in the 1500s, and Denmark lost Norway to Sweden in 1814. A constitutional monarchy was instituted in 1849. Late nineteenth-century social reform, reflected in a new constitution in 1915, laid the groundwork for Denmark's current welfare state. The country remained neutral in World War I. Iceland gained independence following the war but maintained its union with Denmark until 1944. Despite declared neutrality in World War II, Denmark was invaded and occupied by Germany from 1940 to 1945. Compromise and gradual change characterize Danish politics. Its foreign policy stresses ties with developing nations and peaceful solutions to international problems. ■

## DJIBOUTI

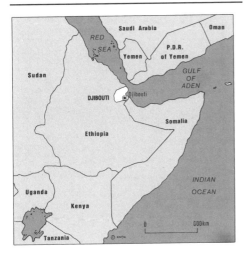

**Official name** Republic of Djibouti
**PEOPLE**
Population 333,000. **Density** 37/mi² (14/km²). **Urban** 78%. **Capital** Djibouti, 120,000. **Ethnic groups** Somali (Issa) 60%, Afar 35%. **Languages** French, Somali, Afar, Arabic. **Religions** Muslim 94%, Christian 6%. **Literacy** 20%.
**POLITICS**
**Government** Republic. **Parties** People's Progress Assembly. **Suffrage** Universal adult. **Memberships** AL, OAU, UN. **Subdivisions** 5 districts.
**ECONOMY**
GDP $339,000,000 **Per capita** $969. **Monetary unit** Franc. **Trade partners** Exports: France, Yemen, Somalia. Imports: France, Ethiopia, Japan. **Exports** Grain, transportation equipment, tobacco. **Imports** Food, textiles and other manufactures, transportation equipment, tobacco.
**LAND**
**Description** Eastern Africa. **Area** 8,958 mi² (23,200 km²). **Highest point** Moussa Ali, 6,768 ft (2,063 m). **Lowest point** Lake Assal, -502 ft (-153 m).

**People.** Characterized by strong cultural unity, Islam, and ethnic ties to Somalia, Somali Issas compose Djibouti's majority. Afars, who make up another main group, are also mostly Muslim and are linked ethnically with Ethiopia. Rivalry between the two groups has marked the nation's history. Because of unproductive land, much of the population is concentrated in the capital city of Djibouti.

**Economy and the Land.** Traditional nomadic herding continues as a way of life for many Djiboutians, despite heat, aridity, and limited grazing area. Several assets promote Djibouti as a port and trade center: a strategic position on the Gulf of Aden, an improved harbor, and a railway linking the city of Djibouti with Addis Ababa in Ethiopia. Marked by mountains that divide a coastal plain from a plateau region, the terrain is mostly desert. The climate is extremely hot and dry.

**History and Politics.** In the ninth century Arab missionaries introduced Islam to the population, and by the 1800s a pattern of conflict between the Issas and Afars had developed. The French purchased the port of Obcock from Afar sultans in 1862, and their territorial control expanded until the region became French Somaliland. The goal of the pro-independence Issas was defeated in elections in 1958 and 1967 when the majority voted for continued French control. The country became the French Territory of Afars and Issas in 1967, and as the Issa population grew, so did demands for independence. A 1977 referendum resulted in the independent Republic of Djibouti. ■

## DOMINICA

**Official name** Commonwealth of Dominica
**PEOPLE**
Population 86,000.
**Density** 282/mi² (109/km²). **Urban** 27%.
**Capital** Roseau, 9,348.
**Ethnic groups** Black 91%, mixed 6%, West Indian 2%. **Languages** English, French. **Religions** Roman Catholic 80%, Methodist, Anglican. **Life expectancy** 59 female, 57 male.
**Literacy** 94%.
**POLITICS**
**Government** Republic.
**Parties** Freedom, Labor.
**Suffrage** Universal, over 18. **Memberships** CW, OAS, UN. **Subdivisions** 10 parishes.
**ECONOMY**
GDP $85,000,000 **Per capita** $1,149. **Monetary unit** East Caribbean dollar.

**Trade partners** Exports: U.K., Jamaica, Trinidad and Tobago. Imports: U.S., U.K., Japan. **Exports** Bananas, soap, copra. **Imports** Manufactures, machinery, transportation equipment.
**LAND**
**Description** Caribbean island. **Area** 305 mi² (790 km²).
**Highest point** Morne Diablotin, 4,747 ft (1,447 m).
**Lowest point** Sea level.

**People.** Dominica's population consists of descendants of black Africans, brought to the island as slaves, and Carib Indians descended from early inhabitants. The Carib population is concentrated in the northeastern part of the island and maintains its own customs and lifestyle. English is widely spoken in urban areas, but villagers, who compose a majority, speak mainly a French-African blend, resulting from French rule and the importation of Africans.

**Economy and the Land.** Of volcanic origin, the island has soils suitable for farming, but a mountainous and densely-forested terrain limits land accessible to cultivation. Agriculture is the economic mainstay, although hurricanes have hindered production. Forestry and fishing offer potential for expansion, and a tropical climate and scenic landscape create a basis for tourism.

**History and Politics.** In the fourteenth century Carib Indians conquered the Arawak who originally inhabited the island. Although Christopher Columbus arrived at Dominica in 1493, Spanish settlement was discouraged by Carib hostilities. French and British rivalry for control of the island followed, and British possession was recognized in 1783. Dominica gained independence in 1978. ■

# DOMINICAN REPUBLIC

10,417 ft (3,175 m). **Lowest point** Lago Enriquillo, -131 ft (-40 m).

**People.** Occupying eastern Hispaniola Island, the Dominican Republic borders Haiti and has a population of mixed ancestry. Haitians, other blacks, Spaniards, and European Jews compose minority groups. Population growth has resulted in unemployment and made it difficult for the government to meet food and service needs.

**Economy and the Land.** Agriculture remains important, with sugar a main component of trade, and sugar refining a major manufacturing activity. Farmland is limited, however, by a northwest-to-southeast mountain range and an arid region west of the range. Mineral exploitation and iron and steel exports contribute to trade, and a number of American firms have subsidiaries here. Tourism is growing, aided by the warm, tropical climate.

**History and Politics.** In 1492 Christopher Columbus arrived at Hispaniola Island. Spanish colonists followed, and the Indian population was virtually wiped out, although some intermingling with Spanish probably occurred. In 1697 the western region of the island, which would become Haiti, was ceded to France. The entire island came under Haitian control as the Republic of Haiti in 1822, and an 1844 revolution established the independent Dominican Republic. Since independence the country has experienced periods of instability, evidenced by military coups and rule, United States military intervention and occupation, and human-rights abuses. Economic instability continues as the government attempts to diversify the economy and lessen dependence on the export of sugar. ■

# ECUADOR

**Official name** Dominican Republic
**PEOPLE**
**Population** 7,094,000. **Density** 379/mi$^2$ (146/km$^2$). **Urban** 56%. **Capital** Santo Domingo, 1,313,172. **Ethnic groups** Mulatto 73%, white 16%, black 11%. **Languages** Spanish. **Religions** Roman Catholic 95%. **Life expectancy** 65 female, 61 male. **Literacy** 67%.
**POLITICS**
**Government** Republic. **Parties** Liberation, Revolutionary, Social Christian Reformist, others. **Suffrage** Universal, over 18 or married. **Memberships** OAS, UN. **Subdivisions** 26 provinces, 1 district.
**ECONOMY**
**GDP** $4,651,000,000 **Per capita** $750. **Monetary unit** Peso. **Trade partners** Exports: U.S., Netherlands. Imports: U.S., Venezuela, Mexico. **Exports** Sugar, iron and steel, coffee, cocoa. **Imports** Petroleum, machinery, manufactures, chemicals, grain and other food.
**LAND**
**Description** Caribbean island (eastern Hispaniola). **Area** 18,704 mi$^2$ (48,442 km$^2$). **Highest point** Pico Duarte,

**Official name** Republic of Ecuador
**PEOPLE**
**Population** 10,650,000. **Density** 97/mi$^2$ (38/km$^2$). **Urban** 52%. **Capital** Quito, 890,355. **Ethnic groups** Mestizo 55%, Amerindian 25%, Spanish 10%, black 10%.

**Languages** Spanish, Quechua, indigenous. **Religions** Roman Catholic 95%. **Life expectancy** 66 female, 62 male. **Literacy** 84%.

## POLITICS
**Government** Republic. **Parties** Democratic Left, Popular Democratic, Social Christian, others. **Suffrage** Universal, over 18. **Memberships** OAS, OPEC, UN. **Subdivisions** 20 provinces.

## ECONOMY
**GDP** $15,982,000,000 **Per capita** $1,731. **Monetary unit** Sucre. **Trade partners** Exports: U.S., Panama. Imports: U.S., Japan, Brazil. **Exports** Petroleum, bananas, fish, coffee. **Imports** Machinery, iron and steel and other manufactures, chemicals.

## LAND
**Description** Western South America. **Area** 109,484 mi² (283,561 km²). **Highest point** Chimborazo, 20,702 ft (6,310 m). **Lowest point** Sea level.

**People.** Ecuador's ethnicity was established by an indigenous Indian population and Spanish colonists. Minority whites, of Spanish or other European descent, live mainly in urban areas or operate large farms called haciendas. Of mixed Spanish-Indian blood, mestizos compose over half the population, although economic and political power is concentrated among whites. Minority Indians speak Quechua or other Indian languages and maintain traditional customs in Andean villages or nomadic jungle tribes. Blacks are concentrated on the northern coastal plain. Recent trends show a movement from the interior highlands to the fertile coastal plain and a rural-to-urban shift. A history of economic inequality has produced a literary and artistic tradition that has focused on social reform.

**Economy and the Land.** Despite an oil boom in the 1970s, Ecuador remains underdeveloped. Minor oil production began in 1911, but since a 1967 petroleum discovery in the *oriente*, a jungle region east of the Andes, Ecuador has become an oil exporter and a member of the Organization of Petroleum Exporting Countries (OPEC). Agriculture remains important for much of the population, although primitive and inefficient practices continue among the poor. Rich soils of the *costa*, extending from the Pacific to the Andes, support most of the export crops. Forestry and fishing have growth potential, and the waters around the Galápagos Islands are rich in tuna. Manufacturing is mainly devoted to meeting domestic needs. The oriente and costa lie on either side of the sierra, a region of highland plateaus between the two Andean chains. Varied altitudes result in a climate ranging from tropical in the lowlands to temperate in the plateaus and cold in the high mountains. A variety of wildlife inhabits the Galápagos Islands, five large and nine small islands about 600 miles (966 km) off Ecuador's coast in the Pacific Ocean.

**History and Politics.** In the fifteenth century Incas conquered and subsequently united the area's various tribes. In the 1500s the Spanish gained control, using Indians and African slaves to work the plantations. Weakened by the Napoleonic Wars, Spain lost control of Ecuador in 1822, and Simón Bolívar united the independent state with the Republic of Greater Colombia. Ecuador left the union as a separate republic in 1830, and subsequent years saw instability and rule by presidents, dictators, and juntas. From 1925 to 1948 no leader was able to complete a full term in office. A new constitution was established in 1978, and a 1979 election installed a president who died in a plane crash in 1981. A 1988 election brought a leftward shift in the government, which is now challenged by a large foreign debt. ∎

# EGYPT

**Official name** Arab Republic of Egypt
## PEOPLE
**Population** 52,830,000. **Density** 137/mi² (53/km²). **Urban** 46%. **Capital** Cairo, 6,052,836. **Ethnic groups** Egyptian (Eastern Hamitic) 90%. **Languages** Arabic. **Religions** Muslim 94%, Coptic Christian and others 6%. **Life expectancy** 60 female, 57 male. **Literacy** 38%.
## POLITICS
**Government** Socialist republic. **Parties** National Democratic, Muslim Brotherhood, New Wafd, Socialist Labor, Socialist Liberal. **Suffrage** Universal, over 18. **Memberships** AL, OAU, UN. **Subdivisions** 26 governorates.
## ECONOMY
**GDP** $39,421,000,000 **Per capita** $848. **Monetary unit** Pound. **Trade partners** Exports: Italy, Israel, Romania. Imports: U.S., W. Germany, Italy. **Exports** Petroleum, cotton, textiles, food. **Imports** Manufactures, machinery, grain and other food, chemicals.
## LAND
**Description** Northeastern Africa. **Area** 386,662 mi² (1,001,449 km²). **Highest point** Mt. Katrina, 8,668 ft (2,642 m). **Lowest point** Qattara Depression, -436 ft (-133 m).

**People.** Egypt's population is relatively homogeneous, and Egyptians compose the largest group. Descended from ancient Nile Valley inhabitants, Egyptians have intermixed somewhat with Mediterranean and Asiatic peoples in the north and with black Africans in the south. Minorities include Bedouins, Arabic-speaking desert nomads; Nubians, black descendants of migrants from the Sudan; and Copts, a Christian group. Islam, the major religion, is also a cultural force, and many Christians as well as Muslims follow Islamic lifestyles. A desert terrain confines about 99 percent of the population to less than 4 percent of the land, in the fertile Nile River valley and along the Suez Canal.

**Economy and the Land.** Egypt's economy has suffered from wars, shifting alliances, and limited natural resources. Government-sponsored expansion and reform in the 1950s concentrated on manufacturing, and most industry was nationalized during the 1960s. Agriculture, centered in the Nile Valley, remains an economic mainstay, and cotton, a principal crop, is both exported and processed. Petroleum, found mainly in the Gulf of Suez, will most likely continue its economic role, and tourism will remain a contributor. Much of Egypt is desert, with hills and mountains in the east and along the Nile River, while the climate is warm and dry.

**History and Politics.** Egypt's recorded history began when King Menes united the region in about 3100 B.C., beginning a series of Egyptian dynasties. Art and architecture flourished during the Age of the Pyramids, from 2700 to 2200 B.C. In time native dynasties gave way to foreign conquerors, including Alexander the Great in the fourth century B.C. The Coptic Christian church emerged between the fourth and sixth centuries A.D., but in the 600s Arabs conquered the area and established Islam as the main religion. Ruling parties changed frequently, and in 1517 the Ottoman Turks added Egypt to their empire. Upon completion of the strategically important Suez Canal in 1869, foreign interest in Egypt increased. In 1875 Egypt sold its share of the canal to Britain, and a rebellion against foreign intervention ended with British occupation in 1882. Turkey sided with Germany in World War I, and the United Kingdom made Egypt a British protectorate in 1914. The country became an independent monarchy in 1922, but the British presence remained. In 1945 Egypt and six other nations formed the Arab League. The founding of Israel in 1948 initiated an era of Arab-Israeli hostilities, including periodic warfare in which Egypt often had a major role. Dissatisfaction over dealings with Israel and continued British occupation of the Suez Canal led to the overthrow of the king, and Egypt became a republic in 1953. Following a power struggle, Gamal Abdel Nasser was elected president in 1956, and the British agreed to remove their troops. Upon the death of Nasser in 1970, Vice President Anwar Sadat came to power. Negotiations between Egyptian president Sadat and Israeli prime minister Menachem Begin began in 1977, and in 1979 the leaders signed a peace treaty ending conflicts between Egypt and Israel. As a result, Egypt was suspended from the Arab League. In 1981 President Sadat was assassinated and was succeeded by Hosni Mubarek, who is faced with pressure from Muslim fundamentalists and discontent over the economy. ■

# EL SALVADOR

**Official name** Republic of El Salvador
**PEOPLE**
**Population** 5,260,000. **Density** 647/mi² (250/km²). **Urban** 39%. **Capital** San Salvador, 459,902. **Ethnic groups**

Mestizo 89%, Amerindian 10%, white 1%. **Languages** Spanish, Nahua. **Religions** Roman Catholic 97%. **Life expectancy** 67 female, 63 male. **Literacy** 62%.
**POLITICS**
**Government** Republic. **Parties** Christian Democratic, National Conciliation, National Republican Alliance, others. **Suffrage** Universal, over 18. **Memberships** OAS, UN. **Subdivisions** 14 departments.
**ECONOMY**
**GDP** $5,732,000,000 **Per capita** $1,169. **Monetary unit** Colon. **Trade partners** Exports: U.S., W. Germany, Guatemala. Imports: U.S., Guatemala, Mexico. **Exports** Coffee and other food, cotton, textiles, paper, clothing. **Imports** Petroleum, pharmaceuticals and other chemicals, manufactures, food.
**LAND**
**Description** Central America. **Area** 8,124 mi² (21,041 km²). **Highest point** Cerro El Pital, 8,957 ft (2,730 m). **Lowest point** Sea level.

**People.** Most Salvadorans are Spanish-speaking mestizos, people of Spanish-Indian descent. An Indian minority is mainly descended from the Pipil, a Nahuatl group related to the Aztecs. The Nahuatl dialect is still spoken among some Indians. El Salvador, the smallest Central American country in area, has the highest population density in mainland Latin America, with inhabitants concentrated in a central valley-and-plateau region.

**Economy and the Land.** El Salvador's economy has been plagued by political instability, low literacy, high population density, and high unemployment. Agriculture remains the economic mainstay, and most arable land has been cultivated. Coffee, cotton, and sugar are produced on large commercial plantations, while subsistence farmers rely on corn, bean, and sorghum crops. East-to-west mountain ranges divide El Salvador into a southern coastal region, central valleys and plateaus, and northern mountains. The climate is subtropical.

**History and Politics.** Maya and Pipil predominated in the area of El Salvador prior to Spanish arrival. In the 1500s Pipil defeated invading Spaniards but were conquered in a subsequent invasion. In 1821 the Spanish-controlled Central American colonies declared independence, and in 1823 they united as the Federation of Central America. By 1838 the problem-ridden federation was in a state of collapse, and as the union dissolved, El Salvador became independent. Instability and revolution soon followed. The expansion of the coffee economy in the late 1800s exacerbated problems by further concentrating wealth and power among large-estate holders. A dictatorship from 1931 to 1944 was followed by instability under various military rulers. In 1969 a brief war with Honduras arose from resentment toward land-ownership laws, border disputes, and nationalistic feelings following a series of soccer games between the two countries. Discontent increased throughout the seventies until a civil war erupted between leftist guerrillas and government forces, accompanied by right-wing death squads and human-rights abuses by the government. During the 1980s, the United States provided extensive military and economic aid in an attempt to moderate the government. However, the election of rightist Alfredo Cristiani in 1989 escalated guerrilla activity. ∎

# EQUATORIAL GUINEA

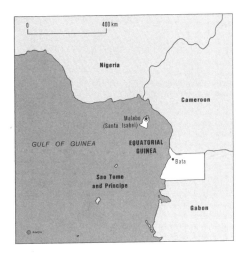

**Official name** Republic of Equatorial Guinea
**PEOPLE**
**Population** 357,000. **Density** 33/mi$^2$ (13/km$^2$). **Urban** 60%. **Capital** Malabo, Bioko I., 30,710. **Ethnic groups** Fang 80%, Bubi 15%. **Languages** Spanish, indigenous, English. **Religions** Roman Catholic 83%, other Christian, tribal religionist. **Life expectancy** 46 female, 42 male. **Literacy** 55%.
**POLITICS**
**Government** Republic. **Parties** Democratic. **Suffrage** Universal adult. **Memberships** OAS, UN. **Subdivisions** 7 provinces.
**ECONOMY**
**GDP** $90,000,000 **Per capita** $321. **Monetary unit** CFA franc. **Trade partners** Spain, Cameroon. **Exports** Cocoa, coffee, wood. **Imports** Food, chemicals, textiles.
**LAND**
**Description** Central Africa. **Area** 10,831 mi$^2$ (28,051 km$^2$). **Highest point** Pico de Santa Isabel, Bioko I., 9,869 ft (3,008 m). **Lowest point** Sea level.

**People.** Several ethnic groups inhabit Equatorial Guinea's five islands, as well as the mainland region of Río Muni. Although the majority Fang, a Bantu people, are concentrated in Río Muni, they also inhabit Bioko, the largest island. Found mainly on Bioko Island are the minority Bubi, also a Bantu people. Coastal groups known as *playeros*, or "those who live on the beach," live on both the mainland and the small islands. The Fernandino, of mixed African heritage, are concentrated on Bioko. Equatorial Guinea is the only black African state with Spanish as its official language.

**Economy and the Land.** Equatorial Guinea's economy is based on agriculture and forestry; cocoa, coffee, and wood are the main products. Cocoa production is centered on fertile Bioko Island, and coffee in Río Muni. The mainland's rain forests also provide for forestry. Mineral exploration has revealed petroleum and natural gas in the waters north of Bioko, and petroleum, iron ore, and radioactive materials exist in Río Muni. Bioko is of volcanic origin, and Río Muni consists of a coastal plain and interior hills. The climate is tropical, with high-temperatures and humidity.

**History and Politics.** Pygmies most likely inhabited the Río Muni area prior to the thirteenth century, when mainland Bubi came to Bioko. From the seventeenth to the nineteenth centuries, Bantu migrations brought first the coastal tribes and then the Fang. Portugal claimed Bioko and part of the mainland in the 1400s, then ceded them to Spain in 1778. From 1827 to 1843, British antislavery activities were based on Bioko, which became the home of many former slaves, the ancestors of the Fernandino population. In 1959 the area became the Spanish Territory of the Gulf of Guinea, and the name was changed to Equatorial Guinea in 1963. Independence was achieved in 1968, and a subsequent dictatorship resulted in human-rights violations, the flight of many residents, and a general deterioration of the economy. A 1979 military coup ended the regime, but ethnic power rivalries continue. The official foreign policy is nonalignment. ∎

# ETHIOPIA

**Official name** People's Democratic Republic of Ethiopia
**PEOPLE**
**Population** 49,628,000. **Density** 103/mi$^2$ (40/km$^2$). **Urban** 12%. **Capital** Addis Ababa, 1,412,575. **Ethnic groups** Oromo (Galla) 40%, Amhara and Tigrean 32%, Sidamo 9%, Shankella 6%, Somali 6%. **Languages** Amharic, Tigrinya, Orominga, Arabic. **Religions** Muslim 45%, Ethiopian Orthodox 35%, Animist 15%. **Life expectancy** 43 female, 39 male. **Literacy** 4%.
**POLITICS**
**Government** Socialist republic. **Parties** Workers'. **Suffrage** Universal, over 18. **Memberships** OAU, UN. **Subdivisions** 25 administrative regions, 5 autonomous regions.
**ECONOMY**
**GDP** $4,857,000,000 **Per capita** $153. **Monetary unit** Birr. **Trade partners** Exports: U.S., W. Germany, Japan. Imports: U.S.S.R., U.S., W. Germany. **Exports** Coffee,

animal hides and other crude materials, petroleum.
**Imports** Machinery, petroleum, manufactures, transportation equipment, chemicals, food.
**LAND**
**Description** Eastern Africa. **Area** 483,123 mi$^2$ (1,251,282 km$^2$). **Highest point** Ras Dashen Mtn., 15,158 ft (4,620 m). **Lowest point** Asālē, -381 ft (-116 m).

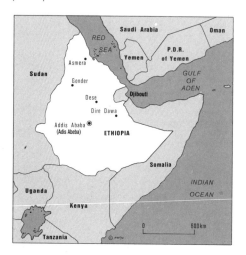

**People.** Ethiopia is ethnically, linguistically, and religiously diverse, but the Oromo, Amhara, and Tigre predominate. The Oromo include agricultural Muslims, Christians, and nomadic herders with traditional religions. Mainly Christian and also agricultural, the Amhara have dominated the country politically. The official language is Amharic; Arabic and indigenous languages are also spoken. Ethiopia's boundaries encompass over forty ethnic groups.

**Economy and the Land.** In addition to problems caused by political instability, drought has plagued Ethiopia's agricultural economy. Existing problems of soil erosion and deforestation resulted in disaster in 1982 when planting-season rains failed to fall in much of the country. The consequences of drought are especially severe in the north and west. Subsistence farming remains a major activity, and much arable land is uncultivated. Mines produce gold, copper, and platinum, and there is potential for expansion. A central plateau is split diagonally by the Great Rift Valley, with lowlands on the west and plains in the southeast. The climate is temperate on the plateau and hot in the lowlands.

**History and Politics.** Ethiopia's history is one of the oldest in the world. Its ethnic patterns were established by indigenous Cushites and Semite settlers, who probably arrived from Arabia about three thousand years ago. Christianity was introduced in the early fourth century. During the 1800s modern Ethiopia began to develop under Emperor Menelik II. Ras Tafari Makonnen became emperor in 1930, taking the name Haile Selassie. Italians invaded in the 1930s and occupied the country until 1941, when Selassie returned to the throne. Discontent with the feudal society increased until Selassie was ousted by the military in 1974. Reform programs and the change in leadership have done little to ease political tensions, which have sometimes erupted in governmental and civilian violence. Government troops continue their battle with separatists in Eritrea, a former Italian colony and autonomous province incorporated into Ethiopia in 1962. In the 1980s, widespread famine and drought aggravated political problems. Internal strife between the Marxist government and secessionist factions hampered worldwide relief efforts. ∎

# FAEROE ISLANDS See DENMARK.

# FALKLAND ISLANDS

**Official name** Falkland Islands
**PEOPLE**
**Population** 2,000. **Density** 0.4/mi$^2$ (0.2/km$^2$). **Urban** 59%. **Capital** Stanley, East Falkland I., 1,200. **Ethnic groups** British descent. **Languages** English. **Religions** Anglican, United Free Church, Roman Catholic.
**POLITICS**
**Government** Dependent territory (U.K.). **Suffrage** Universal, over 18. **Memberships** None. **Subdivisions** None. **Monetary unit** Pound. **Trade partners** Exports: U.K., Netherlands, Japan. Imports: Netherlands Antilles, Japan, U.K.. **Exports** Wool, animal hides. **Imports** Food, alcoholic beverages, wood, clothing, manufactures.
**LAND**
**Description** South Atlantic islands (east of Argentina). **Area** 4,700 mi$^2$ (12,173 km$^2$). **Highest point** Mt. Usborne, East Falkland I., 2,312 ft (705 m). **Lowest point** Sea level.

**People.** Most Falkland Island inhabitants are of British descent, an ancestry reflected in their official language, English, and majority Anglican religion.

**Economy and the Land.** Sheep raising is the main activity, supplemented by fishing. In 1982 Britain funded the Falkland Islands Development Corporation, which began operation in 1984. Situated about 300 miles (482 km) east of southern Argentina, East and West Falkland compose the main and largest islands. Numerous small islands are classified as dependencies. The climate is cool, damp, and windy.

**History and Politics.** Although the British sighted the islands in 1592, the French established the first settlement in 1764, on East Falkland. The British settled on West Falkland the next year. Spain, which ruled the Argentina territories to the west, purchased the French area and drove out the British in 1770. When Argentina gained independence from Spain in 1816, it claimed Spain's right to the islands. Britain reasserted its rule over the islands in the 1830s. The Falklands became a British colony in 1892, with dependencies annexed in 1908. Continued Argentine claim resulted in a 1982 Argentine invasion and occupation. The British won the subsequent battle and continue to govern the Falklands. The dependencies of South Georgia and the South Sandwich Islands became a separate British colony in 1985. ∎

# FIJI

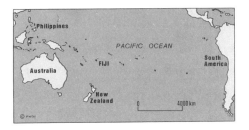

British, who established sugar plantations and brought indentured Indian laborers. The country became independent in 1970. After declaring itself a republic in 1987, Fiji was ejected from the British Commonwealth. ∎

# FINLAND

**Official name** Republic of Fiji
## PEOPLE
**Population** 720,000. **Density** 102/mi$^2$ (39/km$^2$). **Urban** 41%. **Capital** Suva, Viti Levu I., 69,665. **Ethnic groups** Indian 49%, Fijian 46%, European 5%. **Languages** English, Fijian, Hindustani. **Religions** Methodist and other Christian 51%, Hindu 40%, Muslim 8%. **Life expectancy** 71 female, 67 male. **Literacy** 79%.
## POLITICS
**Government** Republic. **Parties** Alliance, Labor, National Federation. **Suffrage** Universal adult. **Memberships** UN. **Subdivisions** 14 provinces.
## ECONOMY
**GDP** $1,162,000,000. **Per capita** $1,672. **Monetary unit** Dollar. **Trade partners** Exports: U.K., U.S., Malaysia. Imports: Australia, Japan, New Zealand. **Exports** Sugar, copra, fish. **Imports** Textiles and other manufactures, petroleum, food, machinery, chemicals.
## LAND
**Description** South Pacific islands. **Area** 7,078 mi$^2$ (18,333 km$^2$). **Highest point** Tomanivi, Viti Levu I., 4,341 ft (1,323 m). **Lowest point** Sea level.

**People.** Fiji's majority population is descended from laborers brought from British India between 1879 and 1916. Most Indians are Hindu, but a Muslim minority exists. Native Fijians are of Melanesian and Polynesian heritage, and most are Christian. English is the official language, a result of British rule; but Indians speak Hindustani, and the main Fijian dialect is Bauan. Tensions between the two groups occasionally arise because plantation owners, who are mainly Indian, must often lease their land from Fijians, the major landowners. About a hundred of the several hundred islands are inhabited.

**Economy and the Land.** The traditional sugar cane crop continues as the basis of Fiji's economy, and agricultural diversification is a current goal. Tourism is another economic contributor, and expansion of forestry is planned. Terrain varies from island to island and is characterized by mountains, valleys, rain forests, and fertile plains. The tropical islands are cooled by ocean breezes.

**History and Politics.** Little is known of Fiji's history prior to the arrival of Europeans. Melanesians probably migrated from Indonesia, followed by Polynesian settlers in the second century. After a Dutch navigator sighted Fiji in 1643, Captain James Cook of Britain visited the island in the eighteenth century. The nineteenth century saw the arrival of European missionaries, traders, and whalers, and several native wars. In 1874 tribal chiefs ceded Fiji to the

**Official name** Republic of Finland
## PEOPLE
**Population** 4,985,000. **Density** 38/mi$^2$ (15/km$^2$). **Urban** 64%. **Capital** Helsinki, 484,263. **Ethnic groups** Finnish (mixed Scandinavian and Baltic), Swedish, Lappic, Gypsy, Tatar. **Languages** Finnish, Swedish, Lapp. **Religions** Lutheran 89%, Eastern Orthodox 1%. **Life expectancy** 78 female, 70 male. **Literacy** 99%.
## POLITICS
**Government** Republic. **Parties** Center-Liberal, Conservative, People's Democratic League, Social Democratic, others. **Suffrage** Universal, over 18. **Memberships** OECD, UN. **Subdivisions** 12 provinces.
## ECONOMY
**GDP** $54,113,000,000. **Per capita** $11,077. **Monetary unit** Markka. **Trade partners** Exports: U.S.S.R., Sweden, U.K. Imports: U.S.S.R., W. Germany, Sweden. **Exports** Paper and other manufactures, machinery, wood and other crude materials. **Imports** Manufactures, machinery, petroleum, transportation equipment, crude materials.
## LAND
**Description** Northern Europe. **Area** 130,559 mi$^2$ (338,145 km$^2$). **Highest point** Haltiatunturi, 4,357 ft (1,328 m). **Lowest point** Sea level.

**People.** The mainly Finnish population includes minorities of Swedes—a result of past Swedish rule—and indigenous Lapps. As part of northern Finland lies within the Arctic Circle, population is concentrated in the south. Finland's rich cultural tradition has contributed much to the arts. Its highly developed social-welfare programs provide free education through the university level, as well as national health insurance.

**Economy and the Land.** Much of Finland's economy is based on its rich forests, which support trade and manufacturing activities. The steel industry is also important. Agriculture focuses on dairy farming and livestock raising; hence many fruits and vegetables must be imported. Coastal islands and lowlands, a central lake region, and northern hills mark Finland's scenic terrain. Summers in the south and central regions are warm, and winters long and cold. Northern Finland—located in the "Land of the Midnight Sun"—has periods of uninterrupted daylight in the summer and darkness in the winter.

**History and Politics.** The indigenous nomadic Lapps migrated north in the first century when the Finns arrived, probably from west-central Russia. A Russian-Swedish struggle for control of the area ended with Swedish rule in the 1100s. Finland was united with Denmark from the fourteenth through the sixteenth centuries. Russia and Sweden fought several wars for control of the country. In 1809 Finland became an autonomous grand duchy within the Russian Empire. After the Russian czar was overthrown in the 1917 Bolshevik Revolution, the new Russian government recognized Finland's declaration of independence. During World War II, Finland fought against the Soviets and, by the peace treaty signed in 1947, lost a portion of its land to the Soviet Union. During the postwar years, Finland and Russia renewed their economic and cultural ties and signed an agreement of friendship and cooperation. Foreign policy emphasizes friendly relations with the Soviet Union and Scandinavia.

# FRANCE

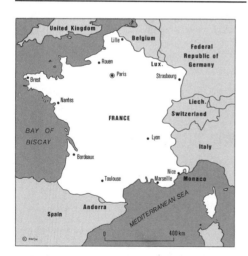

**Official name** French Republic
**PEOPLE**
**Population** 56,210,000. **Density** 266/mi$^2$ (103/km$^2$).
**Urban** 73%. **Capital** Paris, 2,127,100. **Ethnic groups** French (mixed Celtic, Latin, and Teutonic). **Languages** French. **Religions** Roman Catholic 90%, Protestant 2%, Jewish 1%, Muslim 1%. **Life expectancy** 79 female, 71 male. **Literacy** 99%.

**POLITICS**
**Government** Republic. **Parties** Left Radical Movement, Rally for the Republic, Socialist, Union for Democracy, others. **Suffrage** Universal, over 18. **Memberships** EC, NATO, OECD, UN. **Subdivisions** 95 departments, 1 territory.
**ECONOMY**
**GDP** $510,333,000,000 **Per capita** $9,275. **Monetary unit** Franc. **Trade partners** Exports: W. Germany, Italy, U.S. Imports: W. Germany, Italy, Belgium. **Exports** Manufactures, machinery, chemicals, transportation equipment, food. **Imports** Manufactures, machinery, petroleum, chemicals, food.
**LAND**
**Description** Western Europe. **Area** 211,208 mi$^2$ (547,026 km$^2$). **Highest point** Mt. Blanc, 15,771 ft (4,807 m). **Lowest point** Lac de Cazaux et de Sanguinet, -10 ft (-3 m).
*The above information excludes French overseas departments.*

**People.** Many centuries ago, Celtic and Teutonic tribes and Latins established France's current ethnic patterns. The French language developed from the Latin of invading Romans but includes Celtic and Germanic influences as well. Language and customs vary somewhat from region to region, but most people who speak dialects also speak French. France has long contributed to learning and the arts, and Paris is a world cultural center. In addition to mainland divisions, the country has overseas departments and territories.

**Economy and the Land.** The French economy is highly developed. The nation is a leader in agriculture and industry; its problems of inflation and unemployment are common to other modern countries. Soils in the north and northeast are especially productive, and grapes are grown in the south. Minerals include iron ore and bauxite. Industry is diversified, centered in the Paris manufacturing area, and tourism is important. About two-thirds of the country is flat to rolling, and about one-third is mountainous, including the Pyrenees in the south and the Alps in the east. In the west and north, winters are cool and summers mild. Climate varies with altitude. The southern coast has a Mediterranean climate with hot summers and mild winters.

**History and Politics.** In ancient times Celtic tribes inhabited the area that encompasses present-day France. The Romans, who called the region Gaul, began to invade about 200 B.C., and by the 50s B.C. the entire region had come under Roman rule. Northern Germanic tribes—including the Franks, Visigoths, and Burgundians—spread throughout the region as Roman control weakened, and the Franks defeated the Romans in A.D. 486. In the 800s Charlemagne greatly expanded Frankish-controlled territory, which was subsequently divided into three kingdoms. The western kingdom and part of the central kingdom included modern France. In 987 the Capetian dynasty began when Hugh Capet came to the throne, an event which is often considered the start of the French nation. During subsequent centuries, the power of the kings increased and France became a leading world power. Ambitious projects, such as the palace built by Louis XIV at Versailles, and several military campaigns, resulted in financial difficulties. The failing economy and divisions between rich and poor led to the French

## Places and Possessions of FRANCE

| Entity | Status | Area | Population | Capital/Population |
|---|---|---|---|---|
| **Corsica** (Mediterranean island) | Part of France | 3,367 mi² (8,720 km²) | 255,000 | None |
| **French Guiana** (Northeastern South America) | Overseas department | 35,135 mi² (91,000 km²) | 96,000 | Cayenne, 38,091 |
| **French Polynesia** (South Pacific islands) | Overseas territory | 1,544 mi² (4,000 km²) | 194,000 | Papeete, 23,496 |
| **French Southern and Antarctic Territories** (Indian Ocean islands) | Overseas territory | 3,000 mi² (7,770 km²) | 175 | Port-aux-Français |
| **Guadeloupe** (Caribbean islands) | Overseas department | 687 mi² (1,780 km²) | 346,000 | Basse-Terre, 13,656 |
| **Kerguelen Islands** (Indian Ocean) | Part of French Southern and Antarctic Territories | 2,700 mi² (6,993 km²) | 75 | None |
| **Martinique** (Caribbean island) | Overseas department | 425 mi² (1,100 km²) | 347,000 | Fort-de-France, 99,844 |
| **Mayotte** (Southeastern African islands) | Territorial collectivity | 144 mi² (374 km²) | 82,000 | Dzaoudzi (de facto) and Mamoudzou (future), 5,865 |
| **New Caledonia** (South Pacific islands) | Overseas territory | 7,358 mi² (19,058 km²) | 153,000 | Nouméa, 60,112 |
| **Reunion** (Indian Ocean island) | Overseas department | 969 mi² (2,510 km²) | 590,000 | St. Denis, 84,400 |
| **St. Pierre and Miquelon** (North Atlantic islands; south of Newfoundland) | Territorial collectivity | 93 mi² (242 km²) | 6,800 | St. Pierre, 5,371 |
| **Wallis and Futuna** (South Pacific islands) | Overseas territory | 98 mi² (255 km²) | 16,000 | Mata-Utu, 815 |

Revolution in 1789 and the First French Republic in 1792. Napoleon Bonaparte, who had gained prominence during the revolution, overthrew the government in 1799 and established the First Empire, which ended in 1815 with his defeat at Waterloo in Belgium. The subsequent monarchy resulted in discontent, and a 1848 revolution established the Second French Republic with an elected president, who in turn proclaimed himself emperor and set up the Second Empire in 1852. Following a war with Prussia in 1870, the emperor was ousted, and the Third Republic began. This republic ended Germany's invasion in World War I but ended in 1940 when invading Germans defeated the French. By 1942 the Nazis had control of the entire country. The Allies liberated France in 1944, and General Charles de Gaulle headed a provisional government until 1946, when the Fourth Republic was established. Colonial revolts in Africa and French Indochina took their toll on the economy during the fifties. Controversy over a continuing Algerian war for independence brought de Gaulle to power once more and resulted in the Fifth Republic in 1958. Dissension and national strikes erupted during the 1960s, a result of dissatisfaction with the government, and de Gaulle resigned in 1969. In 1987 François Mitterand was re-elected, giving the Socialists a plurality.

■

## FRENCH GUIANA

**Official name** Department of Guiana
**PEOPLE**
**Population** 96,000. **Density** 2.7/mi² (1.1/km²). **Urban** 73%. **Capital** Cayenne, 38,093. **Ethnic groups** Black or mulatto 66%; white 12%; East Indian, Chinese, and Amerindian 12%. **Languages** French. **Religions** Roman Catholic. **Life expectancy** 72 female, 65 male. **Literacy** 82%.

# FRENCH GUIANA

## POLITICS
**Government** Overseas department (France). **Parties** Democratic Action, Rally for the Republic, Socialist, Union for French Democracy. **Suffrage** Universal, over 18. **Memberships** None. **Subdivisions** 2 arrondissements.

## ECONOMY
GDP $181,000,000 **Per capita** $2,742. **Monetary unit** French franc. **Trade partners** Exports: U.S., Japan, France, Guadeloupe. Imports: France, Trinidad and Tobago. **Exports** Fish and shellfish, machinery, wood. **Imports** Manufactures, food, machinery, petroleum, transportation equipment.

## LAND
**Description** Northeastern South America. **Area** 35,135 mi$^2$ (91,000 km$^2$). **Highest point** 2,723 ft (830 m). **Lowest point** Sea level.

**People.** French Guiana has a majority population of black descendants of African slaves and people of mixed African-European ancestry. Population is concentrated in the more accessible coastal area, but the interior wilderness is home to minority Indians and the descendants of slaves who fled to pursue traditional African lifestyles. French is the predominant language, but a French-English creole is also spoken. Two Indo-Chinese refugee settlements were established in 1977 and 1979.

**Economy and the Land.** Shrimp production and a growing timber industry are French Guiana's economic mainstays. The land remains largely undeveloped, however, and reliance on French aid continues. Agriculture is limited by wilderness, but mineral deposits offer potential for mining. The fertile coastal plains of the north give way to hills and mountains along the Brazilian border. Rain forests cover much of the landscape, which features a tropical climate.

**History and Politics.** Indigenous Indians and a hot climate defeated France's attempt at settlement in the early 1600s. The first permanent French settlement was established in 1634, and the area became a French colony in 1667. For almost one hundred years, beginning in the 1850s, penal colonies such as Devils Island brought an influx of European prisoners. The region became a French overseas department in 1946. A minority nationalist group strives for greater autonomy. ■

# FRENCH POLYNESIA

**Official name** Territory of French Polynesia
## PEOPLE
**Population** 194,000. **Density** 126/mi$^2$ (49/km$^2$). **Urban** 62%. **Capital** Papeete, Tahiti I., 23,496. **Ethnic groups** Polynesian 69%, European 12%, Chinese 10%. **Languages** French, Tahitian, Chinese. **Religions** Evangelical and other Protestant 55%, Roman Catholic 32%. **Life expectancy** 63 female, 60 male. **Literacy** 98%.
## POLITICS
**Government** Overseas territory (France). **Parties** Amuitahiraa Mo Porinesia, Ia Mana, Pupu Here Ai'a, Tahoeraa Huiraatira. **Suffrage** Universal adult. **Memberships** None. **Subdivisions** 5 circumscriptions.
## ECONOMY
GDP $1,146,000,000 **Per capita** $7,640. **Monetary unit** CFP franc. **Trade partners** Exports: France, U.S., Italy. Imports: France, U.S., New Zealand. **Exports** Pearls, machinery, copra, precision instruments. **Imports** Manufactures, meat and other food, machinery, transportation equipment.
## LAND
**Description** South Pacific islands. **Area** 1,544 mi$^2$ (4,000 km$^2$). **Highest point** Mt. Orohena, Tahiti I., 7,352 ft (2,241 m). **Lowest point** Sea level.

**People.** Most inhabitants are Polynesian, with minorities including Chinese and French. More than one hundred islands compose the five archipelagoes, and population and commercial activity is concentrated in Papeete on Tahiti. Although per capita income is relatively high, wealth is not equally distributed. Emigration from the poorer islands to Tahiti is common. Polynesia's reputation as a tropical paradise has attracted European and American writers and artists, including French painter Paul Gauguin.

**Economy and the Land.** The islands' economy is based on natural resources; coconut, mother-of-pearl, and tourism contribute to the economy. This South Pacific territory, located south of the equator and midway between South America and Australia, is spread over roughly 1.5 million square miles (3.9 million square km) and is made up of the Marquesas Islands, the Society Islands, the Tuamotu Archipelago, the Gambier Islands, and the Austral Islands. The Marquesas, known for their beauty, form the northernmost group. The Society Islands, southwest of the Marquesas, include Tahiti and Bora-Bora, both popular tourist spots. The Tuamoto Archipelago lies south of the Marquesas and east of the Society Islands, the Gambier Islands are situated at the southern tip of the Tuamotu group, and the Austral Islands lie to the southwest. The region includes both volcanic and coral islands, and the climate is tropical, with a rainy season extending from November to April.

**History and Politics.** The original settlers probably came from Micronesia and Melanesia in the east. Europeans began arriving around the sixteenth century. By the late 1700s they had reached the five major island groups, and visitors to the area included mutineers from the British vessel *Bounty*. By the 1880s the islands had come under French rule, although they did not become an overseas territory until 1946. During European settlement, many Polynesians died as a result of exposure to foreign diseases. The French use several of the islands for nuclear testing. ■

# GABON

**Official name** Gabonese Republic
## PEOPLE
**Population** 1,065,000. **Density** 10/mi$^2$ (4.0/km$^2$). **Urban** 41%. **Capital** Libreville, 235,700. **Ethnic groups** Fang, Eshira, Bapounou, Teke. **Languages** French, Fang, indigenous. **Religions** Roman Catholic and other Christian 55-75%, Fetishism, Muslim. **Life expectancy** 51 female, 47 male. **Literacy** 65%.
## POLITICS
**Government** Republic. **Parties** Democratic. **Suffrage** Universal, over 18. **Memberships** OAU, OPEC, UN. **Subdivisions** 9 provinces.
## ECONOMY
GDP $3,142,000,000 **Per capita** $5,561. **Monetary unit** CFA franc. **Trade partners** Exports: France, U.S., Spain. Imports: France, U.S., Japan. **Exports** Petroleum, wood,

# GALAPAGOS ISLANDS
See ECUADOR.

# GAMBIA

manganese. **Imports** Manufactures, machinery, transportation equipment, food, chemicals.
**LAND**
**Description** Central Africa. **Area** 103,347 mi$^2$ (267,667 km$^2$). **Highest point** 3,346 ft (1,020 m). **Lowest point** Sea level.

**People.** Of Gabon's more than forty ethnic groups, the Fang are a majority and inhabit the area north of the Ogooué River. Other major groups include the Eshira, Bapounou, and Teke. The French, who colonized the area, compose a larger group today than during colonial times. Each of the groups has its own distinct language as well as culture, but French remains the official language.

**Economy and the Land.** Gabon is located astride the equator, and its many resources include petroleum, manganese, uranium, and dense rain forests. The most important activities are oil production, forestry, and mining. The economy depends greatly on foreign investment and imported labor, however, and many native Gabonese continue as subsistence farmers. While the labor shortage hinders economic development, the country has a high per capita income. The terrain is marked by a coastal plain, inland forested hills, and savanna in the east and south. The climate is hot and humid.

**History and Politics.** First inhabited by Pygmies, Gabon was the site of migrations by numerous Bantu peoples during its early history. The thick rain forests isolated the migrant groups from one another and thus preserved their individual cultures. The Portuguese arrived in the fifteenth century, followed by the Dutch, British, and French in the 1700s. The slave and ivory trades flourished, and the Fang, drawn by the prosperity, migrated to the coast in the 1800s. A group of freed slaves founded Libreville, which later became the capital. By 1885 France had gained control of the area, and in 1910 it was united with present-day Chad, the Congo, and the Central African Republic as French Equatorial Africa. Gabon became independent in 1960, and in 1964 French assistance thwarted a military takeover. During the 1970s, Gabon developed major economic ties with the United States and with China. ∎

**Official name** Republic of the Gambia
**PEOPLE**
**Population** 805,000. **Density** 185/mi$^2$ (71/km$^2$). **Urban** 20%. **Capital** Banjul, 44,536. **Ethnic groups** Malinke 40%, Fulani 19%, Wolof 15%, Jola 10%, Serahuli 8%. **Languages** English, Malinke, Wolof, Fula, indigenous. **Religions** Muslim 90%, Christian 9%, tribal religionist 1%. **Life expectancy** 37 female, 34 male. **Literacy** 12%.
**POLITICS**
**Government** Republic. **Parties** National Convention, People's, People's Progressive. **Suffrage** Universal, over 21. **Memberships** CW, OAU, UN. **Subdivisions** 5 divisions, 1 city.
**ECONOMY**
**GDP** $212,000,000 **Per capita** $348. **Monetary unit** Dalasi. **Trade partners** Exports: Switzerland, Netherlands, Guinea-Bissau. Imports: France, U.K., Thailand. **Exports** Peanuts, fish, palm kernels. **Imports** Textiles, food, tobacco, machinery, petroleum, chemicals.
**LAND**
**Description** Western Africa. **Area** 4,361 mi$^2$ (11,295 km$^2$). **Highest point** 174 ft (53 m). **Lowest point** Sea level.

**People.** Gambia's population includes the Mandingo, or Malinke; Fulani; Wolof; Jola; and Serahuli. Most people are Muslim, and language differs from group to group, although the official language is English. Gambians are mainly rural farmers, and literacy is low, with educational opportunities focused in the Banjul area. The population's size varies with the arrival and departure of seasonal Senegalese farm laborers.

**Economy and the Land.** Gambia's economy relies on peanut production, and crop diversification is a current goal. Subsistence crops include rice, and the government hopes increased rice production will decrease dependence on imports and foreign aid. Fishing and tourism have expanded in the past years. In addition, the Gambia River, which provides a route to the African interior, offers potential for an increased role in trade. Dense mangrove swamps border the river, giving way to flat ground that floods in the rainy season. Behind this lie sand hills and plateaus. Low-lying Gambia, with its subtropical climate, is virtually an enclave within Senegal.

**History and Politics.** From the thirteenth to the fifteenth centuries the flourishing Mali Empire included the Gambia area. The Portuguese arrived in the fifteenth century, established slave trading posts, and sold trade rights to Britain in 1588. During the seventeenth and eighteenth centuries France and Britain competed for control of the river trade. By the late 1800s, the Banjul area had become a British colony and the interior a British protectorate. Gambia achieved independence as a monarchy in 1965, and the country became a republic in 1970. In 1982 Gambia and Senegal formed the Confederation of Senegambia, which combined the countries' security and armed forces and strengthened economic ties. The official foreign policy is nonalignment. ■

# GERMANY, EAST

**Official name** German Democratic Republic
**PEOPLE**
**Population** 16,740,000. **Density** 400/mi² (155/km²). **Urban** 77%. **Capital** Berlin (East), 1,236,248. **Ethnic groups** German (Teutonic) 99%. **Languages** German. **Religions** Lutheran and other Protestant 47%, Roman Catholic 7%. **Life expectancy** 75 female, 69 male. **Literacy** 99%.
**POLITICS**
**Government** Socialist republic. **Parties** Socialist Unity. **Suffrage** Universal, over 18. **Memberships** CEMA, UN, Warsaw Pact. **Subdivisions** 14 districts, 1 independent city.
**ECONOMY**
**GNP** $174,700,000,000 **Per capita** $10,486. **Monetary unit** Mark. **Trade partners** U.S.S.R., Eastern European countries, W. Germany. **Exports** Machinery and transportation equipment, manufactures, chemicals, minerals. **Imports** Machinery and transportation equipment, fuel and minerals, food.
**LAND**
**Description** Eastern Europe. **Area** 41,828 mi² (108,333 km²). **Highest point** Fichtelberg, 3,983 ft (1,214 m). **Lowest point** Sea level.

**People.** The population of East Germany is mainly German and German speaking, although there exists a small minority of Slavs. East Germans are mostly Protestant and Lutheran, although many people remain religiously unaffiliated. The standard of living is relatively high, and citizens benefit from extensive educational and social-insurance systems. The arts also receive much government and public support. East and West Germany share a cultural heritage of achievements in music, literature, philosophy, and science.

**Economy and the Land.** Postwar economic expansion emphasized industry and today East Germany is one of the world's largest industrial producers. The economy is centralized; industry is state owned and most agriculture is collectivized. Mineral resources are limited. Northern lakes and low hills, central mountains and productive plains, as well as sandy stretches and southern uplands mark the terrain. The climate is temperate.

**History and Politics.** History of East and West Germany follows WEST GERMANY. ■

# GERMANY, WEST

**Official name** Federal Republic of Germany
**PEOPLE**
**Population** 61,460,000. **Density** 640/mi² (247/km²). **Urban** 86%. **Capital** Bonn, 291,439. **Ethnic groups** German (Teutonic), Danish. **Languages** German. **Religions** Roman Catholic 45%, Evangelical and other Protestant 44%. **Life expectancy** 77 female, 70 male. **Literacy** 99%.
**POLITICS**
**Government** Republic. **Parties** Christian Democratic Union, Christian Social Union, Social Democratic, others. **Suffrage** Universal, over 18. **Memberships** EC, NATO, OECD, UN. **Subdivisions** 11 states.
**ECONOMY**
**GDP** $624,060,000,000 **Per capita** $10,165. **Monetary unit** Mark. **Trade partners** Exports: France, U.S., Netherlands. Imports: Netherlands, France, Italy. **Exports** Manufactures, machinery, transportation equipment, chemicals. **Imports** Manufactures, machinery, petroleum, food, chemicals, transportation equipment.
**LAND**
**Description** Western Europe. **Area** 96,028 mi²

(248,708 km²). **Highest point** Zugspitze, 9,718 ft (2,962 m). **Lowest point** Freepsum Lake, -7 ft (-2 m).

**People.** West Germany, like East Germany, is homogeneous, with a Germanic, German-speaking population. Religious groups include Roman Catholics and Evangelicals. The population, which is generally well educated, numbers about four times that of East Germany, and the country is about twice as large as East Germany in physical size.

**Economy and the Land.** Despite the destruction of World War II and Germany's division into two countries, West Germany has one of the world's strongest economies. Industry is the basis of prosperity, with mining, manufacturing, construction, and utilities important contributors. The Ruhr district, which is the nation's most important industrial region, is located near the Ruhr River in northwest-central Germany and includes cities such as Essen and Dortmund. The Rhine River, the most vital commercial waterway in Europe, is found in the west. Agriculture remains important in the south. Germany's terrain varies from northern plains to western and central uplands and hills that extend to the southern Bavarian Alps. A mild climate is tempered by the sea in the north; in the south the winters are colder because of the Alps.

**History and Politics.** In ancient times Germanic tribes overcame Celtic inhabitants in the area of Germany and established a northern stronghold against Roman expansion of Gaul. As the Roman Empire weakened, the Germanic peoples invaded, deposing the Roman governor of Gaul in the fifth century A.D. The Franks composed the strongest tribe, and in the ninth century Frankish-controlled territory was expanded and united under Charlemagne. The 843 Treaty of Verdun divided Charlemagne's lands into three kingdoms, with the eastern territory encompassing modern Germany. Unity did not follow, however, and Germany remained a disjointed territory of feudal states, duchies, and independent cities. The Reformation, a movement led by German monk Martin Luther, began in 1517 and evolved into the Protestant branch of Christianity. In the eighteenth century, the state of Prussia became the foremost rival of the powerful Austrian state. The rise of Prussian power and growing nationalism eventually united the German states into the German Empire in 1871, and Prussian chancellor Otto von Bismarck installed Prussian King Wilhelm I as emperor. Reconciliation with Austria-Hungary came in 1879, and Germany allied with Austria in World War I in 1914. The empire collapsed as a result of the war, and the Weimar Republic was established in 1918. Instability and disunity arose in the face of economic problems. Promising prosperity and encouraging nationalism, Adolf Hitler of the National Socialist, or Nazi, party became chancellor in 1933. Hitler did away with the freedoms of speech and assembly and began a genocidal program to eliminate Jews and other peoples. Hitler's ambitions led to World War II. In April 1945 Hitler committed suicide, and in May Germany unconditionally surrendered to the Allies. The United States, Britain, the Soviet Union, and France divided Germany into four zones of occupation.

**East Germany.** After World War II, eastern Germany was designated the Soviet-occupied zone. The Communist party combined with the Social Democrats and, following the formation of the western Federal Republic of Germany in 1949, the eastern region proclaimed itself the German Democratic Republic. In 1955 the country became fully independent. Berlin, not included in the occupation zones, was a separate entity under the four Allied nations. When the Soviet Union ceased to participate in Allied negotiations in 1948, the city was divided. The Berlin Wall, separating East from West, existed from 1961 to 1989. The opened border finally allowed freedom of movement between the two Germanys, and has resulted in renewed talk of reunification.

**West Germany.** The Federal Republic of Germany, established in 1949, is composed of the American-, French-, and British-occupied zones. The republic became fully independent in 1955. Military forces of the United States, France, and Britain continue to occupy West Berlin. West German politics have been stable under various chancellors. The government has pledged financial aid to East Germany if economic and political reforms are made. ∎

# GHANA

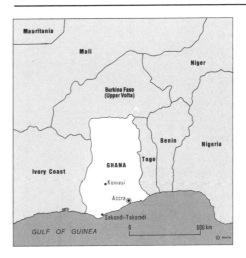

**Official name** Republic of Ghana
**PEOPLE**
**Population** 14,160,000. **Density** 154/mi² (59/km²). **Urban** 32%. **Capital** Accra, 859,640. **Ethnic groups** Akan 44%, Moshi-Dagomba 16%, Ewe 13%, Ga 8%. **Languages** English, Akan, indigenous. **Religions** Tribal religionist 38%, Muslim 30%, Christian 24%. **Life expectancy** 54 female, 50 male. **Literacy** 30%.
**POLITICS**
**Government** Provisional military government. **Parties** None. **Suffrage** Universal over 18. **Memberships** CW, OAU, UN. **Subdivisions** 10 regions.
**ECONOMY**
**GDP** $6,900,000,000 **Per capita** $492. **Monetary unit** Cedi. **Trade partners** Exports: U.S., Japan, Netherlands. Imports: Nigeria, U.K., U.S.. **Exports** Cocoa, aluminum, petroleum, wood. **Imports** Petroleum, manufactures, machinery, transportation equipment, chemicals.
**LAND**
**Description** Western Africa. **Area** 92,098 mi² (238,533 km²). **Highest point** Afadjoto, 2,905 ft (885 m). **Lowest point** Sea level.

**People.** Nearly all Ghanaians are black Africans. The Akan, the majority group, are further divided into the Fanti, who live mainly along the coast, and the Ashanti, who inhabit the forests north of the coast. The Ewe and Ga live in the south and southeast. Other groups include the Guan, living on the Volta River plains, and the Moshi-Dagomba in the north. Ghana's more than fifty languages and dialects reflect this ethnic diversity, and English, the official language, is spoken by a minority. Islam and traditional African religions predominate, but a Christian minority also exists. Most people live in rural areas, and the literacy rate is low.

**Economy and the Land.** Agriculture is the economic base, but Ghana's natural resources are diverse. Production of cocoa, the most important export, is concentrated in the Ashanti region, a belt of tropical rain forest extending north from the coastal plain. Resources include forests and mineral deposits, and exploitation of bauxite, gold, diamonds, and manganese ore is currently underway. Ghana's coastal lowlands give way to scrub and plains, the Ashanti rain forest, and northern savanna. The climate is tropical.

**History and Politics.** The ancestors of today's Ghanaians probably migrated from the northern areas of Mauritania and Mali in the thirteenth century. The Portuguese reached the shore around 1470 and called the area the Gold Coast. Many countries competed for the region, but in 1874 the Gold Coast was made a British colony. By 1901 Britain had extended its control to the inland Ashanti area, which became a colony, and the northern territories, which became a protectorate. The three regions were merged with British Togoland, a onetime German colony under British administration since 1922. In 1957 the four regions united as independent Ghana. Instability resulted, arising from a history of disunity and economic problems. The parliamentary state became a republic in 1960, and civilian rule has alternated with military governments. Ghana follows a foreign policy of nonalignment, and although Ghanaians' loyalties are based on community rather than national allegiance, they are in general agreement on foreign affairs. ■

## GIBRALTAR

**Official name** Gibraltar
**PEOPLE**
**Population** 31,000. **Density** 13,478/mi$^2$ (5,167/km$^2$). **Urban** 100%. **Capital** Gibraltar, 30,000. **Ethnic groups** Gibraltarian (mixed Italian, English, Maltese, Portuguese, and Spanish) 75%, British 14%. **Languages** English, Spanish. **Religions** Roman Catholic 75%, Anglican 9%, Muslim 8%, Jewish 2%, Hindu 1%. **Life expectancy** 75 female, 71 male. **Literacy** 99%.
**POLITICS**
**Government** Dependent territory (U.K.). **Parties** Labor/Association for the Advancement of Civil Rights, Socialist Labor. **Suffrage** Universal adult. **Memberships** None. **Subdivisions** None.
**ECONOMY**
**GNP** $129,000,000 **Per capita** $4,300. **Monetary unit** Pound. **Trade partners** U.K., Morocco, Portugal, Netherlands. **Exports** Tobacco, petroleum, wine. **Imports** Manufactures, fuel, food.

**LAND**
**Description** Southwestern Europe (peninsula on Spain's southern coast). **Area** 2.3 mi$^2$ (6.0 km$^2$). **Highest point** 1,398 ft (426 m). **Lowest point** Sea level.

**People.** Occupying a narrow peninsula on Spain's southern coast, the British colony of Gibraltar has a mixed population of Italian, English, Maltese, Portuguese, and Spanish descent. A number of British residents—many of which are military personnel—also reside here. Most are bilingual in English and Spanish.

**Economy and the Land.** With land unsuited for agriculture and a lack of mineral resources, Gibraltar depends mainly on the British military and tourism. Shipping-related activities and a growing service industry also provide jobs and income. Connected to Spain by an isthmus, Gibraltar consists mainly of the limestone-and-shale ridge known as the Rock of Gibraltar. The climate is mild.

**History and Politics.** Drawn by Gibraltar's strategic location at the Atlantic entrance to the Mediterranean Sea, Phoenicians, Carthaginians, Romans, Vandals, Visigoths, and Moors all played a role in the land's history. After nearly three hundred years under Spanish control, Gibraltar was captured by Britain in 1704, during the War of the Spanish Succession. It was officially ceded to the British in the 1713 Peace of Utrecht. In a 1967 referendum, residents voted to remain under British control. British-Spanish competition for the colony continues. The outcome of the 1988 election makes it clear that a 1987 agreement between Spain and Britain regarding sovereignty does not have popular approval. ■

## GREECE

**Official name** Hellenic Republic
**PEOPLE**
**Population** 10,010,000. **Density** 196/mi$^2$ (76/km$^2$). **Urban** 60%. **Capital** Athens, 885,737. **Ethnic groups** Greek 98%, Turkish 1%. **Languages** Greek. **Religions** Greek

Orthodox 98%, Muslim 1%. **Life expectancy** 76 female, 72 male. **Literacy** 91%.
**POLITICS**
**Government** Republic. **Parties** New Democracy, Panhellenic Socialist Movement, others. **Suffrage** Universal, over 18. **Memberships** EC, NATO, OECD, UN. **Subdivisions** 51 departments.
**ECONOMY**
**GDP** $33,407,000,000 **Per capita** $3,331. **Monetary unit** Drachma. **Trade partners** Exports: W. Germany, Italy, U.S. Imports: W. Germany, Italy, Saudi Arabia. **Exports** Food, clothing, petroleum, textiles, minerals and other crude materials. **Imports** Petroleum, manufactures, machinery, transportation equipment, chemicals.
**LAND**
**Description** Southeastern Europe. **Area** 50,962 mi² (131,990 km²). **Highest point** Mt. Olympus, 9,570 ft (2,917 m). **Lowest point** Sea level.

**People.** Greece has played a central role in European, African, and Asian cultures for thousands of years, but today its population is almost homogeneous. Native Greek inhabitants are united by a language that dates back three thousand years and a religion that influences many aspects of everyday life. Athens, the capital, was the cultural center of an ancient civilization that produced masterpieces of art and literature and broke ground in philosophy, political thought, and science.

**Economy and the Land.** The economy of Greece takes its shape from terrain and location. Dominated by the sea and long a maritime trading power, Greece has one of the largest merchant fleets in the world and depends greatly on commerce. The mountainous terrain and poor soil limit agriculture, although Greece is a leading producer of lemons and olives. The service sector, including tourism, provides most of Greece's national income. Inhabitants enjoy a temperate climate, with mild, wet winters, and hot, dry summers.

**History and Politics.** Greece's history begins with the early Bronze Age cultures of the Minoans and the Mycenaeans. The city-state, or *polis*, began to develop around the tenth century B.C., and Athens, a democracy, and Sparta, an oligarchy, gradually emerged as Greece's leaders. The Persian Wars, in which the city-states united to repel a vastly superior army, ushered in the Golden Age of Athens, a cultural explosion in the fifth century B.C. The Parthenon, perhaps Greece's most famous building, was built at this time. Athens was defeated by Sparta in the Peloponnesian War, and by 338 B.C. Philip II of Macedon had conquered all of Greece. His son, Alexander the Great, defeated the Persians and spread Greek civilization and language all over the known world. Greece became a Roman province in 146 B.C. and part of the Byzantine Empire in A.D. 395, but its traditions had a marked influence on these empires. Absorbed into the Ottoman Empire in the 1450s, Greece had gained independence by 1830 and became a constitutional monarchy about fifteen years later. For much of the twentieth century the nation was divided between republicans and monarchists. During World War II Germany occupied Greece, and postwar instability led to a civil war, which Communist rebels eventually lost. A repressive military junta ruled Greece from 1967 until 1974, when the regime relinquished power to a civilian government. The Greeks then voted for a republic over a monarchy. A Socialist government ruled until 1989. Indecisive election results forced the scheduling of a new election in 1990. ■

# GREENLAND

**Official name** Greenland
**PEOPLE**
**Population** 57,000. **Density** 0.07/mi² (0.03/km²). **Urban** 77%. **Capital** Godthåb, 11,209. **Ethnic groups** Greenlander (Inuit and native-born whites) 86%, Danish 14%. **Languages** Danish, Greenlandic, Inuit dialects. **Religions** Lutheran. **Life expectancy** 66 female, 60 male. **Literacy** 99%.
**POLITICS**
**Government** Self-governing territory (Danish protection). **Parties** Forward (Siumut), Inuit Movement, Polar (Issittrup), Unity (Atassut). **Suffrage** Universal, over 21. **Memberships** None. **Subdivisions** 3 municipalities. **Monetary unit** Danish krone. **Trade partners** Exports: Denmark, W. Germany, France. Imports: Denmark, Norway, Sweden. **Exports** Fish and shellfish, lead and zinc. **Imports** Manufactures, machinery, petroleum, ships and other transportation equipment.
**LAND**
**Description** North Atlantic island. **Area** 840,004 mi² (2,175,600 km²). **Highest point** Gunnbjorn Mtn., 12,139 ft (3,700 m). **Lowest point** Sea level.

**People.** Most Greenlanders are native-born descendants of mixed Inuit-Danish ancestry. Lutheranism, the predominant religion, reflects Danish ties. Descended from an indigenous Arctic people, pure Inuit are a minority and usually follow traditional lifestyles. Most of the island lies within the Arctic Circle, and population is concentrated along the southern coast.

**Economy and the Land.** Fishing is the state's economic backbone. Despite a difficult arctic environment, mining of zinc and lead continues; but iron, coal, uranium, and molybdenum deposits remain undeveloped. The largest island in the world, Greenland is composed of an inland plateau, coastal mountains and fjords, and offshore islands. More than 80 percent of the island lies under permanent ice cap. Greenland is situated in the "Land of the Midnight Sun," and certain areas have twenty-four consecutive hours of daylight in summer and darkness in winter. The climate is cold, with warmer temperatures and more precipitation in the southwest.

**History and Politics.** Following early migration of Arctic Inuit, Norwegian Vikings sighted Greenland in the ninth century, and in the tenth century Erik the Red brought the first settlers from Iceland. Greenland united with Norway in the 1200s, and the two regions, along with several others, came under Danish rule in the 1300s. Denmark retained control of Greenland when Norway left the union in 1814. American troops defended the island during World War II. In 1953 the island became a province of Denmark and in 1979 it gained home rule. ∎

# GRENADA

**Official name** Grenada

**PEOPLE**
**Population** 97,000. **Density** 729/mi² (282/km²). **Urban** 15%. **Capital** St. George's, 4,788. **Ethnic groups** Black 82%, mixed 13%, East Indian 3%. **Languages** English, French. **Religions** Roman Catholic 59%, Anglican 17%, other Protestant. **Life expectancy** 66 female, 60 male. **Literacy** 98%.
**POLITICS**
**Government** Parliamentary state. **Parties** Democratic Labor Congress, New National. **Suffrage** Universal adult. **Memberships** CW, OAS, UN. **Subdivisions** 7 parishes.

**ECONOMY**
**GDP** $96,000,000 **Per capita** $842. **Monetary unit** East Caribbean dollar. **Trade partners** Exports: U.K., Trinidad and Tobago. Imports: U.S., Trinidad and Tobago, U.K.. **Exports** Cocoa, spices, bananas, clothing. **Imports** Food, manufactures, petroleum, chemicals, machinery.
**LAND**
**Description** Caribbean island. **Area** 133 mi² (344 km²). **Highest point** Mt. St. Catherine, 2,756 ft (840 m). **Lowest point** Sea level.

**People.** Grenada's culture bears the influences of former British and French rule. The most widely spoken language is English, although a French patois is also spoken, and the majority of the population is Roman Catholic. Most Grenadians are black, descended from African slaves brought to the island by the British, but there are small East Indian and European populations.

**Economy and the Land.** Rich volcanic soils and heavy rainfall have made agriculture the chief economic activity. Also known as the Isle of Spice, Grenada is one of the world's leading producers of nutmeg and mace. Many tropical fruits are also raised, and the small plots of peasant farmers dot the hilly terrain. Another mainstay of the economy is tourism, with visitors drawn by the beaches and tropical climate. Grenada has little industry; high unemployment has plagued the nation in recent years.

**History and Politics.** The Carib Indians resisted European attempts to colonize Grenada for more than one hundred years after Christopher Columbus discovered the island in 1498. The French established the first settlement in 1650 and slaughtered the Caribs, but the British finally gained control in 1783. In 1974 Grenada achieved full independence under Prime Minister Eric Gairy, despite widespread opposition to his policies. In 1979 foes of the regime staged a coup and installed a Marxist government headed by Maurice Bishop. Power struggles resulted, and a military branch of the government seized power in 1983 and executed Bishop, along with several of his ministers. The United States led a subsequent invasion that deposed the Marxists. A new centrist government was installed in 1984 elections. ∎

# GUADELOUPE See FRANCE.

# GUAM See UNITED STATES.

# GUATEMALA

**Official name** Republic of Guatemala
**PEOPLE**
**Population** 9,059,000. **Density** 215/mi² (83/km²). **Urban** 40%. **Capital** Guatemala, 754,243. **Ethnic groups** Ladino (mestizo and westernized Maya) 56%, Maya 44%. **Languages** Spanish, indigenous. **Religions** Roman Catholic, Protestant, tribal religionist. **Life expectancy** 61 female, 57 male. **Literacy** 55%.

## POLITICS
**Government** Republic. **Parties** Christian Democratic, Democratic Party of National Cooperation, National Centrist Union, Revolutiona. **Suffrage** Universal, over 18. **Memberships** OAS, UN. **Subdivisions** 22 departments.
## ECONOMY
GDP $11,130,000,000 **Per capita** $1,377. **Monetary unit** Quetzal. **Trade partners** Exports: U.S., El Salvador, W. Germany. Imports: U.S., El Salvador, Venezuela. **Exports** Coffee, manufactures, chemicals, cotton, sugar and honey, fruit. **Imports** Petroleum, manufactures, chemicals, machinery, food.
## LAND
**Description** Central America. **Area** 42,042 mi$^2$ (108,889 km$^2$). **Highest point** Volcán Tajumulco, 13,845 ft (4,220 m). **Lowest point** Sea level.

**People.** Guatemala's population is made up of majority ladinos and minority Indians. Ladinos include both mestizos, those of Spanish-Indian origin, and westernized Indians of Mayan descent. Classified on the basis of culture rather than race, ladinos follow a Spanish-American lifestyle and speak Spanish. Nonladino Indians are also of Mayan descent; they generally speak Mayan dialects. Many are poor, uneducated, and isolated from the mainstream of Guatemalan life. Roman Catholicism often combines with traditional Mayan religious practice. Population is concentrated in the central highlands.

**Economy and the Land.** Most Guatemalans practice agriculture in some form. Indians generally operate small, unproductive subsistence farms. Export crops are mainly produced on large plantations on the fertile southern plain that borders the Pacific. Although light industry is growing, it is unable to absorb rural immigrants seeking employment in the cities. Much of the landscape is mountainous, with the Pacific plain and Caribbean lowlands bordering central highlands. Northern rain forests and grasslands are sparsely populated and largely undeveloped. The climate is tropical in low areas and temperate in the highlands.

**History and Politics.** Indians in the region were absorbed into the Mayan civilization that flourished in Central America by the fourth century. In 1523 the Spanish defeated the indigenous Indians and went on to establish one of the most influential colonies in Central America. Guatemala joined Costa Rica, El Salvador, Nicaragua, and Honduras in 1821 to declare independence from Spain, and the former Spanish colonies formed the Federation of Central America in 1823. Almost from the start, the federation was marked by dissension, and by 1838 it had, in effect, been dissolved. Following a series of dictatorships, social and economic reform began in 1944 and continued under two successive presidents. The government was ousted in a United States-backed 1954 coup and military rule established. A presidential assassination, accusations of government corruption and human-rights violations, guerrilla activities, and violence followed. A 1976 earthquake resulted in heavy loss of life and property. Military rule continued until 1985, when the nation returned to civilian rule under Marco Vinicio Cerezo. ∎

# GUERNSEY See UNITED KINGDOM.

# GUINEA

**Official name** Republic of Guinea
## PEOPLE
**Population** 7,178,000. **Density** 76/mi$^2$ (29/km$^2$). **Urban** 22%. **Capital** Conakry, 705,280. **Ethnic groups** Fulani, Malinke, Susu, others. **Languages** French, indigenous. **Religions** Muslim 85%, Christian 10%, Animist 5%. **Life expectancy** 42 female, 39 male. **Literacy** 48%.
## POLITICS
**Government** Provisional military government. **Parties** None. **Suffrage** None. **Memberships** OAU, UN. **Subdivisions** 33 administrative regions.
## ECONOMY
GNP $1,600,000,000 **Per capita** $291. **Monetary unit** Franc. **Trade partners** Exports: U.S., U.S.S.R., W. Germany. Imports: France, U.S.S.R., U.S.. **Exports** Bauxite, alumina, diamonds, coffee, pineapples, bananas, palm kernels. **Imports** Petroleum, metals, machinery and transportation equipment, food.
## LAND
**Description** Western Africa. **Area** 94,926 mi$^2$ (245,857 km$^2$). **Highest point** Mt. Nimba, 5,748 ft (1,752 m). **Lowest point** Sea level.

**People.** Guinea's population is composed of several ethnic groups, with three—the Fulani, Malinke, and Susu—forming nearly half the total. Most Guineans are rural farmers, living in hamlets, and the only true urban center is Conakry. Mortality as well as emigration rates are high. Eight official languages besides French, the language of the colonial power, are taught in the schools.

**Economy and the Land.** Rich soil and a varied terrain suited for diverse crop production have made agriculture an important economic activity. Guinea also has vast mineral reserves, including one of the world's largest bauxite deposits. Centralized economic planning and state enterprise have characterized the republic, but Guinea now encourages private and foreign investments. The terrain is mostly flat along the coast and mountainous in the interior. The climate is tropical on the coast, hot and dry in the north and northeast, and cooler with less humidity in the highlands.

**History and Politics.** As part of the Ghana, Mali, and Songhai empires that flourished in West Africa between the fourth and fifteenth centuries, Guinea was a trading center for gold and slaves. The Portuguese arrived on the coast in the 1400s, and European competition for Guinean trade soon began. In the 1890s France declared the area a colony and named it French Guinea. A movement for autonomy began after World War II with a series of reforms by the French and the growth of a labor movement headed by Sékou Touré, later the nation's first president. The first of the French colonies in West Africa to attain independence, in 1958 Guinea was also the only colony to reject membership in the French Community. In recent years the military set up a provisional government and banned political parties. ∎

# GUINEA-BISSAU

**Official name** Republic of Guinea-Bissau
**PEOPLE**
**Population** 986,000. **Density** 71/mi² (27/km²). **Urban** 27%. **Capital** Bissau, 109,486. **Ethnic groups** Balanta 30%, Fulani 20%, Manjaca 14%, Malinke 13%, Papel 7%. **Languages** Portuguese, Crioulo, indigenous. **Religions** Tribal religionist 65%, Muslim 30%, Christian 5%. **Life expectancy** 45 female, 41 male. **Literacy** 20%.
**POLITICS**
**Government** Republic. **Parties** African Party for Independence. **Suffrage** Universal, over 15.
**Memberships** OAU, UN. **Subdivisions** 9 regions.
**ECONOMY**
**GDP** $190,000,000 **Per capita** $228. **Monetary unit** Peso. **Trade partners** Exports: Spain, Portugal, Switzerland. Imports: Portugal, Sweden, U.S.. **Exports** Oil seeds, fish, plywood, cashews. **Imports** Manufactures, transportation equipment, machinery, food, petroleum, chemicals.
**LAND**
**Description** Western Africa. **Area** 13,948 mi²

(36,125 km²). **Highest point** 860 ft (262 m). **Lowest point** Sea level.

**People.** Guinea-Bissau's largest ethnic group, the Balanta, mainly inhabit the coastal area. Most practice traditional beliefs, although some are Christian. Predominately Muslim peoples, the Fulani and Malinke are concentrated in the northwest. The Manjaca inhabit the northern and central coastal regions. Although the official language is Portuguese, many speak Crioulo, a creole dialect also spoken in Cape Verde.

**Economy and the Land.** Guinea-Bissau's economy is underdeveloped and dependent upon agriculture. Peanuts, cotton, corn, and sorghum are grown in the north, and palm-oil production is concentrated along the coast. Timber is produced primarily in the south. Fishing, especially shrimp production, has increased since 1976. Bauxite deposits have been located, and exploration for additional resources continues. Mineral exploitation is hindered by a lack of transportation routes, however. A swamp-covered coastal plain rises to an eastern savanna. The climate is tropical. The country includes the Bijagos Archipelago, which lies just off the coast.

**History and Politics.** The area of Guinea-Bissau was inhabited by diverse peoples prior to the arrival of the Portuguese in 1446. Ruled as a single colony with Cape Verde, the region soon developed into a base for the Portuguese slave trade. In 1879 it was separated from Cape Verde as Portuguese Guinea, and its status changed to overseas province in 1951. A movement for the independence of Guinea-Bissau and Cape Verde developed in the 1950s, and a coup in Portugal in 1974 resulted in independence the same year. Attempts to unite Guinea-Bissau and Cape Verde were unsuccessful, and a 1980 coup installed an anti-unification government. ∎

# GUYANA

**Official name** Co-operative Republic of Guyana
**PEOPLE**
**Population** 765,000. **Density** 9.2/mi² (3.6/km²). **Urban**

32%. **Capital** Georgetown, 78,500. **Ethnic groups** East Indian 51%, black 30%, mixed 11%, Amerindian 5%. **Languages** English, indigenous. **Religions** Anglican and other Christian 57%, Hindu 33%, Muslim 9%. **Life expectancy** 71 female, 66 male. **Literacy** 92%.
### POLITICS
**Government** Republic. **Parties** People's National Congress, People's Progressive, others. **Suffrage** Universal, over 18. **Memberships** CW, UN. **Subdivisions** 10 districts.
### ECONOMY
**GDP** $462,000,000 **Per capita** $550. **Monetary unit** Dollar. **Trade partners** Exports: U.K., U.S., Venezuela. Imports: Trinidad and Tobago, U.S., U.K.. **Exports** Bauxite, sugar, rice. **Imports** Manufactures, petroleum, dairy products and other food, chemicals.
### LAND
**Description** Northeastern South America. **Area** 83,000 mi² (214,969 km²). **Highest point** Mt. Roraima, 9,094 ft (2,772 m). **Lowest point** Sea level.

**People.** Guyana's population includes descendants of black African slaves and East Indian, Chinese, and Portuguese laborers who were brought to work sugar plantations. Amerindians, the indigenous peoples of Guyana, are a minority. Ninety percent of the people live along the fertile coastal plain, where farming and manufacturing are concentrated.

**Economy and the Land.** Agriculture and mining compose the backbone of the Guyanese economy. Sugar and rice continue to be important crops, and mines produce bauxite, manganese, diamonds, and gold. Guyana's inland forests give way to savanna and a coastal plain. The climate is tropical.

**History and Politics.** First gaining European notice in 1498 with the voyages of Christopher Columbus, Guyana was the stage for competing colonial interests—British, French, and Dutch—until it officially became British Guiana in 1831. Slavery was abolished several years later, causing the British to import indentured laborers, the ancestors of today's majority group. A constitution, adopted in 1953, was suspended when Britain feared a Communist victory at the polls. In the early 1960s, racial tensions erupted into riots between East Indians and blacks. In 1966, the country gained independence, and adopted the name Guyana. Guyana became a republic in 1970 and has pursued socialist policies. The two main political parties continue to reflect its ethnic divisions: the People's National Congress is supported by blacks, and the People's Progressive party by East Indians. ■

# HAITI

**Official name** Republic of Haiti
### PEOPLE
**Population** 6,456,000. **Density** 603/mi² (233/km²). **Urban** 27%. **Capital** Port-au-Prince, 684,284. **Ethnic groups** Black 95%, mulatto and white 5%. **Languages** Creole, French. **Religions** Roman Catholic 75-80%, Protestant 10%. **Life expectancy** 54 female, 51 male. **Literacy** 21%.
### POLITICS
**Government** Provisional military government. **Parties** Christian Democratic, Movement to Install Democracy,

National Alliance Front, Social Christian. **Suffrage** Universal, over 18. **Memberships** OAS, UN. **Subdivisions** 9 departments.
### ECONOMY
**GDP** $2,009,000,000 **Per capita** $379. **Monetary unit** Gourde. **Trade partners** Exports: U.S., France. Imports: U.S., Netherlands Antilles, Canada, Japan. **Exports** Textiles and other manufactures, coffee and other food, aluminum ore. **Imports** Manufactures, food, petroleum, machinery, chemicals, vegetable oil.
### LAND
**Description** Caribbean island (western Hispaniola). **Area** 10,714 mi² (27,750 km²). **Highest point** Morne La Selle, 8,773 ft (2,674 m). **Lowest point** Sea level.

**People.** The world's oldest black republic, Haiti has a population composed mainly of descendants of African slaves. Most people are poor and rural. Although French is the official language, Haitian Creole, a combination of French and West African languages, is more widely spoken. Roman Catholicism is the major religion. Voodooism, which blends Christian and African beliefs, is also practiced.

**Economy and the Land.** Haiti's economy remains underdeveloped. Most people rely on subsistence farming, though productivity is hampered by high population density in productive regions. Coffee is the main commercial crop and export. Recent growth of light industry is partially attributable to tax exemptions and low labor costs. Occupying the western third of Hispaniola Island, Haiti has an overall mountainous terrain and a tropical climate.

**History and Politics.** Christopher Columbus reached Hispaniola in 1492, and the indigenous Arawak Indians almost completely died out during subsequent Spanish settlement. Most Spanish settlers had gone to seek their fortunes in other colonies by the 1600s, and western Hispaniola came under French control in 1697. Slave importation increased rapidly, and in less than a hundred years black Africans far outnumbered the French. In a 1791 revolution led by Toussaint L'Ouverture, Jean Jacques Dessalines, and Henri Christophe, the slaves rose against the French. By 1804 the country achieved independence from France, and the area was renamed Haiti. In the 1820s, Haitians conquered the eastern region of the island, now the Dominican Republic, and it remained part of Haiti until 1844. Instability increased under various dictatorships from 1843 to 1915, and United States marines occupied the country from 1915 to 1934. After a time of alternating military and civilian rule, François Duvalier came to office in 1957, declaring himself president-for-life in 1964. His rule was marked by repression, corruption, and human-rights abuses. His son, Jean-Claude, succeeded him as president-for-life in 1971. The Duvalier dictatorship ended in 1986 when Jean-Claude fled the country. Continued unrest resulted in three different governments between 1987 and 1989. ∎

# HONDURAS

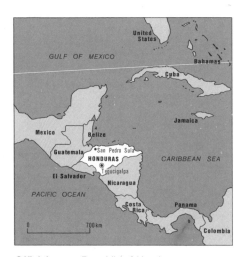

**Official name** Republic of Honduras
**PEOPLE**
**Population** 5,039,000. **Density** 116/mi$^2$ (45/km$^2$). **Urban** 40%. **Capital** Tegucigalpa, 597,500. **Ethnic groups** Mestizo 90%, Amerindian 7%, black 2%, white 1%. **Languages** Spanish, indigenous. **Religions** Roman Catholic 97%. **Life expectancy** 62 female, 58 male. **Literacy** 57%.
**POLITICS**
**Government** Republic. **Parties** Liberal, National, others. **Suffrage** Universal, over 18. **Memberships** OAS, UN. **Subdivisions** 18 departments.
**ECONOMY**
**GDP** $3,480,000,000 **Per capita** $773. **Monetary unit** Lempira. **Trade partners** Exports: U.S., Japan, W. Germany. Imports: U.S., Venezuela, Guatemala. **Exports** Bananas, coffee, minerals, shellfish, lumber. **Imports** Paper and other manufactures, petroleum, chemicals, machinery, food.
**LAND**
**Description** Central America. **Area** 43,277 mi$^2$ (112,088 km$^2$). **Highest point** Cerro Las Minas, 9,347 ft (2,849 m). **Lowest point** Sea level.

**People.** Most Hondurans are mestizos—people of Spanish-Indian descent. Other groups include Indians and descendants of black Africans and Europeans. Most Indians have been assimilated into the majority culture, but a minority continues to practice a traditional Indian lifestyle. The Spanish language predominates, and English is spoken by a small population of British descent on the northern coast and Bay Islands. Poverty is an ongoing problem for the mainly rural population, and economic and educational improvements mostly affect urban inhabitants.

**Economy and the Land.** Honduras has an underdeveloped economy based on banana cultivation. Other activities include livestock raising, coffee production, forestry, and some mining. Honduras's terrain is mostly mountainous, with lowlands along some coastal regions. The climate varies from tropical in the lowlands to temperate in the mountains.

**History and Politics.** Early in its history Honduras was part of the Mayan Empire. By 1502, when Christopher Columbus arrived to claim the region for Spain, the decline of the Maya had rendered the Indians weakened and unable to stave off Spanish settlement. The Spanish colonial period introduced gold and silver mines, cattle ranches, and African slaves. In 1821 Honduras, El Salvador, Nicaragua, Costa Rica, and Guatemala declared independence from Spain and, in 1823, formed the Federation of Central America. The unstable union had virtually collapsed by 1838, and the member states became independent as the federation dissolved. Instability, Guatemalan political influence, and the development of a banana economy based on United States-owned plantations marked the 1800s and early 1900s. Frequent revolutions have characterized the twentieth century, and a dictator governed from 1933 to 1948. Since the 1950s civilian governments have alternated with military coups and rule. Controversies focus on issues of poverty and land distribution. An elected civilian government has ruled since 1982. The country has become an important base for United States activities in Central America, evidenced by ongoing American military maneuvers in the area. ∎

# HONG KONG

**Official name** Hong Kong
**PEOPLE**
**Population** 5,888,000. **Density** 14,222/mi$^2$ (5,493/km$^2$). **Urban** 92%. **Capital** Victoria (Hong Kong), Hong Kong I., 1,175,860. **Ethnic groups** Chinese 95%. **Languages** Chinese (Cantonese), English. **Religions** Buddhist and Taoist 90%, Christian 10%. **Life expectancy** 78 female, 73 male. **Literacy** 77%.
**POLITICS**
**Government** Dependent territory (U.K.). **Parties** None. **Suffrage** Professional or skilled persons. **Memberships** None. **Subdivisions** 19 districts.
**ECONOMY**
**GDP** $34,186,000,000 **Per capita** $6,290. **Monetary unit** Dollar. **Trade partners** Exports: U.S., China. Imports: China, Japan, U.S.. **Exports** Clothing, textiles, photographic equipment, toys, and other manufactures. **Imports** Textiles and other manufactures, machinery, food, chemicals.
**LAND**
**Description** Eastern Asia (islands and mainland area on China's southeastern coast). **Area** 414 mi$^2$ (1,072 km$^2$).

**Highest point** Tai Mo Mtn., 3,140 ft (957 m). **Lowest point** Sea level.

**People.** Hong Kong has a majority Chinese population. Cantonese, a Chinese dialect, is spoken by most of the people, and English and Chinese are the official languages. Major religions are Taoism, Christianity, and Buddhism. Hong Kong is one of the world's most densely populated areas.

**Economy and the Land.** Low taxes, duty-free status, an accessible location, and an excellent natural harbor have helped make Hong Kong an Asian center of trade, finance, manufacturing, and transportation. Situated on the coast of China, Hong Kong borders Guangdong province. The colony consists of the islands of Hong Kong and Lantau, the Kowloon Peninsula, and the New Territories, which include a mainland area and many islands. In addition to mountains, the New Territories contain some level areas suitable for agriculture, while the islands are hilly. The climate is tropical, with hot, rainy summers and cool, humid winters.

**History and Politics.** Inhabited since ancient times, Hong Kong came under Chinese rule around the third century B.C. In 1839 British opium smuggling led to the Opium War between Britain and China, and a victorious Britain received the island of Hong Kong in an 1842 treaty. In 1860 the British gained control of the Kowloon Peninsula, and in 1898 the New Territories came under British rule through a ninety-nine-year lease with China. Hong Kong will be returned to China in 1997 under a negotiated agreement whereby the present economic system will be retained for fifty years. Recent events in China, however, have made many residents uneasy about Hong Kong's future. ∎

# HUNGARY

**Official name** Republic of Hungary
**PEOPLE**
**Population** 10,565,000. **Density** 294/mi² (114/km²). **Urban** 56%. **Capital** Budapest, 2,104,700. **Ethnic groups** Hungarian (Magyar) 99%. **Languages** Hungarian. **Religions** Roman Catholic 68%, Calvinist 20%, Lutheran 5%. **Life expectancy** 74 female, 67 male. **Literacy** 99%.
**POLITICS**
**Government** Republic. **Parties** Socialist, others. **Suffrage** Universal, over 18. **Memberships** CEMA, UN, Warsaw Pact. **Subdivisions** 19 counties, 1 autonomous city.
**ECONOMY**
**GNP** $80,100,000,000 **Per capita** $7,504. **Monetary unit** Forint. **Trade partners** U.S.S.R., W. Germany, E. Germany. **Exports** Manufactures, machinery, food, transportation equipment, chemicals, petroleum. **Imports** Manufactures, machinery, textile fibers and other crude materials.
**LAND**
**Description** Eastern Europe, landlocked. **Area** 35,920 mi² (93,033 km²). **Highest point** Kékes, 3,330 ft (1,015 m). **Lowest point** Tisza River valley, 259 ft (79 m).

**People.** Hungary's major ethnic group and language evolved from Magyar tribes who settled the region in the ninth century. Gypsies, Germans, and other peoples compose minorities. Most people are Roman Catholic, and the government supervises religious activities through a state office. The government also controls educational programs, and the literacy rate is high. Growth of industry since the 1940s has caused a rural-to-urban population shift.

**Economy and the Land.** Following World War II, Hungary pursued a program of industrialization, and the one-time agricultural nation now looks to industry as its main economic contributor. Agriculture is almost completely socialized, and farming remains important, with productivity aided by fertile soils and a mild climate. Economic planning was decentralized in 1968, thus Hungary's economy differs from that of other Soviet-bloc nations, permitting some private enterprise. A flat plain dominates the landscape, and the lack of varied terrain results in a temperate climate throughout the country.

**History and Politics.** In the late 800s Magyar tribes from the east overcame Slavic and Germanic residents and settled the area. Invading Mongols caused much destruction in the thirteenth century. In the early 1500s, after repeated attacks, the Ottoman Turks dominated central Hungary. By the late seventeenth century, the entire region had come under the rule of Austria's Hapsburgs. Hungary succeeded in obtaining equal status with Austria in 1867, and the dual monarchy of Austria-Hungary emerged. Discontent and nationalistic demands increased until 1914, when a Bosnian Serb killed the heir to the Austro-Hungarian throne. Austria-Hungary declared war on Serbia, and World War I began, resulting in both territory and population losses for Hungary. At the end of the war, in 1918, Hungary became a republic, only to revert to monarchical rule in 1919. Hungary entered World War II on the side of Germany, and Adolf Hitler set up a pro-Nazi government in Hungary in 1944. The Soviet Union invaded that same year, and a Hungarian-Allied peace treaty was signed in 1947. Coalition rule evolved into a Communist government in 1949. In 1956 discontent erupted into rebellion, a new premier declared Hungary neutral, and Soviet forces entered Budapest to quell the uprising. A new constitution, which goes into effect in 1990, will help move the nation away from Communist domination. ∎

# ICELAND

**Official name** Republic of Iceland
**PEOPLE**
Population 254,000. **Density** 6.4/mi² (2.5/km²). **Urban** 89%. **Capital** Reykjavík, 88,745. **Ethnic groups** Icelander (mixed Norwegian and Celtic). **Languages** Icelandic. **Religions** Lutheran 95%, other Christian 3%. **Life expectancy** 80 female, 74 male. **Literacy** 100%.
**POLITICS**
Government Republic. **Parties** Independence, Progressive, Social Democratic, others. **Suffrage** Universal, over 18. **Memberships** NATO, OECD, UN. **Subdivisions** 23 counties, 14 independent towns.
**ECONOMY**
GDP $2,663,000,000 **Per capita** $249. **Monetary unit** Krona. **Trade partners** Exports: U.S., U.K., W. Germany. Imports: W. Germany, U.K., Denmark. **Exports** Fish and shellfish, aluminum and other manufactures. **Imports** Manufactures, machinery, petroleum, food, chemicals, crude materials.
**LAND**
Description North Atlantic island. **Area** 39,769 mi² (103,000 km²). **Highest point** Hvannadalshnúkur, 6,952 ft (2,119 m). **Lowest point** Sea level.

**People.** Most Icelanders are of Norwegian or Celtic ancestry, live in coastal cities, and belong to the Lutheran church. Icelandic, the predominant language, has changed little from the Old Norse of the original settlers and still resembles the language of twelfth-century Nordic sagas.

**Economy and the Land.** Fish, found in the island's rich coastal waters, are the main natural resource and export. Iceland has a long tradition based on fishing, but the industry has recently suffered from decreasing markets and catches. Glaciers, lakes, hot springs, volcanoes, and a lava desert limit agricultural land but provide a scenic terrain. Although the island lies just south of the Arctic Circle, the climate is moderated by the Gulf Stream. Summers are damp and cool, and winters relatively mild but windy. Proximity to the Arctic Circle puts Iceland in the "Land of the Midnight Sun," resulting in periods of twenty-four-hour daylight in June.

**History and Politics.** Norwegians began settlement of Iceland around the ninth century. The world's oldest parliament, the Althing, was established in Iceland in A.D. 930. Civil wars and instability during the thirteenth century led to the end of independence in 1262, when Iceland came under Norwegian rule. In the fourteenth century Norway was joined to Denmark's realm, and rule of Iceland passed to the Danes. The Althing was abolished in 1800 but re-established in 1843. In the 1918 Act of Union, Iceland became a sovereign state but retained its union with Denmark under a common king. Germany occupied Denmark in 1940 during World War II; and British troops, replaced by Americans in 1941, protected Iceland from invasion. Following a 1944 plebiscite, Iceland left its union with Denmark and became an independent republic. ∎

# INDIA

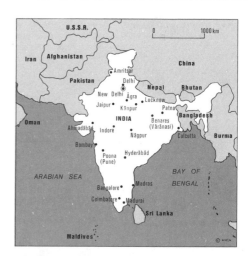

**Official name** Republic of India
**PEOPLE**
Population 841,750,000. **Density** 680/mi² (263/km²). **Urban** 26%. **Capital** New Delhi, 273,036. **Ethnic groups** Indo-Aryan 72%, Dravidian 25%, Mongoloid and other 3%. **Languages** English, Hindi, Hindustani, indigenous. **Religions** Hindu 83%, Muslim 11%, Christian 2%, Sikh 2%. **Life expectancy** 55 female, 56 male. **Literacy** 41%.
**POLITICS**
Government Republic. **Parties** Congress, Communist/Marxist, Telugu Desam, others. **Suffrage** Universal, over 21. **Memberships** CW, UN. **Subdivisions** 25 states, 7 union territories.
**ECONOMY**
GDP $196,904,000,000 **Per capita** $261. **Monetary unit** Rupee. **Trade partners** Exports: U.S.S.R., U.S., Japan. Imports: Iran, U.S., W. Germany. **Exports** Clothing and other manufactures, food, crude materials, machinery,

chemicals. **Imports** Petroleum, iron and steel and other manufactures, machinery, chemicals.
**LAND**
**Description** Southern Asia. **Area** 1,237,062 mi$^2$ (3,203,975 km$^2$). **Highest point** Kānchenjunga, 28,208 ft (8,598 m). **Lowest point** Sea level.
*The above information includes part of Jammu and Kashmir.*

**People.** India's population is composed of two main ethnic groups: the Indo-Aryans and the Dravidians. Found mostly in the north are the Indo-Aryans, a central Asian people who arrived in India around 1500 B.C., pushing the Dravidians to the south, where they remain concentrated today. A Mongoloid minority inhabits the mountains of the far north, and aboriginal groups live in the central forests and mountains. More than fourteen indigenous languages are spoken, as well as English, which is spoken by the majority of educated people. India is second only to China in population, and although Hindus are the religious majority, the country also has one of the world's largest Muslim populations. Christians, Sikhs, Jains, and Buddhists comprise additional religious minorities.

**Economy and the Land.** Economic conditions have improved since India became independent in 1947. Agriculture, upon which most Indians depend, is now more efficient, a result of modernization programs. Industry has expanded as well, and the country ranks high in its number of scientists and skilled laborers. Poverty, unemployment, and underemployment continue to plague the nation, however, partly due to rapid population growth and improved life expectancy. Many natural resources, including coal, iron ore, bauxite, and manganese, remain undeveloped. India comprises three land regions: the Himalayas along the northern border; the Gangetic plain, a fertile northern region; and the peninsula, made up mostly of the Deccan, a plateau region. The climate ranges from temperate to tropical monsoon.

**History and Politics.** India's civilization dates back to 2500 B.C., when the Dravidians flourished in the region. Aryan tribes invaded about one thousand years later, bringing the indigenous beliefs that evolved into Hinduism, and various empires followed. In the sixth or fifth century B.C., Siddhārtha Gautama, who came to be called Buddha, founded Buddhism, a major influence on Indian life until about A.D. 800. Invasions beginning around A.D. 450 brought the Huns, and during the seventh and eighth centuries Arab conquerors introduced Islam. The Mogul Empire, under a series of Muslim rulers, began in the 1500s, and the British East India Company established trading posts in the 1600s. By 1757 the East India Company had become India's major power, and by the 1850s the company controlled nearly all present-day India, Pakistan, and Bangladesh. An Indian rebellion in 1857 caused Britain to take over the East India Company's rule. Demands for independence increased after a controversial massacre of Indians by British troops in 1919. By 1920 Mohandas Gandhi had emerged as the leader of an independence campaign based on nonviolent disobedience and noncooperation. The nation gained independence in 1947, establishing Pakistan as a separate Muslim state because of

Muslim-Hindu hostilities. Recent disputes included a border conflict with China that erupted into fighting in 1959 and 1962 and a disagreement with Pakistan over the mainly Muslim region of Kashmir. Internal dissension and a high birth rate continue to inhibit India's development. Foreign policy is based on nonalignment. ∎

# INDONESIA

**Official name** Republic of Indonesia
**PEOPLE**
**Population** 189,460,000. **Density** 256/mi$^2$ (99/km$^2$).
**Urban** 25%. **Capital** Jakarta, Java I., 7,885,000. **Ethnic groups** Javanese 45%, Sundanese 14%, Madurese 8%, coastal Malay 8%. **Languages** Indonesian, Javanese, Sundanese, Madurese, other indigenous. **Religions** Muslim 87%, Protestant 7%, Catholic 3%, Hindu 2%.
**Life expectancy** 55 female, 52 male. **Literacy** 67%.
**POLITICS**
**Government** Republic. **Parties** Democratic, Golkar, United Development. **Suffrage** Universal, over 18 or married. **Memberships** ASEAN, OPEC, UN.
**Subdivisions** 27 provinces.
**ECONOMY**
**GDP** $85,081,000,000 **Per capita** $512. **Monetary unit** Rupiah. **Trade partners** Japan, U.S., Singapore. **Exports** Petroleum, natural gas, rubber and other crude materials, manufactures. **Imports** Machinery, petroleum, chemicals, iron and steel and other manufactures.
**LAND**
**Description** Southeastern Asian islands. **Area** 741,101 mi$^2$ (1,919,443 km$^2$). **Highest point** Jaya Pk., New Guinea I., 16,503 ft (5,030 m). **Lowest point** Sea level.

**People.** Indonesia is the fifth most populous nation in the world. The majority of the people are of Malay stock, which includes several subgroups, such as Javanese, Sundanese, Madurese, and coastal Malay. More than two hundred indigenous languages are spoken, but the official, unifying language is Indonesian. Most people live in small farm villages and follow ancient customs stressing cooperation. Muslim traders brought Islam to Indonesia, and most of the population is Muslim. Many Indonesians combine spirit worship with Islam or Christianity. Indonesia's rich cultural heritage includes many ancient temples.

**Economy and the Land.** Indonesia is a leading producer of petroleum in the Far East. The area also has large deposits of minerals and natural gas. Agriculture is still a major economic activity, and rice remains an important crop, though overpopulation threatens the economy and food supply. The nation's more than 13,600 islands form a natural barrier between the Indian and Pacific oceans, making the straits between the islands important for world trade and military strategy. Java, the most industrial and heavily populated island, is characterized by volcanic mountains and narrow fertile plains along the northern coast. Indonesia includes most of Borneo, the third largest island in the world. Other major Indonesian islands are Sulawesi, Sumatra, and Irian Jaya (the western half of New Guinea), which also feature inland mountains and limited coastal plains. The climate is tropical, with seasonal monsoons.

**History and Politics.** Indonesian civilization is more than 2,500 years old and has produced two major empires with influence throughout Southeast Asia. The Portuguese arrived in the sixteenth century but were outnumbered by the Dutch, who eventually gained control of most of the islands and established a plantation colony. An independence movement began early in the twentieth century and slowly gained momentum. Japan encouraged Indonesian nationalism during World War II. Shortly after the Japanese surrendered in 1945, Indonesia proclaimed itself an independent republic. Economic and political instability led to an attempted Communist coup in 1965. The government has outlawed the Communist party and strengthened relations with the West, at the same time establishing trade talks with China. Concerns continue over reported human-rights abuses in East Timor. ■

# IRAN

**Official name** Islamic Republic of Iran
**PEOPLE**
**Population** 55,280,000. **Density** 87/mi² (34/km²). **Urban** 52%. **Capital** Tehrān, 5,734,199. **Ethnic groups** Persian 63%, Turkish 18%, other Iranian 13%, Kurdish 3%. **Languages** Farsi, Turkish, Kurdish, Arabic, English, French. **Religions** Shiite Muslim 93%, Sunni Muslim 5%. **Life expectancy** 57 female, 57 male. **Literacy** 37%.
**POLITICS**
**Government** Islamic republic. **Parties** None. **Suffrage** Universal, over 15. **Memberships** OPEC, UN. **Subdivisions** 24 provinces.
**ECONOMY**
**GDP** $168,100,000,000 **Per capita** $3,778. **Monetary unit** Rial. **Trade partners** Exports: Japan, Turkey, Syria, Italy. Imports: W. Germany, Japan, U.K.. **Exports** Petroleum, carpets, fruit and nuts, cement. **Imports** Machinery, military supplies, food, pharmaceuticals.
**LAND**
**Description** Southwestern Asia. **Area** 636,296 mi² (1,648,000 km²). **Highest point** Mt. Demavend, 18,386 ft (5,604 m). **Lowest point** Caspian Sea, -92ft (-28 m).

**People.** Most Iranians are of Aryan ancestry, descended from an Asiatic people who migrated to the area in ancient times. The Aryan groups include majority Persians and minority Gilani, Mazanderani, Kurds, Lur, Bakhtiari, and Baluchi. Turks are the major non-Aryan minority. Until 1935, when the shah officially changed its name, Iran was known as Persia. Farsi, or Persian, remains the main language. Nearly all Iranians are Muslim, mainly of the Shiite sect, and the country is an Islamic republic, with law based on Islamic teachings. Minority religious groups, especially Baha'is, have been victims of persecution. Due to aridity and a harsh mountain-and-desert terrain, the population is concentrated in the west and north.

**Economy and the Land.** Iran's previously rapid economic development has slowed as a result of a 1979 revolution and a war with Iraq. Small-scale farming, manufacturing, and trading appear to be current economic trends. Oil remains the most important export, although output has decreased due to changes in economic policy and other factors. Persian carpets also continue as elements of trade. Iran's terrain consists mainly of a central plateau marked by desert and surrounded by mountains; thus agriculture is limited, and the country remains dependent on imported food. The central region is one of the most arid areas on Earth, and summers throughout most of the country are long, hot, and dry, with higher humidity along the Persian Gulf and Caspian coast. Winters are cold in the mountains of the northwest, but mild on the plain. The Caspian coastal region is generally subtropical.

**History and Politics.** Iran's history is one of the world's oldest, with a civilization dating back several thousand years. Around 1500 B.C., Aryan immigrants began arriving from central Asia, calling the region Iran, or land of the Aryans, and splitting into two groups: the Medes and the Persians. In the sixth century B.C., Cyrus the Great founded the Persian, or Achaemenian, Empire, which came to encompass Babylonia, Palestine, Syria, and Asia Minor. Alexander the Great conquered the region in the fourth century B.C. Various dynasties followed, and Muslim Arabs invaded in the A.D. 600s and established Islam as the major religion. The following centuries saw Iran's boundaries expand and recede under various rulers, and increasing political awareness resulted in a 1906 constitution and parliament. In 1908 oil was discovered in the region, and modernization programs began during the reign of Reza Shah Pahlavi, who came to power in 1925. Despite Iran's declared neutrality in World War II, the Allies invaded, obtaining rights to use the country as a supply route to the Soviet Union. The presence of foreign influences caused nationalism to increase sharply after the war. Mohammad Reza Pahlavi—who succeeded his father, Reza Shah Pahlavi, as shah—instituted social and economic reforms during the sixties, although many Muslims felt the reforms violated religious law, and resented the increasing Western orientation of the country and the absolute power of the shah. Led by Muslim leader Ayatollah Ruholla Khomeini, revolutionaries seized the government in 1979, declaring Iran an Islamic republic based upon fundamental Islamic principles. Khomeini remained the religious leader of Iran until his death in 1989. In 1990 Iran elected the first president of the republic. The country has been involved for many years in conflicts in Lebanon and the Persian Gulf. A cease-fire halted the war with Iraq in 1988. ∎

# IRAQ

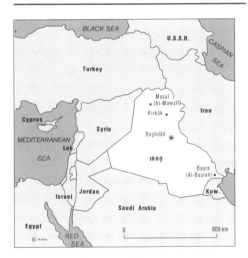

**Official name** Republic of Iraq
## PEOPLE
**Population** 17,745,000. **Density** 105/mi² (40/km²). **Urban** 71%. **Capital** Baghdād, 2,200,000. **Ethnic groups** Arab 75%-80%; Kurdish 15-20%; Turkoman, Assyrian, or other 5%. **Languages** Arabic, Kurdish, Assyrian, Armenian. **Religions** Shiite Muslim 60-65%, Sunni Muslim 32-37%, Christian and others 3%. **Life expectancy** 63 female, 62 male. **Literacy** 45%.
## POLITICS
**Government** Republic. **Parties** Baath, Democratic, Republican. **Suffrage** Universal adult. **Memberships** AL, OPEC, UN. **Subdivisions** 18 provinces.
## ECONOMY
**GDP** $42,338,000,000 **Per capita** $3,144. **Monetary unit** Dinar. **Trade partners** Exports: Pakistan, United Arab Emirates, Greece. Imports: Japan, W. Germany, Italy. **Exports** Food, fuel, chemicals, manufactured goods. **Imports** Machinery and transportation equipment, manufactures, chemicals, food.

## LAND
**Description** Southwestern Asia. **Area** 169,235 mi² (438,317 km²). **Highest point** 11,835 ft (3,607 m). **Lowest point** Sea level.

**People.** Descendants of the founders of one of the world's oldest civilizations inhabit Iraq. Most Iraqis are Muslim Arabs and Arabic speaking. The minority Kurds, also mainly Muslim, are concentrated in the northwest; speak their own language, Kurdish; and follow a non-Arab lifestyle. Kurdish demands for self-rule have led to occasional rebellion.

**Economy and the Land.** Oil is the mainstay of Iraq's economy, and nearly all economic development has focused on the petroleum industry, nationalized in the 1970s. Despite its oil wealth, the Iraqi economy, like the Iranian, has been drained by the continuing Iran-Iraq war. Most farmland lies near the Tigris and Euphrates rivers. The terrain is marked by northeastern mountains, southern and western deserts, and the plains of upper and lower Iraq, which lie between the Tigris and Euphrates rivers. The climate is generally hot and dry.

**History and Politics.** Civilizations such as the Sumerian, Babylonian, and Parthian flourished in the area of the Tigris and Euphrates in ancient times. Once known as Mesopotamia, the region was the setting for many biblical events. After coming under Persian rule in the sixth century B.C., Mesopotamia fell to Alexander the Great in the fourth century B.C. Invading Arabs brought the Muslim religion in the seventh century A.D., and for a time Baghdād was the capital and cultural center of the Arab empire. Thirteenth-century Mongol invaders were followed by Ottoman Turks in the sixteenth century. Ottoman rule continued, and following a British invasion during World War I, Mesopotamia became a British mandate at the end of the war. In 1921 the monarchy of Iraq was established, and independence was gained in 1932. Iraq and other nations formed the Arab League in 1945 and participated in a war against Israel in 1948. Opposition to monarchical rule increased during the 1950s; and after a 1958 military coup, the country was declared a republic. Instability, evidenced by coups, continued into the 1970s. The political climate was further complicated by occasional uprisings by Kurds demanding autonomy. War with Iran continued intermittently through the 1980s with heavy losses on both sides, and the countries agreed to a cease-fire in 1988. ∎

# IRELAND

**Official name** Republic of Ireland
## PEOPLE
**Population** 3,536,000. **Density** 130/mi² (50/km²). **Urban** 57%. **Capital** Dublin, 502,749. **Ethnic groups** Irish (Celtic), English. **Languages** English, Irish Gaelic. **Religions** Roman Catholic 93%, Anglican 3%. **Life expectancy** 76 female, 70 male. **Literacy** 98%.
## POLITICS
**Government** Republic. **Parties** Fianna Fail, Fine Gael, Labor, others. **Suffrage** Universal, over 18. **Memberships** EC, OECD, UN. **Subdivisions** 26 counties.
## ECONOMY
**GDP** $18,394,000,000 **Per capita** $5,117. **Monetary unit**

## 136 IRELAND • ISLE OF MAN • ISRAEL

Pound (punt). **Trade partners** Exports: U.K., W. Germany, U.S. Imports: U.K., U.S., W. Germany. **Exports** Machinery, food, chemicals, manufactures. **Imports** Machinery, manufactures, chemicals, petroleum, food.

### LAND
**Description** Northwestern European island (five-sixths of island of Ireland). **Area** 27,137 mi$^2$ (70,285 km$^2$). **Highest point** Carrauntoohil, 3,406 ft (1,038 m). **Lowest point** Sea level.

**People.** Most of Ireland's population is descended from the Celts, a people who flourished in Europe and Great Britain in ancient times. Irish Gaelic, a form of ancient Celtic, and English are official languages. Most people are Roman Catholic. Protestants mainly belong to the Church of Ireland, a member of the Anglican Communion. With a long literary tradition, the country has contributed greatly to world literature.

**Economy and the Land.** Ireland's economy was agricultural until the 1950s, when a program of rapid industrialization began. This expansion resulted in significant foreign investment, especially by the United States. Most of the Irish labor force is unionized. Agriculture continues to play an important role, however, and food is produced for domestic and foreign consumption. The country of Ireland occupies most of the island but excludes Northern Ireland, which is part of the United Kingdom. The fertile central region features green, rolling hills, suitable for farming and pastureland, and is surrounded by coastal highlands. The climate is temperate maritime, with mild summers and winters and plentiful rainfall.

**History and Politics.** Around the fourth century B.C., Ireland's indigenous population was conquered by Gaels, a Celtic tribe, from continental Europe and Great Britain. Christianity was introduced by St. Patrick in A.D. 432, and periodic Viking raids began near the end of the eighth century. In the twelfth century the pope made the Norman king of England, Henry II, overlord of the island; the English intervened in a dispute between Irish kings; and centuries of British influence began. As British control grew, so did Irish Catholic hostility, arising from seizure of land by English settlers, the Protes-

tant Reformation, and the elimination of political and religious freedoms. The Protestant majority of present-day Northern Ireland was established in the 1600s, when land taken from the Irish was distributed to English and Scottish Protestants. In 1801 the British Act of Union established the United Kingdom of Great Britain, and Northern Ireland. Religious freedom was regained in 1829, but the struggle for independence continued. Most of the Irish depended upon potatoes as a staple food, and hundreds of thousands died or emigrated in the 1840s when the crop failed because of a plant disease. Following an armed rebellion, the Irish Free State, a dominion of Great Britain, was created in 1921, with the predominantly Protestant countries in the north remaining under British rule. The nation became a republic in 1949. Many Irish citizens and Catholics in Northern Ireland continue to demand unification of the country, and the struggle occasionally erupts into violence. Neutrality remains the basis of foreign policy, and the nation is a strong supporter of European unity. ■

## ISLE OF MAN See UNITED KINGDOM.

## ISRAEL

**Official name** State of Israel

### PEOPLE
**Population** 4,460,000. **Density** 556/mi$^2$ (215/km$^2$). **Urban** 90%. **Capital** Jerusalem, 468,900. **Ethnic groups** Jewish 83%, Arab and others 17%. **Languages** Hebrew, Arabic, English, Yiddish. **Religions** Jewish 82%, Muslim 14%, Christian 2%, Druze 2%. **Life expectancy** 76 female, 73 male. **Literacy** 88%.

### POLITICS
**Government** Republic. **Parties** Labor Alignment, Likud, others. **Suffrage** Universal, over 18. **Memberships** UN. **Subdivisions** 6 districts.

### ECONOMY
**GDP** $24,559,000,000 **Per capita** $5,889. **Monetary unit** Shekel. **Trade partners** Exports: U.S., U.K., W. Germany. Imports: U.S., Belgium, W. Germany. **Exports** Diamonds and other manufactures, chemicals, fruit and other food. **Imports** Manufactures, machinery, petroleum, chemicals, food.

### LAND
**Description** Southwestern Asia. **Area** 8,019 mi$^2$ (20,770 km$^2$). **Highest point** Mt. Meron, 3,963 ft (1,208 m). **Lowest point** Dead Sea, -1,319 ft (-402 m). *The above information excludes Israeli occupied areas.*

**People.** Most Israelis are Jewish immigrants or descendants of Jews who settled in the region in the late 1800s. The two main ethnic groups are the Ashkenazim of central and eastern European origin and the Sephardim of the Mediterranean and Middle East. The non-Jewish population is predominantly Arab and Muslim, and many Palestinians inhabit the Israeli-occupied West Bank, whose status is still in dispute. Hebrew and Arabic are the official languages, and both are used on documents and currency. Conflict between conservative and liberal Jewish groups has spilled over into the nation's political life.

**Economy and the Land.** Despite drastic levels of inflation and a constant trade deficit, Israel has experienced continuous economic growth. Skilled labor supports the market economy based on services, manufacturing, and commerce. Taxes are a major source of revenue, as are grants and loans from other countries, and income from tourism. The country is poor in natural resources, but through improved irrigation and soil conservation, Israel now produces much of its own food. Because of its limited natural resources, Israel must import most of the raw materials it needs for industry. The region's varied terrain includes coastal plains, central mountains, the Jordan Rift Valley, and the desert region of the Negev. Except in the Negev, the climate is temperate.

**History and Politics.** Israel comprises much of the historic region of Palestine, known in ancient times as Canaan and the site of most biblical history. Hebrews arrived in this region around 1900 B.C. The area experienced subsequent immigration and invasion by diverse peoples, including Assyrians, Babylonians, and Persians. In 63 B.C. it became part of the Roman Empire, was renamed Judaea and finally, Palestine. In the A.D. 600s, invading Arabs brought Islam to the area, and by the early 1500s, when Ottoman Turks conquered the region, Muslims comprised a majority. During the late 1800s, as a result of oppression in eastern Europe, many Jews immigrated to Palestine, hoping to establish a Jewish state. This movement, called Zionism, and the increasing Jewish population, led to Arab-Jewish tensions. Turkey sided with Germany in World War I, and after the war the Ottoman Empire collapsed. Palestine became a mandated territory of Britain in 1920. Jewish immigration and Arab-Jewish hostility increased during the years of Nazi Germany. Additional unrest arose from conflicting interpretations of British promises and the terms of the mandate. In 1947 Britain turned to the United Nations for help, and in 1948 the nation of Israel was established. Neighboring Arab countries invaded immediately, and war ensued, during which Israel gained some land. A truce was signed in 1949, but Arab-Israeli wars broke out periodically throughout the fifties, sixties, and seventies. Israel signed a peace treaty with Egypt in 1979, annexed the Golan Heights in 1981, and returned the Sinai to Egypt the following year. The years since have seen increasing trouble with the Palestinian refugee problem and the administration of the occupied territories of the West Bank and the Gaza Strip. ■

# ITALY

**Official name** Italian Republic
**PEOPLE**
**Population** 57,625,000. **Density** 495/mi$^2$ (191/km$^2$). **Urban** 67%. **Capital** Rome, 2,815,457. **Ethnic groups** Italian (Latin). **Languages** Italian. **Religions** Roman Catholic 99%. **Life expectancy** 78 female, 71 male. **Literacy** 97%.
**POLITICS**
**Government** Republic. **Parties** Christian Democratic, Communist, Socialist, others. **Suffrage** Universal, over 18. **Memberships** EC, NATO, OECD, UN. **Subdivisions** 20 regions.
**ECONOMY**
**GDP** $358,669,000,000 **Per capita** $6,299. **Monetary unit** Lira. **Trade partners** W. Germany, France, U.S.. **Exports** Clothing and other manufactures, machinery, chemicals. **Imports** Petroleum, iron and steel and other manufactures, machinery, food, chemicals.
**LAND**
**Description** Southern Europe. **Area** 116,324 mi$^2$ (301,277 km$^2$). **Highest point** Mt. Blanc (Monte Bianco), 15,771 ft (4,807 m). **Lowest point** Sea level.

**People.** Italy is populated mainly by Italian Roman Catholics. Most speak Italian; however, dialects often differ from region to region. Despite an ethnic homogeneity, the people exhibit diversity in terms of politics and culture. The country has about twelve political parties, and northern inhabitants are relatively prosperous, employed primarily in industry, whereas southerners are generally farmers and often poor. The birthplace of the Renaissance, Italy has made substantial contributions to world culture.

**Economy and the Land.** The Italian economy is based on private enterprise, although the government is involved in some industrial and commercial activities. Industry and commercial agriculture are centered in the north, which produces steel, textiles, and chemicals. A hilly terrain makes parts of the south unsuited for crop raising, and livestock grazing is a main activity. Tourism is also important; visitors are drawn by the northern Alps, the sunny south, and the Italian cultural tradition. The island of Sicily, lying off the southwest coast, produces fruits, olives, and grapes. Sardinia, a western island, engages in some sheep and wheat raising. Except for the northern Po Valley, narrow areas along the coast, and a small section of the southern peninsula, Italy's terrain is mainly rugged and mountainous. In 1987, landslides in the Alps destroyed Sant'Antonio Morignone, isolating it from the rest of the country. The climate varies from cold in the Alps to mild and Mediterranean in other regions.

**History and Politics.** Early influences in Italy included Greeks, Etruscans, and Celts. From the fifth century B.C. to the fifth century A.D., the dominant people were Romans descended from Sabines and neighboring Latins, who inhabited the Latium coast. Following the demise of the Roman Empire, rulers and influences included Byzantines; Lombards, an invading Germanic tribe; and the Frankish King Charlemagne, whom the pope crowned emperor of the Romans in 800. During the eleventh century, Italy became a region of city-states, and its cultural life led to the Renaissance, which started in the 1300s. As the city-states weakened, Italy fell victim to invasion and rule by France, Spain, and Austria, with these countries controlling various regions at different times. In 1861 Victor Emmanuel II, the king of Sardinia, proclaimed Italy a kingdom, and by 1871 the nation included the entire peninsula, with Rome as the capital and Victor Emmanuel as king. In 1922 Benito Mussolini, the leader of Italy's Fascist movement, came to power. By 1925 Mussolini was ruling as dictator, and an almost continuous period of warfare followed. In World War II the country allied with Germany, and a popular resistance movement evolved. The monarchy was ended by plebiscite in 1946, and the country became a republic. There are now many political parties, but the Christian Democratic, Communist, and Socialist parties are dominant. Italy's Communist party is the world's largest nonruling Communist party. ∎

# IVORY COAST

**Official name** Republic of the Ivory Coast
**PEOPLE**
**Population** 11,845,000. **Density** 95/mi$^2$ (37/km$^2$). **Urban** 42%. **Capital** Abidjan (de facto), 1,500,000; Yamoussoukro (future), 80,000. **Ethnic groups** Baule 23%, Bete 18%, Senoufou 15%, Malinke 11%, other African. **Languages** French, indigenous. **Religions** Animist 63%, Muslim 25%, Christian 12%. **Life expectancy** 52 female, 49 male. **Literacy** 25%.
**POLITICS**
**Government** Republic. **Parties** Democratic. **Suffrage** Universal, over 21. **Memberships** OAU, UN. **Subdivisions** 49 provinces.
**ECONOMY**
**GDP** $6,980,000,000 **Per capita** $807. **Monetary unit** CFA franc. **Trade partners** Exports: France, U.S., Netherlands. Imports: France, W. Germany, Nigeria. **Exports** Cocoa, coffee, wood and other crude materials, petroleum. **Imports** Machinery, petroleum, rice and other food, manufactures.
**LAND**
**Description** Western Africa. **Area** 124,518 mi$^2$ (322,500 km$^2$). **Highest point** Mt. Nimba, 5,748 ft (1,752 m). **Lowest point** Sea level.

**People.** Ivory Coast is composed almost entirely of black Africans from more than sixty ethnic groups. French is the nation's official language, a result of former French rule, but many indigenous languages are spoken as well. Traditional religions predominate, though a significant number of Ivorians are Muslim or Christian. Most Ivorians live in huts in small villages, but increased numbers have moved to the cities to find work. Overcrowding is a major problem in the cities.

**Economy and the Land.** Once solely dependent upon the export of cocoa and coffee, Ivory Coast now produces and exports a variety of agricultural goods. Forest land, when cleared, provides rich soil for agriculture—still the country's main activity. Petroleum, textile, and apparel industries also contribute to the strong economy. Ivory Coast pursues a policy of economic liberalism in which foreign investment is encouraged. As a result, foreigners hold high-level positions in most Ivory Coast industries. The hot, humid coastal region gives way to inland tropical forest. Beyond the forest lies savanna, and to the northwest are highlands.

**History and Politics.** Ivory Coast once consisted of many African kingdoms. French sailors gave the region its present name when they began trading for ivory and other goods in 1483. Missionaries arrived in 1637, but European settlement was hindered by the rugged coastline and intertribal conflicts. Ivory Coast became a French colony in 1893. Movements toward autonomy began after World War II, and in 1960 Ivory Coast declared itself an independent republic. The nation has enjoyed political stability since independence and has maintained close economic ties with France. Ivory Coast has one political party, which controls the government. Foreign policy stresses favorable relations with the West. ∎

# JAMAICA

**Official name** Jamaica
## PEOPLE
**Population** 2,386,000. **Density** 562/mi² (217/km²). **Urban** 54%. **Capital** Kingston, 586,930. **Ethnic groups** African 76%, Afro-European 15%, East Indian and Afro-East Indian 3%, white 3%. **Languages** English, Creole. **Religions** Pentecostal and other Protestant, Anglican, Roman Catholic. **Life expectancy** 76 female, 70 male. **Literacy** 96%.
## POLITICS
**Government** Parliamentary state. **Parties** Labor, People's National. **Suffrage** Universal, over 18. **Memberships** CW, OAS, UN. **Subdivisions** 14 parishes.
## ECONOMY
**GDP** $2,026,000,000 **Per capita** $934. **Monetary unit** Dollar. **Trade partners** Exports: U.S., Canada, U.K. Imports: U.S., Netherlands Antilles, Venezuela. **Exports** Alumina and aluminum ores, sugar and other food, manufactures. **Imports** Petroleum, grain and other food, manufactures, machinery, chemicals.
## LAND
**Description** Caribbean island. **Area** 4,244 mi² (10,991 km²). **Highest point** Blue Mountain Pk., 7,402 ft (2,256 m). **Lowest point** Sea level.

**People.** Most Jamaicans are of African or Afro-European descent, and the majority are Christian. English is the official language, but many Jamaicans also speak Creole. Population is concentrated on the coastal plains, where the main commercial crops are also grown.

**Economy and the Land.** Agriculture is the traditional mainstay, and more than a third of the population is engaged in farming. Sugar cane and bananas are principal crops. Mining is also important, and Jamaica is a leading producer of bauxite. The tropical climate, tempered by ocean breezes, makes the island a popular tourist destination. A mountainous inland region is surrounded by coastal plains and beaches.

**History and Politics.** Christopher Columbus claimed the island for Spain in 1494. As the enslaved native population died out, blacks were brought from Africa to work plantations. Britain invaded and gained control of Jamaica in the seventeenth century, and for a time the island was one of the most important sugar and slave centers of the New World. In 1838 the British abolished slavery, the plantation economy broke down, and most slaves became independent farmers. Local political control began in the 1930s, and the nation became fully independent in 1962. Since independence the nation has faced problems of unemployment, inflation, and poverty, with periodic social unrest. Jamaica maintains a foreign policy of nonalignment. ■

# JAPAN

**Official name** Japan
## PEOPLE
**Population** 123,350,000. **Density** 846/mi² (326/km²). **Urban** 77%. **Capital** Tōkyō, Honshū I., 8,353,674. **Ethnic groups** Japanese 99%, Korean. **Languages** Japanese. **Religions** Buddhist and Shinto. **Life expectancy** 80 female, 74 male. **Literacy** 99%.
## POLITICS
**Government** Constitutional monarchy. **Parties** Clean Government (Komeito), Democratic Socialist, Liberal Democratic, Socialist, others. **Suffrage** Universal, over 20. **Memberships** OECD, UN. **Subdivisions** 47 prefectures.
## ECONOMY
**GDP** $1,325,203,000,000 **Per capita** $11,025. **Monetary unit** Yen. **Trade partners** Exports: U.S., China. Imports: U.S., Saudi Arabia, Indonesia. **Exports** Machinery, motor vehicles and other transportation equipment, manufactures. **Imports** Fuels, minerals and other crude materials, manufactures, food, machinery.
## LAND
**Description** Eastern Asian islands. **Area** 145,870 mi² (377,801 km²). **Highest point** Mt. Fuji, Honshū I., 12,388 ft (3,776 m). **Lowest point** Hachiro-gata reclamation area, Honshū I., -13 ft (-4 m).

**People.** The Japanese constitute Japan's major ethnic group, while minorities include Koreans and Chinese. Shintoism and Buddhism are the principal religions. Almost all the population lives on the coastal plains. Japan's culture blends East and West, with karate, tea ceremonies, and kimonos balanced by baseball, fast food, and business suits. Although its arts have been greatly influenced by China, Japan has developed distinctive music, literature, and painting.

**Economy and the Land.** One of the world's leading industrial powers, Japan is remarkable for its economic growth rate since World War II, considering it has few natural resources. It has also become famous for its innovative technology and continues to be a major user of robots in industry. Manufacturing is the basis of the economy, and Japan is a leading producer of ships, machinery, cars, and electronic equipment. Its chemical, iron, and steel industries are extremely profitable. Agriculture's part in the economy is small, since little of the rugged island terrain is arable. Fishing still plays a significant role in Japan's economy, though exports in this area have not been as high in recent years. Overseas trade has expanded rapidly since the 1960s, as Japan requires raw materials for its many industries. Trade barriers and the competitiveness of Japanese products overseas have led to trade deficits among Western nations. Japan's mountainous terrain includes both active and dormant volcanoes; earthquakes occasionally occur. The climate ranges from subtropical to temperate.

**History and Politics.** Legend states that Japan's first emperor was descended from the sun goddess and came to power around 600 B.C. The arrival of Buddhism, Confucianism, and new technologies from China in the fifth and sixth centuries A.D. revolutionized society. Feuding nobles controlled Japan between 1192 and 1867 and ruled as *shoguns*, or generals, in the name of the emperor. The warrior class, or *samurai*, developed early in this period. The arrival of Europeans in the sixteenth century caused fear of an invasion among the shoguns, and in the 1630s they dissolved all foreign contacts. Japan's isolation lasted until 1854, when Commodore Matthew Perry of the United States opened the nation to the West with a show of force. The subsequent Meiji Restoration modernized Japan by adopting Western technologies and legal systems, and by stressing industrialization and education. Japan embarked on military expansion in the late nineteenth century, annexing Korea in 1910 and adding to its holdings after participating in World War I as a British ally. It occupied Manchuria in 1931 and invaded China in 1937. As part of the Axis powers in World War II, Japan attacked United States military bases in Pearl Harbor, Hawaii, in 1941. After the United States dropped atomic bombs on Hiroshima and Nagasaki in 1945, Japan surrendered. Allied forces occupied the nation until 1952. By that time the Japanese approved a constitution that shifted political power from the emperor to the people and also abolished the military. In the years since, Japan has emerged as one of the world's fastest growing economies. ■

## JERSEY See UNITED KINGDOM.

## JORDAN

**Official name** Hashemite Kingdom of Jordan
**PEOPLE**
**Population** 3,011,000. **Density** 86/mi² (33/km²). **Urban** 64%. **Capital** 'Ammān, 833,500. **Ethnic groups** Arab 98%, Circassian 1%, Armenian 1%. **Languages** Arabic. **Religions** Sunni Muslim 95%, Christian 5%.

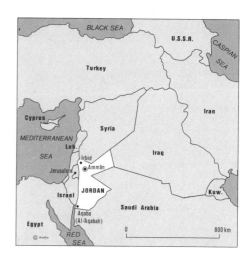

**Life expectancy** 66 female, 62 male. **Literacy** 65%.
**POLITICS**
**Government** Constitutional monarchy. **Parties** Muslim Brotherhood. **Suffrage** Universal, over 20. **Memberships** AL, UN. **Subdivisions** 8 governorates.
**ECONOMY**
**GDP** $4,067,000,000 **Per capita** $1,643. **Monetary unit** Dinar. **Trade partners** Exports: Iraq, Saudi Arabia, India. Imports: Saudi Arabia, U.S., Japan. **Exports** Fertilizer, chemicals, manufactures, vegetables and other food. **Imports** Manufactures, petroleum, food, machinery, transportation equipment, chemicals.
**LAND**
**Description** Southwestern Asia. **Area** 35,135 mi² (91,000 km²). **Highest point** Mt. Ramm, 5,755 ft (1,754 m). **Lowest point** Dead Sea, -1,319 ft (-402 m). *The above information excludes the West Bank.*

**People.** Most Jordanians are Arabs, but there are Circassian, Armenian, and Kurdish minorities, as well as a small nomadic population, the Bedouins, in desert areas. A large number of Jordanians are Palestinian refugees, displaced by Arab-Israeli wars, who have been granted citizenship by the government. Many Palestinians also live on the West Bank, a disputed area occupied by Jordan until Israel gained control in 1967. Arabic is the official language, and most people are Sunni Muslim, legacies of the Muslim conquest in A.D. 600s.

**Economy and the Land.** A nation with few natural resources, limited rainfall, and little arable land, Jordan has suffered further economic damage from an influx of refugees and the chronic political instability of the Middle East. In a 1967 war with Israel, Jordan lost the economically active West Bank, which made up about half the country's farmland. Agriculture remains the most important activity, and tourism has helped boost a weak economy that relies heavily on foreign aid and investment from the United States and Arab nations. There is some light industry and mining. The Jordan River divides Jordan into the West Bank and the East Bank, and the terrain is marked by deserts, mountains, and rolling plains. The climate ranges from Mediterranean in the west to desert in the east.

**History and Politics.** Jordan is the site of one of

the world's oldest settlements, dating back to about 8000 B.C. The area came under the rule of the Hebrews, Assyrians, Egyptians, Persians, Greeks, and Romans, and, around A.D. 636 Arab Muslims. Rule by the Ottoman Turks began in the sixteenth century, and in World War I Arab armies helped the British defeat Turkey. At the end of the war present-day Israel and Jordan became the British mandate of Palestine, which in 1922 was divided into the mandates of Transjordan, lying east of the Jordan River, and Palestine, lying to the west. Transjordan gained full independence in 1946. In 1948 the Palestine mandate created Israel, and Arab-Israeli fighting ensued. After capturing the West Bank, Transjordan was renamed Jordan in 1949. During the Arab-Israeli Six-Day War in 1967, this region and the Jordanian section of Jerusalem fell to Israel. After each war, Jordan's Palestinian-refugee population grew. A 1970 civil war pitted the government against Palestinian guerrillas, who, like Jordan, desired control of the West Bank. The guerrillas were expelled following the war, but subsequent Arab-Israeli hostilities led to Jordan's recognition of the Palestine Liberation Organization. In 1988, Jordan relinquished all claims to the Israeli-held West Bank area, although it continues to be involved in discussions on the fate of the Palestinians. Jordan is a constitutional monarchy headed by a king. ∎

# KENYA

**Official name** Republic of Kenya
**PEOPLE**
**Population** 25,350,000. **Density** 113/mi² (44/km²). **Urban** 20%. **Capital** Nairobi, 1,103,600. **Ethnic groups** Kikuyu 21%, Luhya 14%, Luo 13%, Kamba 11%, Kalenjin 11%, Kisii 6%, Meru 5%. **Languages** English, Swahili, indigenous. **Religions** Protestant 38%, Roman Catholic 28%, Animist 26%, Muslim 6%. **Life expectancy** 55 female, 51 male. **Literacy** 47%.
**POLITICS**
**Government** Republic. **Parties** African National Union.

**Suffrage** Universal, over 18. **Memberships** CW, OAU, UN. **Subdivisions** 7 provinces, 1 capital district.
**ECONOMY**
**GDP** $5,769,000,000 **Per capita** $304. **Monetary unit** Shilling. **Trade partners** Exports: U.K., W. Germany, Uganda. Imports: U.K., United Arab Emirates, Japan. **Exports** Coffee, petroleum, tea, fruit and vegetables, crude materials. **Imports** Petroleum, machinery, chemicals, manufactures, transportation equipment.
**LAND**
**Description** Eastern Africa. **Area** 224,961 mi² (582,646 km²). **Highest point** Mt. Kenya (Kirinyaga), 17,058 ft (5,199 m). **Lowest point** Sea level.

**People.** Nearly all Kenyans are black Africans belonging to one of more than forty different groups, each with its own language and culture. Some groups are nomadic, like the Masai. Arab and European minorities—found mostly along the coast—reflect Kenya's history of foreign rule. Most Kenyans live in the southwestern highlands, raising crops or livestock. Over half of the citizens practice a form of Christianity, while the rest pursue indigenous beliefs or Islam. Swahili, a blend of Bantu and Arabic, is the official language; it serves as a communication link among Kenya's many ethnic groups. English is also spoken. The national slogan of *harambee*, or "pull together," illustrates the need for cooperation among Kenya's diverse groups. The government promotes such national unity.

**Economy and the Land.** Scenic terrain, tropical beaches, and abundant wildlife have given Kenya a thriving tourist industry, and land has been set aside for national parks and game preserves. Agriculture is the primary activity, even though the northern three-fifths of the country is semidesert. The most productive soils are found in the southwestern highlands, and coffee is the main export crop. Much of the land is also used for raising livestock, another leading economic contributor. Oil from other nations is refined in Kenya, and food processing and cement production are also significant activities. Kenya's climate varies from arid in the north to temperate in the highlands and tropical along the coast.

**History and Politics.** Remains of early humans dating back more than two million years have been found in Kenya. Settlers from other parts of Africa arrived about 1000 B.C. A thousand years later Arab traders reached the coast, and controlled the area by the eighth century A.D. The Portuguese ruled the coast between 1498 and the late 1600s. Kenya came under British control in 1895 and was known as the East African Protectorate. Opposition to British rule began to mount in the 1940s as Kenyans demanded a voice in government. The Mau Mau rebellion of the fifties, an armed revolt, was an outgrowth of this discontent. Kenya gained independence from Britain in 1963 and became a republic in 1964. Its first president was Jomo Kenyatta, a Kikuyu who had been an active leader in the previous revolt. Recent administrations have pursued a policy of Africanization, under which land and other holdings have been transferred from European to African hands. ∎

# KERGUELEN ISLANDS
See FRANCE.

# KIRIBATI

**Official name** Republic of Kiribati
**PEOPLE**
**Population** 70,000. **Density** 250/mi$^2$ (96/km$^2$). **Urban** 34%. **Capital** Bairiki, Tarawa Atoll, 2,086. **Ethnic groups** Kiribatian (Micronesian). **Languages** English, Gilbertese. **Religions** Roman Catholic 53%, Congregationalist 41%, Bahai 2%. **Life expectancy** 54 female, 50 male. **Literacy** 90%.
**POLITICS**
**Government** Republic. **Parties** Christian Democratic, Gilbertese National. **Suffrage** Universal, over 18. **Memberships** CW. **Subdivisions** 6 districts.
**ECONOMY**
**GDP** $28,000,000 **Per capita** $475. **Monetary unit** Australian dollar. **Trade partners** Exports: Denmark, U.S., American Samoa. Imports: Australia, Japan, New Zealand. **Exports** Phosphates. **Imports** Machinery, food, manufactures, petroleum, beverages and tobacco.
**LAND**
**Description** Central Pacific islands. **Area** 280 mi$^2$ (726 km$^2$). **Highest point** On Banaba I., 246 ft (75 m). **Lowest point** Sea level.

**People.** The people of Kiribati, a nation of thirty-three islands in the central Pacific, are mostly Micronesian. Almost all the population lives on the Gilbert Islands in small villages and practices Roman Catholicism or Protestantism. English, the official language, and Gilbertese are spoken.

**Economy and the Land.** A small, unskilled work force combined with small land area and few natural resources have given Kiribati a subsistence economy. Phosphate and copra are the main exports. Kiribati depends on economic aid from Australia, New Zealand, and Great Britain. The islands of Kiribati are almost all coral reefs, composed of hard sand and little soil; many surround a lagoon. The climate is tropical.

**History and Politics.** Kiribati was invaded by Samoa in the 1400s. From 1916 the islands were part of the British Gilbert and Ellice Islands Colony. Fighting between the United States and Japan took place during World War II on Tarawa Island. The Ellice Islands became independent in 1978 as the nation of Tuvalu and the Republic of Kiribati came into existence a year later. ∎

# KOREA, NORTH

**Official name** Democratic People's Republic of Korea
**PEOPLE**
**Population** 22,790,000. **Density** 490/mi$^2$ (189/km$^2$). **Urban** 64%. **Capital** Pyŏngyang, 1,283,000. **Ethnic groups** Korean 100%. **Languages** Korean. **Religions** Shamanist, Chondoist, Buddhist. **Life expectancy** 71 female, 65 male. **Literacy** 95%.
**POLITICS**
**Government** Socialist republic. **Parties** Workers'.

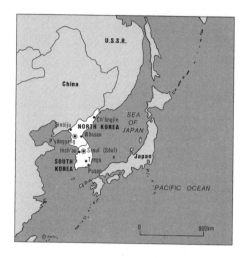

**Suffrage** Universal, over 17. **Memberships** None. **Subdivisions** 9 provinces, 4 special cities.
**ECONOMY**
**GNP** $24,000,000,000 **Per capita** $1,209. **Monetary unit** Won. **Trade partners** U.S.S.R., China, Eastern European countries, Japan. **Exports** Minerals, metal products, food, manufactures. **Imports** Petroleum, machinery, coal, grain.
**LAND**
**Description** Eastern Asia. **Area** 46,540 mi$^2$ (120,538 km$^2$). **Highest point** Paektu Mtn., 9,003 ft (2,744 m). **Lowest point** Sea level.

**People.** Despite a history of invasions, North Korea has a homogeneous population with virtually no minorities. Several dialects of Korean are spoken, and North Koreans use the Hankul, or Korean, alphabet exclusively. Korean religions have included Shamanism and Buddhism with Chondoist sects, though the government discourages religious activity. Urban population has grown rapidly since 1953 due to an emphasis on manufacturing. The nation remains more sparsely populated than South Korea.

**Economy and the Land.** The division of the Korean peninsula after World War II left North Korea with most of the industry and natural resources but little agricultural land and few skilled workers. The country has succeeded in becoming one of the most industrialized nations in Asia and in overcoming its agricultural problems. Most industry is government owned, and mines produce a variety of minerals. Farming is collectivized, and output has been aided by irrigation and other modern practices. The Soviet Union and China aided North Korea's development, but the theory of self-reliance was the government's guiding principle. A central mountainous region is bounded by coastal plains, and the climate is temperate.

**History and Politics.** History of North and South Korea follows SOUTH KOREA. ∎

# KOREA, SOUTH

**Official name** Republic of Korea
**PEOPLE**
**Population** 42,590,000. **Density** 1,114/mi² (430/km²). **Urban** 65%. **Capital** Seoul, 10,513,000. **Ethnic groups** Korean. **Languages** Korean. **Religions** Shamanist, Christian, Buddhist, Confucian, Chondoist. **Life expectancy** 71 female, 65 male. **Literacy** 88%.
**POLITICS**
**Government** Republic. **Parties** Democratic Justice, Peace and Democracy, Reunification Democratic, others. **Suffrage** Universal, over 20. **Memberships** None. **Subdivisions** 13 provinces.
**ECONOMY**
**GDP** $86,180,000,000 **Per capita** $2,037. **Monetary unit** Won. **Trade partners** U.S., Japan. **Exports** Clothing and other manufactures, machinery, ships and boats. **Imports** Machinery, petroleum, manufactures, crude materials, ships and boats.
**LAND**
**Description** Eastern Asia. **Area** 38,230 mi² (99,016 km²). **Highest point** Halla Mtn., 6,398 ft (1,950 m). **Lowest point** Sea level.

**People.** The homogeneous quality of South Korea's population is similar to that of North Korea. Population density, however, is much greater in South Korea, where two million Koreans migrated following World War II. The major language, Korean, is written predominantly in the Hankul, or Korean, alphabet, with some Chinese characters. Buddhism is practiced by most South Koreans, although Confucianism has influenced much of life.

**Economy and the Land.** South Korea was traditionally the peninsula's agricultural zone, and following the 1945 partition of the country, the south was left with little industry and few resources but abundant manpower. The economy has advanced rapidly since 1953, and today agriculture and industry are of almost equal importance. Rice, barley, and beans are principal crops; machinery and textiles are significant manufactured products. Central mountains give way to plains in the south and west, and the climate is temperate.

**History and Politics.** Korea's strategic location between Russia, China, and Japan has made it prey to foreign powers. China conquered the northern part of the peninsula in 108 B.C., influencing culture, religion, and government. Mongols controlled Korea for most of the thirteenth and fourteenth centuries. The rule of the Yi dynasty lasted from 1392 to 1910, when Japan annexed Korea. In 1945, following Japan's defeat in World War II, Soviet troops occupied northern Korea while the United States military occupied the south. The Soviet Union, the United States, and Great Britain tried to aid unification of the country but failed. The Soviets opposed a subsequent plan for United Nations–supervised elections. Separate governments were formed in 1948: the northern Democratic People's Republic of Korea and the southern Republic of Korea. Both governments claimed the peninsula, and relations became strained. After several border clashes, North Korea invaded South Korea in 1950. Chinese Communists fought on the side of North Korea, and United States/United Nations forces aided the south. An armistice ended the war in 1953, but a permanent peace treaty has never been signed. Both countries continue to claim the entire peninsula. Sporadic fighting has broken out between the north and south in recent years, and tense relations have stalled steps toward reunification.

**North Korea.** The Democratic People's Republic of Korea was established in 1948, several months after the formation of South Korea. The country incurred about 2.5 million casualties during the war with South Korea. Following the war, the government moved quickly to modernize industry and the military; North Korea maintains one of the world's largest armies. Despite its ties to the Soviet Union and China, North Korea strives for an independent foreign policy based on self-reliance.

**South Korea.** The Republic of Korea was established on August 15, 1948. The country has since experienced a presidential overthrow, military rule, and a presidential assassination. In 1980 it adopted its fifth constitution since 1948, which initiated the Fifth Republic. Students have since pressed for free elections, withdrawal of United States troops, and reunification with North Korea.

# KUWAIT

**Official name** State of Kuwait
**PEOPLE**
**Population** 1,971,000. **Density** 286/mi² (111/km²). **Urban** 94%. **Capital** Kuwait, 44,335. **Ethnic groups** Kuwaiti 40%, other Arab 39%, Southern Asian 9%, Iranian 4%. **Languages** Arabic, English. **Religions** Sunni Muslim 45%, Shiite Muslim 30%, Christian 6%. **Life expectancy** 74 female, 70 male. **Literacy** 68%.
**POLITICS**
**Government** Constitutional monarchy. **Parties** None. **Suffrage** Limited adult male. **Memberships** AL, OPEC, UN. **Subdivisions** 4 governorates.
**ECONOMY**
**GDP** $19,744,000,000 **Per capita** $10,878. **Monetary unit** Dinar. **Trade partners** Exports: Japan, Iraq, Italy. Imports: Japan, W. Germany, U.S.. **Exports** Petroleum,

manufactures. **Imports** Manufactures, machinery, transportation equipment, food.
**LAND**
**Description** Southwestern Asia. **Area** 6,880 mi$^2$ (17,818 km$^2$). **Highest point** 922 ft (281 m). **Lowest point** Sea level.

**People.** Kuwait's recent prosperity has drawn emigrants from the Persian Gulf and beyond, giving it a diverse population; there are Palestinian, Iranian, and Pakistani minorities. The population has risen dramatically since the thirties, when the oil industry began. Arabic is the official language; English is also taught and widely spoken. Almost all residents of Kuwait observe Islam, the state religion. Most belong to the Sunni branch, but there is a sizable Shiite community.

**Economy and the Land.** The economy centers on the largely government-controlled petroleum industry. Kuwait is one of the world's largest oil producers, and its oil reserves are among the world's most extensive. However, oil production and refining require a limited work force, and Kuwait has recently tried to diversify to create more jobs. Commercial fishing is gaining importance in Kuwait's economy. Because of the desert terrain, agriculture is marginal. Kuwait's climate is subtropical.

**History and Politics.** Arab nomads settled Kuwait Bay around A.D. 1700. The Al Sabah dynasty has ruled the nation since the mid-1700s. Alarmed by Turk and Arabic expansion, in 1899 Kuwait signed an agreement with Britain to guarantee Kuwait's defense. Drilling for oil began in 1936, and by 1945 Kuwait had become a major exporter. Independence came in 1961. Iraq immediately made a claim to the state but was discouraged from attacking by the arrival of British troops. Official border agreements have never been made between Kuwait and Iraq. Kuwait briefly cut off oil shipments to Western nations in retaliation for their support of Israel in the 1967 and 1973 Arab-Israeli wars. Kuwait's remarkable oil wealth, which transformed it from a poor nation into an affluent one, has enabled it to offer its citizens a wide range of benefits and to aid other Arab states. Poised at the tip of the Persian Gulf, Kuwait must always be sensitive to the interests of its many neighbors. Kuwait allied itself with Iraq in the 1980-1988 Iran/Iraq war. ∎

# LAOS

**Official name** Lao People's Democratic Republic
**PEOPLE**
**Population** 3,980,000. **Density** 44/mi$^2$ (17/km$^2$). **Urban** 16%. **Capital** Viangchan (Vientiane), 377,000. **Ethnic groups** Lao 50%; Thai 20%; Phoutheung 15%; Miao, Hmong, Yao, and others 15%. **Languages** Lao, French, Thai, indigenous. **Religions** Buddhist 85%, Animist and others 15%. **Life expectancy** 51 female, 48 male. **Literacy** 85%.
**POLITICS**
**Government** Socialist republic. **Parties** People's Revolutionary. **Suffrage** Universal, over 18. **Memberships** UN. **Subdivisions** 17 provinces.
**ECONOMY**
**GNP** $765,000,000 **Per capita** $190. **Monetary unit** Kip.

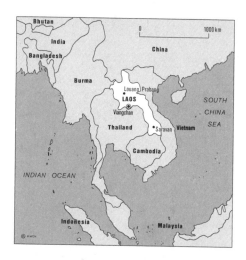

**Trade partners** Exports: Thailand, Malaysia. Imports: Thailand, U.S.S.R, Japan, France. **Exports** Wood, tin, coffee. **Imports** Rice and other food, petroleum, machinery, transportation equipment.
**LAND**
**Description** Southeastern Asia, landlocked. **Area** 91,429 mi$^2$ (236,800 km$^2$). **Highest point** Mt. Bia, 9,249 ft (2,818 m). **Lowest point** Mekong River valley, 230 ft (70 m).

**People.** Laos is populated by many ethnic groups, each with its own customs, religion, and language. Its history of culturally diverse communities is mirrored in the political divisions of recent years. The Lao are numerically and politically dominant, and Lao is the official language. Small Vietnamese and Chinese minorities exist. Most of Lao's residents are rice farmers.

**Economy and the Land.** Years of warfare, a landlocked position, and a poor transportation system have hindered the development of Laos's economy. Although agriculture is the basis of the economy, very little of the fertile land is cultivated. Substantial mineral deposits and large timber reserves also have not been exploited to their potential. Manufacturing is limited, partly because of an unskilled work force. Situated in a mountainous, densely-forested region, Laos has a tropical climate and experiences seasonal monsoons.

**History and Politics.** By A.D. 900 the forerunners of the Lao had arrived from southern China. The first united Lao kingdom was founded in 1353 and included much of modern Thailand. It dissolved into three rival states by the early 1700s, setting the stage for interference by Burma, Vietnam, and Sigam, present-day Thailand. In 1899 France made Laos part of French Indochina. Laos gained some autonomy in 1949, but this period saw the growth of Communist and anti-Communist factions whose rivalry would prevent any unified government until 1975. Although Geneva peace agreements declared Laos neutral in 1954 and 1962, the nation became increasingly embroiled in the Vietnam War as both sides in that conflict entered Laos. A protracted civil war began in 1960 between the Pathet Lao, a Communist faction aided by the North

Vietnamese, and government forces backed by the Thai and South Vietnamese. A cease-fire was signed in 1973 and a new coalition government was formed a year later. Following Communist victories in Vietnam and Kampuchea, the Pathet Lao gained control in 1975 and established the Lao People's Democratic Republic. Opposed to Communist rule, many Lao fled the country for refuge in Thailand and the United States. Laos retains close ties with Vietnam. ∎

# LEBANON

**Official name** Republic of Lebanon

**PEOPLE**
**Population** 3,377,000. **Density** 841/mi² (325/km²). **Urban** 80%. **Capital** Beirut, 509,000. **Ethnic groups** Arab 93%, Armenian 6%. **Languages** Arabic, French, Armenian, English. **Religions** Muslim 75%, Christian 25%, Jewish. **Life expectancy** 67 female, 63 male. **Literacy** 68%.
**POLITICS**
**Government** Republic. **Parties** Progressive Socialist, Liberal Nationalist, Phalangist, others. **Suffrage** Females, over 21 (with elementary education); males, over 21. **Memberships** AL, UN. **Subdivisions** 6 governorates.

**ECONOMY**
**GDP** $2,656,000,000 **Per capita** $811. **Monetary unit** Pound. **Trade partners** Exports: Saudi Arabia, Iraq, Jordan. Imports: Syria, U.S., W. Germany, France. **Exports** Fruit and vegetables, manufactures. **Imports** Food, textiles and clothing, machinery and transportation eqipment, metals.
**LAND**
**Description** Southwestern Asia. **Area** 4,015 mi² (10,400 km²). **Highest point** Mt. Sawda, 10,115 ft (3,083 m). **Lowest point** Sea level.

**People.** Traditionally home to many diverse groups, Lebanon has recently been shaken by the conflicting demands of its population. Almost all Lebanese are of Arab stock, and Arabic and French are the official languages. Palestinian refugees have settled here since the creation of Israel in 1948, many of them living in refugee camps. Lebanon's religious makeup is notable for its variety, encompassing seventeen recognized sects. Islam is now the majority religion, although Christianity continues to be a strong presence. Muslims are divided among the majority Shiite, minority Sunni, and Druze sects, while most Christians are Maronites.

**Economy and the Land.** Situated strategically between the West and the Middle East, Lebanon has long been a center of commerce. Its economy is fueled by the service sector, particularly banking. Prolonged fighting, beginning with the 1975 civil war, has greatly damaged all economic activity. Much of the work force is engaged in agriculture, and various crops are grown. The coastal area consists of a plain, behind which lie mountain ranges separated by a fertile valley. The climate is Mediterranean.

**History and Politics.** The Phoenicians settled parts of Lebanon about 3000 B.C. and were followed by Egyptian, Assyrian, Persian, Greek, and Roman rulers. Christianity came to the area during the Byzantine Empire, around A.D. 325, and Islam followed in the seventh century. In 1516 Lebanon was incorporated into the Ottoman Empire. Between the end of World War I, when the Ottoman Empire collapsed, and 1943, when Lebanon became independent, the nation was a French mandate. After independence, Muslims and Christians shared government power. Opposition to Lebanon's close ties to the West led to a 1958 insurrection, which United States marines put down at the government's request. The Palestine Liberation Organization (PLO), a group working to establish a Palestinian state, began operating from bases in Lebanon. This led to clashes with Israel in the late 1970s and early 1980s. The presence of the PLO divided Muslims, who generally supported it, from Christians, who opposed it. The increasing Muslim population also demanded a greater voice in the government. Civil war between Muslims and Christians broke out in 1975, and fighting slowed the next year with the requested aid of Syrian deterrent forces. Internal instability continued, however, along with Israeli-Palestinian hostilities. In June 1982 Israel invaded Lebanon, driving the PLO from Beirut and the south. Hundreds of Palestinian refugees were killed by the Christian Lebanese forces in September. A multinational peacekeeping force left after falling victim to terrorist attacks. Israel began a gradual withdrawal from Lebanon in 1985, but maintains a buffer zone in southern Lebanon. Syrian troops also occupy parts of the country. International attempts to reconcile warring factions have been unsuccessful. ∎

# LESOTHO

**Official name** Kingdom of Lesotho
**PEOPLE**
**Population** 1,772,000. **Density** 151/mi² (58/km²). **Urban** 17%. **Capital** Maseru, 109,382. **Ethnic groups** Sotho 100%. **Languages** English, Sesotho, Zulu, Xhosa. **Religions** Roman Catholic and other Christian 80%, tribal religionist 20%. **Life expectancy** 52 female, 46 male. **Literacy** 60%.
**POLITICS**
**Government** Constitutional monarchy. **Parties** Basotho National, Basutoland Congress, Marematlou Freedom. **Suffrage** Universal adult. **Memberships** CW, OAU, UN. **Subdivisions** 10 districts.
**ECONOMY**
**GDP** $401,000,000 **Per capita** $281. **Monetary unit** Loti. **Trade partners** South Africa. **Exports** Wool, wheat, cattle, peas, beans, corn, hides and skins, tourism, diamonds. **Imports** Corn, building materials, clothing,

**146** LESOTHO • LIBERIA

vehicles, machinery, pharmaceuticals.
**LAND**
**Description** Southern Africa, landlocked. **Area** 11,720 mi² (30,355 km²). **Highest point** Mt. Ntlenyana, 11,425 ft (3,482 m). **Lowest point** 5,000 ft (1,500 m).

**People.** The Sotho, a black African group, comprise almost all of Lesotho's population. Most Sotho live in the lowlands and raise livestock and crops. The official languages are Sesotho, a Bantu tongue, and English, and the traditional religion is based on ancestor worship, though many Sotho are Christian. A system of tribal chieftaincy is followed locally.

**Economy and the Land.** Surrounded by South Africa and having few resources, Lesotho is almost entirely dependent on South Africa for economic survival. Much of the male population must seek employment there, usually spending several months a year in South African mines or industries. Agriculture remains at the subsistence level, and soil erosion threatens production. Livestock raising represents a significant part of Lesotho's economy. Wool and mohair are among the chief exports. Diamond mining, one of the few industries, employs a small portion of the population. Most of the terrain is mountainous; the fairly high elevations give Lesotho a temperate climate.

**History and Politics.** Refugees from tribal wars in southern Africa arrived in what is now Lesotho between the sixteenth and nineteenth centuries A.D. Chief Moshoeshoe united the Sotho tribes in 1818 and led them in war against the Boers, settlers of Dutch or Huguenot descent. At Moshoeshoe's request, Basutoland came under British protection in 1868. It resisted attempts at absorption by the Union of South Africa and became the independent kingdom of Lesotho in 1966. The government of Prime Minister Leabua Jonathan, threatened by an apparent defeat at the polls, suspended the constitution in 1970 and set up a provisional assembly in 1973. Opposition to the Jonathan administration has erupted in periodic violence. Lesotho, although unforgiving of South Africa's racial policies, is forced by its geographic and economic situation to cooperate with its powerful neighbor. After claims by South Africa that Lesotho was harboring rebel groups, Lesotho agreed to expel rebels opposing South African policies. ■

# LIBERIA

**Official name** Republic of Liberia
**PEOPLE**
**Population** 2,670,000. **Density** 70/mi² (27/km²). **Urban** 40%. **Capital** Monrovia, 421,058. **Ethnic groups** Indigenous black 95%, descendants of freed American slaves 5%. **Languages** English, indigenous. **Religions** Animist 70%, Muslim 20%, Christian 10%. **Life expectancy** 51 female, 47 male. **Literacy** 21%.
**POLITICS**
**Government** Republic. **Parties** Action, National Democratic, others. **Suffrage** Universal, over 18. **Memberships** OAU, UN. **Subdivisions** 11 counties, 2 territories.
**ECONOMY**
**GDP** $811,000,000 **Per capita** $369. **Monetary unit** U.S. dollar. **Trade partners** Exports: W. Germany, U.S., Italy. Imports: U.S., W. Germany, Netherlands. **Exports** Iron ore, rubber, wood, cocoa, coffee. **Imports** Rice and other food, petroleum, manufactures, machinery.
**LAND**
**Description** Western Africa. **Area** 38,250 mi² (99,067 km²). **Highest point** Mt. Wuteve, 4,528 ft (1,380 m). **Lowest point** Sea level.

**People.** Most Liberians belong to about twenty indigenous black groups. Few are descended from the freed American slaves who founded modern Liberia, but this group—known as Americo-Liberians—has traditionally been politically dominant. The official language is English, and more than twenty other tongues are also spoken. Most people are farmers and practice traditional religious beliefs, although Islam and Christianity also have adherents. Liberia is the only black African state to escape colonialism.

**Economy and the Land.** Liberia owes its healthy economy largely to an open-door policy, which has made its extensive resources attractive to foreign nations. Two of the most important activities, iron-ore mining and rubber production, were developed by Western firms. Large timber reserves have not yet been fully exploited. Liberia also profits from the vast merchant fleet registered under its flag. The land is characterized by a coastal plain, plateaus, and low mountains, while the hot, humid climate is marked by distinct wet and dry seasons.

**History and Politics.** Early settlers are thought to have migrated from the north and east between the twelfth and seventeenth centuries A.D. Trade between Europeans and coastal groups developed after the Portuguese visited the area in the late 1400s. The American Colonization Society, a private United States organization devoted to resetting freed slaves, purchased land in Liberia, and in 1822 the first settlers landed at the site of Monrovia. The settlers declared their independence in 1847, setting up a government based on the United States model and creating Africa's first independent republic. For the next century, the Liberian government endured attempts at colonization by France and Britain, as well as internal tribal opposition. The string of Americo-Liberian rulers was broken in 1980, when a small group of soldiers of African descent toppled the government and imposed martial law. Civilian rule and some degree of harmony were restored in a 1985 election. ∎

# LIBYA

**Official name** Socialist People's Libyan Arab Jamahiriya
**PEOPLE**
Population 4,143,000. Density 6.1/mi² (2.4/km²). Urban 65%. Capital Tripoli, 858,500. Ethnic groups Arab-Berber 97%. Languages Arabic. Religions Sunni Muslim 97%. Life expectancy 60 female, 57 male. Literacy 39%.
**POLITICS**
Government Socialist republic. Parties None. Suffrage Universal adult. Memberships AL, OAU, OPEC, UN. Subdivisions 13 municipalities.

**ECONOMY**
GDP $29,884,000,000 Per capita $9,472. Monetary unit Dinar. Trade partners Exports: U.S., Italy, W. Germany. Imports: Italy, W. Germany, U.K.. Exports Petroleum. Imports Metal goods and other manufactures, machinery, food, motor vehicles.
**LAND**
Description Northern Africa. Area 679,362 mi² (1,759,540 km²). Highest point Bette, 7,438 ft (2,267 m). Lowest point Sabkhat Ghuzzayil, -154 ft (-47 m).

**People.** Libya, originally settled by Berbers, is largely a mix of Arab and Berber today. Almost all Libyans live along the coast, with some nomadic groups in desert areas. Large migrations from rural areas to the cities have accompanied Libya's oil-based prosperity. Islam is the majority religion, and nearly all Libyans speak Arabic. Traditional social orders still exist, despite centuries of foreign rule.

**Economy and the Land.** The discovery of oil in 1959 propelled Libya from the ranks of the world's poorest nations to one of its leading oil producers. It has used these revenues to develop industry and agriculture to diversify its economy. Most of Libya is covered by the Sahara Desert, and the limited agriculture has been further hurt by Libyan farmers migrating to the cities. The climate is desert except for the coast, which has moderate temperatures.

**History and Politics.** For much of its history, Libya was dominated by Mediterranean empires: Phoenician, Carthaginian, Greek, and Roman. In the seventh century A.D. the area was taken by Muslim Arabs, whose language and religion transformed Libyan culture. Although the Ottoman Turks conquered the region in the sixteenth century, local rulers remained virtually autonomous. Italy invaded Libya in 1911, and the country became an Italian colony in 1912. Following World War II, British and French forces occupied the area until a United Nations resolution made Libya an independent nation in 1951. A monarchy ruled until 1969, when a military coup established a republic headed by Colonel Mu'ammar al-Qadhafi. Under his leadership, Libya has backed Arab unity and the Palestinian cause, opposed foreign influences, and created a welfare system. Libya's support of terrorist activities led to a controversial United States air strike against the country in 1986, and several nations have instituted economic sanctions against Libya. ∎

# LIECHTENSTEIN

**Official name** Principality of Liechtenstein
**PEOPLE**
Population 28,000. Density 452/mi² (175/km²). Urban 24%. Capital Vaduz, 4,919. Ethnic groups Liechtensteiner (Alemannic) 66%, Swiss 15%, Austrian 7%, German 4%. Languages German. Religions Roman Catholic 83%, Protestant 7%. Life expectancy 74 female, 65 male. Literacy 100%.
**POLITICS**
Government Constitutional monarchy. Parties Fatherland Union, Progressive Citizens'. Suffrage Universal adult. Memberships None. Subdivisions 11 communes.
**ECONOMY**
GDP $710,000,000 Per capita $26,296. Monetary unit

# LIECHTENSTEIN • LUXEMBOURG

Swiss franc. **Trade partners** Switzerland. **Exports** Machinery and transportation equipment, manufactures, metals, chemicals. **Imports** Machinery and transportation equipment, manufactures, metals.
**LAND**
**Description** Central Europe, landlocked. **Area** 62 mi$^2$ (160 km$^2$). **Highest point** Vorder-Grauspitz, 8,527 ft (2,599 m). **Lowest point** Ruggleller Riet, 1,411 ft (430 m).

**People.** In spite of its location at the crossroads of Europe, Liechtenstein has retained a largely homogeneous ethnicity. Almost all Liechtensteiners are descended from the Alemanni, a Germanic tribe, and many speak the Alemanni dialect. German, however, is the official language. Roman Catholicism is the most widely practiced religion but a Protestant minority also exists. Most of the country is mountainous, and population is concentrated on the fertile plains adjacent to the Rhine River, which forms the country's western boundary. Most Liechtensteiners work in factories or in trades.

**Economy and the Land.** The last few decades have seen the economy shift from agricultural to highly industrialized. Despite this growth in industry, Liechtenstein has not experienced a serious pollution problem, and the government continues its work to prevent the problem from occurring. An economic alliance with Switzerland dating from 1923 has been profoundly beneficial to Liechtenstein: the two nations form a customs union and use the same currency. Other important sources of revenue are tourism, the sale of postage stamps, and taxation of foreign businesses headquartered here. Most of Liechtenstein, one of the world's smallest nations, is covered by the Alps; nonetheless, its climate is mild.

**History and Politics.** Early inhabitants of what is now Liechtenstein included the Celts, Romans, and Alemanni, who arrived about A.D. 500. The area became part of the empire of the Frankish King Charlemagne in the late 700s, and following Charlemagne's death, it was divided into the lordships of Vaduz and Schellenberg. By 1719, when the state became part of the Holy Roman Empire, the Austrian House of Liechtenstein had purchased both lordships, uniting them as the Imperial Principality of Liechtenstein. The nation's independence dates from the abolition of the empire by France's Napoleon Bonaparte in 1806. Liechtenstein was neutral in both world wars and has remained unaffected by European conflicts. The government is a hereditary constitutional monarchy; the prince is the head of the House of Liechtenstein, thus chief of state, and the prime minister is the head of government. In 1984, women gained the right to vote. ∎

# LUXEMBOURG

**Official name** Grand Duchy of Luxembourg
**PEOPLE**
**Population** 381,000. **Density** 382/mi$^2$ (147/km$^2$). **Urban** 81%. **Capital** Luxembourg, 78,924. **Ethnic groups** Luxembourger (mixed Celtic, French, and German). **Languages** French, Luxembourgish, German, English. **Religions** Roman Catholic 97%, Jewish and Protestant 3%. **Life expectancy** 74 female, 68 male. **Literacy** 99%.
**POLITICS**
**Government** Constitutional monarchy. **Parties** Christian Socialist, Liberal, Socialist Workers, others. **Suffrage** Universal, over 18. **Memberships** EC, NATO, OECD, UN. **Subdivisions** 3 districts.
**ECONOMY**
**GDP** $3,567,000,000 **Per capita** $9,773. **Monetary unit** Franc. **Trade partners** W. Germany, Belgium, France. **Exports** Iron and steel products. **Imports** Minerals, metals, foodstuffs, machinery.
**LAND**
**Description** Western Europe, landlocked. **Area** 998 mi$^2$ (2,586 km$^2$). **Highest point** Buurgplaatz, 1,834 ft (559 m). **Lowest point** Confluence of Moselle and Sûre rivers, 427 ft (130 m).

**People.** Luxembourg's population bears the imprint of foreign influences, yet retains an individual character. Most Luxembourgers are a blend of Celtic, French, and German stock. German and French are official languages, as is Luxembourgish, an indigenous German dialect. Roman Catholicism is observed by virtually all the population. There are significant communities of guest workers from sev-

LUXEMBOURG • MACAO • MADAGASCAR

eral European nations.

**Economy and the Land.** Luxembourg's steel industry forms the basis of its economy, and the country has compensated for a worldwide drop in the steel market by developing financial services, notably banking. Manufacturing of plastics and chemicals is also important, as is tourism. Luxembourg's trade benefits from the country's membership in the European Community and the Benelux union. Luxembourg has two distinct regions: the mountainous, wooded north and the open, rolling south, known as Bon Pays. The climate is temperate.

**History and Politics.** The present city of Luxembourg developed from a castle built in A.D. 963 by Count Siegfried of Ardennes. Several heavily fortified towns grew up around the castle, and the area became known as the "Gibraltar of the North" because of those fortifications. The duchy remained semiautonomous until the Burgundians conquered the area in 1443. Various European powers ruled Luxembourg for most of the next four centuries, and in 1815 the duchy was elevated to a grand duchy. It became autonomous in 1839 and was recognized in 1867 as an independent state. Despite Luxembourg's declaration of neutrality, Germany occupied the country in both world wars. Luxembourg maintains a pro-Western, pan-European stance in its foreign relations. ∎

# MACAO

**Official name** Macao
**PEOPLE**
**Population** 454,000. **Density** 68,788/mi² (26,706/km²). **Urban** 98%. **Capital** Macao, Macao I., 429,000. **Ethnic groups** Chinese 95%, Portuguese 3%. **Languages** Portuguese, Chinese (Cantonese). **Religions** Buddhist, Roman Catholic. **Literacy** 79%.
**POLITICS**
**Government** Chinese territory under Portuguese administration. **Parties** None. **Suffrage** Portuguese, Chinese, and foreign residents, over 18. **Memberships** None. **Subdivisions** 2 districts.
**ECONOMY**
**GNP** $1,030,000,000 **Per capita** $3,323. **Monetary unit** Pataca. **Trade partners** Exports: U.S., Hong Kong, W. Germany. Imports: Hong Kong, China, Japan. **Exports** Clothing and other manufactures, machinery. **Imports** Textiles and other manufactures, food, machinery, crude materials.
**LAND**
**Description** Eastern Asia (islands and peninsula on China's southeastern coast). **Area** 6.6 mi² (17 km²). **Highest point** Coloane Alto, I. de Coloane, 571 ft (174 m). **Lowest point** Sea level.

**People.** Situated on the southeastern China coast, 17 miles (27.4 km) west of Hong Kong, Macao is populated almost entirely by Chinese. An overseas province of Portugal, the island includes people of Portuguese and mixed Chinese-Portuguese descent. Several Chinese dialects are widely spoken, and Portuguese is the official language. Buddhism is Macao's principal religion; a small percentage of its population are Roman Catholics.

**Economy and the Land.** Tourism, gambling, and light industry help make up Macao's economy; however, its leading industries are textiles and light manufacturing, which employ the majority of the labor force. Macao has been likened to Hong Kong because of its textile exports, yet it remains a heavy importer, relying on China for drinking water and much of its food supply. The province consists of the city of Macao, located on a peninsula, and the nearby islands of Taipa and Coloane. The climate is maritime tropical, with cool winters and warm summers.

**History and Politics.** Macao became a Portuguese trading post in 1557. It flourished as the midpoint for trade between China and Japan but declined when Hong Kong became a trading power in the mid-1800s. Macao remained a neutral port during World War II and was economically prosperous. Although the government is nominally directed by Portugal, any policies relating to Macao are subject to China's approval. Macao is the oldest European settlement in the Far East. It will be returned to China in 1999 under a negotiated agreement whereby the present capitalist system will be maintained for 50 years. ∎

# MADAGASCAR

**Official name** Democratic Republic of Madagascar
**PEOPLE**
**Population** 11,615,000. **Density** 51/mi² (20/km²). **Urban** 22%. **Capital** Antananarivo, 663,000. **Ethnic groups** Merina 15%, Betsimisaraka 9%, Betsileo 7%, Tsimihety 4%, Antaisaka 4%, other tribes. **Languages** Malagasy, French. **Religions** Animist 52%, Christian 41%, Muslim 7%. **Life expectancy** 50 female, 49 male. **Literacy** 81%.
**POLITICS**
**Government** Republic. **Parties** Advance Guard of the Revolution, Militants for the Establishment of a Proletarian Regime. **Suffrage** Universal, over 18. **Memberships** OAU, UN. **Subdivisions** 6 provinces.
**ECONOMY**
**GDP** $2,345,000,000 **Per capita** $240. **Monetary unit**

## 150 MADAGASCAR • MADEIRA ISLANDS • MALAWI

Franc. **Trade partners** Exports: France, U.S., Singapore. Imports: France, Saudi Arabia. **Exports** Spices, coffee, petroleum, shellfish. **Imports** Petroleum, machinery, rice and other grains, chemicals, manufactures.
**LAND**
**Description** Southeastern African island. **Area** 226,658 mi$^2$ (587,041 km$^2$). **Highest point** Maromokotro, 9,436 ft (2,876 m). **Lowest point** Sea level.

**People.** Most of the population is of mixed African and Indonesian descent. Those who live on the coast, the *cotiers*, are of predominantly African origin, while those on the inland plateau have Asian roots. There is a long-standing rivalry between the *cotiers* and the inland groups, most of whom belong to the Merina people. The official languages are French and Malagasy. Sizable Christian communities exist, but most Malagasy practice indigenous beliefs that involve ancestor worship.

**Economy and the Land.** Madagascar is chiefly an agricultural nation, with the majority of the work force engaged in farming or herding. Overpopulation and outmoded cultivation have recently cut into yields of rice, an important crop, and other products. Varied mineral resources, including oil, point to possible expansion. The climate is tropical on the coastal plains and moderate in the inland highlands.

**History and Politics.** Madagascar's first settlers are thought to be Indonesians, who brought African wives and slaves around two thousand years ago. Arab traders established themselves on the coast in the seventh century. The Portuguese first sighted the island in the 1500s, and other Europeans followed. The Merina kingdom, based in the central plateau, gained control over most of the island in the 1790s. French influence grew throughout the nineteenth century, and in 1896 France made the island a colony after subduing the Merina. Resentment of French rule continued, culminating in an armed revolt in 1947. Full independence came in 1960. After twelve years of rule by the same president, a coup placed the military in power. A new constitution was adopted in 1975 that established the Democratic Republic of Madagascar. ∎

# MADEIRA ISLANDS
See PORTUGAL.

# MALAWI

**Official name** Republic of Malawi
**PEOPLE**
**Population** 8,335,000. **Density** 182/mi$^2$ (70/km$^2$). **Urban** 12%. **Capital** Lilongwe, 175,000. **Ethnic groups** Chewa, Nyanja, Tumbuka, Yao, Lomwe, others. **Languages** Chichewa, English, Tumbuka. **Religions** Protestant 55%, Roman Catholic 20%, Muslim 20%. **Life expectancy** 46 female, 44 male. **Literacy** 25%.
**POLITICS**
**Government** Republic. **Parties** Congress. **Suffrage** Universal, over 21. **Memberships** CW, OAU, UN. **Subdivisions** 3 regions.
**ECONOMY**
**GDP** $1,203,000,000 **Per capita** $185. **Monetary unit** Kwacha. **Trade partners** Exports: U.K., U.S., Netherlands. Imports: South African countries, U.K., W. Germany. **Exports** Tobacco, sugar, tea, textiles,

peanuts. **Imports** Textiles and other manufactures, machinery, chemicals, petroleum, food.
**LAND**
**Description** Southern Africa, landlocked. **Area** 45,747 mi$^2$ (118,484 km$^2$). **Highest point** Sapitwa, 9,849 ft (3,002 m). **Lowest point** Shire River valley, 120 ft (37 m).

**People.** Almost all Malawians are black Africans descended from Bantu peoples. The Chewa constitute the majority in the central area, while the Nyanja are dominant in the south and the Tumbuka in the north. Chichewa and English are official languages. The majority of the population is rural, and traditional village customs are prevalent. For the most part, the society is matriarchal. Many Malawians combine Christian or Muslim beliefs with traditional religious practices.

**Economy and the Land.** A landlocked nation with limited resources and a largely unskilled work force, Malawi relies almost entirely on agriculture. A recent series of poor harvests, combined with a tripling of the population between 1950 and 1989, has contributed to the decline in agricultural output. Among the main exports are tea and tobacco. Many Malawians work part of the year as miners in South Africa, Zambia, and Zimbabwe. Malawi, situated along the Great Rift Valley, has a varied terrain with highlands, plateaus, and lakes. The climate is subtropical, and rainfall varies greatly from north to south.

**History and Politics.** Archaeological findings indicate that Malawi has been inhabited for at least fifty thousand years. Bantu-speaking peoples, ancestors of the Malawians, immigrated from the north around A.D. 1400 and soon formed centralized kingdoms. In the 1830s, other Bantu groups, involved in the slave trade, invaded the region. The arrival of Scottish missionary David Livingstone in 1859 began a period of British influence; in 1891 the territory became the British protectorate of Nyasaland. Beginning in 1953, Nyasaland was part of the larger Federation of Rhodesia and Nyasaland. Malawi attained independence in 1964 and became a republic in 1966, with nationalist leader Dr. H.

Kamuzu Banda as its first president. The Malawi Congress party appointed Banda as president-for-life in 1970. ∎

## MALAYSIA

**Official name** Malaysia
**PEOPLE**
**Population** 17,480,000. **Density** 135/mi² (52/km²). **Urban** 38%. **Capital** Kuala Lumpur, 937,817. **Ethnic groups** Malay and other indigenous 60%, Chinese 31%, Indian 8%. **Languages** Malay, Chinese dialects, English, Tamil. **Religions** Muslim 53%, Buddhist 17%, Chinese religions 12%, Hindu 7%. **Life expectancy** 69 female, 65 male. **Literacy** 83%.
**POLITICS**
**Government** Constitutional monarchy. **Parties** Democratic Action, Islamic, National Front. **Suffrage** Universal, over 21. **Memberships** ASEAN, CW, UN. **Subdivisions** 13 states, 2 federal territories.
**ECONOMY**
**GDP** $31,231,000,000 **Per capita** $2,015. **Monetary unit** Ringgit. **Trade partners** Exports: Singapore, Japan, U.S. Imports: Japan, U.S., Singapore. **Exports** Petroleum, machinery, wood, rubber, tin and other manufactures, palm oil. **Imports** Machinery, manufactures, petroleum, food, transportation equipment, chemicals.
**LAND**
**Description** Southeastern Asia (includes part of the island of Borneo). **Area** 129,251 mi² (334,758 km²). **Highest point** Mt. Kinabalu, Borneo I., 13,455 ft (4,101 m). **Lowest point** Sea level.

**People.** Malaysia's location at one of Southeast Asia's maritime crossroads has left it with a diverse population, including Malays, Chinese, Indians, and native non-Malay groups. The mostly rural Malays dominate politically, while the predominantly urban Chinese are very active in economic life. Considerable tension exists between the two groups. Although most Malays speak Malay and practice Islam, Malaysia's ethnic groups have resisted assimilation; Chinese, Indian, and Western languages and beliefs are also part of the culture. Most Malaysians live in Peninsular Malaysia.

**Economy and the Land.** The economy is one of the healthiest in the region, supported by multiple strengths in agriculture, mining, forestry, and fishing. The nation is one of the world's leading producers of rubber, palm oil, and tin, and one of the Far East's largest petroleum exporters. Manufacturing is also being developed. Malaysia consists of the southern portion of the Malay Peninsula and the states of Sarawak and Sabah on northern Borneo. The land is characterized by swampy areas, mountains, and rain forests. The climate is tropical and very humid.

**History and Politics.** The Malay Peninsula has been inhabited since the late Stone Age. Hindu and Buddhist influences were widespread from the ninth through the fourteenth centuries A.D., after which Islam was introduced. In 1511 the Portuguese seized Melaka, a trading center, but were soon replaced, first by the Dutch in 1641 and then by the British in 1795. By the early 1900s, Britain was in control of present-day Malaysia and Singapore, the areas which were occupied by Japan during World War II. Following the war, the Federation of Malaya was created, a semiautonomous state under British authority. A guerrilla war ensued, waged by Chinese Communists and others who opposed the British. The country gained full independence in 1963 with the unification of Malaysia. Singapore seceded in 1965. As a result of the impact of large numbers of Vietnamese refugees, Malaysia announced that as of April 1989 it could accept no more. ∎

## MALDIVES

**Official name** Republic of Maldives
**PEOPLE**
**Population** 211,000. **Density** 1,835/mi² (708/km²). **Urban** 20%. **Capital** Male, Male I., 46,334. **Ethnic groups** Maldivian (mixed Sinhalese, Dravidian, Arab, and black). **Languages** Divehi. **Religions** Sunni Muslim. **Life expectancy** 50 female, 53 male. **Literacy** 82%.

## MALDIVES • MALI • MALTA

**POLITICS**
**Government** Republic. **Parties** None. **Suffrage** Universal, over 21. **Memberships** CW, UN. **Subdivisions** 19 districts, 1 capital city.
**ECONOMY**
GDP $84,000,000 **Per capita** $480. **Monetary unit** Rufiyaa. **Trade partners** Japan, Sri Lanka, Thailand. **Exports** Fish, clothing. **Imports** Fuel, food, machinery, transportation equipment, textiles.
**LAND**
**Description** Indian Ocean islands. **Area** 115 mi$^2$ (298 km$^2$). **Highest point** On Male I., 80 ft (24 m). **Lowest point** Sea level.

**People.** Most Maldivians are descended from Sinhalese peoples from Sri Lanka; southern Indians, or Dravidians; and Arabs. Nearly all Maldivians are Sunni Muslims and speak Divehi. The population is concentrated on Male, the capital island.

**Economy and the Land.** The nation draws on its advantages as a union of twelve hundred islands to fuel its economy: tourism, shipping, and fishing are the mainstays. With limited arable land and infertile soil, agriculture is marginal. The Maldives, flat coral islands, form a chain of nineteen atolls. Seasonal monsoons mark the tropical climate.

**History and Politics.** The Maldives are believed to have been originally settled by southern Indian peoples. Arab sailors brought Islam to the islands in the twelfth century A.D. Although a Muslim sultanate remained in power with only two interruptions from 1153 until 1968, the Portuguese and Dutch controlled the islands intermittently between the 1500s and the 1700s. The Maldives were a British protectorate from 1887 to 1965, when they achieved independence. They declared the country a republic three years later. The Republic of Maldives is nonaligned and maintains close ties with other Islamic nations. ∎

# MALI

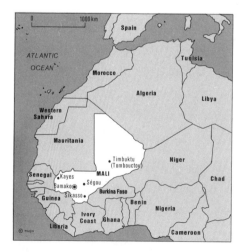

**Official name** Republic of Mali
**PEOPLE**
**Population** 9,293,000. **Density** 19/mi$^2$ (7.5/km$^2$). **Urban** 18%. **Capital** Bamako, 740,000. **Ethnic groups** Malinke 50%, Fulani 17%, Voltaic 12%, Songhai 6%. **Languages** French, Bambara, indigenous. **Religions** Sunni Muslim 90%, Animist 9%, Christian 1%. **Life expectancy** 44 female, 40 male. **Literacy** 9%.
**POLITICS**
**Government** Republic. **Parties** Democratic Union of the People. **Suffrage** Universal, over 21. **Memberships** OAU, UN. **Subdivisions** 8 districts.
**ECONOMY**
GDP $538,000,000 **Per capita** $70. **Monetary unit** CFA franc. **Trade partners** France, Ivory Coast, W. Germany. **Exports** Cotton, clothing, livestock and other food, peanut oil. **Imports** Petroleum, machinery, manufactures, transportation equipment, food.
**LAND**
**Description** Western Africa, landlocked. **Area** 478,767 mi$^2$ (1,240,000 km$^2$). **Highest point** Hombori Mtn., 3,789 ft (1,155 m). **Lowest point** Senegal River valley, 72 ft (22 m).

**People.** The majority of Malians belong to one of several black groups, although there is a small non-black nomadic population. Most Malians are farmers who live in small villages. The official language is French, but most people communicate in Bambara, a market language. The population is concentrated in the basins of the Niger and Senegal rivers in the south. Heirs of three ancient empires, Malians have produced a distinct culture.

**Economy and the Land.** One of the world's poorest nations, Mali depends primarily on agriculture but is limited by a climate that produces drought and a terrain that is almost half desert. Mineral reserves have not been exploited because of poor transportation and power facilities. Food processing and textiles account for most industry. A landlocked country, Mali faces a growing national debt due to its dependence on foreign goods. The climate is hot and dry, with alternating dry and wet seasons.

**History and Politics.** Parts of present-day Mali once belonged to the Ghana, Mali, and Songhai empires. These wealthy empires, which ruled from about A.D. 300 to 1600, traded with the Mediterranean world and were centers of Islamic learning. Fierce native resistance delayed colonization by the French until 1904, when French Sudan, as the area was called, was made part of French West Africa. In 1959 it joined Senegal to form the Federation of Mali. Senegal soon withdrew from the union, and French Sudan declared itself the Republic of Mali in 1960. A military coup overthrew the republic, a socialist state, in 1968. In 1979, the country reestablished civilian rule. ∎

# MALTA

**Official name** Republic of Malta
**PEOPLE**
**Population** 347,000. **Density** 2,844/mi$^2$ (1,098/km$^2$). **Urban** 85%. **Capital** Valletta, 9,263. **Ethnic groups** Maltese (mixed Arab, Sicilian, Norman, Spanish, Italian, and English). **Languages** English, Maltese. **Religions** Roman Catholic 98%. **Life expectancy** 74 female, 69 male. **Literacy** 88%.
**POLITICS**
**Government** Republic. **Parties** Labor, Nationalist. **Suffrage** Universal, over 18. **Memberships** CW, UN.

MALTA • MARSHALL ISLANDS • MARTINIQUE • MAURITANIA  **153**

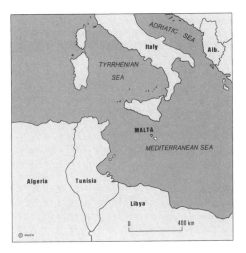

**Subdivisions** 6 regions.
**ECONOMY**
GDP $1,017,000,000 **Per capita** $2,825. **Monetary unit** Lira. **Trade partners** Exports: W. Germany, U.K., Italy. Imports: Italy, U.K., W. Germany. **Exports** Clothing, eyeglasses, and other manufactures; machinery. **Imports** Textiles and other manufactures, machinery, food, petroleum, chemicals.
**LAND**
**Description** Mediterranean island. **Area** 122 mi$^2$ (316 km$^2$). **Highest point** 829 ft (253 m). **Lowest point** Sea level.
**People.** Malta's diverse population reflects centuries of rule by Arabs, Normans, and British. The official languages are English and Maltese, the latter a blend of Arabic and a Sicilian dialect of Italian. Roman Catholicism is practiced by the majority of residents. Malta is one of the world's most densely populated nations.

**Economy and the Land.** Situated strategically between Europe and Africa, Malta became an important military site for foreign powers with the opening of the Suez Canal in 1869. Its economy, shaped by the patterns of war and peace in the Mediterranean, has recently turned toward commercial shipbuilding, construction, manufacturing, and tourism. Its soil is poor, and most food is imported. Although there are many natural harbors and hundreds of miles of coastline, fishing is not a major source of income. Malta, with its hilly terrain, is subtropical in summer and temperate the rest of the year.

**History and Politics.** The Phoenicians and Carthaginians first colonized the island of Malta between 1000 and 600 B.C. After becoming part of the Roman and Byzantine empires, Malta was ruled successively by Arabs, Normans, and various feudal lords. In the 1500s the Holy Roman Emperor Charles V ceded Malta to the Knights of St. John of Jerusalem, an order of the Roman Catholic church. The Knights' reign, marked by cultural and architectural achievements, ended with surrender to France's Napoleon Bonaparte in 1798. The Maltese resisted French rule, however, and offered control to Britain, becoming part of the United Kingdom in 1814. Throughout both world wars, Malta was a vital naval base for the Allied forces. It achieved independence from Britain in 1964 and became a republic ten years later. In 1979 the last British and North Atlantic Treaty Organization (NATO) military forces departed, and Malta declared its neutrality and nonalignment. ∎

## MARSHALL ISLANDS
See UNITED STATES.

## MARTINIQUE See FRANCE.

## MAURITANIA

**Official name** Islamic Republic of Mauritania
**PEOPLE**
**Population** 2,008,000. **Density** 5.1/mi$^2$ (2.0/km$^2$). **Urban** 35%. **Capital** Nouakchott, 285,000. **Ethnic groups** Mixed Moor and black 40%, Moor 30%, black 30%. **Languages** Arabic, French, indigenous. **Religions** Sunni Muslim 100%. **Life expectancy** 46 female, 42 male. **Literacy** 17%.
**POLITICS**
**Government** Provisional military government. **Parties** None. **Suffrage** Universal adult. **Memberships** AL, OAU, UN. **Subdivisions** 12 regions, 1 capital district.
**ECONOMY**
GDP $697,000,000 **Per capita** $386. **Monetary unit** Ouguiya. **Trade partners** Exports: Japan, France, Spain. Imports: France, Spain, Senegal. **Exports** Iron ore, fish. **Imports** Machinery and transportation equipment, wheat, manufactures, fuel.
**LAND**
**Description** Western Africa. **Area** 395,956 mi$^2$ (1,025,520 km$^2$). **Highest point** Mt. Jill, 3,002 ft (915 m). **Lowest point** Sebkha de Ndrhamcha, -10 ft (-3 m).
**People.** Most Mauritanians are Moors, descendants of Arabs and Berbers, or of mixed Arab, Berber, and black descent. The Moors, who speak Arabic, are mostly nomadic herdsmen. The remainder of the population is composed of black Africans, who speak several languages and farm in the

Senegal River valley. Virtually all Mauritanians are Muslim. Proportionally, the nomadic population has declined recently because of long periods of drought, although overall population is increasing.

**Economy and the Land.** Mauritania's economy is based on agriculture, with many farmers producing only subsistence-level outputs. Crop production, confined chiefly to the Senegal River valley, has recently fallen because of drought and outmoded cultivation methods. Mining of high-grade iron-ore deposits is the main industrial activity, although fishing and fish processing are also important. Inadequate transportation and communication systems and a war with Western Sahara have crippled the economy. In addition to the river valley, land regions include a northern desert and southeastern grasslands. Mauritania has a hot, dry climate.

**History and Politics.** Berbers began settling in parts of the area around A.D. 300 and established a network of caravan trading routes. From this time until the late 1500s, sections of the south were dominated by the Ghana, the Mali, and finally the Songhai empires. Contact with Europeans grew between the 1600s and 1800s, and in 1920 France made Mauritania a colony. Mauritania attained independence in 1960, although Morocco claimed the area and did not recognize the state until 1970. During the late seventies, Mauritania became embroiled in a war with Morocco and the Polisario Front, a Western Saharan nationalist group, for control of Western Sahara. Mauritania withdrew its claim to the area in 1979. A coup in 1978 ended seventeen years of presidential rule and established a military government. Local elections were held in the late 1980s in a first step towards democratization. ■

# MAURITIUS

**Official name** Mauritius
**PEOPLE**
**Population** 1,105,000. **Density** 1,402/mi$^2$ (542/km$^2$).
**Urban** 42%. **Capital** Port Louis, Mauritius I., 139,730.

**Ethnic groups** Indo-Mauritian 68%, Creole 27%, Sino-Mauritian 3%, Franco-Mauritian 2%. **Languages** English, Creole, French, Bhojpuri. **Religions** Hindu 30%, Roman Catholic 28%, Muslim 16%, Tamil 7%. **Life expectancy** 69 female, 64 male. **Literacy** 67%.
**POLITICS**
**Government** Parliamentary state. **Parties** Labor, Militant Socialist Movement, Militant Movement, Social Democratic, others. **Suffrage** Universal, over 18.
**Memberships** CW, OAU, UN. **Subdivisions** 9 districts.
**ECONOMY**
**GDP** $1,061,000,000 **Per capita** $1,035. **Monetary unit** Rupee. **Trade partners** Exports: U.K., France, U.S. Imports: Bahrain, France, South African countries.
**Exports** Sugar, clothing and other manufactures.
**Imports** Textiles and other manufactures, grain and other food, petroleum, machinery.
**LAND**
**Description** Indian Ocean island. **Area** 788 mi$^2$ (2,040 km$^2$). **Highest point** Piton de la Petite Rivière Noire, 2,717 ft (828 m). **Lowest point** Sea level.
*The above information includes dependencies.*

**People.** Mauritius's diverse ethnicity is largely the product of its past as a sugar-producing colony. Creoles are descendants of African slaves and European plantation owners, while the Indian community traces its roots to laborers who replaced the Africans after slavery was abolished. There are also people of Chinese and French descent. Franco-Mauritians now compose most of the nation's elite. English is the official tongue, but French, a French creole, and many other languages are also spoken. Religious activity is similarly varied and includes followers of Hinduism, Christianity, Islam, and Tamil.

**Economy and the Land.** Sugar remains fundamental to the economy: almost all arable land is covered by sugar cane, and sugar and its by-products make up the majority of exports. Attempts have been made at diversification, with tea and tobacco recently introduced. Inflation, unemployment, overpopulation, and low sugar prices cloud the economic outlook. The nation includes the island of Mauritius, Rodrigues Island, Agalega Islands, and Cargados Carajos Shoals. The climate is tropical.

**History and Politics.** Although visited by Arab, Malay, and Portuguese sailors between the tenth and sixteenth centuries A.D., Mauritius was uninhabited until 1598, when the Dutch claimed it. They abandoned the island in 1710, and five years later the French made it their colony. During the 1700s, the French used Mauritius, which they called Île de France, as a naval base and established plantations worked by imported slaves. The British ousted the French in 1810 and outlawed slavery soon afterward. In the nineteenth century indentured workers from India replaced the slaves. Mauritius began its history as an independent state in 1968 with a system of parliamentary democracy. In 1982, the Militant Socialist Movement succeeded the Labor Party, which had been in power for fourteen years. ■

# MAYOTTE See FRANCE.

# MEXICO

**Official name** United Mexican States
**PEOPLE**
**Population** 85,090,000. **Density** 113/mi² (43/km²). **Urban** 70%. **Capital** Mexico City, 8,831,079. **Ethnic groups** Mestizo 60%, Amerindian 30%, white 9%. **Languages** Spanish, indigenous. **Religions** Roman Catholic 97%, Protestant 3%. **Life expectancy** 68 female, 64 male. **Literacy** 83%.
**POLITICS**
**Government** Republic. **Parties** Cardenist Front of the Nationalist Reconstruction, Institutional Revolutionary, National Action, other. **Suffrage** Universal, over 18. **Memberships** OAS, UN. **Subdivisions** 31 states, 1 federal district.
**ECONOMY**
**GDP** $177,475,000,000 **Per capita** $2,256. **Monetary unit** Peso. **Trade partners** Exports: U.S., Japan, Spain. Imports: U.S.. **Exports** Petroleum, food, manufactures, machinery. **Imports** Machinery, chemicals, manufactures, hides and other crude materials, food.
**LAND**
**Description** Southern North America. **Area** 756,066 mi² (1,958,201 km²). **Highest point** Pico de Orizaba, 18,406 ft (5,610 m). **Lowest point** Laguna Salada, -26 ft (-8 m).

**People.** Most Mexicans are mestizos, descended from Indians and the Spaniards who conquered Mexico in the 1500s. Spanish is spoken by most inhabitants, and Roman Catholicism is the most popular religion. Another major ethnic group is comprised of indigenous Indians, or Amerindians, some of whom speak only Indian languages and hold traditional religious beliefs. Mexico's rapid population growth has contributed to poverty among rural dwellers, spurring a migration to the cities. Due to its mild climate and fertile soils, Mexico's central plateau is home to most of the population.

**Economy and the Land.** Mexico is a leading producer of petroleum and silver, a growing manufacturer of iron, steel, and chemicals, and an exporter of coffee and cotton. Foreign visitors—drawn by archaeological sites and warm, sunny weather—make tourism an important activity. Despite economic gains made since the mid-1900s in agriculture and industry, Mexico recently has been troubled by inflation, declining oil prices, rising unemployment, and a trade deficit that has grown with the need for imported materials. In recent years the peso has been significantly devalued, and banks have been nationalized to help reduce a massive international debt. Austerity plans and foreign aid are expected to help revitalize the economy. Terrain and climate are greatly varied, ranging from tropical jungles along the coast to desert plains in the north. A temperate central plateau is bounded by rugged mountains in the south, east, and west.

**History and Politics.** Farm settlements grew in the Valley of Mexico between 6500 and 1500 B.C., and during the subsequent three thousand years Mexico gave birth to the great civilizations of the Olmec, Maya, Toltec, and Aztec Indians. The Aztec Empire was overthrown by the Spanish in 1521, and Mexico became the viceroyalty of New Spain. Although there was much dissatisfaction with Spanish rule, rebellion did not begin until 1810. Formal independence came in 1821. Mexico lost considerable territory, including Texas, to the United States during the Mexican War, from 1846 to 1848. During subsequent years, power changed hands frequently as liberals demanding social and economic reforms battled conservatives. A brief span of French imperial rule, from 1864 to 1867, interrupted the struggle. Following a revolution that started in 1910, a new constitution was adopted in 1917, and progress toward reform began, culminating in the separation of church and state and the redistribution of land. A 1988 election was won by the Institutional Revolutionary candidate but parties on both the right and the left showed significant strength. ■

# MICRONESIA, FEDERATED STATES OF See UNITED STATES.

# MIDWAY ISLANDS
See UNITED STATES.

# MONACO

**Official name** Principality of Monaco
**PEOPLE**
**Population** 29,000. **Density** 41,429/mi² (15,263/km²). **Urban** 100%. **Capital** Monaco, 29,000. **Ethnic groups** French 47%, Monegasque 17%, Italian 16%, English 4%, Belgian 2%, Swiss 1%. **Languages** French, English, Italian, Monegasque. **Religions** Roman Catholic 95%. **Literacy** 99%.
**POLITICS**
**Government** Constitutional monarchy. **Parties** Action, Democractic Union Movement, National and Democratic Union, Socialist. **Suffrage** Universal adult. **Memberships** None. **Subdivisions** 3 communes. **Monetary unit** French franc.
**LAND**
**Description** Southern Europe (on the southeastern coast of France). **Area** 0.7 mi² (1.9 km²). **Highest point** 459 ft (140 m). **Lowest point** Sea level.

**People.** Monaco is inhabited mostly by French citizens, while Monegasques—citizens of indigenous descent—and various Europeans form the rest of the population. Many foreigners have taken up residence, drawn by the country's tax benefits. French is the official language. Monegasque, a blend of French and Italian, is also spoken, as are French, Italian and English. Most residents are Roman Catholic.

**Economy and the Land.** Monaco's beautiful seaside location, mild Mediterranean climate, and famous gambling casino in Monte Carlo make it a popular tourist haven. Consequently, tourism forms the backbone of the economy. Production of chemicals, food products, and perfumes, among other light industries, are additional sources of income. Monaco also profits from many foreign businesses, which are attracted by the favorable tax climate and headquartered in the principality. France and Monaco form a customs union for a mutually beneficial trade system; the French franc is Monaco's official currency. The world's second smallest independent state in area—after Vatican City—Monaco has four regions: the old city of Monaco-Ville, site of the royal palace; Monte Carlo, the resort and major tourist center; La Condamine, the port area; and Fontvieille, the rapidly growing industrial section.

**History and Politics.** Known to the Phoenicians, Greeks, and Romans, the region became a Genoese colony in the twelfth century A.D. Around the turn of the fourteenth century, the area was granted to the Grimaldi family of Genoa. France, Spain, and Sardinia had intermittent control of Monaco from 1400 until 1861, when its autonomy was recognized by the Franco-Monegasque Treaty. Another treaty, providing for French protection of Monaco, was signed in 1918. The absolute rule of Monaco's princes ended with the 1911 constitution. ■

# MONGOLIA

**Official name** Mongolian People's Republic
**PEOPLE**
**Population** 2,155,000. **Density** 3.6/mi$^2$ (1.4/km$^2$). **Urban** 51%. **Capital** Ulan Bator, 488,200. **Ethnic groups** Mongol 90%, Kazakh 4%, Chinese 2%, Russian 2%.
**Languages** Khalkha Mongol, Kazakh, Russian, Chinese.
**Religions** Shamanic, Tibetan Buddhist, Muslim. **Life expectancy** 64 female, 60 male. **Literacy** 80%.
**POLITICS**
**Government** Socialist republic. **Parties** People's Revolutionary. **Suffrage** Universal, over 18.
**Memberships** CEMA, UN. **Subdivisions** 18 provinces, 3 municipalities.
**ECONOMY**
**GDP** $1,670,000,000 **Per capita** $886. **Monetary unit** Tugrik. **Trade partners** U.S.S.R.. **Exports** Livestock, animal products, wool, hides, minerals, metals. **Imports** Machinery, petroleum, clothing, building materials, sugar, tea, chemicals.
**LAND**
**Description** Central Asia, landlocked. **Area** 604,250 mi$^2$ (1,565,000 km$^2$). **Highest point** 14,350 ft (4,374 m). **Lowest point** Höh Lake, 1,814 ft (553 m).

**People.** Mongols, a central Asian people, make up the vast majority of Mongolia's population. Khalkha Mongol is the predominant language. Turkic-speaking Kazakhs, as well as Russians and Chinese, comprise minorities. Tibetan Buddhism was once the most common religion; however, the government now discourages religious practice. The traditional nomadic way of life is becoming less common, as recent government policies have led to urbanization and settled agriculture.

**Economy and the Land.** Mongolia's economy, long based on the raising of livestock, has been shaped by the ideal grazing land found in most of the country. But significant economic changes have occurred since 1924, including the collectivization and modernization of farming, the introduction of industry, and the exploitation of mineral resources. Although dependent on Soviet aid, Mongolia has made considerable progress toward diversifying and developing its economy. Mongolia's terrain varies from mountains in the north and west to steppe in the east and desert in the south. Located in the heart of Asia, remote from any moderating body of water, Mongolia has a rigorous continental climate with little precipitation.

**History and Politics.** Mongolian tribes were united under the warlord Genghis Khan around A.D. 1200, and he and his successors built one of history's largest land empires. In 1691 the Manchu dynasty of China subdued Outer Mongolia, as the area was then known, but allowed the Mongol rulers autonomy. Until the Mongols ousted the Chinese in 1911, Outer Mongolia remained a Chinese province. In 1912 the state accepted Russian protection but was unable to prevent a subsequent Chinese advance, and in 1919 Outer Mongolia again became a Chinese province. In 1921 a combined Soviet and Mongolian force defeated Chinese and Belorussian, or White Russian, troops, and the Mongolian People's Republic was declared in 1924. A mutual-assistance pact was signed by Mongolia and Russia in 1966. In 1989, the Soviets agreed to withdraw most of their troops from Mongolia. ∎

# MONTSERRAT
See UNITED KINGDOM.

# MOROCCO

**Official name** Kingdom of Morocco
## PEOPLE
**Population** 25,930,000. **Density** 150/mi² (58/km²). **Urban** 45%. **Capital** Rabat, 518,616. **Ethnic groups** Arab-Berber 99%. **Languages** Arabic, Berber dialects, French. **Religions** Sunni Muslim 99%. **Life expectancy** 60 female, 57 male. **Literacy** 30%.
## POLITICS
**Government** Constitutional monarchy. **Parties** Constitutional Union, Istiqlal, National Assembly of Independents, Popular Movement, others. **Suffrage** Universal, over 20. **Memberships** AL, UN. **Subdivisions** 35 provinces, 8 prefectures.
## ECONOMY
**GDP** $11,892,000,000 **Per capita** $547. **Monetary unit** Dirham. **Trade partners** Exports: France, Spain, India. Imports: France, U.S., Saudi Arabia. **Exports**

Phosphates, chemicals, clothing and other manufactures, oranges, fish. **Imports** Petroleum, manufactures, food, machinery, crude materials, chemicals.
## LAND
**Description** Northwestern Africa. **Area** 172,414 mi² (446,550 km²). **Highest point** Mt. Toubkal, 13,665 ft (4,165 m). **Lowest point** Sebkha Tah, -180 ft (-55 m).
*The above information excludes Western Sahara.*

**People.** Moroccans, virtually homogeneous in race and culture, are mostly a mix of Arab and Berber stocks and speak Arabic. A few Berber dialects are spoken in rural mountain areas, and French and Spanish, the colonial tongues, are common in business and government. The majority of people are Sunni Muslim. The population is concentrated west of the Atlas Mountains, which border the Sahara Desert. Rural people are migrating to cities, where the standard of living is higher.

**Economy and the Land.** Although agriculture employs much of the work force and is an important activity, the nation depends on mining for most of its income. Morocco is a leading exporter of phosphates, but has other mineral reserves as well. Fishing and tourism are growing sources of revenue. Recently, severe drought, rising dependency on imported oil, and a costly war in Western Sahara have slowed productivity, while investments by Arab countries have bolstered the economy. Morocco, with its varied terrain of desert, forests, and mountains, has an equally varied climate that is semitropical along the coast, and desert beyond the Atlas Mountains.

**History and Politics.** In ancient times, Morocco was a province of Carthage and Rome. Vandals and Byzantine Greeks, the subsequent rulers, were followed in the A.D. 700s by Arabs, who brought Islam. Morocco's strategic position awakened the interest of colonial powers in the 1800s, and by 1912 the area was divided into French and Spanish protectorates. A nationalist movement began in the 1920s, occasionally bringing violence, but not until 1956 did Morocco become independent from France. The last of Spain's holdings in Morocco were returned in 1969. War broke out in 1976, when Morocco claimed the northern part of Western Sahara and was challenged by the Saharan nationalist Polisario Front. Although Mauritania, which had been involved in the war and had been fighting for southern Western Sahara, surrendered its claim in 1979, Morocco has continued to battle the Polisario Front. ∎

# MOZAMBIQUE

**Official name** People's Republic of Mozambique
## PEOPLE
**Population** 15,535,000. **Density** 50/mi² (19/km²). **Urban** 19%. **Capital** Maputo, 755,300. **Ethnic groups** Makua, Lomwe, Thonga, others. **Languages** Portuguese, indigenous. **Religions** Tribal religionist 60%, Roman Catholic and other Christian 30%, Muslim. **Life expectancy** 46 female, 44 male. **Literacy** 27%.
## POLITICS
**Government** Socialist republic. **Parties** Front for the Liberation. **Suffrage** Universal adult. **Memberships** OAU, UN. **Subdivisions** 10 provinces, 1 independent city.
## ECONOMY
**GDP** $1,840,000,000 **Per capita** $142. **Monetary unit**

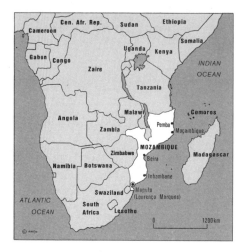

armed campaign against the Portuguese. In 1975 Mozambique became an independent state dedicated to eliminating white-minority rule in the area. Nevertheless, Mozambique has economic ties to South Africa, and in 1984 the two nations pledged to deny refuge to each other's foes. Continued guerrilla fighting and food shortages have created a crisis situation in Mozambique. ■

# NAMIBIA

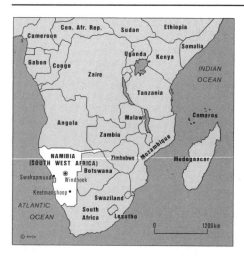

Metical. **Trade partners** Exports: U.S., E. Germany, Japan. Imports: U.S.S.R., South African countries, France. **Exports** Fish, cashews, tea, cotton, sugar. **Imports** Food, fuel, machinery and transportation equipment, chemicals.
**LAND**
**Description** Southern Africa. **Area** 308,642 mi$^2$ (799,379 km$^2$). **Highest point** Monte Binga, 7,992 ft (2,436 m). **Lowest point** Sea level.

**People.** Black Africans belonging to about ten groups compose the vast majority of the population. Most black Mozambicans live in rural areas, while small European and Asian minorities live primarily in urban centers. Traditional African religions are followed by a majority, while others practice Islam and Christianity. Although Portuguese is the official language, most blacks speak Bantu tongues.

**Economy and the Land.** Mozambique's underdeveloped economy is largely the product of its colonial past, during which its human and natural resources were neglected. Recent political developments in southern Africa have created more economic woes, as lucrative trade agreements with racially divided neighbors have ceased. While the mainstays of the economy are agriculture and transport services, fishing and mining are also being developed. The Marxist government has allowed some private enterprise, and foreign aid is important. The climate is tropical or subtropical along the coastal plain that covers nearly half of the country, with cooler conditions in the western high plateaus and mountains.

**History and Politics.** Bantu-speaking peoples settled in present-day Mozambique around the first century A.D. Subsequent immigrants included Arab traders in the 800s and the Portuguese in the late 1400s. European economic interest in the area was hindered by lucrative trading with other colonies, and Mozambique wasn't recognized as a Portuguese colony until 1885. Policies instituted by the Portuguese benefited European settlers and Portugal while overlooking the welfare of Mozambique and its native inhabitants. In the early 1960s, the country made clear its opposition to foreign rule, with the formation of the Mozambique Liberation Front, a Marxist nationalist group that initiated an

**Official name** Namibia
**PEOPLE**
**Population** 1,386,000. **Density** 4.4/mi$^2$ (1.7/km$^2$). **Urban** 51%. **Capital** Windhoek, 120,000. **Ethnic groups** Ovambo 49%, Kavango 9%, Damara 8%, Herero 7%, white 7%, mixed 7%. **Languages** Afrikaans, English, German, indigenous. **Religions** Lutheran and other Protestant, Roman Catholic, Animist. **Life expectancy** 50 female, 47 male. **Literacy** 23%.
**POLITICS**
**Government** Republic. **Parties** Democratic Turnhalle Alliance, South West Africa People's Organization. **Suffrage** Universal adult. **Memberships** None. **Subdivisions** 26 districts.
**ECONOMY**
**GDP** $860,000,000 **Per capita** $782. **Monetary unit** South African rand. **Trade partners** South Africa, W. Germany, U.K., U.S.. **Exports** Diamonds, copper, lead, uranium. **Imports** Food, building materials, manufactures.
**LAND**
**Description** Southern Africa. **Area** 317,818 mi$^2$ (823,144 km$^2$). **Highest point** Brandberg, 8,461 ft (2,579 m). **Lowest point** Sea level.
*The above information excludes Walvis Bay.*

**People.** The largest ethnic group is black African, composed of many indigenous peoples. South Africans, Britons, and Germans constitute the white minority. Black Namibians speak various native dialects, while the majority of whites speak Afrikaans. Blacks still follow traditional customs and religions, but a considerable number have converted to Christianity.

**Economy and the Land.** Namibia's economy is based on the mining of diamonds, copper, lead, and other minerals. Agriculture makes a marginal contribution, but livestock raising is important.

Manufacturing remains undeveloped because of an unskilled work force, and Namibia imports most of its finished goods from South Africa, its partner in a customs union. A variety of factors, including continuing drought and political instability, have held back economic growth. Namibia consists of a high plateau that encompasses the Namib Desert and part of the Kalahari Desert. The climate is subtropical.

**History and Politics.** Bushmen were probably the area's first inhabitants, followed by other African peoples. European exploration of the coast began in the A.D. 1500s, but the coastal desert prevented foreign penetration. In 1884 Germany annexed all of the territory except for the coastal enclave of Walvis Bay, which had been claimed by Britain in 1878. After South African troops ousted the Germans from the area during World War I, the League of Nations mandated Namibia, then known as South West Africa, to South Africa. Following World War II, the United Nations requested that the territory become a trusteeship. South Africa refused to cooperate. In 1966 the United Nations revoked South Africa's mandate, yet South Africa kept control of Namibia. Beginning in the sixties, the South West Africa People's Organization, a Namibian nationalist group with Communist support, made guerrilla raids on South African forces from bases in Zambia and, later, from Angola. In 1989, after years of continued pressure, an assembly was elected to draft a constitution. Independence was achieved in March 1990. ∎

# NAURU

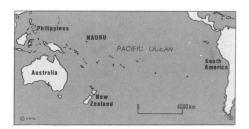

**Official name** Republic of Nauru
**PEOPLE**
**Population** 9,000. **Density** 1,111/mi² (429/km²). **Capital** Yaren District. **Ethnic groups** Nauruan 58%, other Pacific Islander 26%, Chinese 8%, European 8%. **Languages** Nauruan, English. **Religions** Congregationalist and other Protestant 67%, Roman Catholic 33%. **Literacy** 99%.
**POLITICS**
**Government** Republic. **Parties** Democratic, Nauru. **Suffrage** Universal adult. **Memberships** CW. **Subdivisions** 14 districts.
**ECONOMY**
**GNP** $160,000,000 **Per capita** $20,513. **Monetary unit** Australian dollar. **Trade partners** Exports: Australia, New Zealand. Imports: Australia, U.K., New Zealand, Japan. **Exports** Phosphates. **Imports** Food, fuel, water.
**LAND**
**Description** South Pacific island. **Area** 8.1 mi² (21 km²). **Highest point** 210 ft (64 m). **Lowest point** Sea level.

**People.** Indigenous Nauruans are a mix of Polynesian, Micronesian, and Melanesian stock, and many residents are from other Pacific islands. Nauruan is the language of most inhabitants, but English is widely spoken. Nearly all Nauruans are Christian.

**Economy and the Land.** The economy depends primarily on its sole resource, phosphates; the government is establishing trust funds to support islanders when the resource is depleted. With limited agriculture, nearly all food must be imported. Nauru is one of the smallest countries in the world. Most of the coral island is a plateau, and the climate is tropical.

**History and Politics.** Nauru was most likely settled by castaways from nearby islands. Noted by a British explorer in 1798, Nauru remained autonomous until it came under German control in 1881. In 1914 Germany surrendered the island, and it was subsequently mandated to Australia, Britain, and New Zealand. World War II brought occupation by Japan. Nauru reverted to Australian rule in 1947 as a trusteeship. It became independent in 1968 and gained control of European interests in the phosphate industry in 1970. ∎

# NEPAL

**Official name** Kingdom of Nepal
**PEOPLE**
**Population** 18,930,000. **Density** 333/mi² (129/km²). **Urban** 8%. **Capital** Kathmandu, 235,160. **Ethnic groups** Newar, Indian, Tibetan, Gurung, Magar, Tamang, Bhotia, others. **Languages** Nepali, Maithili, Bhojpuri, other indigenous. **Religions** Hindu 90%, Buddhist 5%, Muslim 3%. **Life expectancy** 45 female, 47 male. **Literacy** 21%.
**POLITICS**
**Government** Constitutional monarchy. **Parties** None. **Suffrage** Universal, over 21. **Memberships** UN. **Subdivisions** 14 zones.
**ECONOMY**
**GDP** $2,288,000,000 **Per capita** $136. **Monetary unit** Rupee. **Trade partners** Exports: India, U.S. Imports: India, Japan. **Exports** Rice and other food, carpets and

other textiles, clothing, leather goods. **Imports** Textiles and other manufactures, machinery, chemicals, food, petroleum.

**LAND**
**Description** Southern Asia, landlocked. **Area** 56,827 mi² (147,181 km²). **Highest point** Mt. Everest, 29,028 ft (8,848 m). **Lowest point** 197 ft (60 m).

**People.** Nepal's mixed population results from migrations over the centuries from India, Tibet, and central Asia. Most of Nepal's ruling families have been of Indian descent, and Nepali, the official language, is derived from Sanskrit, an ancient Indian language. Although the majority of the population practices Hinduism, Nepal is the birthplace of Buddha and has been greatly influenced by Buddhism as well. The importance of both religions is reflected in the more than twenty-seven hundred shrines in the Kathmandu Valley. Most Nepalese are rural farmers.

**Economy and the Land.** Because of geographic remoteness and a political policy of isolation lasting until the 1950s, Nepal's economy is one of the least developed in the world. Agriculture, concentrated chiefly in the south, is the most significant activity, even though most of Nepal is covered by the Himalayas, the world's highest mountains. This range—which includes Mount Everest, the world's highest peak—has made tourism increasingly lucrative. Nepal has potential in hydroelectricity and forestry, but inadequate transportation routes, overpopulation, and deforestation present obstacles to development. Nepal has received financial aid from many nations, partly because of its strategic location between India and China. The climate varies from subtropical in the flat, fertile south to temperate in the central hill country. Himalayan summers are cool and winters severe.

**History and Politics.** Several small Hindu-Buddhist kingdoms had emerged in the Kathmandu Valley by about A.D. 300. These states were unified in the late 1700s by the founder of the Shah dynasty. The Rana family wrested control from the Shahs in 1846 and pursued an isolationist course, which thwarted foreign influence but stunted economic growth. Opposition to the Ranas mounted during the 1930s and 1940s, and in 1951 the Shah monarchy was restored by a revolution. In 1962 the king established a government that gave the crown dominance and abolished political parties. A 1980 referendum narrowly upheld this system. ∎

# NETHERLANDS

**Official name** Kingdom of the Netherlands
**PEOPLE**
**Population** 14,825,000. **Density** 919/mi² (355/km²). **Urban** 88%. **Capital** Amsterdam (designated), 679,140; The Hague (seat of government), 443,961. **Ethnic groups** Dutch (mixed Scandinavian, French, and Celtic) 99%, Indonesian and others 1%. **Languages** Dutch. **Religions** Roman Catholic 40%, Dutch Reformed and other Protestant 31%. **Life expectancy** 80 female, 73 male. **Literacy** 99%.
**POLITICS**
**Government** Constitutional monarchy. **Parties** Christian Democratic Appeal, Labor, Liberal, others. **Suffrage** Universal, over 18. **Memberships** EC, NATO, OECD, UN. **Subdivisions** 12 provinces.
**ECONOMY**
**GDP** $124,983,000,000 **Per capita** $8,640. **Monetary unit** Guilder. **Trade partners** Exports: W. Germany, Belgium, France. Imports: W. Germany, Belgium, U.K.. **Exports** Manufactures, chemicals, food, petroleum, machinery, natural gas. **Imports** Manufactures, machinery, petroleum, oil seeds and other crude materials.
**LAND**
**Description** Western Europe. **Area** 16,133 mi² (41,785 km²). **Highest point** Vaalserberg, 1,053 ft (321 m). **Lowest point** Prins Alexander polder, -22 ft (-7 m).

**People.** The major ethnic group is the Dutch, for the most part a mixture of French, Scandinavian, and Celtic peoples. There are small minorities from the former Dutch possessions of Indonesia and Su-

## Places and Possessions of the NETHERLANDS

| Entity | Status | Area | Population | Capital/Population |
|---|---|---|---|---|
| **Aruba** (Caribbean island) | Self-governing territory | 75 mi² (193 km²) | 63,000 | Oranjestad, 19,800 |
| **Curaçao** (Caribbean island) | Island territory of Netherlands Antilles | 171 mi² (444 km²) | 178,000 | Willemstad, 31,883 |
| **Netherlands Antilles** (Caribbean islands) | Self-governing territory | 309 mi² (800 km²) | 207,000 | Willemstad, 31,883 |

riname. Dutch is the official language, but many Netherlanders also speak English or German. Although most Dutch are Christian, the nation has a history of religious tolerance that has drawn countless refugees.

**Economy and the Land.** A variety of manufacturing strengths—notably the metal, chemical, and food-processing industries—fuels the prosperous economy. Tourism and the production of natural gas are also important. Due to a lack of natural resources, the Netherlands must import many goods. The country benefits from its strategic position and has enjoyed success in shipping and trade. Much of the Netherlands, including most farmland, has been reclaimed from the sea through artificial drainage. The land is almost uniformly flat, and proximity to the sea produces a mild, damp climate. The Kingdom of the Netherlands includes the Netherlands Antilles, two groups of Caribbean islands, and Aruba.

**History and Politics.** The Germanic tribes of the area were conquered in 58 B.C. by the Romans, who were driven out in the A.D. 400s by the Franks. As part of the Low Countries with Belgium and Luxembourg, the Netherlands was dominated successively by Charlemagne, the dukes of Burgundy, the Hapsburgs, and rulers of Spain. Spanish persecution of Dutch Protestants led to a revolt that in 1581 created the Republic of the United Netherlands. In the 1600s the Netherlands became a maritime as well as a colonial power and produced many masterpieces in painting. But a series of wars with England and France ending in 1714 spelled the end of Dutch influence, and the nation fell to France in 1795. With the defeat of Napoleon Bonaparte of France in 1815, the Netherlands was united with Belgium and became an independent kingdom. Belgium seceded in 1830. The Netherlands declared its neutrality in both world wars but was occupied by Germany from 1940 to 1945. The war cost the country many lives and much of its economic strength. Membership in several international economic unions aided recovery. Since the war, the Netherlands has abandoned neutrality and now maintains a pro-Western stance in foreign affairs. ■

# NETHERLANDS ANTILLES
See NETHERLANDS.

# NEW CALEDONIA

**Official name** Territory of New Caledonia and Dependencies
**PEOPLE**
**Population** 153,000. **Density** 21/mi$^2$ (8.0/km$^2$). **Urban** 76%. **Capital** Nouméa, New Caledonia I., 60,112. **Ethnic groups** Melanesian 43%, French 37%, Wallisian 8%, Polynesian 4%, Indonesian 4%, Vietnamese 2%.
**Languages** French, Malay-Polynesian languages.
**Religions** Roman Catholic 60%, Protestant 30%. **Life expectancy** 67 female, 61 male. **Literacy** 91%.
**POLITICS**
**Government** Overseas territory (France). **Parties** Kanak Socialist National Liberation Front, National Front, Rally for the Republic. **Suffrage** Universal adult. **Memberships** None. **Subdivisions** 4 regions.
**ECONOMY**
**GDP** $824,000,000 **Per capita** $5,644. **Monetary unit** CFP franc. **Trade partners** Exports: France, Japan, Australia. Imports: France, Australia, U.S.. **Exports** Nickel, ferro-alloys. **Imports** Manufactures, petroleum, food, machinery, automobiles, chemicals.
**LAND**
**Description** South Pacific islands. **Area** 7,358 mi$^2$ (19,058 km$^2$). **Highest point** Mt. Panié, New Caledonia I., 5,341 ft (1,628 m). **Lowest point** Sea level.

**People.** The largest ethnic group in New Caledonia, a group of Pacific islands northeast of Australia, is the Melanesian, or Kanak. People of French descent make up the second largest group, with Asians and Polynesians composing significant minorities. New Caledonia's status as an overseas French territory is reflected in its languages, which include French as well as regional dialects, and in a population that is largely Christian.

**Economy and the Land.** The principal economic activity, the mining and smelting of nickel, has fallen off in recent years. Small amounts of coffee and copra are exported, and tourism is important in the capital. Possessing few resources, New Caledonia imports almost all finished products from France. The main island, also called New Caledonia, is mountainous and accounts for almost 90 percent of the territory's land area. Smaller islands include the Isle of Pines, Loyalty and Bélep islands. The climate is tropical.

**History and Politics.** New Caledonia was settled by Melanesians about 2000 B.C. Europeans first reached the main island in 1774, when Captain James Cook of Britain gave it its present name. In 1853 France annexed New Caledonia and used the main island as a penal colony until the turn of the century. During World War II the islands served as a base for the United States military. Officially a French overseas territory since 1946, New Caledonia experienced violence in the 1980s, stemming from the desire of the Kanak population for independence. ■

# NEW ZEALAND

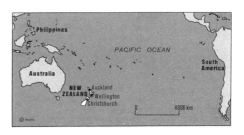

**Official name** New Zealand
**PEOPLE**
**Population** 3,408,000. **Density** 33/mi$^2$ (13/km$^2$). **Urban** 84%. **Capital** Wellington, North I., 137,495. **Ethnic**

groups European origin 86%, Maori 9%, Samoan and other Pacific islander 3%. **Languages** English, Maori. **Religions** Anglican 24%, Presbyterian 18%, Roman Catholic 15%, Methodist 5%. **Life expectancy** 77 female, 71 male. **Literacy** 99%.

## POLITICS
**Government** Parliamentary state. **Parties** Democratic, Labor, National. **Suffrage** Universal, over 18. **Memberships** CW, OECD, UN. **Subdivisions** 85 counties.

## ECONOMY
**GDP** $23,367,000,000 **Per capita** $7,406. **Monetary unit** Dollar. **Trade partners** Exports: Australia, Japan, U.S. Imports: Japan, Australia, U.S.. **Exports** Meat, manufactures, wool and other crude materials, dairy products, fruit. **Imports** Textiles and other manufactures, machinery, petroleum, chemicals.

## LAND
**Description** South Pacific islands. **Area** 103,519 mi² (268,112 km²). **Highest point** Mt. Cook, South I., 12,349 ft (3,764 m). **Lowest point** Sea level.

**People.** The majority of New Zealanders are descended from Europeans, mostly Britons, who arrived in the 1800s. Of Polynesian descent, the indigenous Maori form the largest minority. After a period of decline following the arrival of the Europeans, the Maori population has been increasing. The major languages are English, the official tongue, and Maori. Most New Zealanders live on North Island. Christian religions are observed by many residents, and the Maori have incorporated some Christian elements into their beliefs.

**Economy and the Land.** Success in agriculture and trade has allowed New Zealand to overcome its small work force, remoteness from major markets, and a relative lack of natural resources. A terrain with much ideal grazing land and a climate that is temperate year-round have encouraged cattle and sheep farming. Manufacturing, including the food-processing and paper industries, is an expanding sector, as is tourism. New Zealand consists of two large islands—North Island and South Island—and many smaller islands scattered throughout the South Pacific. The nation administers several island territories. The scenic terrain is greatly varied, ranging from fjords and mountains to a volcanic plateau.

**History and Politics.** The Maori, the original settlers, are thought to have arrived around A.D. 1000. In 1642 they fought off the Dutch, the first Europeans to reach the area. Captain James Cook of Britain charted the islands in the late 1700s. Soon after, European hunters and traders, drawn by the area's whales, seals, and forests, began to arrive. Maori chiefs signed the 1840 Treaty of Waitangi, establishing British sovereignty, and British companies began to send settlers to New Zealand. Subsequent battles between settlers and Maori ended with the Maori's defeat in 1872, but European diseases and weapons continued to reduce the Maori population. In 1907 New Zealand became a self-governing dominion of Britain; formal independence came forty years later. New Zealand supported Britain in both world wars, but foreign policy has recently focused on Southeast Asia and the South Pacific. The country has banned vessels carrying nuclear weapons through its waters, which has strained relations with the United States. ∎

# NICARAGUA

**Official name** Republic of Nicaragua
## PEOPLE
**Population** 3,555,000. **Density** 71/mi² (27/km²). **Urban** 57%. **Capital** Managua, 644,588. **Ethnic groups** Mestizo 69%, white 17%, black 9%, Amerindian 5%. **Languages** Spanish, English, indigenous. **Religions** Roman Catholic 95%. **Life expectancy** 61 female, 59 male. **Literacy** 58%.

## POLITICS
**Government** Republic. **Parties** National Opposition Union, Sandinista National Liberation Front. **Suffrage** Universal, over 16. **Memberships** OAS, UN. **Subdivisions** 16 departments.

## ECONOMY
**GDP** $3,560,000,000 **Per capita** $1,203. **Monetary unit** Cordoba. **Trade partners** Exports: U.S., W. Germany,

## Places and Possessions of NEW ZEALAND

| Entity | Status | Area | Population | Capital/Population |
|---|---|---|---|---|
| **Cook Islands** (South Pacific) | Self-governing territory | 91 mi² (236 km²) | 18,000 | Avarua, 9,525 |
| **Niue** (South Pacific island) | Self-governing territory | 102 mi² (263 km²) | 1,600 | Alofi, 894 |
| **Tokelau** (South Pacific islands) | Island territory | 4.6 mi² (12 km²) | 1,700 | None |

Japan. Imports: Mexico, U.S.. **Exports** Coffee, textile fibers, sugar and honey, meat, shellfish, chemicals. **Imports** Manufactures, petroleum, machinery, pharmaceuticals and other chemicals.
**LAND**
**Description** Central America. **Area** 50,193 mi² (130,000 km²). **Highest point** Pico Mogotón, 6,913 ft (2,107 m). **Lowest point** Sea level.

**People.** Nicaraguan society closely reflects the nation's history as a Spanish colony: most of its inhabitants are Spanish speaking, Roman Catholic, and mestizo, a mix of Indian and European stocks. Indian and black communities are found mostly in the Caribbean region. The educational level has improved in the past decade.

**Economy and the Land.** Nicaragua is chiefly an agricultural nation, relying on the production of textiles, coffee, and sugar. Years of instability before a 1979 revolution, a large foreign debt inherited from the previous regime, and a continuing civil war have severely hindered economic prosperity. The nation also suffers from a reliance on imported goods. In 1985 the currency was sharply devalued, and the United States, formerly a chief trading partner, announced a trade embargo. Basic consumer goods are in short supply. The terrain includes a low-lying Pacific region, central highlands, and a flat Caribbean area. The climate is tropical.

**History and Politics.** Spanish conquistadores, who came via Panama in 1522 to what is now Nicaragua, found a number of independent Indian states. Nicaragua was ruled by Spain as part of Guatemala until it became independent in 1821. In 1823 the former Spanish colonies of the region formed the Federation of Central America, a union which collapsed in 1838, resulting in the independent Republic of Nicaragua. For the next century, Nicaragua was the stage both for conflict between the Liberal and Conservative parties and for United States military and economic involvement. Members of the Somoza family, who had close ties to America, directed a repressive regime from 1936 to 1979, when the widely-supported Sandinistas overthrew the government. The Sandinistas, led by Daniel Ortega, are opposed by rival political parties and the Contras, who are rebels linked to the former Somoza administration and backed by the United States. Five Central American countries reached an agreement in 1987 on a plan to dismantle Contra forces. In 1990 elections, Ortega was defeated by Violeta Chamorro of the National Opposition Union.
■

# NIGER

**Official name** Republic of Niger
**PEOPLE**
**Population** 7,609,000. **Density** 16/mi² (6.0/km²). **Urban** 16%. **Capital** Niamey, 399,100. **Ethnic groups** Hausa 56%, Djerma 22%, Fulani 9%, Taureg 8%, Beriberi 4%. **Languages** French, Hausa, Djerma, indigenous. **Religions** Muslim 80%, Animist and Christian 20%. **Life expectancy** 44 female, 41 male. **Literacy** 10%.
**POLITICS**
**Government** Provisional military government. **Parties**

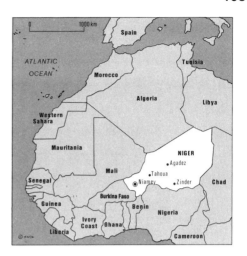

None. **Suffrage** Universal adult. **Memberships** OAU, UN. **Subdivisions** 7 departments.
**ECONOMY**
**GDP** $1,830,000,000 **Per capita** $320. **Monetary unit** CFA franc. **Trade partners** Exports: France, Japan, Nigeria. Imports: France, Nigeria, Algeria. **Exports** Uranium, livestock. **Imports** Textiles and other manufactures, food, machinery, petroleum.
**LAND**
**Description** Western Africa, landlocked. **Area** 489,191 mi² (1,267,000 km²). **Highest point** Indoukâl-n-Taghès, 6,634 ft (2,022 m). **Lowest point** Niger River valley, 650 ft (200 m).

**People.** Nearly all Nigerois are black Africans belonging to culturally diverse groups. The Hausa and the Djerma, farmers who live mostly in the south, constitute the two largest groups. The remaining Nigerois are nomadic herders who inhabit the northern desert regions. Although the official language is French, most inhabitants speak indigenous tongues. Islam is the most commonly observed religion, but some Nigerois follow indigenous and Christian beliefs.

**Economy and the Land.** Niger's economy is chiefly agricultural, although arable land is scarce and drought common. The raising of livestock, grain, beans, and peanuts accounts for most farming activity. Uranium mining, a growing industry, has become less productive recently due to a slump in the world uranium market. Mountains and the Sahara Desert cover most of northern Niger, while the south is savanna. The climate is hot and dry.

**History and Politics.** Because of its central location in northern Africa, Niger was a crossroads for many peoples during its early history and was dominated by several African empires before European explorers arrived in the 1800s. The area was placed within the French sphere of influence in 1885, but not until 1922 did France make Niger a colony of French West Africa. Gradual moves toward autonomy were made during the forties and fifties, and Niger became fully independent in 1960. Unrest caused in part by a prolonged drought led to a coup in 1974 and the establishment of a military government. Civilians now have some part in the political system. Niger maintains close ties to France. ■

# NIGERIA

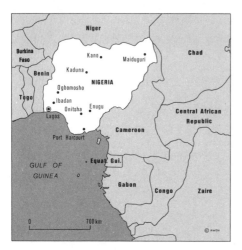

**Official name** Federal Republic of Nigeria
## PEOPLE
**Population** 111,010,000. **Density** 311/mi² (120/km²). **Urban** 23%. **Capital** Lagos (de facto), 1,123,000; Abuja (future). **Ethnic groups** Hausa, Fulani, Yoruba, Ibo, others. **Languages** English, Hausa, Fulani, Yorbua, Ibo, indigenous. **Religions** Muslim 50%, Christian 40%, Animist 10%. **Life expectancy** 50 female, 47 male. **Literacy** 38%.
## POLITICS
**Government** Provisional military government. **Parties** None. **Suffrage** None. **Memberships** CW, OAU, OPEC, UN. **Subdivisions** 21 states, 1 capital territory.
## ECONOMY
**GDP** $67,291,000,000 **Per capita** $805. **Monetary unit** Naira. **Trade partners** Exports: U.S., Netherlands, France. Imports: U.K., W. Germany, Japan. **Exports** Petroleum, cocoa. **Imports** Manufactures, machinery, transportation equipment, food, chemicals.
## LAND
**Description** Western Africa. **Area** 356,669 mi² (923,768 km²). **Highest point** Mt. Waddi, 7,936 ft (2,419 m). **Lowest point** Sea level.

**People.** Nigeria, Africa's most populous nation, contains more than two hundred distinct black African groups. The largest groups are the Hausa and the Fulani, who dominate the north; the Yoruba, found primarily in the southwest; and the Ibo, who live in the southeast and have historically been active in government and trade. Most Hausa and Fulani are Muslim, and a sizable Christian community is found mainly in the south. Nigerians commonly combine traditional beliefs with Islam or Christianity. Indigenous tongues are more widely spoken than English, the official language. Competition among Nigeria's many ethnic groups has threatened national unity.

**Economy and the Land.** Nigeria's economy is based on mining and agriculture. Petroleum is very important to the Nigerian economy, but a number of factors—including unskilled labor, poor power facilities, and the worldwide dip in oil prices—have silenced the oil boom of the 1970s and slowed development in other areas. In 1983 and 1985 the government expelled millions of illegal aliens in an effort to revive the economy. The terrain is diverse, encompassing tropical forest, savanna, and semi-desert. The climate is predominantly tropical.

**History and Politics.** From around 500 B.C. to about A.D. 200 the region was home to the sophisticated Nok civilization. Later cultures that dominated parts of the area included the Hausa, Fulani, and Yoruba. The Portuguese arrived in the 1400s, but the British gained control over the following centuries, uniting the region in 1914 as the Colony and Protectorate of Nigeria. Nigerian calls for self-rule culminated in independence in 1960. Internal tensions began to wrack the new nation, and in 1966 two military coups took place. After subsequent massacres of Ibo, that group declared eastern Nigeria the autonomous state of Biafra. A three-year civil war followed, ending in 1970 with Biafra's surrender. Government development and the oil boom speeded economic recovery. Subsequent years have seen coups and elections install short-lived regimes, and political instability continues. ■

# NIUE See NEW ZEALAND.

# NORFOLK ISLAND
See AUSTRALIA.

# NORTHERN MARIANA ISLANDS See UNITED STATES.

# NORWAY

**Official name** Kingdom of Norway
## PEOPLE
**Population** 4,202,000. **Density** 28/mi² (11/km²). **Urban** 73%. **Capital** Oslo, 448,747. **Ethnic groups** Norwegian (Scandinavian), Lappic. **Languages** Norwegian, Lapp. **Religions** Lutheran 94%, other Protestant and Roman Catholic 4%. **Life expectancy** 80 female, 73 male. **Literacy** 99%.
## POLITICS
**Government** Constitutional monarchy. **Parties** Center, Christian People's, Conservative, Labor, others. **Suffrage** Universal, over 18. **Memberships** NATO, OECD, UN. **Subdivisions** 19 counties.
## ECONOMY
**GDP** $58,371,000,000 **Per capita** $14,065. **Monetary unit** Krone. **Trade partners** Exports: U.K., W. Germany, Sweden. Imports: Sweden, W. Germany, U.K.. **Exports** Petroleum, natural gas, aluminum and other manufactures, ships and boats. **Imports** Manufactures, machinery, transportation equipment, crude materials, chemicals.
## LAND
**Description** Northern Europe. **Area** 149,412 mi² (386,975 km²). **Highest point** Glittertinden, 8,104 ft (2,470 m). **Lowest point** Sea level.
*The above information includes Svalbard and Jan Mayen.*

## OMAN

**People.** Because of its relatively remote location in far northern Europe, Norway has seen few population migrations and possesses a virtually homogeneous population, which is predominantly Germanic, Norwegian speaking, and Lutheran. Small communities of Lapps and Finns live in the far north, while most Norwegians live in the south and along the coast. The people enjoy many government-provided social services and programs.

**Economy and the Land.** Norway's economy, based on shipping, trade, and the mining of offshore oil and natural gas, takes its shape from the nation's proximity to several seas. Shipbuilding, fishing, and forestry are also important activities. Norway is a leading producer of hydroelectricity. Combined with some government control of the economy, these lucrative activities have given the nation a high standard of living and fairly low unemployment. Most of Norway is a high plateau covered with mountains. The Gulf Stream gives the nation a much milder climate than other places at the same latitude.

**History and Politics.** Parts of present-day Norway were inhabited by about 9000 B.C. Germanic tribes began immigrating to the area about 2000 B.C. Between A.D. 800 and 1100, Viking ships from Norway raided coastal towns throughout Western Europe and also colonized Greenland and Iceland. Unified around 900, Norway was subsequently shaken by civil war, plague, and the end of its royal line. It entered a union with Denmark in 1380, becoming a Danish province in 1536. Around the end of the Napoleonic Wars, in 1814, Norway became part of Sweden. A long struggle against Swedish rule ended in 1905 as Sweden recognized Norwegian independence, and a Danish prince was made king. Norway was neutral in World War I but endured German occupation during World War II. In 1967 the government initiated a wide-ranging social-welfare system. Norway retains relations with Western nations and the Soviet Union, but does not allow foreign military bases or nuclear arms on its soil. ∎

**Official name** Sultanate of Oman
### PEOPLE
**Population** 1,325,000. **Density** 16/mi$^2$ (6.2/km$^2$). **Urban** 9%. **Capital** Muscat, 50,000. **Ethnic groups** Arab, Baluchi, Zanzibari, Indian. **Languages** Arabic, English, Baluchi, Urdu, Indian dialects. **Religions** Ibadite Muslim 75%, Sunni Muslim, Shiite Muslim, Hindu. **Life expectancy** 54 female, 51 male. **Literacy** 20%.
### POLITICS
**Government** Monarchy. **Parties** None. **Suffrage** None. **Memberships** AL, UN. **Subdivisions** 10 provinces.
### ECONOMY
**GDP** $10,019,000,000 **Per capita** $9,775. **Monetary unit** Rial. **Trade partners** Exports: United Arab Emirates, U.S. Imports: United Arab Emirates, Japan, U.K.. **Exports** Petroleum, motor vehicles, fish and other food, machinery, aircraft. **Imports** Machinery, manufactures, transportation equipment, food.
### LAND
**Description** Southwestern Asia. **Area** 82,030 mi$^2$ (212,457 km$^2$). **Highest point** Mt. Sham, 9,957 ft (3,035 m). **Lowest point** Sea level.

**People.** Most of Oman's population is Arab, Arabic speaking, and belongs to the Ibadite sect of Islam. Other forms of Islam are also practiced. There is a significant foreign community that includes Indians, Pakistanis, and East African blacks. Many of them are guest workers in the oil industry.

**Economy and the Land.** Although oil production is the economic mainstay, Oman's reserves are not as vast as those of some other Arab states, and the government is seeking to diversify. The mining of natural gas and copper is being developed, as are agriculture and fishing. A central position in the politically volatile Persian Gulf and revolutionary internal strife have led Oman to devote a considerable portion of its budget to defense. Land regions include a coastal plain and interior mountains and desert. Oman's land borders are undefined and in dispute. A desert climate prevails over most areas except the coast, which has humid conditions.

**History and Politics.** Islam came to Muscat and Oman, as the nation was known before 1970, in the seventh century A.D. The Portuguese gained control of parts of the coast in 1508 but were driven out in 1650 by the Arabs. At about this time the hereditary sultanate—which absorbed the political power formerly held by the Ibadite religious leaders, or imams—was founded. Close relations with Britain, cemented in a 1798 agreement and subsequent treaties, have continued to the present. Conflicts between the sultan and Omanis, who wanted to be ruled exclusively by their imam, erupted intermittently after 1900, and in 1959 the sultan defeated the rebels with British help and outlawed the office of imam. Marxist insurgency was put down in 1975. Sultan Qaboos bin Said, who overthrew his father's regime in 1970, has liberalized some policies and worked to modernize the nation. Oman is a moderate, pro-Western Arab state. ∎

## ORKNEY ISLANDS
See UNITED KINGDOM.

## PACIFIC ISLANDS, TRUST TERRITORY OF THE
See UNITED STATES.

## PAKISTAN

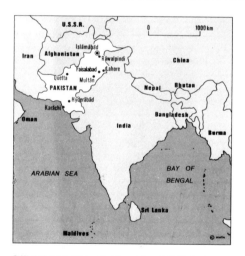

**Official name** Islamic Republic of Pakistan
**PEOPLE**
**Population** 112,360,000. **Density** 331/mi$^2$ (128/km$^2$).
**Urban** 30%. **Capital** Islāmābād, 201,000. **Ethnic groups** Punjabi, Sindhi, Pathan, Baluchi. **Languages** English, Urdu, Punjabi, Pashto, Sindhi, Saraiki. **Religions** Sunni Muslim 77%, Shiite Muslim 20%, Christian 1%, Hindu 1%. **Life expectancy** 49 female, 51 male. **Literacy** 26%.
**POLITICS**
**Government** Islamic republic. **Parties** Muslim League, People's, others. **Suffrage** Universal, over 21.
**Memberships** UN. **Subdivisions** 4 provinces, 1 federal area, 1 territory.

**ECONOMY**
**GDP** $33,136,000,000 **Per capita** $327. **Monetary unit** Rupee. **Trade partners** Exports: Japan, U.S. Saudi Arabia. Imports: U.S., Japan, Saudi Arabia. **Exports** Cotton fabric and other textiles, rice and other food, raw cotton, clothing. **Imports** Petroleum, machinery, manufactures, chemicals, food, transportation equipment.
**LAND**
**Description** Southern Asia. **Area** 339,732 mi$^2$ (879,902 km$^2$). **Highest point** K2, 28,250 ft (8,611 m). **Lowest point** Sea level.
*The above information includes part of Jammu and Kashmir.*

**People.** Pakistan's varied ethnicity is the product of centuries of incursions by different races. Today each people is concentrated in a different region and speaks its own language; Urdu, the official language, is not widely spoken. The Punjabis compose the largest ethnic group and traditionally have been influential in government and commerce. Virtually all of Pakistan, which was created as a Muslim homeland, follows Islam. Spurred by poor living conditions and a lack of jobs, many Pakistanis work abroad.

**Economy and the Land.** Despite recent progress in manufacturing, agriculture remains the economic mainstay. Improvement in farming techniques has increased productivity. Government planning and foreign assistance have aided all sectors, but Pakistan remains troubled by population growth, unskilled labor, a trade deficit, and an influx of refugees fleeing the war in Afghanistan. Pakistan's terrain includes mountains, fertile plains, and desert. The climate is continental, with extremes in temperature.

**History and Politics.** Around 2500 B.C., the Indus Valley civilization flourished in the area of modern Pakistan. Various empires and immigrants followed, including Aryans, Persians, and Greeks. Invading Arabs introduced Islam to the region in the A.D. 700s. In the 1500s, the Mogul Empire of Afghanistan came to include nearly all of present-day Pakistan, India, and Bangladesh, and as that empire declined, various peoples ruled the area. Through wars and treaties, the British presence in Asia expanded, and by the early twentieth century British India included all of modern Pakistan. Because of hostilities between British India's Muslims and Hindus, the separate Muslim nation of Pakistan was created when British India gained independence in 1947. With its boundaries drawn around the Muslim population centers, Pakistan was formed from the northeastern and northwestern parts of India, and its eastern region was separated from the west by more than 1,000 miles (1,600 km). East Pakistanis felt that power was unfairly concentrated in the west, and in 1971 a civil war erupted. Aided by India, East Pakistan won the war and became the independent nation of Bangladesh. After the death of President Mohammed Zia in 1988, the people elected Benazir Bhutto, who has revived the People's party of her father, a previous president. ∎

## PALAU See UNITED STATES.

## PANAMA

**Official name** Republic of Panama
**PEOPLE**
**Population** 2,396,000. **Density** 81/mi$^2$ (31/km$^2$). **Urban** 52%. **Capital** Panamá, 389,172. **Ethnic groups** Mestizo 70%, West Indian 14%, white 10%, Amerindian 6%. **Languages** Spanish, English, indigenous. **Religions** Roman Catholic 93%, Protestant 6%. **Life expectancy** 73 female, 69 male. **Literacy** 87%.
**POLITICS**
**Government** Republic. **Parties** Coalition for National Liberation, Opposition Democratic Alliance. **Suffrage** Universal, over 18. **Memberships** OAS, UN. **Subdivisions** 9 provinces, 1 intendency.
**ECONOMY**
**GDP** $4,881,000,000 **Per capita** $2,265. **Monetary unit** Balboa. **Trade partners** Exports: U.S., Costa Rica, W. Germany. Imports: U.S., Mexico, Japan. **Exports** Bananas, shellfish, sugar, petroleum, coffee. **Imports** Petroleum, manufactures, machinery, chemicals, food, transportation equipment.
**LAND**
**Description** Central America. **Area** 29,762 mi$^2$ (77,082 km$^2$). **Highest point** Volcán Barú, 11,401 ft (3,475 m). **Lowest point** Sea level.

**People.** Most Panamanians are mestizos, a mixture of Spanish and Indian stocks. Indigenous Indians, blacks from the West Indies, and whites form the remaining population. A Spanish legacy is reflected by the official language, Spanish, and the predominance of Roman Catholicism. Most people live near the Panama Canal. A wealthy elite has traditionally directed the government and economy.

**Economy and the Land.** Because of its location, Panama has been a strategic center for trade and transportation. The 1914 opening of the Panama Canal, connecting the Atlantic and Pacific oceans, accentuated these strengths and has provided additional revenue and jobs; the canal area is now Panama's most economically developed region.

Agriculture is an important activity; and oil refining, food processing, fishing, and financial services all contribute to the economy as well. Panama will have to adjust to the economic and technical losses that will accompany the end of United States operation of the canal in 1999. The country has a mountainous interior and a tropical climate.

**History and Politics.** Originally inhabited by Indians, Panama became a Spanish colony in the early 1500s and served as a vital transportation center. In 1821 it overcame Spanish rule and entered the Republic of Greater Colombia. After Colombia vetoed a United States plan to build a canal across the narrow isthmus, Panama, encouraged by the United States, seceded from the republic and became independent in 1903. Eleven years later, America completed the canal and established control over it and the Panama Canal Zone. Dissatisfaction with this arrangement resulted in several anti-American riots in the fifties and sixties. A 1968 coup placed the Panamanian National Guard in power, and the movement to end American control of the Canal Zone gained momentum. In 1979, the sovereignty of the Canal Zone was transferred to Panama; it will gain control of the canal in 1999. Some representation has been returned to civilians, but the military, under General Manuel Noriega, exercised repressive control until United States military forces invaded and overthrew Noriega in December 1989. ∎

## PAPUA NEW GUINEA

**Official name** Papua New Guinea
**PEOPLE**
**Population** 3,653,000. **Density** 20/mi$^2$ (7.9/km$^2$). **Urban** 14%. **Capital** Port Moresby, New Guinea I., 123,624. **Ethnic groups** Melanesian, Papuan, Negrito, Micronesian, Polynesian. **Languages** English, Motu, Pidgin, indigenous. **Religions** Animist 50%, Lutheran and other Protestant 37%, Roman Catholic 13%. **Life expectancy** 53 female, 51 male. **Literacy** 32%.

## PAPUA NEW GUINEA

### POLITICS
**Government** Parliamentary state. **Parties** Pangu, People's Democratic Movement, People's Progress, others. **Suffrage** Universal adult. **Memberships** CW, UN. **Subdivisions** 19 provinces, 1 capital district.

### ECONOMY
**GDP** $2,292,000,000 **Per capita** $674. **Monetary unit** Kina. **Trade partners** Exports: Japan, W. Germany, Australia. Imports: Australia, Japan, Singapore. **Exports** Copper, coffee, copra products, cocoa, palm oil, wood, tea. **Imports** Manufactures, machinery, food, petroleum, transportation equipment, chemicals.

### LAND
**Description** South Pacific islands. **Area** 178,704 mi$^2$ (462,840 km$^2$). **Highest point** Mt. Wilhelm, New Guinea I., 14,793 ft (4,509 m). **Lowest point** Sea level.

**People.** Almost all inhabitants are Melanesians belonging to several thousand culturally diverse and geographically isolated communities. More than seven hundred languages are spoken, but most people also speak Motu or a dialect of English. European missionaries brought Christianity, but faiths based on spirit and ancestor worship predominate. The traditions of village life remain strong.

**Economy and the Land.** The economic supports are agriculture, which employs most of the work force, and copper and gold mining. Papua New Guinea has other mineral resources, as well as potential for forestry. The nation consists of the eastern half of New Guinea Island, plus New Britain, New Ireland, Bougainville, and six hundred smaller islands. Terrain includes mountains, volcanoes, broad valleys, and swamps; the climate is tropical.

**History and Politics.** Settlers from Southeast Asia are thought to have arrived as long as fifty thousand years ago. Isolated native villages were found by the Spanish and Portuguese in the early 1500s. In 1884 Germany annexed the northeastern part of the island of New Guinea and its offshore islands, and Britain took control of the southeastern section and its islands. Australia assumed administration of the British territory, known as Papua, in 1906 and seized the German regions, or German New Guinea, during World War I. The League of Nations granted Australia a mandate to New Guinea in 1920. After being occupied by Japan in World War II, Papua and New Guinea were united as an Australian territory from 1945 to 1946. Papua New Guinea gained independence in 1975. The island of Bougainville seceded a few months later but rejoined the nation in 1976. Papua New Guinea has close ties with Australia and a moderate foreign policy. ∎

## PARAGUAY

**Official name** Republic of Paraguay
### ECONOMY
**GDP** $5,808,000,000 **Per capita** $1,798. **Monetary unit** Guarani. **Trade partners** Exports: Brazil, Netherlands, Argentina. Imports: Brazil, Argentina, Algeria. **Exports** Cotton, soybeans, wood, vegetable oil, animal food, chemicals. **Imports** Machinery and transportation equipment, manufactures, petroleum.

### PEOPLE
**Population** 4,221,000. **Density** 27/mi$^2$ (10/km$^2$). **Urban** 44%. **Capital** Asunción, 455,517. **Ethnic groups** Mestizo 95%, white and Amerindian 5%. **Languages** Spanish, Guarani. **Religions** Roman Catholic 90%, Mennonite and other Protestant. **Life expectancy** 68 female, 63 male. **Literacy** 88%.

### POLITICS
**Government** Republic. **Parties** Authentic Radical Liberal, Colorado, others. **Suffrage** Universal, over 18. **Memberships** OAS, UN. **Subdivisions** 20 departments.

### LAND
**Description** Central South America, landlocked. **Area** 157,048 mi$^2$ (406,752 km$^2$). **Highest point** 2,625 ft (800 m). **Lowest point** Confluence of Paraná and Paraguay rivers, 151 ft (46 m).

**People.** Paraguay's population displays a homogeneity unusual in South America; most people are a mix of Spanish and Guarani Indian ancestry, are Roman Catholic, and speak both Spanish and Guarani. The small number of unassimilated Guarani live mostly in western Paraguay, known as the Gran Chaco. There are some foreign communities, mostly German, Japanese, and Brazilian. Culture combines Spanish and Indian traditions.

**Economy and the Land.** Agriculture—based on cotton, soybeans, and cattle—forms the keystone of the economy. Forestry also contributes significantly to Paraguay's exports. The lack of direct access to the sea, unskilled labor, and a history of war and instability have resulted in an underdeveloped economy; manufacturing in particular has suffered. The world's largest hydroelectric project, the Itaipu Dam, was completed in 1988. Paraguay has two distinct regions, divided by the Paraguay River: the semiarid Gran Chaco plains in the west, and the temperate, fertile east, where most farming takes place.

**History and Politics.** The indigenous Guarani formed an agricultural society centered around what is now Asunción. Portuguese and Spanish explorers arrived in the early 1500s, and the region subsequently gained importance as the center of Spanish holdings in southern South America. During the 1700s, Jesuit missionaries worked to convert thousands of Indians to Roman Catholicism. After gaining independence in 1811, Paraguay was ruled until 1870 by three successive dictators: José Gaspar Rodríguez de Francia, who held power from 1814 to 1840 and sealed Paraguay off from foreign influence; Carlos Antonio López, who reversed this isolationism during his rule from 1841 to 1862; and his son, Francisco Solano López, who led Paraguay into a disastrous war against Uruguay, Argentina, and Brazil that cost the nation half its population. A war against Bolivia from 1932 to 1935 increased Paraguay's territory but further weakened its stability. Alternating weak and repressive regimes followed until 1989, when a military coup ended the thirty-five year regime of General Stroessner. His successor, General Rodriguez, then won a multi-candidate election and promised to turn over the government to an elected civilian in 1993. ∎

# PERU

**Official name** Republic of Peru
**PEOPLE**
**Population** 22,085,000. **Density** 45/mi$^2$ (17/km$^2$). **Urban** 67%. **Capital** Lima, 371,122. **Ethnic groups** Amerindian 45%, mestizo 37%, white 15%. **Languages** Quechua, Spanish, Aymara. **Religions** Roman Catholic 89%, Protestant 5%. **Life expectancy** 61 female, 57 male. **Literacy** 83%.
**POLITICS**
**Government** Republic. **Parties** American Popular Revolutionary Alliance, Popular Action, Popular Christian, United Left. **Suffrage** Universal, over 18. **Memberships** OAS, UN. **Subdivisions** 24 departments, 1 constitutional province.
**ECONOMY**
**GDP** $14,394,000,000 **Per capita** $737. **Monetary unit** Inti. **Trade partners** U.S., Japan. **Exports** Petroleum, copper and other metals, mineral ores, coffee and other food. **Imports** Manufactures, machinery, food, transportation equipment, chemicals.
**LAND**
**Description** Western South America. **Area** 496,225 mi$^2$ (1,285,216 km$^2$). **Highest point** Nevado Huascarán, 22,133 ft (6,746 m). **Lowest point** Sea level.

**People.** Peru's Indian population constitutes the nation's largest ethnic group and the largest Indian concentration in North or South America. Although whites make up the third largest group after Indians and mestizos, they have historically controlled much of the wealth. The Indians are often geographically and culturally remote from the ruling classes and generally live in poverty. Most Peruvians practice Roman Catholicism, a Spanish inheritance.

**Economy and the Land.** Considerable natural resources have made Peru a leader in the production of minerals—notably copper, lead, and silver—and in fishing. The food-processing, textile, and oil-refining industries also contribute. Productivity has been slowed by a mountainous terrain that impedes transport and communication, earthquakes and other natural disasters, a largely unskilled work force, and years of stringent military rule. Climate varies from arid and mild in the coastal desert to temperate but cool in the Andean highlands and hot and humid in the eastern jungles and plains.

**History and Politics.** Several Indian cultures arose in the region between 900 B.C. and A.D. 1200, the last of which was the Incan. Excavation began in 1987 of the richest burial ground of a pre-Hispanic ruler ever discovered, further documenting the sophistication of these cultures. Builders of an empire stretching from Colombia to Chile, the Inca were conquered by the Spanish by 1533. For almost the next three hundred years, Peru was a harshly ruled Spanish colony and center for colonial administration. Peru achieved independence from Spain in 1821, largely through the efforts of José de San Martín of Argentina and Simón Bolívar of Venezuela, although Spain did not formally recognize Peruvian independence until 1879. Military officers ruled the country through the rest of the century. In 1883, Chile and Bolivia defeated Peru in the War of the Pacific, and the country lost its valuable southern nitrate region. A reform party, despite being banned by the government, gained momentum in the 1930s and 1940s. Fernando Belaúnde Terry, a moderate reformer, was elected in 1963. A military junta ousted him in 1968, nationalizing some industries and instituting land reform. Inflation and unemployment caused dissatisfaction and a 1975 coup. Elections in 1980 and 1985 restored democratic leadership. ∎

# PHILIPPINES

**Official name** Republic of the Philippines
**PEOPLE**
**Population** 60,835,000. **Density** 525/mi$^2$ (203/km$^2$). **Urban** 40%. **Capital** Manila, Luzon I., 1,630,485. **Ethnic groups** Christian Malay 92%, Muslim Malay 4%, Chinese 2%. **Languages** English, Pilipino, Tagalog, Cebuano. **Religions** Roman Catholic 83%, Protestant 9%, Muslim 5%, Buddhist and others 3%. **Life expectancy** 64 female, 60 male. **Literacy** 83%.
**POLITICS**
**Government** Republic. **Parties** Democratic Socialist Coalition, PDP-Laban, Struggle for a Democratic Philippines, Union for National. **Suffrage** Universal adult. **Memberships** ASEAN, UN. **Subdivisions** 74 provinces, 60 chartered cities.
**ECONOMY**
**GDP** $32,787,000,000 **Per capita** $595. **Monetary unit** Peso. **Trade partners** Exports: U.S., Japan, Singapore. Imports: U.S., Japan, Saudi Arabia. **Exports** Clothing and other manufactures, food, raw materials, copra oil. **Imports** Petroleum, machinery, manufactures chemicals, food.

# PHILIPPINES • PITCAIRN • POLAND

### LAND
**Description** Southeastern Asian islands. **Area** 115,831 mi² (300,000 km²). **Highest point** Mt. Apo, Mindanao I., 9,692 ft (2,954 m). **Lowest point** Sea level.

**People.** Nearly all Filipinos are descended from Malay peoples. The majority are Roman Catholic, a reflection of centuries of Spanish rule. A Muslim minority has begun agitating for autonomy. Although nearly ninety native languages and dialects are spoken, Pilipino and English are the official languages. The wide gap between rich and poor, inherited from a plantation economy, has concentrated wealth in the hands of the landowners.

**Economy and the Land.** Philippines is a primarily agricultural nation, relying on rice, sugar, coconuts, and wood. Fishing is an important activity. Considerable reserves of copper, nickel, and chromite make mining important. Manufacturing is developing through government incentives. A dependence on imported goods, along with inadequate but growing power and transport systems, has hampered growth. The archipelago of more than seven thousand islands is marked by mountains, volcanoes, forests, and inland plains. The climate is tropical and includes a typhoon season.

**History and Politics.** The islands are thought to have been settled by Negritos about thirty thousand years ago. Beginning about 3000 B.C., Malay immigrants arrived. By 1565 the area was under Spanish control, and the Roman Catholic church had considerable influence throughout the Spanish period. In the late 1800s, a movement for independence developed but was put down first by the Spanish and then by the United States, which gained the islands in 1898 after defeating Spain in the Spanish-American War. During World War II Japan occupied the Philippines. Independence came in 1946 and was followed by a rebellion by Communists demanding land reform; the rebels were defeated in 1954. Ferdinand Marcos was elected president in 1965 and, in the face of opposition from many quarters, declared martial law in 1972. Marcos lifted martial law in 1981 but was defeated in a 1986 presidential election by Corazon Aquino, wife of assassinated opposition leader Benigno Aquino. Marcos eventually fled the island, and Aquino assumed power. Reforms have been instituted; but coup attempts, leftist insurgency groups, and unresolved social and economic problems still plague the country. ■

## PITCAIRN See UNITED KINGDOM.

## POLAND

**Official name** Republic of Poland
### PEOPLE
**Population** 37,840,000. **Density** 313/mi² (121/km²). **Urban** 61%. **Capital** Warsaw, 1,664,700. **Ethnic groups** Polish (mixed Slavic and Teutonic) 99%, Ukrainian, Byelorussian. **Languages** Polish. **Religions** Roman Catholic 95%. **Life expectancy** 75 female, 67 male. **Literacy** 99%.
### POLITICS
**Government** Republic. **Parties** Solidarity, United Workers'. **Suffrage** Universal, over 18. **Memberships** CEMA, UN, Warsaw Pact. **Subdivisions** 49 provinces.
### ECONOMY
**GNP** $240,600,000,000 **Per capita** $6,493. **Monetary unit** Zloty. **Trade partners** Exports: U.S.S.R., W. Germany, Czechoslovakia. Imports: U.S.S.R., W. Germany, E. Germany. **Exports** Machinery, manufactures, coal, transportation equipment, crude materials. **Imports** Machinery, manufactures, petroleum, crude materials, food, chemicals.
### LAND
**Description** Eastern Europe. **Area** 120,728 mi² (312,683 km²). **Highest point** Rysy, 8,199 ft (2,499 m). **Lowest point** Raczki Elbląskie, -6 ft (-2 m).

**People.** Poland's homogeneous population is partially a result of Nazi persecution during World War II, which virtually obliterated the Jewish community and led to the emigration of most minorities. Roman Catholicism, practiced by almost all Poles, remains a unifying force. The urban population has risen in the postwar period because of government emphasis on industrialization.

**Economy and the Land.** Government policies

since the war have transformed Poland from an agricultural nation into an industrial one. It is a leading producer of coal and has several metal-processing industries. Machinery and textiles are important products. Although most industries are government controlled, the majority of farms are privately owned. Poland's poor soil and short growing season have kept it from achieving agricultural self-sufficiency. Shortages in consumer goods have been chronic since the 1970s, when the failure of Polish goods in world markets compounded debts to the West. Poland has a mostly flat terrain—except for mountains in the south—and a temperate climate.

**History and Politics.** Slavic tribes inhabited the region of modern Poland several thousand years ago. The Piast dynasty began in the A.D. 900s and established Roman Catholicism as the official religion. In the sixteenth century, the Jagiellonian dynasty guided the empire to its height of expansion. A subsequent series of upheavals and wars weakened Poland, and from the 1770s to the 1790s it was partitioned three times, finally disappearing as an independent state. In 1918, following the Allies' World War I victory, Poland regained its independence and, through the 1919 Treaty of Versailles, much of its former territory. World War II began with Germany's invasion of Poland in 1939. With the end of the war, Poland came under Communist control and Soviet domination. Antigovernment strikes and riots, some spurred by rising food prices, erupted periodically. In the first free election since Communist control, the trade union, Solidarity, won an overwhelming victory in 1989. ■

# PORTUGAL

**Official name** Portuguese Republic
**PEOPLE**
**Population** 10,495,000. **Density** 296/mi$^2$ (114/km$^2$). **Urban** 32%. **Capital** Lisbon, 807,167. **Ethnic groups** Portuguese (Mediterranean), black. **Languages** Portuguese. **Religions** Roman Catholic 97%, Protestant 1%. **Life expectancy** 75 female, 68 male. **Literacy** 71%.
**POLITICS**
**Government** Republic. **Parties** Democratic Renewal, Social Democratic, Socialist, others. **Suffrage** Universal, over 18. **Memberships** EC, NATO, OECD, UN. **Subdivisions** 18 districts, 2 autonomous regions.

**ECONOMY**
**GDP** $20,687,000,000 **Per capita** $2,055. **Monetary unit** Escudo. **Trade partners** Exports: W. Germany, U.S., France. Imports: W. Germany, U.K., France. **Exports** Clothing and other manufactures, machinery, crude materials, chemicals. **Imports** Petroleum, manufactures, machinery, crude materials, food, chemicals.
**LAND**
**Description** Southwestern Europe. **Area** 35,516 mi$^2$ (91,985 km$^2$). **Highest point** Ponta do Pico, Ilha do Pico, Azores Is., 7,713 ft (2,351 m). **Lowest point** Sea level.

**People.** Although many foreign invaders have been drawn by Portugal's long coastline, today the population is relatively homogeneous. One group of invaders, the Romans, laid the basis for the chief language, Portuguese, which developed from Latin. The only significant minority is composed of black Africans from former colonies. Most Portuguese are rural and belong to the Roman Catholic church, which has had a strong influence on society.

**Economy and the Land.** The mainstays of agriculture and fishing were joined in the mid-1900s by manufacturing, chiefly of textiles, clothing, cork products, metals, and machinery. A variety of social and political ills contributing to Portugal's status as one of Europe's poorest nations include: past wars with African colonies, an influx of colonial refugees, and intraparty violence. Tourism is increasingly important, but agriculture has suffered from outdated techniques and a rural-to-urban population shift.

## Places and Possessions of PORTUGAL

| Entity | Status | Area | Population | Capital/Population |
| --- | --- | --- | --- | --- |
| **Azores** (North Atlantic islands) | Autonomous region | 868 mi$^2$ (2,247 km$^2$) | 259,000 | Ponta Delgada, 21,187 |
| **Macao** (Eastern Asia; islands and peninsula on China's southeastern coast) | Chinese territory under Portuguese administration | 6.6 mi$^2$ (17 km$^2$) | 454,000 | Macao, 429,000 |
| **Madeira Islands** (North Atlantic islands; northwest of Africa) | Autonomous region | 307 mi$^2$ (794 km$^2$) | 278,000 | Funchal, 44,111 |

The terrain is mostly plains and lowlands, with some mountains; the climate is mild and sunny.

**History and Politics.** Inhabited by an Iberian people about five thousand years ago, the area was later visited by Phoenicians, Celts, and Greeks before falling to the Romans around the first century B.C. The Romans were followed by Germanic Visigoths and in A.D. 711 by North African Muslims, who greatly influenced Portuguese art and architecture. Spain absorbed Portugal in 1094, and Portugal declared its independence in 1143. About one hundred years later, the last of the Muslims were expelled. Portugal's golden age—during which its navigators explored the globe and founded colonies in South America, Africa, and the Far East—lasted from 1385 to the late 1500s. Rival European powers soon began to seize Portuguese holdings. In 1580, Spain invaded Portugal, ruling until 1640, when the Spanish were driven out and independence reestablished. After the 1822 loss of Brazil, Portugal's most valuable colony, and decades of opposition, a weakened monarchy was overthrown in 1910. The hardships of World War I battered the newly-established republic, and in 1926 its parliamentary democracy fell to a military coup. Antonio Salazar became prime minister in 1932, ruling as a virtual dictator until 1968. Salazar's favored treatment of the rich and his refusal to relinquish Portugal's colonies aggravated the economic situation. A 1974 coup toppled Salazar's successor and set up a military government, events that sparked violence among political parties. Almost all Portuguese colonies gained independence during the next two years. A democratic government was adopted in 1976; varying coalitions have since ruled the nation. Elections in 1987 resulted in the first majority government won by the Social Democrats. ∎

# PUERTO RICO

**Official name** Commonwealth of Puerto Rico
**PEOPLE**
**Population** 3,368,000. **Density** 958/mi² (370/km²). **Urban** 71%. **Capital** San Juan, 424,600. **Ethnic groups** Puerto Rican (mixed Spanish and black). **Languages** Spanish, English. **Religions** Roman Catholic 85%. **Life expectancy** 78 female, 71 male. **Literacy** 88%.
**POLITICS**
**Government** Commonwealth (U.S. protection). **Parties** New Progressive, Popular Democratic, others. **Suffrage** Universal, over 18. **Memberships** None. **Subdivisions** 78 municipalities.
**ECONOMY**
**GDP** $21,109,000,000 **Per capita** $6,301. **Monetary unit** U.S. dollar. **Trade partners** Exports: U.S., Virgin Is. (U.S.), Dominican Republic. Imports: U.S., Venezuela, Iran. **Exports** Clothing, pharmaceuticals and other chemicals, petroleum, machinery. **Imports** Petroleum, fish, food, metals.
**LAND**
**Description** Caribbean island. **Area** 3,515 mi² (9,104 km²). **Highest point** Cerro de Punta, 4,389 ft (1,338 m). **Lowest point** Sea level.

**People.** Puerto Rico's chief language, Spanish, and religion, Roman Catholicism, reflect this American Commonwealth's past under Spanish rule. Most of the population is descended from Spaniards and black African slaves. A rising population has caused housing shortages and unemployment. Many Puerto Ricans live in the United States, mostly in New York City.

**Economy and the Land.** Once dependent on such plantation crops as sugar and coffee, Puerto Rico is now a manufacturing nation, specializing in food processing and electrical equipment. Commonwealth incentives for foreign investors aided this transformation, also known as Operation Bootstrap, after World War II. Foreign visitors, attracted by the tropical climate, make tourism another important activity. Economic development has been hurt by a lack of natural resources and by fluctuations in the United States economy. The island's terrain is marked by mountains, lowlands, and valleys.

**History and Politics.** The original inhabitants, the Arawak Indians, were wiped out by Spanish colonists, who first settled the island in 1508. Despite successive attacks by the French, English, and Dutch, Puerto Rico remained under Spanish control until 1898, when the United States took possession after the Spanish-American War. A civil government under a United States governor was set up in 1900; seventeen years later Puerto Ricans were made United States citizens. In 1952 the island became a self-governing Commonwealth. This status was upheld in a referendum in 1967, but fierce, occasionally violent internal debate continues over whether Puerto Rico should be a state, a Commonwealth, or an independent nation. ∎

# QATAR

**Official name** State of Qatar
**PEOPLE**
**Population** 417,000. **Density** 94/mi² (36/km²). **Urban** 88%. **Capital** Doha, 217,294. **Ethnic groups** Arab 40%, Pakistani 18%, Indian 18%, Iranian 10%. **Languages** Arabic, English. **Religions** Muslim 95%. **Life expectancy** 70 female, 65 male. **Literacy** 34%.

## REUNION

### POLITICS
**Government** Monarchy. **Parties** None. **Suffrage** None. **Memberships** AL, OPEC, UN. **Subdivisions** None.
### ECONOMY
**GDP** $6,532,000,000 **Per capita** $23,329. **Monetary unit** Riyal. **Trade partners** Exports: Japan, Netherlands, France. Imports: Japan, U.K., France. **Exports** Petroleum, chemicals. **Imports** Machinery, manufactures, automobiles and other transportation equipment.
### LAND
**Description** Southwestern Asia. **Area** 4,416 mi$^2$ (11,437 km$^2$). **Highest point** Aba al Bawl Hill, 344 ft (105 m). **Lowest point** Sea level.

**People.** Qatar's population is distinguished by a relatively high proportion of Iranians, Pakistanis, and Indians, who began arriving during the oil boom of the 1950s. Most Qataris are Sunni Muslims and live in or near Doha, the capital. In recent years, the government has encouraged the nomadic Bedouins to take up settled lifestyles. Despite a political trend toward a modern welfare state, Qatar retains many elements of a traditional Islamic society.

**Economy and the Land.** Oil provides the great majority of Qatar's income, while extensive reserves of natural gas await exploitation. The government has made moves toward economic diversification, investing in agriculture and industry; fertilizer and cement are important new products. Most of Qatar is stony desert, and the climate is hot and arid.

**History and Politics.** No strong central government existed in Qatar before Saudi Muslims gained control in the late eighteenth century. Ottoman Turks occupied the region from 1872 to 1916, when Qatar became a British protectorate. Although oil was discovered in 1940 on the western side of Qatar's peninsula, the outbreak of World War II postponed exploitation for another nine years. Qatar became independent in 1971 after failing to agree on the terms of a union with eight Persian Gulf sheikdoms—today the United Arab Emirates and Bahrain. Oil revenues have been used to improve housing, transportation, and public health. Qatar maintains friendly relations with the West and neighboring Arab states. ∎

**Official name** Department of Reunion
### PEOPLE
**Population** 590,000. **Density** 609/mi$^2$ (235/km$^2$). **Urban** 60%. **Capital** St. Denis, 84,400. **Ethnic groups** Reunionese (mixed French, African, Malagasy, Chinese, Pakistani, and Indian). **Languages** French, Creole. **Religions** Roman Catholic 94%. **Life expectancy** 74 female, 66 male. **Literacy** 79%.
### POLITICS
**Government** Overseas department (France). **Parties** Communist, Rally for the Republic, Union for Democracy, others. **Suffrage** Universal adult. **Memberships** None. **Subdivisions** 4 arrondissements.
### ECONOMY
**GDP** $1,709,000,000 **Per capita** $3,165. **Monetary unit** French franc. **Trade partners** Exports: France, Portugal. Imports: France, Bahrain. **Exports** Sugar, fish and shellfish, rum. **Imports** Machinery, manufactures, food, transportation equipment, chemicals, petroleum.
### LAND
**Description** Indian Ocean island. **Area** 969 mi$^2$ (2,510 km$^2$). **Highest point** Piton des Neiges, 10,069 ft (3,069 m). **Lowest point** Sea level.

**People.** Reunion has a racially mixed population, mainly descended from French settlers, African slaves, and Asian laborers. French is the official language, but most inhabitants speak a creole dialect. The mainly Roman Catholic population is densely concentrated in the lowland areas along the coast. Social stratification is rigid.

**Economy and the Land.** Reunion's traditional sugar crop continues as its economic mainstay, although commercial fishing and shellfish are also important. Unemployment is a problem, and the island remains dependent upon French aid. Volcanoes, including one active and several extinct, mark the mountainous terrain. The tropical climate is subject to occasional cyclones and trade winds, which bring high rainfall to the south and southeast.

**History and Politics.** Although known to the Arabs and the Portuguese, Reunion was uninhabited when French settlement began in the 1660s. First called Île Bourbon, the island originally served as a stopover on the French shipping route to India. The French soon developed coffee and sugar plantations, bringing slaves from Africa to work them. British-French rivalry for control of the area led to brief British rule during the early 1800s. The name was changed to Reunion in 1848, and after the abolition of slavery, indentured laborers were brought from Indochina, India, and eastern Africa. Reunion was a French colony until 1946, when it became an overseas department. ∎

# ROMANIA

**Official name** Romania
**PEOPLE**
Population 23,210,000. **Density** 253/mi$^2$ (98/km$^2$). **Urban** 49%. **Capital** Bucharest, 1,989,823. **Ethnic groups** Romanian (mixed Latin, Thracian, Slavic, and Celtic) 89%, Hungarian 8%, German 2%. **Languages** Romanian, Hungarian, German. **Religions** Romanian Orthodox 80%, Roman Catholic 6%. **Life expectancy** 73 female, 68 male. **Literacy** 96%.
**POLITICS**
**Government** Socialist republic. **Parties** National Salvation Front. **Suffrage** Universal, over 18. **Memberships** CEMA, UN, Warsaw Pact. **Subdivisions** 40 counties, 1 municipality.
**ECONOMY**
**GNP** $123,700,000,000 **Per capita** $5,411. **Monetary unit** Leu. **Trade partners** Exports: U.S.S.R., Italy, W. Germany. Imports: U.S.S.R., Iran, Egypt. **Exports** Machinery and transportation equipment; fuel, minerals, and metals. **Imports** Fuel, minerals, and metals; machinery and transportation equipment; chemicals.
**LAND**
**Description** Eastern Europe. **Area** 91,699 mi$^2$ (237,500 km$^2$). **Highest point** Moldoveanu, 8,346 ft (2,544 m). **Lowest point** Sea level.

**People.** The majority population of Romania belongs to the Romanian Orthodox church and traces its roots to Latin-speaking Romans, Thracians, Slavs, and Celts. Minorities, concentrated in Transylvania and areas north and west of Bucharest, are mainly Roman Catholic Hungarians and Germans. Other minorities include Gypsies, Serbs, Croats, Ukrainians, Greeks, Turks, and Armenians. Almost all inhabitants speak Romanian, although minority groups often speak other languages.

**Economy and the Land.** When Romania became a Communist country in the 1940s, the government began to turn the country from agriculture to industry. The economy is now based on such major products as iron and steel. Although Romania remains less developed than many other European countries, it has experienced post-war growth in its gross national product. Most agriculture is collectivized, and corn and wheat are major crops. The terrain is marked by a south-to-northeast plateau that curves around several mountain ranges, including the Carpathians, found in the northern and central regions. The climate is continental, with cold, snowy winters and warm summers.

**History and Politics.** First colonized by the Dacians, a Thracian tribe, around the fourth century B.C., the area became the Roman province of Romania in the second century A.D. Invading Bulgars, Goths, Huns, Magyars, Slavs, and Tartars followed the Romans. Between 1250 and 1350, the independent Romanian principalities of Walachia and Moldavia emerged. In the fifteenth and sixteenth centuries, Ottoman Turks conquered the principalities, and following a Russian-Turkish war, Russians occupied the states. In 1861 Walachia and Moldavia were united as Romania, in 1878 they gained independence, and in 1881 Romania was proclaimed a kingdom. Oppression and a concentration of land and wealth among the aristocracy marked the nation's government, and in 1907 its army quelled a rebellion. In 1919, after a World War I alliance with the Allies, Romania gained Transylvania and other territories. Instability and dissatisfaction, spurred by worldwide economic depression, continued through the 1930s. With the cooperation of Romanian leadership, Germany occupied the country in World War II. In 1944 Soviet troops entered Romania, and the nation subsequently joined the Allies. A Communist government was established in 1945, and in 1947 the king was forced to abdicate and Romania officially became a Communist country. Initially Romania's policies were closely tied to those of the Soviet Union; but renewed nationalism in the sixties led to several independent policy decisions. Nicolae Ceausescu's twenty-four years of harsh, repressive leadership led to a popular revolt and his execution in 1989. An interim government plans elections in 1990. ∎

# RWANDA

**Official name** Republic of Rwanda
**PEOPLE**
Population 7,463,000. **Density** 734/mi$^2$ (283/km$^2$). **Urban** 6%. **Capital** Kigali, 181,600. **Ethnic groups** Hutu 89%, Tutsi 10%, Twa. **Languages** French, Kinyarwanda. **Religions** Roman Catholic 52%, Protestant 21%, Animist 9%. **Life expectancy** 48 female, 45 male. **Literacy** 35%.
**POLITICS**
**Government** Republic. **Parties** National Revolutionary

Movement for Development. **Suffrage** Universal adult. **Memberships** OAU, UN. **Subdivisions** 10 prefectures.

### ECONOMY
**GDP** $1,587,000,000 **Per capita** $295. **Monetary unit** Franc. **Trade partners** Exports: Belgium, Kenya. Imports: Kenya, Belgium, Japan. **Exports** Coffee, tea, tin and other minerals, crude vegetable materials, animal feed. **Imports** Textiles and other manufactures, transportation equipment, petroleum.

### LAND
**Description** Eastern Africa, landlocked. **Area** 10,169 mi$^2$ (26,338 km$^2$). **Highest point** Volcan Karisimbi, 14,787 ft (4,507 m). **Lowest point** 3,100 ft (950 m).

**People.** Most Rwandans are Hutu, mainly farmers of Bantu stock. Minorities include the Tutsi, a pastoral people that dominated politically until a Hutu rebellion in 1959, and the Twa, Pygmies descended from the original population. Both French and Kinyarwanda are official languages, but most speak Kinyarwanda, a Bantu tongue. Roman Catholicism is the major religion, and minority groups practice indigenous beliefs as well as Protestantism and Islam. A high population density and a high birthrate characterize Rwanda.

**Economy and the Land.** Agriculture is the major activity, although plagued by the erosion and overpopulation of arable land. Many Rwandans practice subsistence farming, while coffee and tea are major export crops. The production and export of minerals, partly fueled by foreign investment, is also important. Tourism is small but growing; Rwanda is one of the last refuges of the mountain gorilla. The country's landlocked position and underdeveloped transportation system hinder economic growth. The terrain consists mainly of grassy uplands and hills, with volcanic mountains in the west and northwest, while the climate is mild.

**History and Politics.** The Twa, the region's original inhabitants, were followed by the Hutu. The Tutsi most likely arrived about the fourteenth century, subjugating the weaker Hutu and becoming the region's dominant force. The areas of present-day Rwanda and Burundi became part of German East Africa in the 1890s. In 1919, following World War I, the region was mandated to Belgium as Ruanda-Urundi, and following World War II, Ruanda-Urundi was made a United Nations trust territory under Belgian administration. In 1959 a Hutu revolt against Tutsi domination resulted in the death of many Tutsi and the flight of many more. After gaining independence in 1962, the former territory split into the countries of Rwanda and Burundi. The military overthrew the nation's first president in 1973.

∎

## ST. CHRISTOPHER AND NEVIS

**Official name** Federation of St. Christopher and Nevis

### PEOPLE
**Population** 46,000. **Density** 442/mi$^2$ (171/km$^2$). **Urban** 45%. **Capital** Basseterre, St. Christopher I., 14,725. **Ethnic groups** Black 94%, mixed 3%, white 1%. **Languages** English. **Religions** Anglican 33%, Methodist 29%, Moravian 9%, Roman Catholic 7%. **Life expectancy** 70 female, 66 male. **Literacy** 98%.

### POLITICS
**Government** Parliamentary state. **Parties** Labor, People's Action Movement, Reformation. **Suffrage** Universal, over 18. **Memberships** CW, OAS, UN. **Subdivisions** 14 parishes.

### ECONOMY
**GDP** $65,000,000 **Per capita** $1,444. **Monetary unit** East Caribbean dollar. **Trade partners** Exports: U.K., U.S., Trinidad and Tobago. Imports: U.S., U.K., Trinidad and Tobago. **Exports** Sugar, clothing and other manufactures, machinery. **Imports** Manufactures, meat and other food, machinery, petroleum, chemicals.

### LAND
**Description** Caribbean islands. **Area** 104 mi$^2$ (269 km$^2$). **Highest point** Mt. Liamuiga, St. Christopher I., 3,792 ft (1,156 m). **Lowest point** Sea level.

**People.** Most of the inhabitants of the islands of St. Christopher, often called St. Kitts, and Nevis are of black African descent. The primarily rural population is concentrated along the coast. English is spoken throughout the islands, and most people are Protestant, especially Anglican, evidence of former British rule.

**Economy and the Land.** Agriculture and tourism are the economic mainstays of St. Christopher and Nevis. Sugar cane is a major crop, cultivated mainly on St. Christopher, while Nevis produces cotton, fruits, and vegetables. Agriculture also provides for sugar processing, the major industrial activity. A tropical climate, beaches, and a scenic mountainous terrain provide an ideal setting for tourism.

**History and Politics.** The islands were first inhabited by Arawak Indians, who were displaced by the warlike Caribs. In 1493 Christopher Columbus sighted the islands, and in the 1600s British settlement of both islands began, along with French settlement on St. Christopher. Sugar plantations were soon established, and slaves were imported from Africa. Britain's control of the islands was recognized by the 1783 Treaty of Paris, and for a time St. Christopher, Nevis, and Anguilla were ruled as a single colony. Anguilla became a separate dependency of Britain in 1980, and St. Christopher and Nevis gained independence in 1983. ∎

## ST. HELENA See UNITED KINGDOM.

## ST. LUCIA

Official name St. Lucia

**PEOPLE**
**Population** 151,000. **Density** 634/mi² (245/km²). **Urban** 40%. **Capital** Castries, 53,933. **Ethnic groups** Black 90%, mixed 6%, East Indian 3%. **Languages** English, French. **Religions** Roman Catholic 86%, Anglican 3%, Seventh Day Adventist 4%. **Life expectancy** 75 female, 67 male. **Literacy** 67%.
**POLITICS**
**Government** Parliamentary state. **Parties** Labor, United Workers'. **Suffrage** Universal, over 18. **Memberships** CW, OAS, UN. **Subdivisions** 11 quarters.

**ECONOMY**
**GDP** $151,000,000 **Per capita** $1,258. **Monetary unit** East Caribbean dollar. **Trade partners** Exports: U.K., Jamaica, U.S. Imports: U.S., U.K., Trinidad and Tobago. **Exports** Bananas, paper containers and other manufactures, machinery, beverages. **Imports** Metals and other manufactures, food, machinery, chemicals, petroleum.
**LAND**
**Description** Caribbean island. **Area** 238 mi² (616 km²). **Highest point** Mt. Gimie, 3,117 ft (950 m). **Lowest point** Sea level.

**People.** St. Lucia's population is composed mainly of descendants of black African slaves, and minority groups include people of African-European descent, whites, and East Indians. During the colonial period, the island frequently shifted from British to French control, and its culture reflects both British and French elements. Although English is widely spoken, many St. Lucians speak a French dialect. Roman Catholicism is the main religion, and the Protestant minority includes Anglicans.

**Economy and the Land.** Agriculture remains important, and principal crops include bananas and cocoa. Tax incentives and relative political stability have caused an increase in industrial development and foreign investment, mainly from the United States. Tourism is becoming increasingly important, with visitors drawn by the tropical climate, scenic mountainous terrain, and beaches.

**History and Politics.** Arawak Indians arrived between the A.D. 200s and 400s, and were conquered by the Caribs between the ninth and eleventh centuries. Dutch, French, and British rivalry for control began in the seventeenth century, but the Europeans were unable to subdue the Caribs. The first successful settlement was established by the French in 1651. After many years of alternating French and British control, St. Lucia came under British rule through the 1814 Treaty of Paris. The island gained full independence in 1979. ∎

## ST. PIERRE AND MIQUELON See FRANCE.

## ST. VINCENT AND THE GRENADINES

Official name St. Vincent and the Grenadines
**PEOPLE**
**Population** 114,000. **Density** 760/mi² (294/km²). **Urban** 14%. **Capital** Kingstown, St. Vincent I., 19,028. **Ethnic groups** Black 82%, mixed 14%, East Indian 2%, white 1%. **Languages** English, French. **Religions** Anglican 42%, Methodist 21%, Roman Catholic 12%, Baptist 6%. **Life expectancy** 60 female, 58 male. **Literacy** 96%.
**POLITICS**
**Government** Parliamentary state. **Parties** Labor, New Democratic. **Suffrage** Universal, over 18. **Memberships** CW, OAS, UN. **Subdivisions** 5 parishes.

**ECONOMY**
**GDP** $102,000,000 **Per capita** $729. **Monetary unit** East Caribbean dollar. **Trade partners** Exports: U.K., Trinidad and Tobago. Imports: U.S., U.K., Trinidad and Tobago. **Exports** Bananas, root crops, wheat flour, manufactures, nuts. **Imports** Food, metals and other manufactures, chemicals, petroleum.
**LAND**
**Description** Caribbean islands. **Area** 150 mi² (388 km²). **Highest point** Soufrière, St. Vincent I., 4,048 ft (1,234 m). **Lowest point** Sea level.

**People.** The people of St. Vincent are mainly descended from black African slaves. The colonial influences of Britain and France are evident in the languages and religions. English is the official language, though a French patois is also spoken. Most people are Anglican, Methodist, or Roman Catholic.

**Economy and the Land.** St. Vincent's economy is based on agriculture, especially banana production. Tourism also plays a role, both on the main island of St. Vincent and in the Grenadines. St. Vincent is the largest island, and about one hundred smaller islands make up the Grenadines. The terrain is mountainous, with coastlines marked by sandy beaches, and the climate is tropical.

**History and Politics.** The indigenous Arawak Indians were conquered by the Caribs about 1300. Christopher Columbus probably reached the area in 1498. Although the Caribs fought the Europeans, the British began settling St. Vincent in the 1760s. A period of French control began in 1779, and the islands were returned to the British in 1783. St. Vincent and the Grenadines remained under British rule until they gained independence in 1979. ∎

# SAN MARINO

**Official name** Republic of San Marino
**PEOPLE**
**Population** 24,000. **Density** 1,000/mi² (393/km²). **Urban** 74%. **Capital** San Marino, 4,137. **Ethnic groups** Sanmarinese (mixed Latin, Adriatic, and Teutonic), Italian. **Languages** Italian. **Religions** Roman Catholic. **Literacy** 96%.
**POLITICS**
**Government** Republic. **Parties** Christian Democratic, Communist, Socialist, Socialist Unity. **Suffrage** Universal adult. **Memberships** None. **Subdivisions** 9 municipalities.
**Monetary unit** Italian lira. **Trade partners** Italy. **Exports** Building materials, wood, food, wine, hides, ceramics. **Imports** Manufactures.
**LAND**
**Description** Southern Europe, landlocked. **Area** 24 mi² (61 km²). **Highest point** Monte Titano, 2,425 ft (739 m). **Lowest point** 164 ft (50 m).

**People.** San Marino, completely surrounded by Italy, has strong ethnic ties to the Italians, combining Latin, Adriatic, and Teutonic roots. Italian is the main language, and Roman Catholicism the major religion. Despite San Marino's similarities to Italy, its tradition of independence has given its citizens a strong national identity.

**Economy and the Land.** Close economic ties between San Marino and Italy have produced a mutually beneficial customs union: Italians have no customs restrictions at San Marino's borders, and San Marino receives annual budget subsidiary payments from Italy. Most San Marinese are employed in agriculture; livestock raising is a main activity, and crops include wheat and grapes. Tourism and the sale of postage stamps are major economic contributors, as is industry, which produces construction materials for export. Located in the Apennine Mountains, San Marino has a rugged terrain and a generally moderate climate.

**History and Politics.** San Marino is considered the world's oldest republic. Tradition has it that Marinus, a Christian stonecutter seeking religious freedom in a time of repressive Roman rule, founded the state in the fourth century A.D. Partly because of the protection afforded by its mountainous terrain, San Marino has been able to maintain continuous independence despite attempted invasions. In the 1300s the country became a republic, and the pope recognized its independent status in 1631. San Marino signed its first treaty of friendship with Italy in 1862. In its foreign relations, the country maintains a distinct identity and status. ∎

# SAO TOME AND PRINCIPE

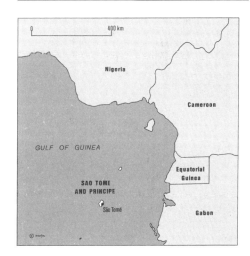

**Official name** Democratic Republic of Sao Tome and Principe
**PEOPLE**
**Population** 123,000. **Density** 331/mi² (128/km²). **Urban** 38%. **Capital** São Tomé, São Tomé I., 17,380. **Ethnic groups** Black, mixed black and Portuguese, Portuguese. **Languages** Portuguese, indigenous languages. **Religions** Roman Catholic, African Protestant, Seventh

Day Adventist. **Life expectancy** 45 female, 43 male. **Literacy** 57%.
## POLITICS
**Government** Republic. **Parties** Movement for the Liberation. **Suffrage** Universal, over 18. **Memberships** OAU, UN. **Subdivisions** 7 districts.
## ECONOMY
**GDP** $37,700,000 **Per capita** $428. **Monetary unit** Dobra. **Trade partners** Netherlands, Portugal, U.S., W. Germany. **Exports** Cocoa, copra, coffee, palm oil. **Imports** Food, machinery, fuel.
## LAND
**Description** Western African islands. **Area** 372 mi$^2$ (964 km$^2$). **Highest point** Pico do São Tomé, São Tomé I., 6,640 ft (2,024 m). **Lowest point** Sea level.

**People.** Descendants of African slaves and people of Portuguese-African heritage compose most of Sao Tome and Principe's population. Colonial rule by Portugal is evidenced by the predominance of the Portuguese language and Roman Catholicism. The majority of the population lives on São Tomé.

**Economy and the Land.** Cocoa dominates Sao Tome and Principe's economy. Copra and palm-oil production are also important, and fishing plays an economic role as well. Through the development of vegetable crops, the government hopes to diversify agricultural output, as much food must now be imported. Part of an extinct volcanic mountain range, Sao Tome and Principe have a mostly mountainous terrain. The climate is tropical.

**History and Politics.** When Portuguese explorers arrived in the 1400s, Sao Tome and Principe were uninhabited. Early settlers included Portuguese convicts and exiles. Cultivation of the land and importation of slaves led to a thriving sugar economy by the mid-1500s. In the 1800s, following slave revolts and the decline of sugar production, coffee and cocoa became the islands' mainstays, and soon large Portuguese plantations called *rocas* were established. Slavery was abolished by Portugal in 1876, but an international controversy arose in the early 1900s when it was found that Angolan contract workers were being treated as virtual slaves. Decades of unrest led to the 1953 Batepa Massacre, in which Portuguese rulers killed several hundred rioting African workers. A movement for independence began in the late 1950s, and following a 1974 change of government in Portugal, Sao Tome and Principe became independent in 1975. The country has established ties with other former Portuguese colonies in northern Africa since gaining independence. ∎

# SAUDI ARABIA

**Official name** Kingdom of Saudi Arabia
## PEOPLE
**Population** 14,645,000. **Density** 18/mi$^2$ (6.8/km$^2$). **Urban** 72%. **Capital** Riyadh, 1,250,000. **Ethnic groups** Arab 90%, Afro-Asian 10%. **Languages** Arabic. **Religions** Muslim 100%. **Life expectancy** 63 female, 59 male. **Literacy** 35%.
## POLITICS
**Government** Monarchy. **Parties** None. **Suffrage** None. **Memberships** AL, OPEC, UN. **Subdivisions** 14 emirates.

## ECONOMY
**GDP** $79,152,000,000 **Per capita** $7,215. **Monetary unit** Riyal. **Trade partners** Exports: Japan, France, U.S. Imports: Japan, U.S., W. Germany. **Exports** Petroleum, natural gas. **Imports** Metals and other manufactures, machinery, rice and other food, motor vehicles.
## LAND
**Description** Southwestern Asia. **Area** 830,000 mi$^2$ (2,149,690 km$^2$). **Highest point** Mt. Sawda 10,522 ft (3,207 m). **Lowest point** Sea level.

**People.** Saudi Arabia is inhabited primarily by Arab Muslims descended from Semitic peoples who settled in the region several thousand years ago. The petroleum industry has attracted a sizable minority of Arabs from other nations, Europeans, and non-Arab Muslims from Africa and Asia. The country's official language is Arabic, although English is used among educated Saudis in business and international affairs. Islam dominates Saudi life, and nearly all the people belong to the religion's Sunni branch. Various forms of Christianity and traditional religions are practiced among foreign workers and indigenous minority groups. Most live in urban areas, but some Bedouin tribes preserve their nomadic way of life.

**Economy and the Land.** The economy of Saudi Arabia has been shaped by its vast deserts and huge petroleum and natural gas reserves. The hot, mostly arid climate has prevented agricultural abundance and stability: the country must import nearly all its food. Oil was discovered in the 1930s, but the country did not begin rapid economic development until the reserves were aggressively exploited following World War II. Saudi Arabia is the world's leading exporter of petroleum, possessing the largest concentration of known oil reserves in the world. The government is seeking to diversify the economy, improve transportation and communication lines, and build agricultural output. Private enterprise and foreign investment are encouraged. Saudi Arabia is divided into the western highlands bordering the Red Sea, a central plateau, northern deserts, the huge Rub al Khali desert in the south, and the eastern lowlands. Only the coastal regions receive appreciable rainfall, and some inland desert areas may go without rain for several years.

**History and Politics.** Even though what is now Saudi Arabia established prosperous trade routes thousands of years ago, its history begins with the founding of Islam by Muhammad in the early 600s A.D. By the end of that century, Mecca and Medina were established as political and religious centers of Islam and remain so today. The territory split into numerous states that warred among themselves for over a thousand years. The Ottoman Turks gained control over the coastal region of Hejaz in the early 1500s, while Britain set up protectorates along the southern and eastern coasts of Arabia during the 1800s. The Saud family dynasty, founded in the 1400s, managed to remain a dominant religious and political force. Members of the dynasty fought to establish the supremacy of Islamic law and unite the various clans into one nation. In 1932 Ibn Saud proclaimed the Kingdom of Saudi Arabia and established a Saud monarchy that has continued despite dissension within the royal family. Since the 1960s Saudi Arabia has aggressively sought to upgrade local governments, industry, education, the status of women, and the standard of living, while maintaining Islamic values and traditions. Saudi Arabia is a dominant member of the Organization of Petroleum Exporting Countries (OPEC). Despite disagreements with the West and continuing conflicts with Israel, the country maintains strong diplomatic and economic ties with Western nations. ∎

# SENEGAL

**Official name** Republic of Senegal
**PEOPLE**
**Population** 7,367,000. **Density** 97/mi² (37/km²). **Urban** 36%. **Capital** Dakar, 1,428,084. **Ethnic groups** Wolof 41%, Serer 15%, Fulani 12%, Tukulor 11%, Diola 5%, Malinke 6%. **Languages** French, Wolof, indigenous. **Religions** Muslim 92%, Animist 6%, Roman Catholic and other Christian 2%. **Life expectancy** 45 female, 42 male. **Literacy** 47%.
**POLITICS**
**Government** Republic. **Parties** Democratic, Socialist, others. **Suffrage** Universal adult. **Memberships** OAU, UN. **Subdivisions** 10 regions.

**ECONOMY**
**GDP** $2,642,000,000 **Per capita** $397. **Monetary unit** CFA franc. **Trade partners** Exports: France, U.K. Imports: France, Nigeria. **Exports** Petroleum, phosphate, fish and shellfish, manufactures, chemicals. **Imports** Petroleum, food, manufactures, machinery, chemicals, transportation equipment.
**LAND**
**Description** Western Africa. **Area** 75,955 mi² (196,722 km²). **Highest point** 1,906 ft (581 m). **Lowest point** Sea level.

**People.** Most Senegalese are black Africans from many ethnic groups, each with its own customs and language. The country has many immigrants from other African nations. While French is the official language, Wolof is widely spoken. Islam is the major religion, followed by Animist and Christian beliefs. Senegal is mainly a rural nation of subsistence farmers.

**Economy and the Land.** The mainstays of the economy are petroleum, agriculture, fishing, and mining. Tourism is a rapidly growing new industry. Petroleum, chemicals, phosphates, and fish products rank as Senegal's primary exports. Agricultural output is often hurt by irregular weather patterns, and the country must import nearly all its energy. Senegal has one of the finest transportation systems in Africa. Small plateaus, low massifs, marshy swamps, and a sandy coast highlight the terrain, which is mainly flat. The climate is marked by dry and rainy seasons, with differing precipitation patterns in the south and the more arid north.

**History and Politics.** The area that is now Senegal has been inhabited by black Africans since prehistoric times. When Europeans first established trade ties with the Senegalese in the mid-1400s, the country had been divided into several independent kingdoms. By the early 1800s, France had gained control of the region and in 1895 made Senegal part of French West Africa. In 1959 Senegal joined with French Sudan, or present-day Mali, to form the Federation of Mali, which became independent in 1960. However, Senegal withdrew from the federation later in the year to found the independent Republic of Senegal. The new parliamentary government was plagued by coup attempts and an economy crippled by the severe droughts of the late 1960s and early 1970s. In 1982 Senegal formed a union with Gambia, called the Confederation of Senegambia, to strengthen economic and military ties between the two countries. Senegal maintains close ties to France and follows a pro-Western foreign policy. ∎

# SEYCHELLES

**Official name** Republic of Seychelles
**PEOPLE**
**Population** 69,000. **Density** 394/mi² (152/km²). **Urban** 50%. **Capital** Victoria, Mahé I., 23,000. **Ethnic groups** Seychellois (mixed Asian, African, and European). **Languages** English, French, Creole. **Religions** Roman Catholic 90%, Anglican 8%. **Life expectancy** 73 female, 66 male. **Literacy** 58%.
**POLITICS**
**Government** Republic. **Parties** People's Progressive

# SIERRA LEONE

Front. **Suffrage** Universal, over 18. **Memberships** CW, OAU, UN. **Subdivisions** None.
**ECONOMY**
**GDP** $152,000,000 **Per capita** $2,338. **Monetary unit** Rupee. **Trade partners** Exports: Bahrain, Singapore, U.S. Imports: Bahrain, U.K., South African countries. **Exports** Petroleum, telecommunications equipment and other machinery, fish. **Imports** Petroleum, manufactures, grain and other food, machinery, chemicals.
**LAND**
**Description** Indian Ocean islands. **Area** 175 mi$^2$ (453 km$^2$). **Highest point** Morne Seychellois, Mahé I., 2,969 ft (905 m). **Lowest point** Sea level.

**People.** The majority of Seychellois are of mixed African, European, and Asian ancestry. The islands' culture combines French and African elements, and although the official languages of French and English are widely spoken, most also speak a creole dialect of French. Many of the more than one hundred islands are coral atolls, unable to support human life. The population is concentrated on Mahé, the largest island, while the remainder live mainly on Praslin and La Digue islands.

**Economy and the Land.** The basis of the economy is tourism, with foreign visitors attracted by the tropical climate, white-sand beaches, and exotic flora and wildlife found on the granite islands. Mountainous granite islands, which contain fertile soils for growing cinnamon and coconuts, and flat coral islands comprise Seychelles.

**History and Politics.** The Portuguese reached the uninhabited islands in the early 1500s. For more than two hundred years, the islands served as little more than pirates' havens. France claimed them in 1756; by the 1770s white planters and African slaves had begun to settle Mahé. After a French-English war, France ceded the islands to Britain in 1814. Seychelles achieved independence in 1976.

# SHETLAND ISLANDS
See UNITED KINGDOM.

**Official name** Republic of Sierra Leone
**PEOPLE**
**Population** 4,116,000. **Density** 147/mi$^2$ (57/km$^2$). **Urban** 28%. **Capital** Freetown, 469,776. **Ethnic groups** Temne 30%, Mende 30%, Creole 2%, other African. **Languages** English, Krio, indigenous. **Religions** Muslim 30%, Animist 30%, Christian 10%. **Life expectancy** 36 female, 33 male. **Literacy** 15%.
**POLITICS**
**Government** Republic. **Parties** All People's Congress. **Suffrage** Universal, over 21. **Memberships** CW, OAU, UN. **Subdivisions** 3 regions, 1 area.
**ECONOMY**
**GDP** $1,627,000,000 **Per capita** $438. **Monetary unit** Leone. **Trade partners** Exports: Belgium, Netherlands, U.K. Imports: Nigeria, U.K., W. Germany. **Exports** Diamonds, bauxite and other minerals, cocoa, coffee. **Imports** Petroleum, manufactures, rice and other food, machinery, motor vehicles.
**LAND**
**Description** Western Africa. **Area** 27,925 mi$^2$ (72,325 km$^2$). **Highest point** Bintimani, 6,381 ft (1,945 m). **Lowest point** Sea level.

**People.** The population of Sierra Leone is divided into nearly twenty main ethnic groups. The two major groups are the Temne in the north and west and the Mende in the south. Descendants of freed American slaves, who settled in Freetown on the coast, make up a sizable Creole minority. English is the official language, but most of the people speak local African tongues. The Creoles speak Krio, a dialect of English. Most people practice Islam or various local religions, and a small number are Christian.

**Economy and the Land.** Sierra Leone is one of the world's largest producers of industrial and commercial diamonds. The nation also mines bauxite and rutile. Poor soil, a fluctuating tropical climate, and traditional farming methods keep crop yields low. Rice, coffee, and cocoa are important crops. To improve agricultural production, the government is clearing some of the coastal mangrove swamplands. The interior of Sierra Leone is marked by a broad coastal plain in the north and by mountains and plateaus that rise along the country's northern and eastern borders. During the wet season Sierra Leone receives heavy rainfall in the Freetown area and significantly less in the north.

**History and Politics.** When the Portuguese reached the region in 1460, they found the area inhabited by the Temne. The British followed the Portuguese in the 1500s. Europeans took slaves from the area for the New World until Britain abolished the slave trade. In 1787 Englishman Granville Sharp settled nearly four hundred freed black American slaves in what is now Freetown. Britain declared the peninsula a colony in 1808 and a protectorate in 1896. In 1961, Sierra Leone became an independent nation with a constitution and parliamentary form of government. A military takeover in 1967 was short lived, and the constitution was rewritten in 1971 to make the country a republic. Though officially nonaligned, Sierra Leone maintains close ties to Britain and other Western nations. ■

# SINGAPORE

**Official name** Republic of Singapore
**PEOPLE**
**Population** 2,710,000. **Density** 11,016/mi$^2$ (4,261/km$^2$). **Urban** 100%. **Capital** Singapore, 2,631,000. **Ethnic groups** Chinese 76%, Malay 15%, Indian 6%. **Languages** Chinese (Mandarin), English, Malay, Tamil. **Religions** Taoist 29%, Buddhist 27%, Muslim 16%, Christian 10%, Hindu 4%. **Life expectancy** 75 female, 69 male. **Literacy** 83%.
**POLITICS**
**Government** Republic. **Parties** Democratic, People's Action, others. **Suffrage** Universal, over 20.
**Memberships** ASEAN, CW, UN. **Subdivisions** None.
**ECONOMY**
**GDP** $17,510,000,000 **Per capita** $6,880. **Monetary unit** Dollar. **Trade partners** Exports: U.S., Malaysia, Japan. Imports: Japan, U.S., Malaysia. **Exports** Machinery, petroleum, manufactures, chemicals, rubber. **Imports** Petroleum, machinery, manufactures, food, transportation equipment, chemicals.

**LAND**
**Description** Southeastern Asian island. **Area** 246 mi$^2$ (636 km$^2$). **Highest point** Timah Hill, 545 ft (166 m). **Lowest point** Sea level.

**People.** Singapore is one of the most densely populated nations in the world. Most of the population is Chinese. A significant minority is Malay, and the remainder is European or Indian. Singapore's languages include Chinese, English, Malay, and Tamil. The main religions—Taoism, Buddhism, Islam, Christianity, and Hinduism—reflect the cultural diversity of the nation. A mixture of Western and traditional customs and dress characterize Singapore's society. Nearly all the population lives in the city of Singapore on Singapore Island.

**Economy and the Land.** Singapore is a leading Asian economic power. The city of Singapore is well known as a financial center and major harbor for trade. The nation's factories produce a variety of goods, such as chemicals, electronic equipment, and machinery, and are among the world leaders in petroleum refining. Singapore has few natural resources, however, and little arable land. Most agricultural output is consumed domestically; the country must import much of its raw materials and food. The nation consists of one main island, which is characterized by wet lowlands, and many small offshore islets. Cool sea breezes and a tropical climate make Singapore an attractive spot for tourists.

**History and Politics.** Present-day Singapore has been inhabited since prehistoric times. From the 1100s to the 1800s, Singapore served mainly as a trading center and refuge for pirates. The British East India Company, the major colonial force in India, realized Singapore's strategic importance to British trade and gained possession of the harbor in 1819. Singapore became a crown colony in 1826. As the port prospered, the island's population grew rapidly. Following World War II, the people of Singapore moved from internal self-government to independence in 1965. The government continues to work in partnership with the business community to further Singapore's growth. In foreign policy, the nation remains nonaligned, but as a small country dependent on trade, Singapore is interested in maintaining wide contacts. ■

# SOLOMON ISLANDS

**Official name** Solomon Islands
**PEOPLE**
**Population** 312,000. **Density** 28/mi$^2$ (11/km$^2$). **Urban** 10%. **Capital** Honiara, Guadalcanal I., 30,499. **Ethnic groups** Melanesian 93%, Polynesian 4%, Micronesian 2%. **Languages** English, Malay-Polynesian languages. **Religions** Church of Melanesia 34%, Roman Catholic 19%, South Sea Evangelical 17%. **Literacy** 60%.
**POLITICS**
**Government** Parliamentary state. **Parties** People's Alliance, United, others. **Suffrage** Universal, over 21.
**Memberships** CW, UN. **Subdivisions** 7 Provinces.

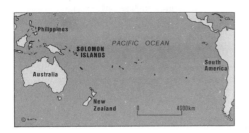

### ECONOMY
**GDP** $152,000,000 **Per capita** $608. **Monetary unit** Dollar. **Trade partners** Exports: Japan, U.K., Netherlands. Imports: Australia, Japan, Singapore. **Exports** Fish and shellfish, copra, wood, palm oil. **Imports** Manufactures, petroleum, machinery, grain and other food, chemicals.

### LAND
**Description** South Pacific islands. **Area** 10,954 mi$^2$ (28,370 km$^2$). **Highest point** Mt. Makarakomburu, Guadalcanal I., 8,028 ft (2,447 m). **Lowest point** Sea level.

**People.** Over 90 percent of the people are Melanesian, and the remainder are Polynesian, European, Chinese, and Micronesian. English is the official language, but some ninety local languages are also spoken. The dominant religion is Protestantism, and religious minorities include Roman Catholics and followers of local traditions. The population is primarily rural, and much of its social structure is patterned on traditional village life.

**Economy and the Land.** The economy is based on subsistence farming and exports of fish, wood, copra, and some spices and palm-oil. Food, machinery, gasoline, and manufactured goods must be imported. Terrain ranges from forested mountains to low-lying coral atolls. The climate is warm and moist, with heavy annual rainfall.

**History and Politics.** Hunter-gatherers lived on the islands as early as 1000 B.C. Because of disease and native resistance, early attempts at colonization failed, and Europeans did not firmly establish themselves until the mid-1800s. Britain declared the islands a protectorate in 1893. The area was the site of fierce battles between the Japanese and Allied forces during World War II, and following the war, moves were made toward independence. In 1978, the Solomon Islands adopted a constitution and became a sovereign nation. ∎

# SOMALIA

**Official name** Somali Democratic Republic
### PEOPLE
**Population** 8,332,000. **Density** 34/mi$^2$ (13/km$^2$). **Urban** 34%. **Capital** Mogadishu, 600,000. **Ethnic groups** Somali 85%. **Languages** Arabic, Somali, English, Italian. **Religions** Sunni Muslim. **Life expectancy** 43 female, 39 male. **Literacy** 60%.
### POLITICS
**Government** Socialist republic. **Parties** Revolutionary Socialist. **Suffrage** Universal, over 18. **Memberships** AL, OAU, UN. **Subdivisions** 16 regions.

### ECONOMY
**GDP** $2,551,000,000 **Per capita** $563. **Monetary unit** Shilling. **Trade partners** Exports: Saudi Arabia, Italy. Imports: U.K., Italy, W. Germany. **Exports** Livestock, fruit and vegetables. **Imports** Telecommunications equipment and other machinery, transportation equipment.
### LAND
**Description** Eastern Africa. **Area** 246,201 mi$^2$ (637,657 km$^2$). **Highest point** Shimber Berris, 7,897 ft (2,407 m). **Lowest point** Sea level.

**People.** Unlike the population in many African nations, the people of Somalia are remarkably homogeneous in their language, culture, and identity. Most are nomadic or seminomadic herders; only a quarter of the people have settled in permanent communities in southern Somalia. While Arabic and Somali are official languages, English and Italian are also spoken. Nearly all the Somali people are Sunni Muslims.

**Economy and the Land.** Somalia is a developing country that has not exploited its rich deposits of iron ore and gypsum. There is little manufacturing. The economy is agricultural, though activity is restricted to the vicinity of the rivers and certain coastal districts. A hot climate with recurring droughts, as well as a lack of railroads and paved highways, hamper economic development. The terrain ranges from central and southern flatlands to northern hills.

**History and Politics.** In the A.D. 800s or 900s, Arabs converted the ancestors of the Somalis who settled the region to Islam. They fought many religious wars with the Christian kingdom of Ethiopia between the 1300s and 1500s. The British, Italians, and French arrived in the region in the latter half of the 1800s and divided the Somali territory among themselves, with Ethiopia seizing Ogaden in the west. After World War II, Italy was made administrator of its former colony to prepare it for independence. In 1960 British Somaliland and Italian Somalia joined to form an independent republic. Since that time, Somalia has had many border clashes with Kenya and Ethiopia over the rights of Somalis living in these countries to determine their own destiny. Military leaders staged a successful coup in 1969, and subsequently changed the nation's name to Somali Democratic Republic and abolished all political parties. In 1976, however, the Somali Revolutionary Socialist party was formed. ■

# SOUTH AFRICA

**Official name** Republic of South Africa
**PEOPLE**
**Population** 36,790,000. **Density** 85/mi² (33/km²). **Urban** 56%. **Capital** Pretoria (administrative), 443,059; Cape Town (legislative), 776,617; Bloemfontein (judicial), 104,381. **Ethnic groups** Black 69%, white 18%, mulatto (coloured) 10%, Indian 3%. **Languages** Afrikaans, English, Zulu, Xhosa, other indigenous. **Religions** Black Independent 21%, Dutch Reformed 14%, Roman Catholic 10%. **Life expectancy** 55 female, 52 male. **Literacy** 59%.
**POLITICS**
**Government** Republic. **Parties** African National Congress, Conservative, National, Progressive Federal, others. **Suffrage** Coloreds, Indians, and whites, over 18. **Memberships** UN. **Subdivisions** 4 provinces.
**ECONOMY**
**GDP** $54,834,000,000 **Per capita** $2,042. **Monetary unit** Rand. **Trade partners** U.S., W. Germany, Japan, U.K., South African countries. **Exports** Gold, food, coal, iron and steel, diamonds, metals, minerals. **Imports** Machinery, manufactures, transportation equipment, chemicals.
**LAND**
**Description** Southern Africa. **Area** 433,680 mi² (1,123,226 km²). **Highest point** eNjesuthi, 11,306 ft (3,446 m). **Lowest point** Sea level.
*The above information excludes Bophuthatswana, Ciskei, Transkei, and Venda.*

**People.** The government of South Africa classifies the country's population into four groups: black, white, colored, and Asian. Black African groups make up the majority population. The minority whites are either Afrikaners—of Dutch, German, and French descent—or British. Coloreds, people of mixed white, black, and Asian heritage, and Asians, primarily from India, make up the remaining population. Afrikaans and English are the official languages, although the blacks, coloreds, and Asians speak their own languages as well. The dominant religions are Christian; however, many groups follow traditional practices. The South African government enforces apartheid, a policy of racial segregation widely criticized for violating the rights of blacks, coloreds, and Asians.

**Economy and the Land.** The discovery of gold and diamonds in South Africa in the late 1800s shaped the nation's prosperous economy. Revenues from mining promoted industry, and today South Africa is one of the richest and most highly developed countries in Africa. Mining remains a mainstay, as does agriculture; the nation is almost self-sufficient in food production. Many effects of apartheid, including discriminatory systems of education and job reservation, have kept the majority population from the benefits of national prosperity. The varied landscape features coastal beaches, plateaus, mountains, and deep valleys. The climate is temperate. The Republic of South Africa includes the enclave of Walvis Bay, situated on Africa's southwest coast.

**History and Politics.** Southern Africa has been inhabited for many thousands of years. Ancestors of the area's present African population had settled there by the time Portuguese explorers reached the Cape of Good Hope in the late 1400s. The first white settlers, ancestors of today's Afrikaners, established colonies in the seventeenth century. Britain gained control of the area in the late eighteenth century, and relations between Afrikaners and the British soon became strained. To escape British rule, many Afrikaners migrated northward to lands occupied by black Africans. The discovery of gold and diamonds in the late 1800s brought an influx of Europeans and further strained relations between Afrikaners and the British, with both groups striving for control of valuable mineral deposits. Two wars broke out, and in 1902 the British defeated the Afrikaners, or Boers, and incorporated the Boer territories into the British Empire. The British also subdued black Africans, and in 1910 they formed the white-controlled Union of South Africa. Afrikaner nationalism grew in the early twentieth century and led to the formation of the National party, which gained control in 1924 and again in 1948. The party began the apartheid system of separation of the races in the late forties, and subsequent decades saw increasing apartheid legislation and racial tension. In the 1970s and early 1980s, blacks were forcibly moved to nominally independent homelands and stripped of their South African citizenship. Foreign and internal pressure to dismantle apartheid has resulted in the beginnings of reform. ■

# SOUTH GEORGIA
See UNITED KINGDOM.

# SOVIET UNION

**Official name** Union of Soviet Socialist Republics
**PEOPLE**
**Population** 289,010,000. **Density** 34/mi² (13/km²). **Urban** 66%. **Capital** Moscow, 8,769,000. **Ethnic groups** Russian 52%, Ukrainian 16%, Uzbek 5%, Byelorussian

**184** SOVIET UNION • SPAIN

4%. **Languages** Russian and other Slavic languages, various ethnic languages. **Religions** Russian Orthodox 18%, Muslim 9%. **Life expectancy** 75 female, 67 male. **Literacy** 100%.
**POLITICS**
**Government** Socialist republic. **Parties** Communist. **Suffrage** Universal, over 18. **Memberships** CEMA, UN, Warsaw Pact. **Subdivisions** 15 soviet socialist republics.
**ECONOMY**
**GNP** $2,062,600,000,000 **Per capita** $7,484. **Monetary unit** Ruble. **Trade partners** Exports: E. Germany, Czechoslovakia, Poland. Imports: E. Germany, Czechoslovakia, Bulgaria. **Exports** Petroleum, machinery and transportation equipment, natural gas. **Imports** Machinery, grain, transportation equipment, chemicals, sugar, iron and steel.
**LAND**
**Description** Eastern Europe and northern Asia. **Area** 8,600,387 mi$^2$ (22,274,900 km$^2$). **Highest point** Communism Pk., 24,590 ft (7,495 m). **Lowest point** Vpadina Karagije (near Caspian Sea), -433 ft (-132 m).

**People.** The varied population of the Soviet Union is composed of more than one hundred distinct groups. Nearly three-quarters of the people are Eastern Slavs, and more than 70 percent of this group are Russians. The remaining Slavs are Ukrainians, Byelorussians, and Uzbek. The rest of the population belongs to Turkic, Finno-Ugric, Caucasian, other Indo-European groups, and a mixture of peoples, including Inuit. Each group speaks its own language, although Russian is the most widely used. Religious practice is discouraged by the state, and churches have no legal status—although Russian Orthodox, Islam, Catholicism, Protestantism, Judaism, and other religions are actively practiced.

**Economy and the Land.** The Soviet Union is one of the world's leading industrial powers. Mining, steel production, and other heavy industries predominate. The economy is controlled by the state, and economic policies are administered through a series of five-year plans, which emphasize industrial and technological growth. The Soviet economy suffers from low productivity, energy shortages, and a lack of skilled labor, problems the government hopes can be eased by greater use of technology and science. The Soviet Union trades primarily with members of the eastern-bloc Council for Mutual Economic Assistance, although trade with the West has risen sharply in the past few years. Geographically, the Soviet Union is the largest nation in the world. Its terrain is widely varied and richly endowed with minerals. Though the country contains some of the world's most fertile land, long winters and hot, dry summers keep many crop yields low.

**History and Politics.** Inhabited as early as the Stone Age, what is now the Soviet Union was much later invaded successively by Scythians, Sarmatians, Goths, Huns, Bulgars, Slavs, and others. By A.D. 989 Byzantine cultural influence had become predominant. Various groups and regions were slowly incorporated into a single state. In 1547 Ivan IV was crowned czar of all Russia, beginning a tradition of czarist rule that lasted until the 1917 Russian Revolution, when the Bolsheviks came to power and named Vladimir Ilyich Lenin as head of the first Soviet government. The Bolsheviks established a Communist state and weathered a bitter civil war. Joseph Stalin succeeded Lenin as head of state in 1924 and initiated a series of political purges that lasted through the 1930s. The Sovlet Union became embroiled in World War II, siding with the Allies, losing over twenty million people, and suffering widespread destruction of its cities and countryside. It emerged from the war with extended influence, however, having annexed part of Finland and many Eastern European nations. Following Stalin's death in 1953, the Soviet Union experienced a liberalization of policies under Nikita Krushchev. In 1964 Leonid Brezhnev worked to consolidate and strengthen the power of the Secretariat and Politburo of the Communist party. Mikhail S. Gorbachev took office in 1985 and introduced a new era of leadership, reform, and government restructure. ■

# SPAIN

**Official name** Spanish State
**PEOPLE**
**Population** 39,520,000. **Density** 203/mi$^2$ (78/km$^2$). **Urban**

## Places and Possessions of SPAIN

| Entity | Status | Area | Population | Capital/Population |
|---|---|---|---|---|
| Balearic Islands (Mediterranean Sea) | Province | 1,936 mi$^2$ (5,014 km$^2$) | 772,000 | Palma, 242,900 |
| Canary Islands (North Atlantic; northwest of Africa) | Part of Spain | 2,808 mi$^2$ (7,273 km$^2$) | 1,651,000 | None |
| Spanish North Africa (Cities on northern coast of Morocco) | Five possessions | 12 mi$^2$ (32 km$^2$) | 100,000 | None |

76%. **Capital** Madrid, 3,100,507. **Ethnic groups** Spanish (mixed Mediterranean and Teutonic). **Languages** Spanish (Castilian), Catalan, Galician, Basque. **Religions** Roman Catholic 99%. **Life expectancy** 78 female, 71 male. **Literacy** 93%.

### POLITICS
**Government** Constitutional monarchy. **Parties** Popular, Social Democratic Center, Socialist Workers, others. **Suffrage** Universal, over 18. **Memberships** EC, NATO, OECD, UN. **Subdivisions** 50 provinces.

### ECONOMY
**GDP** $164,254,000,000 **Per capita** $4,265. **Monetary unit** Peseta. **Trade partners** Exports: France, U.S., W. Germany. Imports: U.S., W. Germany, France. **Exports** Manufactures, transportation equipment, machinery, food, petroleum, chemicals. **Imports** Petroleum, machinery, manufactures, crude materials, food.

### LAND
**Description** Southwestern Europe. **Area** 194,885 mi$^2$ (504,750 km$^2$). **Highest point** Pico de Teide, Tenerife I., Canary Is., 12,188 ft (3,715 m). **Lowest point** Sea level.

**People.** The population of Spain is a mixture of ethnic groups from northern Europe and the area surrounding the Mediterranean Sea. Spanish is the official language; however, several regional dialects of Spanish are commonly spoken. The Basque minority, one of the oldest surviving ethnic groups in Europe, lives mainly in the Pyrenees in northern Spain, preserving its own language and traditions. Since the 1978 constitution, Spain has not had an official religion, yet nearly all its people are Roman Catholic. Spain has a rich artistic tradition, blending Moorish and Western cultures.

**Economy and the Land.** Spain has benefited greatly from an economic-restructuring program that began in the 1950s. The nation has concentrated on developing industry, which now employs over 30 percent of the population. The chemical industry, high technology, electronics, and tourism are important sources of revenue. The agricultural contribution to the economy has declined to about half of peak production. Spain's terrain is mainly composed of a dry plateau area; mountains cover the northern section, and plains extend down the country's eastern coast. The climate in the eastern and southern regions is Mediterranean, while the northwest has more rainfall and less sunshine throughout the year.

**History and Politics.** Spain is among the oldest inhabited regions in Europe. A Roman province for centuries, Spain was conquered by the Visigoths in the A.D. 500s, only to change hands again in the 700s when the Arab-Berbers, or Moors, seized control of all but a narrow strip of northern Spain. Christian kings reclaimed the country from the eleventh to the fourteenth centuries. Controlled by the three kingdoms of Navarre, Aragon, and Castile, Spain was united in the late 1400s under King Ferdinand and Queen Isabella. At the height of its empire, Spain claimed territory in North and South America, northern Africa, Italy, and the Canary Islands. However, a series of wars burdened Spain financially, and in the 1500s, under King Philip II, the country entered a period of decline. Throughout the 1700s and 1800s, the nation lost most of its colonial possessions through treaty or revolution. In 1936 a bitter civil war erupted between an insurgent fascist group and supporters of the republic. General Francisco Franco, leader of the successful insurgent army, ruled as dictator of Spain from the end of the war until his death in 1975. Spain enjoyed phenomenal economic growth during the 1950s and 1960s; however, that growth declined in the 1970s. Since Franco's death, King Juan Carlos has led the country toward a more democratic form of government. ■

# SRI LANKA

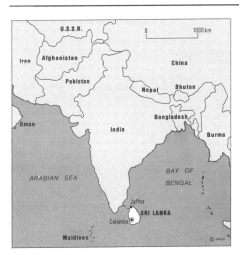

**Official name** Democratic Socialist Republic of Sri Lanka

### PEOPLE
**Population** 16,935,000. **Density** 678/mi$^2$ (262/km$^2$). **Urban** 21%. **Capital** Colombo (de facto), 623,000; Sri Jayawardenapura (future). **Ethnic groups** Sinhalese 74%, Ceylon Tamil 12%, Ceylon Moor 7%, Indian Tamil 5%. **Languages** English, Sinhala, Tamil. **Religions** Buddhist 70%, Hindu 15%, Christian 8%, Muslim 7%. **Life expectancy** 70 female, 67 male. **Literacy** 86%.

## SRI LANKA

### POLITICS
**Government** Socialist republic. **Parties** Freedom, Tamil Independents, United National, others. **Suffrage** Universal, over 18. **Memberships** CW, UN. **Subdivisions** 24 districts.

### ECONOMY
**GDP** $5,808,000,000 **Per capita** $361. **Monetary unit** Rupee. **Trade partners** Exports: U.S., Iraq, Egypt. Imports: Japan, Saudi Arabia, U.S.. **Exports** Tea, clothing, petroleum, rubber. **Imports** Petroleum, textiles and other manufactures, machinery, food, chemicals.

### LAND
**Description** Southern Asian island. **Area** 24,962 mi² (64,652 km²). **Highest point** Pidurutalagala, 8,281 ft (2,524 m). **Lowest point** Sea level.

**People.** The two principal groups in Sri Lanka are the majority Sinhalese and the minority Tamils. Other minorities include the Moors; Burghers, who are descendants of Dutch, Portuguese, and British colonists; Malays; and Veddah aborigines. Sinhala, Tamil, and English are official languages. Most Sinhalese are Buddhist, most Tamils are Hindu, and the majority of the Moors and Malays are Muslims.

**Economy and the Land.** Sri Lanka's economy is based on agriculture, which employs nearly half the people in producing tea, rubber, and coconuts. Sri Lanka also hopes to become self-sufficient in rice, thus reducing imports of this staple. Industrial production has increased, and major exports include rubber and textile products. The country also sponsors several internal-development programs. However, continuing high government subsidy and welfare policies threaten economic growth. A low coastal plain, mountainous and forested southern interior, and tropical climate characterize Sri Lanka.

**History and Politics.** The Sinhalese dynasty was founded by a northern Indian prince in about 500 B.C. Later, the Tamils from southern India settled in the north of Sri Lanka. European control began in the 1500s, when the Portuguese and Dutch ruled the island. It became a British possession in 1796 and the independent nation of Ceylon in 1948. In 1972 it changed its name to Sri Lanka. Tensions between the ruling Sinhalese and the minority Tamils have often erupted in violence. Sri Lanka pursues a policy of nonalignment in foreign affairs. ∎

## SUDAN

**Official name** Democratic Republic of the Sudan
### PEOPLE
**Population** 24,775,000. **Density** 26/mi² (9.9/km²). **Urban** 21%. **Capital** Khartoum, 476,218. **Ethnic groups** Black 52%, Arab 39%, Beja 6%. **Languages** Arabic, indigenous, English. **Religions** Sunni Muslim 70%, indigenous 20%, Christian 5%. **Life expectancy** 49 female, 47 male. **Literacy** 31%.

### POLITICS
**Government** Provisional military government. **Parties** Democratic Unionist, National Islamic Front, Umma, others. **Suffrage** Universal adult. **Memberships** AL, OAU, UN. **Subdivisions** 18 provinces.

### ECONOMY
**GDP** $7,678,000,000 **Per capita** $375. **Monetary unit** Pound. **Trade partners** Exports: Saudi Arabia, China, W. Germany. Imports: Saudi Arabia, U.K., U.S.. **Exports** Oil seeds, textile fibers, grain, livestock, gum arabic. **Imports** Machinery, sugar and other food, manufactures, transportation equipment.

### LAND
**Description** Eastern Africa. **Area** 967,500 mi² (2,505,813 km²). **Highest point** Kinyeti, 10,456 ft (3,187 m). **Lowest point** Sea level.

**People.** Sudan's population is composed of two distinct cultures—black African and Arab. African blacks of diverse ethnicity are a majority and are concentrated in the south, where they practice traditional lifestyles and beliefs and speak indigenous languages. Arabic-speaking Muslims, belonging to several ethnic groups, live mainly in northern and central regions.

**Economy and the Land.** The economy is based on agriculture; and irrigation has made arid Sudan a leading producer of cotton, although the land is vulnerable to drought. Forests provide for production of gum arabic, used in making candy and perfumes, while other crops include peanuts and sesame seeds. Economic activity is concentrated near the Nile River and its branches, as well as near water holes and wells. The mostly flat terrain is marked by eastern and western mountains; southern forests and savanna give way to swampland, scrubland, and northern desert. The climate varies from desert in the north to tropical in the south.

**History and Politics.** Egypt mounted repeated invasions of what is now northern Sudan beginning about 300 B.C. Sudan remained a collection of small independent states until 1821, when Egypt conquered and unified the northern portion. Egypt was unable to establish control over the south, which was often raided by slavers. In 1881 a Muslim leader began uniting various groups in a revolt against Egyptian rule, and success came four years later. His successor ruled until 1898, when British and Egyptian forces reconquered the land. Renamed the Anglo-Egyptian Sudan, the region was ruled jointly by Egypt and Britain, with British administration dominating. Since gaining independence in 1956, a series of military coups, a continuing civil war, and severe famine have burdened Sudan with political and economic instability. ∎

# SURINAME

**Official name** Republic of Suriname
## PEOPLE
**Population** 405,000. **Density** 6.4/mi² (2.5/km²). **Urban** 46%. **Capital** Paramaribo, 67,905. **Ethnic groups** East Indian 37%, Creole 31%, Javanese 15%, black 10%, Amerindian 3%, Chinese 2%. **Languages** Dutch, Sranan Tongo, English, Hindustani, Javanese. **Religions** Hindu 27%, Protestant 25%, Roman Catholic 23%, Muslim 20%. **Life expectancy** 71 female, 66 male. **Literacy** 65%.
## POLITICS
**Government** Republic. **Parties** New Democratic, Front for Democracy and Development. **Suffrage** Universal adult. **Memberships** OAS, UN. **Subdivisions** 9 districts.
## ECONOMY
**GDP** $963,000,000 **Per capita** $2,568. **Monetary unit** Guilder. **Trade partners** Exports: Netherlands, U.S., W. Germany. Imports: U.S., Trinidad and Tobago, Netherlands. **Exports** Alumina, bauxite, aluminum, rice, wood. **Imports** Machinery, petroleum, iron and steel, cotton, flour, meat, dairy products.
## LAND
**Description** Northeastern South America. **Area** 63,251 mi² (163,820 km²). **Highest point** Juliana Mtn., 4,035 ft (1,230 m). **Lowest point** Sea level.

**People.** Descendants of East Indians and Creoles—of mixed European-black African heritage—compose Suriname's two major groups. Black African slaves and contract laborers, imported from the east, resulted in various ethnic populations. Minority groups include the Javanese; Bush Negroes, a black group; Amerindians, descendants of Arawak and Caribs; Chinese; and Europeans. Dutch is the official language, but most groups have preserved their distinct language, culture, and religion.

**Economy and the Land.** The economy is based on mining and metal processing, and bauxite and alumina are the major exports. Agriculture plays an economic role as well and, together with fishing and forestry, offers potential for expansion. A narrow coastal swamp, central forests and savanna, and southern jungle-covered hills mark the country's terrain. The climate is tropical.

**History and Politics.** Prior to the arrival of Europeans, present-day Suriname was inhabited by indigenous Indians. Christopher Columbus sighted the coast in 1498, but the area's lack of gold slowed Spanish and Portuguese exploration. The British established the first settlement in 1651, and in 1665 Jews from Brazil erected the first synagogue in the Western Hemisphere. In 1667 the British traded the area to the Netherlands for the Dutch colony of New Amsterdam—present-day Manhattan, New York. Subsequent wars and treaties shifted ownership of Suriname among the British, French, and Dutch until 1815, when the Netherlands regained control. In 1954, Suriname became an autonomous part of the Netherlands, with status equal to that of the Netherlands and the Netherlands Antilles. Suriname gained independence in 1975. In 1980, the military seized power and established a military-civilian government soon after. In 1987, a new constitution, as well as an election, moved Suriname towards greater political stability. ∎

# SWAZILAND

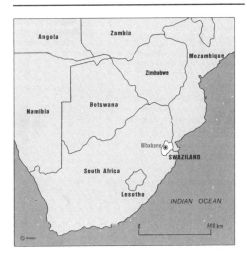

**Official name** Kingdom of Swaziland
## PEOPLE
**Population** 787,000. **Density** 117/mi² (45/km²). **Urban** 26%. **Capital** Mbabane (de facto), 53,000; Lobamba (future). **Ethnic groups** Swazi 95%, European 2%, Zulu 1%. **Languages** English, siSwati. **Religions** African Protestant and other Christian 57%, tribal religionist 43%. **Life expectancy** 50 female, 47 male. **Literacy** 55%.
## POLITICS
**Government** Monarchy. **Parties** Imbokodvo National Movement. **Suffrage** Universal adult. **Memberships** CW, OAU, UN. **Subdivisions** 4 districts.
## ECONOMY
**GDP** $571,000,000 **Per capita** $960. **Monetary unit** Lilangeni. **Trade partners** South Africa, U.K., U.S.. **Exports** Sugar, asbestos, wood, fruit. **Imports** Motor vehicles, chemicals, petroleum, food.
## LAND
**Description** Southern Africa, landlocked. **Area** 6,704 mi² (17,364 km²). **Highest point** Emlembe, 6,109 ft (1,862 m). **Lowest point** Usutu river valley, 70 ft (21 m).

**People.** About 95 percent of the people of Swaziland are black Africans called Swazi, though small minorities of white Europeans and Zulus also live in the country. The two official languages are English and siSwati. Government and official business is conducted primarily in English. More than half the Swazi belong to Christian churches, while others practice traditional African religions.

**Economy and the Land.** Most Swazi are subsistence farmers. Cattle are highly prized for their own sake but are being used increasingly for milk, meat, and profit. Europeans own nearly half the land in Swaziland and raise most of the cash crops, including fruits, sugar, tobacco, cotton, and wood. About half the nation's income comes from European-owned mining operations, and major exports include asbestos. Swaziland also has deposits of coal, pottery clay, gold, and tin. The country's mountains and forests have brought a growing tourist industry. The climate is temperate.

**History and Politics.** According to legend, the Swazi originally came from the area near Maputo. British traders and Dutch farmers from South Africa first reached Swaziland in the 1830s; more whites arrived in the 1880s when gold was discovered. Swazi leaders unknowingly granted many concessions to the whites at this time. After the Boer War, Britain assumed administration of Swaziland and ruled until 1967. Swaziland became independent in 1968. The British designed a constitution, but many Swazi thought it disregarded their traditions and interests. In 1973, King Sobhuza abolished this constitution, suspended the legislature, and appointed a commission to produce a new constitution. Sobhuza ruled until his death in 1982, and King Mswati III was installed in 1986. ■

# SWEDEN

**Official name** Kingdom of Sweden
**PEOPLE**
**Population** 8,503,000. **Density** 49/mi$^2$ (19/km$^2$). **Urban** 83%. **Capital** Stockholm, 663,217. **Ethnic groups** Swedish (Scandinavian) 92%, Finnish, Lappic. **Languages** Swedish. **Religions** Lutheran (Church of Sweden) 94%, Roman Catholic 2%. **Life expectancy** 79 female, 73 male. **Literacy** 99%.
**POLITICS**
**Government** Constitutional monarchy. **Parties** Moderate, Liberal, Social Democratic, others. **Suffrage** Universal, over 18. **Memberships** OECD, UN. **Subdivisions** 24 counties.
**ECONOMY**
**GDP** $100,247,000,000 **Per capita** $12,027. **Monetary unit** Krona. **Trade partners** Exports: U.S., W. Germany, Norway. Imports: W. Germany, U.K., U.S.. **Exports** Paper and other manufactures, machinery, transportation equipment, wood. **Imports** Manufactures, machinery, petroleum, chemicals, transportation equipment.
**LAND**
**Description** Northern Europe. **Area** 173,732 mi$^2$ (449,964 km$^2$). **Highest point** Kebnekaise, 6,926 ft (2,111 m). **Lowest point** Sea level.

**People.** The most significant minorities in the largely urban Swedish population are Swedes of Finnish origin and a small number of Lapps. Sweden is also the home of immigrants from other Nordic countries, Yugoslavia, Greece, and Turkey. Swedish is the main language, although Finns and Lapps often speak their own tongues. English is the leading foreign language, especially among students and younger people.

**Economy and the Land.** Sweden has one of the highest standards of living in the world. Taxes are also high, but the government provides exceptional benefits for most citizens, including free education and medical care, pension payments, four-week vacations, and payments for child care. The nation is industrial and bases its economy on its three most important natural resources—timber, iron ore, and water power. The iron and steel industry produces high-quality steel used in ball bearings, precision tools, agricultural machinery, aircraft, automobiles, and ships. Swedish farmers rely heavily on dairy products and livestock, and most farms are part of Sweden's agricultural-cooperative movement. Sweden's varied terrain includes mountains, forests, plains, and sandy beaches. The climate is temperate, with cold winters in the north. Northern Sweden lies in the "Land of the Midnight Sun" and experiences periods of twenty-four hours of daylight in summer and darkness in winter.

**History and Politics.** Inhabitants of what is now Sweden began to trade with the Roman Empire about 50 B.C. Sailing expeditions by Swedish Vikings began about A.D. 800. In the fourteenth century the kingdom came under Danish rule, but declared its independence in 1523. The Swedish king offered protection to the followers of Martin Luther, and Lutheranism was soon declared the state religion. By the late 1660s, Sweden had become one of the great powers of Europe; it suffered a military defeat by Russia in 1709, however, and gradually lost most of its European possessions. An 1809 constitution gave most of the executive power of the government to the king. Despite this, the power of the Parliament gradually increased, and parliamentary rule was adopted in 1917. A 1975 constitution reduced the king's role to a ceremonial one. Sweden remained neutral during both world wars. Except for 1976-82, when Sweden was run by a conservative coalition, the country has had a Socialist government. ■

# SWITZERLAND

**Official name** Swiss Confederation

# SWITZERLAND

and western Germanic tribes began a series of invasions, and in the 800s the region became part of the empire of the Frankish king Charlemagne. In 1291 leaders of the three Swiss cantons, or regions, signed an agreement declaring their freedom and promising mutual aid against any foreign ruler. The confederation was the beginning of modern Switzerland. Over the next few centuries Switzerland became a military power, expanding its territories until 1515, when it was defeated by France. Soon after, Switzerland adopted a policy of permanent neutrality. The country was again conquered by France during the French Revolution; however, after Napoleon's final defeat in 1815, the Congress of Vienna guaranteed Switzerland's neutrality, a guarantee that has never been broken. ∎

## SYRIA

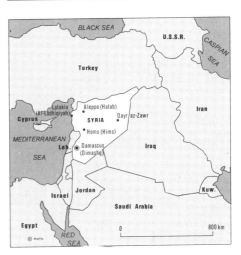

### PEOPLE
Population 6,623,000. Density 415/mi$^2$ (160/km$^2$). Urban 58%. Capital Bern, 137,134. Ethnic groups German 65%, French 18%, Italian 10%, Romansch 1%. Languages German, French, Italian, Romansch. Religions Roman Catholic 48%, Protestant 44%. Life expectancy 80 female, 73 male. Literacy 99%.
### POLITICS
Government Republic. Parties Christian Democratic People's, People's, Radical Democratic, Social Democratic, others. Suffrage Universal, over 20. Memberships OECD. Subdivisions 26 cantons.
### ECONOMY
GDP $92,776,000,000 Per capita $14,306. Monetary unit Franc. Trade partners Exports: W. Germany, U.S., France. Imports: W. Germany, France, Italy. Exports Watches and other manufactures, machinery, chemicals. Imports Manufactures, machinery, chemicals, petroleum, transportation equipment.
### LAND
Description Central Europe, landlocked. Area 15,943 mi$^2$ (41,293 km$^2$). Highest point Dufourspitze, 15,203 ft (4,634 m). Lowest point Lago Maggiore, 633 ft (193 m).

**People.** About seven hundred years ago, the Swiss began joining together for mutual defense, but preserved their regional differences in language and customs. The country has four official languages—German, French, and Italian—and the fourth, Romansch, is spoken by a minority. Dialects often differ from community to community. The population is concentrated on a central plain located between mountain ranges.

**Economy and the Land.** The Alps and Jura Mountains cover nearly 70 percent of Switzerland, making much of the land unsuited for agriculture but a good basis for a thriving tourist industry. The central plain contains rich cropland and holds Switzerland's major cities and manufacturing facilities, many specializing in high-quality, precision products. Switzerland is also an international banking and finance center. Straddling the ranges of the central Alps, Switzerland features mountains, hills, and plateaus. The temperate climate varies with altitude.

**History and Politics.** Helvetic Celts inhabited the area of present-day Switzerland when Julius Caesar conquered the region, annexing it to the Roman Empire. As the Roman Empire declined, northern

**Official name** Syrian Arab Republic
### PEOPLE
Population 11,915,000. Density 167/mi$^2$ (64/km$^2$). Urban 50%. Capital Damascus, 1,259,000. Ethnic groups Arab 90%, Kurdish, Armenian, and others 10%. Languages Arabic, Kurdish, Armenian, Aramaic, Circassian. Religions Sunni Muslim 74%, other Muslim 16%, Christian 10%. Life expectancy 64 female, 61 male. Literacy 40%.
### POLITICS
Government Socialist republic. Parties Arab Socialist Resurrectionist (Baath). Suffrage Universal, over 18. Memberships AL, UN. Subdivisions 13 provinces, 1 capital district.
### ECONOMY
GDP $20,267,000,000 Per capita $1,933. Monetary unit Pound. Trade partners Exports: Romania, Italy, France. Imports: Iran, W. Germany, France. Exports Petroleum, cotton and other textile fibers, textiles. Imports Petroleum, food, manufactures, machinery, chemicals, transportation equipment.
### LAND
Description Southwestern Asia. Area 71,498 mi$^2$ (185,180 km$^2$). Highest point Mt. Hermon, 9,232 ft (2,814 m). Lowest point Near Sea of Galilee, -655 ft (-200 m).

**People.** Most Syrians are Arabic-speaking descendants of Semites, a people who settled the region in ancient times. The majority are Sunni Muslim, and Islam is a powerful cultural force. Only a small percentage are Christian. Non-Arab Syrians include Kurds and Armenians, who speak their own languages and maintain their own customs. French is widely understood, and English is spoken in larger cities. The population is evenly divided between urban and rural settlements.

**Economy and the Land.** Syria is a developing country with great potential for economic growth. Textile manufacturing is a major industry, and oil, the main natural resource, provides for expanding activity in oil refining. The plains and river valleys are fertile, but rainfall is irregular and irrigation is necessary to sustain agriculture. Most farms are small; cotton and wheat are their major products. The terrain is marked by mountains, the Euphrates River valley, and a semiarid plateau. The climate is hot and dry, with relatively cold winters.

**History and Politics.** Syria was the site of one of the world's most ancient civilizations, and Damascus and other Syrian cities were centers of world trade as early as 2500 B.C. Greater Syria, as the area was called until the end of World War I, originally included much of modern Israel, Jordan, Lebanon, and parts of Turkey. The region was occupied and ruled by several empires, including the Phoenician, Assyrian, Babylonian, Persian, and Greek, before coming under Roman rule in 64 B.C. During subsequent years, Christianity arose in the part of Greater Syria called Palestine. In 636 the region fell to Arab Muslims, who governed until 1260, when Egypt gained control. Syria became part of the Turkish Ottoman Empire in 1516. During World War I, Syria aided Britain in defeating the Turks and Germans in return for independence. After the war, however, the League of Nations divided Greater Syria into four mandates—Syria, Lebanon, Palestine, and Transjordan—and placed Syria under French control. When Syria gained independence in 1946, many nationals wanted to reunite Greater Syria, but the United Nations made part of Palestine into the Jewish state of Israel. Tensions between Israel and Syria erupted in war in 1967 and 1973 and remain unresolved. In the 1980s, Syria assumed a role in Lebanon's affairs and maintains a military presence there. ■

# TAIWAN

**Official name** Republic of China
**PEOPLE**
**Population** 20,345,000. **Density** 1,464/mi$^2$ (565/km$^2$).
**Urban** 66%. **Capital** T'aipei, 2,637,100. **Ethnic groups** Taiwanese 84%, Chinese 14%, aborigine 2%.
**Languages** Chinese dialects. **Religions** Buddhist, Confucian, and Taoist 93%, Christian 5%. **Life expectancy** 74 female, 69 male. **Literacy** 86%.
**POLITICS**
**Government** Republic. **Parties** Democratic Progressive, Kuomintang. **Suffrage** Universal, over 20. **Memberships** None. **Subdivisions** 16 counties, 7 independent cities.
**ECONOMY**
**GNP** $60,000,000,000 **Per capita** $3,143. **Monetary unit** Dollar. **Trade partners** Exports: U.S., Japan. Imports:

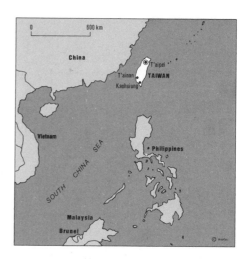

Japan, U.S., Saudi Arabia. **Exports** Machinery, textiles, metals, food, wood. **Imports** Machinery, petroleum, chemicals, metals, food.
**LAND**
**Description** Eastern Asian island. **Area** 13,900 mi$^2$ (36,002 km$^2$). **Highest point** Yu Mtn., 13,114 ft (3,997 m). **Lowest point** Sea level.

**People.** The majority of Taiwan's inhabitants are descendants of Chinese who migrated from the coast of China in the eighteenth and nineteenth centuries. In 1949, when the Communists came to power in mainland China, many educated Chinese fled to Taiwan. A small group of aborigines, which lives in the mountains in central Taiwan, is most likely of Malay-Polynesian origin. Taiwan's languages are mainly various dialects of Chinese, a Fujian dialect, and a dialect known as "Hakka." Most religious practices combine Buddhist and Taoist beliefs with the Confucian ethical code.

**Economy and the Land.** Since World War II, Taiwan's economy has changed from agriculture to industry. A past emphasis on light industry, producing mainly consumer goods, has shifted to technology and heavy industry. Although only one-quarter of the island is arable, farmland is intensely cultivated, with some areas producing two and three crops a year. Even though rice, sugar cane, fruits, tea, and fishing are important, much food must be imported. The island's terrain is marked by steep eastern mountains sloping to a fertile western region. The capital of T'aipei administers the Penghu Islands and about twenty offshore islands as well as the island of Taiwan. The climate is maritime subtropical.

**History and Politics.** Chinese migration to Taiwan began as early as A.D. 500. Dutch traders claimed the island in 1624 as a base for trade with China and Japan. It was ruled by China's Manchu dynasty from 1683 until 1895, when China ceded Taiwan to Japan after the first Sino-Japanese war. Following World War II, China regained possession of Taiwan. A civil war in mainland China between Nationalist and Communist forces ended with the victory of the Communists in 1949. Nationalist leader Chiang Kai-shek fled to Taiwan, proclaiming T'aipei the provisional capital of Nationalist China. In 1971 the People's Republic of China replaced Taiwan in the United Nations. Even though Nationalist China still maintains it is the legitimate ruler of all China, nearly all nations now recognize the mainland's People's Republic of China. ∎

# TANZANIA

**Official name** United Republic of Tanzania
**PEOPLE**
**Population** 25,220,000. **Density** 69/mi² (27/km²). **Urban** 22%. **Capital** Dar es Salaam (de facto), 1,300,000; Dodoma (future), 54,000. **Ethnic groups** African 99%. **Languages** English, Swahili, indigenous. **Religions** Animist 35%, Muslim 35%, Christian 30%. **Life expectancy** 53 female, 49 male. **Literacy** 46%.
**POLITICS**
**Government** Republic. **Parties** Revolutionary. **Suffrage** Universal, over 18. **Memberships** CW, OAU, UN. **Subdivisions** 25 regions.
**ECONOMY**
**GDP** $6,401,000,000 **Per capita** $297. **Monetary unit** Shilling. **Trade partners** Exports: W. Germany, U.K., India. Imports: U.K., Japan, W. Germany. **Exports** Coffee, cotton, nuts, diamonds, cloves, sisal, tobacco. **Imports** Petroleum, machinery, buses and other transportation equipment, manufactures.
**LAND**
**Description** Eastern Africa. **Area** 364,900 mi² (945,087 km²). **Highest point** Kilimanjaro, 19,340 ft (5,895 m). **Lowest point** Sea level.

**People.** The largely rural African population of Tanzania consists of more than 130 ethnic groups; most speak a distinct language. Religious beliefs are nearly evenly divided among Christian, Muslim, and traditional religions.

**Economy and the Land.** Agriculture accounts for the most export earnings and employs 80 percent of the work force. Yet two-thirds of the land cannot be cultivated because of lack of water and tsetse-fly infestation. Mainland farmers grow cassava, corn, and beans, while other cash crops include coffee and cashews. Zanzibar and Pemba islands are famous sources of cloves. Diamonds, salt, and iron are important mineral resources. Hot, humid coastal plains; an arid central plateau; and temperate lake and highland areas characterize mainland Tanzania. The climate is equatorial and includes monsoons.

**History and Politics.** The northern mainland has fossil remains of some of humanity's earliest ancestors. Subsequent early inhabitants were gradually displaced by Bantu farmers and Nilotes. Arabs were trading with coastal groups as early as the eighth century, and by the early 1500s the Portuguese had claimed the coastal region. They were displaced in the 1700s by Arabs, who subsequently established a lucrative slave trade. Germans began colonizing the coast in 1884 and six years later signed an agreement with Great Britain, which secured German dominance along the coast and made Zanzibar a British protectorate. After World War I, Britain received part of German East Africa from the League of Nations as a mandate and renamed it Tanganyika. The area became a trust territory under the United Nations following World War II. The country achieved independence in 1961, and two years later Zanzibar received its independence as a constitutional monarchy under the sultan. A 1964 revolt by the African majority overthrew the sultan, and Zanzibar and Tanganyika subsequently united and became known as Tanzania. ∎

# TASMANIA See AUSTRALIA.

# THAILAND

**Official name** Kingdom of Thailand
**PEOPLE**
**Population** 55,925,000. **Density** 282/mi² (109/km²). **Urban** 20%. **Capital** Bangkok, 5,446,708. **Ethnic groups**

Thai 84%, Chinese 12%. **Languages** Thai, indigenous.
**Religions** Buddhist 98%, Muslim 1%. **Life expectancy**
65 female, 61 male. **Literacy** 88%.
**POLITICS**
**Government** Constitutional monarchy. **Parties** Citizens, Democratic, Social Action, Thai Nation (Chart Thai), United. **Suffrage** Universal, over 20. **Memberships** ASEAN, UN. **Subdivisions** 73 provinces.
**ECONOMY**
**GDP** $38,343,000,000 **Per capita** $734. **Monetary unit** Baht. **Trade partners** Exports: U.S., Japan, Netherlands. Imports: Japan, U.S., Saudi Arabia. **Exports** Rice and other good, clothing and other manufactures, rubber, machinery. **Imports** Machinery, petroleum, manufactures, chemicals, transportation equipment.
**LAND**
**Description** Southeastern Asia. **Area** 198,115 mi² (513,115 km²). **Highest point** Mt. Inthanon, 8,530 ft (2,600 m). **Lowest point** Sea level.

**People.** Thailand's society is relatively homogeneous. More than 85 percent of its people speak varying dialects of Thai and share a common culture and common religion, Buddhism. Malay-speaking Muslims and Chinese immigrants compose small minorities. Thai society is rural, with most people living in the rice-growing regions. The government has sponsored a successful family-planning program, which has greatly reduced the annual birth rate.

**Economy and the Land.** With an economy based on agriculture, Thailand exports large quantities of rice each year. Forests produce teak and rattan, and tin is another valuable natural resource. Tourism is the largest source of foreign income. Future industrialization may hinge on deposits of coal and natural gas. The cost of caring for thousands of refugees from Vietnam, Laos, and Cambodia has been a major drain on the Thai economy. A mountainous and heavily forested nation, Thailand has a tropical climate, dominated by monsoons, high temperatures, and humidity.

**History and Politics.** Thai communities were established as early as 4000 B.C., although a Thai kingdom founded in the thirteenth century A.D. began the history of modern Thailand. In the late 1700s Burmese armies overwhelmed the kingdom. Rama I, founder of the present dynasty, helped to drive the invaders from the country in 1782. He subsequently renamed the country Siam and established a capital at Bangkok. Siam allowed Europeans to live within its borders during the period of colonial expansion, but the nation never succumbed to foreign rule. As a result, Siam was the only South and Southeast Asian country never colonized by a European power. In 1932 a revolt changed the government from an absolute monarchy to a constitutional monarchy. Military officers assumed control in 1938, and the nation reverted to its former name, Thailand, in 1939. The country was invaded by Japan in World War II. Following the war, Thailand was ruled by military officers until 1973, when civilians seized control and instigated a period of democracy that ended in 1976, when the military again took control. A new constitution was passed in 1978, followed by elections in 1979. ∎

# TOGO

**Official name** Republic of Togo
**PEOPLE**
**Population** 3,508,000. **Density** 160/mi² (62/km²). **Urban** 22%. **Capital** Lomé, 369,926. **Ethnic groups** Ewe 25%, Kabye 15%, Mina, others. **Languages** French, indigenous. **Religions** Animist 70%, Christian 20%, Muslim 10%. **Life expectancy** 52 female, 49 male. **Literacy** 16%.
**POLITICS**
**Government** Republic. **Parties** Rally of the People. **Suffrage** Universal adult. **Memberships** OAU, UN. **Subdivisions** 21 circumscriptions.

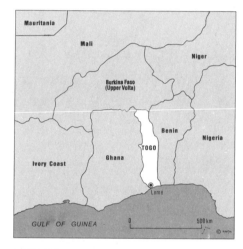

**ECONOMY**
**GDP** $747,000,000 **Per capita** $267. **Monetary unit** CFA franc. **Trade partners** Exports: Netherlands, France, Yugoslavia. Imports: France, Netherlands, W. Germany. **Exports** Phosphates, cocoa, cotton, cement. **Imports** Textiles and other manufactures, food, chemicals, petroleum.
**LAND**
**Description** Western Africa. **Area** 21,925 mi² (56,785 km²). **Highest point** Pic Baumann, 3,235 ft (986 m). **Lowest point** Sea level.

**People.** Almost all the people of Togo are black Africans, coming primarily from the Ewe, Kabye, and Mina ethnic groups. Most of the population lives in the south and practices traditional religions. Significant Christian and Muslim minorities exist.

**Economy and the Land.** Togo is an agricultural country, but productive land is scarce. Fishing is a major industry in the coastal areas. Togo has one of the world's largest phosphate reserves. Much of Togo is mountainous, with a sandy coastal plain. The climate is hot and humid.

**History and Politics.** Togo's original inhabitants were probably the ancestors of the present-day central mountain people. Ewes entered the south in the 1300s, and refugees from war-torn northern countries settled in the north between the 1500s and 1800s. For two hundred years, European ships raided the coastal region in search of slaves. In 1884 Germany claimed the territory. After World

War I, Togoland became a League of Nations mandate governed by Britain and France. The mandate was made a United Nations trust territory following World War II and remained under British and French administration. British Togoland voted to join the Gold Coast and nearby British-administered territories in 1957 and became the independent nation of Ghana. French Togoland voted to become a republic in 1956 with internal self-government within the French Union, although the United Nations did not accept this method of ending the trusteeship. Togo peacefully severed its ties with France in 1960 and gained independence the same year. Internal political strife and military dominance of the government have characterized Togo's years of independence. ∎

## TOKELAU See NEW ZEALAND.

## TONGA

**Official name** Kingdom of Tonga
**PEOPLE**
Population 97,000. **Density** 334/mi² (129/km²). **Urban** 20%. **Capital** Nuku'alofa, Tongatapu I., 21,265. **Ethnic groups** Tongan (Polynesian) 98%. **Languages** Tongan, English. **Religions** Methodist 47%, Roman Catholic 16%, Free Church 14%, Church of Tonga 9%. **Life expectancy** 61 female, 57 male. **Literacy** 100%.
**POLITICS**
**Government** Constitutional monarchy. **Parties** None. **Suffrage** Literate adults, over 21 (males must be taxpayers). **Memberships** CW. **Subdivisions** 3 island groups.
**ECONOMY**
GDP $61,000,000 **Per capita** $570. **Monetary unit** Pa'anga. **Trade partners** Exports: New Zealand, Australia, U.S. Imports: New Zealand, Australia, Japan. **Exports** Copra, fruits and vegetables, manufactures, spices, crude materials. **Imports** Manufactures, meat and other food, petroleum, machinery, chemicals, wood.
**LAND**
**Description** South Pacific islands. **Area** 290 mi² (750 km²). **Highest point** 3,432 ft (1,046 m). **Lowest point** Sea level.

**People.** Almost all Tongans are Polynesian and follow Methodist and other Christian religions. About two-thirds of the population lives on the main island of Tongatapu.

**Economy and the Land.** Tonga's economy is dominated by both subsistence and plantation agriculture, while manufacturing is almost nonexistent. Most of the islands are coral reefs, and many have fertile soil. The climate is subtropical.

**History and Politics.** Tonga has been settled since at least 500 B.C. In the late 1700s, a civil war broke out among three lines of kings who sought to establish rulership. In 1822 Wesleyan Methodist missionaries converted one of the warring kings to Christianity. His faction prevailed, and he ruled as George Tupou I, founder of the present dynasty. Tonga came under British protection in 1900 but retained its autonomy in internal matters. The nation became fully independent in 1970 and maintains close relations with Great Britain, as well as its Pacific neighbors. ∎

## TRINIDAD AND TOBAGO

**Official name** Republic of Trinidad and Tobago

**PEOPLE**
Population 1,248,000. **Density** 630/mi² (243/km²). **Urban** 64%. **Capital** Port of Spain, Trinidad I., 65,906. **Ethnic groups** Black 41%, East Indian 41%, mixed 16%, white 1%. **Languages** English, Hindi, French, Spanish. **Religions** Roman Catholic 33%, Anglican and other Protestant 29%, Hindu 25%. **Life expectancy** 71 female, 66 male. **Literacy** 95%.
**POLITICS**
**Government** Republic. **Parties** National Alliance for Reconstruction, People's National Movement. **Suffrage** Universal, over 18. **Memberships** CW, OAS, UN. **Subdivisions** 10 administrative areas.
**ECONOMY**
GDP $7,558,000,000 **Per capita** $6,095. **Monetary unit** Dollar. **Trade partners** Exports: U.S., U.K. Imports: U.S., U.K., Canada. **Exports** Petroleum, chemicals. **Imports** Manufactures, machinery, food, transportation equipment, chemicals.
**LAND**
**Description** Caribbean islands. **Area** 1,980 mi² (5,128 km²). **Highest point** El Cerro Del Aripo, Trinidad I., 3,085 ft (940 m). **Lowest point** Sea level.

**People.** The two islands of Trinidad and Tobago form a single country, but Trinidad has nearly all the land mass and population. About 80 percent of all Trinidadians are either black African or East Indian, and about 20 percent are European, Chinese, and of mixed descent. Most Tobagonians are black African. The official language is English, and Christianity and Hinduism are the major religions.

**Economy and the Land.** Agriculture and tourism are important, but the economy is based on oil, which accounts for about 80 percent of the nation's exports. Trinidad is also one of the world's chief sources of natural asphalt and possesses supplies of natural gas. Tropical rain forests, scenic beaches, and fertile farmland characterize the islands.

**History and Politics.** Trinidad was occupied by Arawak Indians when Christopher Columbus arrived and claimed the island for Spain in 1498. The island remained under Spanish rule until 1797, when the British captured it and ruled for more than 150 years. Tobago changed hands among the Dutch,

French, and British until 1814, when Britain took control. In 1888 Trinidad and Tobago became a single British colony and achieved independence in 1962. A separatist movement on Tobago has caused the government to give that island more control over its internal affairs. ∎

# TUNISIA

**Official name** Republic of Tunisia
**PEOPLE**
**Population** 8,079,000. **Density** 128/mi$^2$ (49/km$^2$). **Urban** 57%. **Capital** Tunis, 596,654. **Ethnic groups** Arab 98%, European 1%. **Languages** Arabic, French. **Religions** Muslim 98%, Christian 1%. **Life expectancy** 61 female, 60 male. **Literacy** 46%.
**POLITICS**
**Government** Republic. **Parties** Constitutional Democratic Rally, others. **Suffrage** Universal, over 21. **Memberships** AL, OAU, UN. **Subdivisions** 23 governorates.
**ECONOMY**
**GDP** $8,214,000,000 **Per capita** $1,126. **Monetary unit** Dinar. **Trade partners** Exports: France, U.S., Italy. Imports: France, Italy, W. Germany. **Exports** Petroleum, clothing, fertilizer and other chemicals, food. **Imports** Textiles and other manufactures, machinery, food, petroleum.
**LAND**
**Description** Northern Africa. **Area** 63,170 mi$^2$ (163,610 km$^2$). **Highest point** Mt. Chambi, 5,066 ft (1,544 m). **Lowest point** Chott el Gharsa, -56 ft (-17 m).

**People.** Tunisians are descended from a mix of Berber and Arab ethnic groups. Nearly all Tunisians are Muslim. Arabic is the official language, but French is widely spoken. Tunisia is a leader in the Arab world in promoting rights for women. A large middle class and equitable land distribution characterize its society.

**Economy and the Land.** Tunisia is an agricultural country; wheat, barley, citrus fruits, and olives are important crops. Oil from deposits discovered in the 1960s supplies domestic needs and serves as a major export, along with phosphates and other chemicals. Tourism is a growing industry, and despite an unemployment problem, Tunisia has a more balanced economy than many of its neighbors. Tunisia's terrain ranges from a well-watered and fertile northern area to more arid central and southern regions.

**History and Politics.** Phoenicians began the Carthaginian Empire in Tunisia about 1100 B.C. In 146 B.C. Romans conquered Carthage and ruled Tunisia for six hundred years. Arab Muslims from the Middle East gained control of most of North Africa in the seventh century, influencing the religion and overall culture of the region. Tunisia became part of the Turkish Ottoman Empire in the late 1500s, and in 1881 France succeeded in establishing a protectorate in the area. Nationalistic calls for Tunisian independence began before World War I and gained momentum by the 1930s. When Tunisia gained independence in 1956, more than half of the European population emigrated, severely damaging the economy. A year later Tunisia abolished its monarchy and became a republic. After a thirty-year rule, Habib Bourguiba was deposed in 1987. Tunisia continues to maintain a balance between pro-Western and Arab positions. ∎

# TURKEY

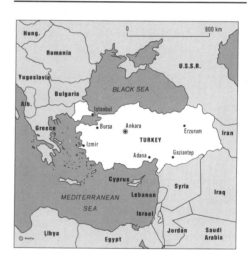

**Official name** Republic of Turkey
**PEOPLE**
**Population** 54,075,000. **Density** 180/mi$^2$ (69/km$^2$). **Urban** 46%. **Capital** Ankara, 2,235,035. **Ethnic groups** Turkish 85%, Kurdish 12%. **Languages** Turkish, Kurdish, Arabic. **Religions** Muslim 98%. **Life expectancy** 63 female, 60 male. **Literacy** 69%.
**POLITICS**
**Government** Republic. **Parties** Correct Way, Motherland, Social Democratic Populist. **Suffrage** Universal, over 19. **Memberships** NATO, OECD, UN. **Subdivisions** 67 provinces.
**ECONOMY**
**GDP** $52,701,000,000 **Per capita** $1,039. **Monetary unit** Lira. **Trade partners** Exports: W. Germany, Iraq, Iran. Imports: Iran, W. Germany, U.S.. **Exports** Clothing and other manufactures, nuts and other food, crude

materials. **Imports** Petroleum, machinery, chemicals, manufactures, iron and steel.
**LAND**
**Description** Southeastern Europe and southwestern Asia. **Area** 300,948 mi$^2$ (779,452 km$^2$). **Highest point** Mt. Ararat, 16,804 ft (5,122 m). **Lowest point** Sea level.

**People.** Most Turks are descended from an Asian people who migrated from Russia and Mongolia around A.D. 900. About half the Turkish population lives in cities and half in rural areas. Kurds, the largest minority, live in the country's mountainous regions. Arabs and whites compose smaller minorities. The population is mainly Sunni Muslim. The changing status of women and the influence of Islam on daily life are key issues in Turkish society.

**Economy and the Land.** More than half the workers in this developing country are farmers, but industrialization has increased greatly since 1950. The most productive lands are in the mild coastal regions, although wheat and barley are grown in the desertlike plateau area. The government owns or controls many important industries, transportation services, and utilities, while most small farms and manufacturing companies are privately owned. The climate is Mediterranean along the coast, but temperature extremes are typical in the inland plateau.

**History and Politics.** Hittites began to migrate to the area from Europe or central Asia around 2000 B.C. Successive dominant groups included Phrygians, Greeks, Persians, and Romans. Muslims and Christians battled in the area during the Crusades of the eleventh and twelfth centuries. In the 1300s, Ottoman Turks began to build what would become a vast empire for six hundred years. Mustafa Kemal founded the Republic of Turkey in 1923, after the collapse of the Ottoman Empire. In 1960 the Turkish government was overthrown by Turkish military forces, who subsequently set up a provisional government, adopted a new constitution, and held free elections. In the sixties and seventies, disputes with Greece over Cyprus, populated by majority Greeks and minority Turks, flared into violence, and radical groups committed terrorist acts against the government. Turkey's generals assumed power in 1980 and restored order to the country. The government returned to civilian rule in 1984 under Prime Minister Turgut Ozal, who was re-elected in 1987. ∎

# TURKS AND CAICOS ISLANDS See UNITED KINGDOM.

# TUVALU

**Official name** Tuvalu
**PEOPLE**
**Population** 8,800. **Density** 880/mi$^2$ (338/km$^2$). **Capital** Funafuti, Funafuti I., 2,191. **Ethnic groups** Tuvaluan (Polynesian) 91%, Kiribatian 5%. **Languages** Tuvaluan, English. **Religions** Tuvalu Church 97%. **Life expectancy** 60 female, 57 male. **Literacy** 50%.

**POLITICS**
**Government** Parliamentary state. **Parties** None. **Suffrage** Universal adult. **Memberships** CW. **Subdivisions** 1 town council, 7 island councils.
**ECONOMY**
**GNP** $4,000,000 **Per capita** $513. **Monetary unit** Australian dollar. **Trade partners** Australia, Fiji, New Zealand, Japan, U.K.. **Exports** Copra, developed cinema film. **Imports** Grain and other food, manufactures, petroleum, machinery, chemicals.
**LAND**
**Description** South Pacific islands. **Area** 10 mi$^2$ (26 km$^2$). **Highest point** 16 ft (5 m). **Lowest point** Sea level.

**People.** The small island nation of Tuvalu has a largely Polynesian population centered in rural villages. Tuvaluans speak the Tuvaluan language, derived from Polynesian, and many also speak English, reflecting ties with England.

**Economy and the Land.** The soil of the Tuvaluan coral-reef islands is poor, and there are few natural resources other than coconut palms. Copra and developed film are the primary exports, and many Tuvaluans weave mats and baskets for export. Tuvalu has minimal manufacturing and no mining. The nation consists of nine islands, most of them atolls surrounding lagoons. The climate is tropical.

**History and Politics.** Tuvalu's first inhabitants were probably Samoan immigrants. The islands were not seen by Europeans until 1568 and came under British control in the 1890s. Then called the Ellice Islands by Europeans, they were combined with the nearby Gilbert Islands in 1916 to form the Gilbert and Ellice Islands Colony. The island groups were separated in 1975. The Ellice Islands were renamed Tuvalu and gained independence in 1978. One year later, the Gilbert Islands became independent Kiribati. ∎

# UGANDA

**Official name** Republic of Uganda
**PEOPLE**
**Population** 17,300,000. **Density** 186/mi$^2$ (72/km$^2$). **Urban** 10%. **Capital** Kampala, 460,000. **Ethnic groups** Ganda,

Nkole, Gisu, Soga, Turkana, Chiga, Lango, Acholi. **Languages** English, Luganda, Swahili, indigenous. **Religions** Roman Catholic 33%, Protestant 33%, Muslim 16%, Animist. **Life expectancy** 51 female, 47 male. **Literacy** 52%.

### POLITICS
**Government** Provisional military government. **Parties** Conservative, Democratic, Patriotic Movement, People's Congress. **Suffrage** Universal adult. **Memberships** CW, OAU, UN. **Subdivisions** 10 provinces.

### ECONOMY
**GDP** $5,900,000,000 **Per capita** $422. **Monetary unit** Shilling. **Trade partners** Exports: U.S., U.K., Spain. Imports: Kenya, U.K., Japan. **Exports** Coffee, cotton, copper, tea. **Imports** Machinery and transportation equipment, manufactures, chemicals, food.

### LAND
**Description** Eastern Africa, landlocked. **Area** 93,104 mi² (241,139 km²). **Highest point** Margherita Pk., 16,763 ft (5,109 m). **Lowest point** Albert Nile River valley, 2,000 ft (650 m).

**People.** Primarily a rural nation, Uganda has a largely African population, which is composed of various ethnic groups. Numerous differences divide Uganda's peoples and have traditionally inspired conflict. Though English is the official language, Luganda and Swahili are widely used, along with indigenous Bantu and Nilotic languages. Most Ugandans are Christian, but Muslims and followers of traditional beliefs compose significant minorities.

**Economy and the Land.** Despite attempts to diversify the economy, the country remains largely agricultural. Uganda meets most of its own food needs and grows coffee, cotton, and tea commercially. Copper deposits account for most mining activity. Though Uganda straddles the equator, temperatures are modified by altitude. Most of the country is plateau, and Uganda benefits from its proximity to several major lakes.

**History and Politics.** Arab traders who traveled to the interior of Uganda in the 1830s found sophisticated kingdoms that had developed over several centuries. Trying to track the source of the Nile River, British explorers arrived in the 1860s and were followed by European missionaries. Britain quickly became a dominant force in eastern Africa, and part of modern Uganda became a British protectorate in 1894. Subsequent border adjustments brought Uganda to its present boundaries in 1926. After increasing demands for independence, moves toward autonomy began in the mid-1950s. Independence came in 1962, followed by internal conflicts and power struggles. In 1971 Major General Idi Amin Dada led a successful coup against President Obote and declared himself president. His dictatorship was rife with corruption, economic decline, and disregard for human rights. A force of Tanzanian troops and Ugandan exiles drove Amin out of Uganda in 1979. President Obote returned to power in 1980 but was forced from office in a 1985 military coup. A struggle within the military regime continues. ∎

# UNITED ARAB EMIRATES

**Official name** United Arab Emirates

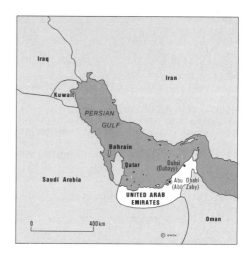

### PEOPLE
**Population** 2,183,000. **Density** 68/mi² (26/km²). **Urban** 78%. **Capital** Abu Dhabi, 242,975. **Ethnic groups** South Asian 50%, native Emirian 19%, other Arab 23%. **Languages** Arabic, English, Farsi, Hindi, Urdu. **Religions** Muslim 89%, Christian 6%. **Life expectancy** 70 female, 65 male. **Literacy** 68%.

### POLITICS
**Government** Federation of monarchs. **Parties** None. **Suffrage** None. **Memberships** AL, OPEC, UN. **Subdivisions** 7 emirates.

### ECONOMY
**GDP** $27,081,000,000 **Per capita** $16,926. **Monetary unit** Dirham. **Trade partners** Exports: Japan, France, U.S. Imports: Japan, U.S., U.K.. **Exports** Petroleum. **Imports** Iron and steel and other manufactures, machinery, transportation equipment.

### LAND
**Description** Southwestern Asia. **Area** 32,278 mi² (83,600 km²). **Highest point** Sea level.

**People.** The United Arab Emirates is a predominantly urban federation of seven independent states, each with its own ruling emir. The indigenous population is mostly Arab and Muslim, but only a small percentage of residents are United Arab Emirates citizens. Other groups include foreigners attracted by jobs in industry, especially Asians and Western Europeans. Arabic is the official language, but Farsi and English are widely spoken. The nation's population enjoys one of the highest per capita incomes in the world, as well as free medical and educational facilities.

**Economy and the Land.** Most of the United Arab Emirates is desert, which explains agriculture's small economic role. However, the federation is rich in oil, and major deposits—primarily in Abu Dhabi—account for nearly all of the Emirian national budget. The United Arab Emirates has tried to diversify its economy through production of natural gas, ammonia, and building materials. To attract tourists, airport expansion and hotel development are also on the rise.

**History and Politics.** Centuries ago, Arab rulers gained control of the region, formerly called the Trucial Coast, and Islam spread to the area in the A.D. 600s. In 1820 Arabian emirs signed the first of a number of treaties with the United Kingdom. Mutual self-interest led to an 1892 treaty that granted Britain exclusive rights to Trucial territory and government activity in return for military protection. Britain formally withdrew from Trucial affairs in 1971, and six of the Trucial emirates entered into a loose federation called the United Arab Emirates, which included Abu Dhabi, Dubai, Ash Shāriqah, 'Ajmān, Umm al Qaywayn, and Al Fujayrah. The seventh, Ra's al Khaymah, joined in early 1972. Because each emirate has a great deal of control over its internal affairs and economic development, the growth of federal powers has been slow. Defense spending is on the increase, however, and growing Arab nationalism may lead to a more centralized government. ■

# UNITED KINGDOM

**Official name** United Kingdom of Great Britain and Northern Ireland
**PEOPLE**
**Population** 57,335,000. **Density** 608/mi$^2$ (235/km$^2$). **Urban** 92%. **Capital** London, England, 6,851,400. **Ethnic groups** English 82%, Scottish 10%, Irish 2%, Welsh 2%. **Languages** English, Welsh, Gaelic. **Religions** Anglican 45%, Roman Catholic 9%, Presbyterian 3%, Methodist 1%. **Life expectancy** 77 female, 71 male. **Literacy** 99%.
**POLITICS**
**Government** Constitutional monarchy. **Parties**

## Places and Possessions of The UNITED KINGDOM

| Entity | Status | Area | Population | Capital/Population |
|---|---|---|---|---|
| Anguilla (Caribbean island) | Dependent territory | 35 mi$^2$ (91 km$^2$) | 7,000 | The Valley, 1,042 |
| Ascension (South Atlantic island) | Dependency of St. Helena | 34 mi$^2$ (88 km$^2$) | 1,300 | Georgetown |
| Bermuda (North Atlantic islands; east of North Carolina) | Dependent territory | 21 mi$^2$ (54 km$^2$) | 57,000 | Hamilton, 1,676 |
| British Indian Ocean Territory (Indian Ocean islands) | Dependent territory | 23 mi$^2$ (60 km$^2$) | None | None |
| Cayman Islands (Caribbean Sea) | Dependent territory | 100 mi$^2$ (259 km$^2$) | 25,000 | George Town, 11,500 |
| Channel Islands (Northwestern European) | Dependent territory | 75 mi$^2$ (194 km$^2$) | 138,000 | None |
| Falkland Islands (South Atlantic; east of Argentina) | Dependent territory | 4,700 mi$^2$ (12,173 km$^2$) | 2,000 | Stanley, 1,200 |
| Gibraltar (Southwestern Europe; Peninsula on Spain's southern coast) | Dependent territory | 2.3 mi$^2$ (6.0 km$^2$) | 30,000 | Gibraltar, 30,000 |
| Guernsey (Northwestern European islands) | Bailiwick of Channel Islands | 30 mi$^2$ (78 km$^2$) | 57,000 | St. Peter Port, 16,085 |
| Hong Kong (Eastern Asia; islands and mainland area on China's southeastern coast) | Dependent territory | 414 mi$^2$ (1,072 km$^2$) | 5,888,000 | Victoria (Hong Kong), 1,175,860 |
| Isle of Man (Northwestern European island) | Self-governing territory | 221 mi$^2$ (572 km$^2$) | 67,000 | Douglas, 20,368 |
| Jersey (Northwestern European island) | Bailiwick of Channel Islands | 45 mi$^2$ (116 km$^2$) | 81,000 | St. Helier, 27,083 |
| Montserrat (Caribbean island) | Dependent territory | 39 mi$^2$ (102 km$^2$) | 12,000 | Plymouth, 1,568 |
| Orkney Islands (North Atlantic) | Part of Scotland | 377 mi$^2$ (976 km$^2$) | 19,000 | Kirkwall, 5,713 |
| Pitcairn (South Pacific islands) | Dependent territory | 19 mi$^2$ (49 km$^2$) | 60 | Adamstown, 59 |
| Shetland Islands (North Atlantic) | Part of Scotland | 553 mi$^2$ (1,433 km$^2$) | 22,000 | Lerwick, 6,333 |
| South Georgia and the South Sandwich Islands (South Atlantic Islands) | Dependent territory | 1,450 mi$^2$ (3,755 km$^2$) | None | None |
| St. Helena (South Atlantic islands) | Dependent territory | 162 mi$^2$ (419 km$^2$) | 7,600 | Jamestown, 1,413 |
| Tristan da Cunha (South Atlantic islands) | Dependency of St. Helena | 40 mi$^2$ (104 km$^2$) | 300 | Edinburgh |
| Turks and Caicos Islands (Caribbean Sea) | Dependent territory | 166 mi$^2$ (430 km$^2$) | 11,000 | Grand Turk, 3,146 |
| Virgin Islands, British (Caribbean Sea) | Dependent territory | 59 mi$^2$ (153 km$^2$) | 13,000 | Road Town, 2,479 |

Conservative, Labor, Liberal, Social and Liberal Democratic, others. **Suffrage** Universal, over 18.

**Memberships** CW, EC, NATO, OECD, UN. **Subdivisions** 4 political divisions (England, Northern Ireland, Scotland, and Wales).
**ECONOMY**
**GDP** $454,540,000,000 **Per capita** $8,111. **Monetary unit** Pound sterling. **Trade partners** Exports: U.S., W. Germany, France. Imports: W. Germany, U.S., France. **Exports** Manufactures, machinery, petroleum, chemicals, transportation equipment. **Imports** Manufactures, machinery, transportation equipment, petroleum, food, chemicals.
**LAND**
**Description** Northwestern European islands. **Area** 94,248 mi$^2$ (244,100 km$^2$). **Highest point** Ben Nevis, Scotland, 4,406 ft (1,343 m). **Lowest point** Holme Fen, England, -9 ft (-3 m).

**People.** The ancestry of modern Britons reflects many centuries of invasions and migrations from Scandinavia and the European continent. Today Britons are a mixture of Celtic, Roman, Anglo-Saxon, Norse, and Norman influences. English is the official language, although Celtic languages such as Welsh and Scottish Gaelic are also spoken. Anglican is the dominant religion in England, while many Scots practice Presbyterianism. A sizable minority is Roman Catholic. The population is primarily urban and suburban, with a significant percentage living in the southeastern corner of England.

**Economy and the Land.** A land of limited natural resources, the United Kingdom has relied on trading and, more recently, manufacturing to achieve economic strength. Access to the sea is a traditional economic and political asset. The country maintains a large merchant fleet, which at one time dominated world trade. The industrial revolution developed quickly in Great Britain, and the country continues to be a leading producer of transportation equipment, metal products, and other manufactured goods. Although climate and limited acreage have hindered agricultural development, intensive, mechanized farming methods have allowed the nation to produce half of its food supply. Livestock raising is especially important. Additional contributors to the country's industry are extensive deposits of coal and iron, which make mining important. London is well known as an international financial center. The United Kingdom includes Scotland, England, Wales, Northern Ireland, and several offshore islands. The varied terrain is marked by several mountain ranges, moors, rolling hills, and plains. The climate is tempered by the sea and is subject to frequent changes. Great Britain administers many overseas possessions.

**History and Politics.** Little is known of the earliest inhabitants of Britain, but evidence such as Stonehenge indicates the existence of a developed culture before the Roman invasion in the 50s B.C. Britain began to trade with the rest of Europe while under Roman rule. The Norman period after A.D. 1066 fostered the establishment of many cultural and political traditions that continue to be reflected in British life. Scotland came under the British Crown in 1603, and in 1707 England and Scotland agreed to unite as Great Britain. Ireland had been conquered by the early seventeenth century, and the 1801 British Act of Union established the United Kingdom of Great Britain and Ireland. Although colonial and economic expansion had taken Great Britain to the Far East, America, Africa, and India, the nation's influence began to diminish at the end of the nineteenth century as the industrial revolution strengthened other nations. World War I significantly weakened the United Kingdom and during the period following World War II, which saw the demise of an empire, many colonies gained independence. Margaret Thatcher of the Conservative party has governed the country since 1979. ∎

# UNITED STATES

**Official name** United States of America
**PEOPLE**
**Population** 250,150,000. **Density** 68/mi$^2$ (26/km$^2$). **Urban** 74%. **Capital** Washington, D.C., 638,432. **Ethnic groups** White 85%, black 12%. **Languages** English, Spanish. **Religions** Baptist and other Protestant 32%, Roman Catholic 22%, Jewish 2%. **Life expectancy** 78 female, 71 male. **Literacy** 91%.

## Places and Possessions of the UNITED STATES

| Entity | Status | Area | Population | Capital/Population |
|---|---|---|---|---|
| **American Samoa** (South Pacific islands) | Unincorporated territory | 77 mi² (199 km²) | 44,000 | Pago Pago, 3,075 |
| **Guam** (North Pacific island) | Unincorporated territory | 209 mi² (541 km²) | 154,000 | Agana, 896 |
| **Johnston Atoll** (North Pacific island) | Unincorporated territory | 0.5 mi² (1.3 km²) | 300 | None |
| **Marshall Islands** (North Pacific) | Republic in free association with U.S. | 70 mi² (181 km²) | 43,000 | Majuro (island) |
| **Micronesia, Federated States of** (North Pacific islands) | Republic in free association with U.S. | 271 mi² (702 km²) | 90,000 | Kolonia, 5,549 |
| **Midway Islands** (North Pacific) | Unincorporated territory | 2.0 mi² (5.2 km²) | 500 | None |
| **Navassa Island** (Caribbean Sea) | Unincorporated territory | 1.9 mi² (4.9 km²) | None | None |
| **Northern Mariana Islands** (North Pacific) | Commonwealth | 184 mi² (477 km²) | 24,000 | Saipan (island) |
| **Pacific Islands, Trust Territory of the** (North Pacific) | United Nations trusteeship (U.S. administration) | 196 mi² (508 km²) | 15,000 | None |
| **Palau (Belau)** (North Pacific) | Part of Trust Territory of the Pacific Islands | 196 mi² (508 km²) | 15,000 | Koror, 6,222 |
| **Puerto Rico** (Caribbean island) | Commonwealth | 3,515 mi² (9,104 km²) | 3,368,000 | San Juan, 424,600 |
| **Virgin Islands of the United States** (Caribbean Sea) | Unincorporated territory | 133 mi² (344 km²) | 114,000 | Charlotte Amalie, 11,842 |
| **Wake Island** (North Pacific) | Unincorporated territory | 3.0 mi² (7.8 km²) | 300 | None |

## POLITICS

**Government** Republic. **Parties** Democratic, Republican. **Suffrage** Universal, over 18. **Memberships** NATO, OECD, OAS, UN. **Subdivisions** 50 states, 1 district.

## ECONOMY

**GDP** $3,959,610,000,000 **Per capita** $16,662. **Monetary unit** Dollar. **Trade partners** Exports: Canada, Japan, Mexico. Imports: Japan, Canada, W. Germany. **Exports** Machinery, aircraft and other transportation equipment, manufactures. **Imports** Manufactures, machinery, transportation equipment, petroleum, food.

## LAND

**Description** Central North America. **Area** 3,679,245 mi² (9,529,202 km²). **Highest point** Mt. McKinley, Alaska, 20,320 ft (6,194 m). **Lowest point** Death Valley, California, -282 ft (-86 m).

**People.** The diverse population of the United States is mostly composed of whites, many descended from eighteenth- and nineteenth-century immigrants; blacks, mainly descended from African slaves; peoples of Spanish and Asian origin; and indigenous Indians, Inuit, and Hawaiians. Religions encompass the world's major faiths; Protestantism, Roman Catholicism, and Judaism predominate. English is the official language, though Spanish is spoken by many, and other languages are often found in ethnic enclaves.

**Economy and the Land.** The United States is an international economic power, and all sectors of the economy are highly developed. Fertile soils produce high crop yields, with considerable land under cultivation. Mineral output includes petroleum and natural gas, coal, copper, lead, and zinc; but high consumption makes the United States dependent on foreign oil. The country is a leading manufacturer, with a well-developed service sector. Mountains, prairies, woodlands, and deserts mark its vast terrain. The climate varies regionally, from mild year-round along the Pacific coast and in the South to temperate in the Northeast and Midwest. In addition to forty-eight contiguous states, the country includes the subarctic state of Alaska and the tropical state of Hawaii, an island group in the Pacific.

**History and Politics.** Thousands of years ago, Asiatic peoples, ancestors of American Indians, crossed the Bering Strait land bridge and spread across North and South America. Vikings reached North America around A.D. 1000, and Christopher Columbus arrived in 1492. Following early explorations by Portugal and Spain, England established a colony at Jamestown, Virginia, in 1607. Thirteen British colonies waged a successful war of independence against England from 1775 to 1783. United States expansion continued westward throughout the nineteenth century. The issues of black slavery and states' rights led to the American Civil War from 1861 to 1865, a struggle that pitted the North against the South and resulted in the end of slavery. Opportunities for prosperity accompanied the industrial revolution in the late nineteenth century and led to a large influx of immigrants. From 1917 to 1918, the country joined with the Allies in World War I. A severe economic depression began in 1929, and the United States did not really recover until World War II stimulated industry and the economy in general. In 1945, the use of the atomic bomb on Japan ended the war and changed the course of history. The Civil Rights Act of 1964 and the Vietnam War, 1961-75, ushered in an era of great social progress and turmoil in the United States. Technological advances were unparalleled with man's entry into space and the first landing on the moon in 1969. The 1980s saw increasing concern with a deteriorating environment and the nuclear arms race. ∎

# URUGUAY

**Official name** Oriental Republic of Uruguay
## PEOPLE
**Population** 3,120,000. **Density** 46/mi² (18/km²). **Urban** 85%. **Capital** Montevideo, 1,246,500. **Ethnic groups** White 88%, mestizo 8%, black 4%. **Languages** Spanish. **Religions** Roman Catholic 66%, Protestant 2%, Jewish 2%. **Life expectancy** 74 female, 67 male. **Literacy** 94%.
## POLITICS
**Government** Republic. **Parties** Broad Front, Colorado, National (Blanco). **Suffrage** Universal, over 18. **Memberships** OAS, UN. **Subdivisions** 19 departments.
## ECONOMY
**GDP** $5,054,000,000 **Per capita** $1,725. **Monetary unit** New Peso. **Trade partners** Exports: U.S., Brazil, Argentina. Imports: Brazil, Nigeria, Argentina. **Exports** Clothing and other manufactures, wool, meat, grain, fish. **Imports** Petroleum, chemicals, machinery, manufactures, crude materials, food.
## LAND
**Description** Eastern South America. **Area** 68,500 mi² (177,414 km²). **Highest point** Cerro Catedral, 1,686 ft (514 m). **Lowest point** Sea level.

**People.** Most Uruguayans are white descendants of nineteenth- and twentieth-century immigrants from Spain, Italy, and other European countries. Mestizos, of Spanish-Indian ancestry, and blacks round out the population. Spanish is the official language, and Roman Catholicism is the major religion, with small Protestant and Jewish minorities. Many Uruguayans claim to follow no religion.

**Economy and the Land.** Uruguay's fertile soil, grassy plains, and temperate climate provide the basis for agriculture and are especially conducive to livestock raising. The country has virtually no mineral resources, and petroleum exploration has been unrewarding. However, refinement of imported fuel is a major industry, and Uruguay has significant hydroelectric potential.

**History and Politics.** Uruguay's original inhabitants were Indians. In the 1680s, the Portuguese established the first European settlement, followed by a Spanish settlement in the 1720s. By the 1770s, Spain had gained control of the area, but in the 1820s Portugal once again came to power, annexing present-day Uruguay to Brazil. When nationalistic feelings in the early nineteenth century led to an 1828 war by Uruguayan patriots and Argentina against Brazil, the country achieved independence. Political unrest, caused in part by economic depression, resurfaced in the 1970s, leading to military intervention in the government and the jailing of thousands of political prisoners. The country restored its civilian government in 1985. ∎

# VANUATU

**Official name** Republic of Vanuatu
## PEOPLE
**Population** 158,000. **Density** 34/mi² (13/km²). **Urban** 25%. **Capital** Port-Vila, Efate I., 14,184. **Ethnic groups** Ni-Vanuatu 94%, European 2%, other Pacific Islander 1%. **Languages** Bislama, English, French. **Religions** Presbyterian 37%, Anglican 15%, Roman Catholic 15%, other Protestant. **Literacy** 20%.
## POLITICS
**Government** Republic. **Parties** National (Vanua'aku Pati), Union of Moderate Parties. **Suffrage** Universal adult. **Memberships** CW, UN. **Subdivisions** 11 island councils.
## ECONOMY
**GDP** $103,000,000 **Per capita** $805. **Monetary unit** Vatu. **Trade partners** Exports: Netherlands, Belgium, France. Imports: Australia, Japan, New Zealand. **Exports** Copra, meat, cocoa. **Imports** Manufactures, food, machinery, petroleum, transportation equipment.
## LAND
**Description** South Pacific islands. **Area** 4,706 mi² (12,189 km²). **Highest point** Mt. Tabwémasana, Espíritu Santo I., 6,165 ft (1,879 m). **Lowest point** Sea level.

**People.** The majority of Vanuatuans are Melanesian. Europeans and Polynesians compose minorities. Languages include English and French, the languages of former rulers; and Bislama, a mixture of English and Melanesian. Most Vanuatuans are Christian, although indigenous religions are also practiced.

**Economy and the Land.** The economy is based on agriculture, and copra is the primary export crop. Fishing is also important, as is the growing tourist business. Narrow coastal plains, mountainous interiors, and a mostly hot, rainy climate characterize the more than eighty islands of Vanuatu.

**History and Politics.** In 1606 Portuguese explorers encountered indigenous Melanesian inhabitants on islands that now compose Vanuatu. Captain James Cook of Britain charted the islands in 1774 and named them the New Hebrides after the Hebrides islands of Scotland. British and French merchants and missionaries began to settle the islands in the early 1800s. To resolve conflicting interests, Great Britain and France formed a joint naval commission to oversee the area in 1887 and a condominium government in 1906. Demands for autonomy began in the 1960s, and the New Hebrides became the independent Republic of Vanuatu in 1980. ■

## VATICAN CITY

**Official name** State of the Vatican City
**PEOPLE**
**Population** 800. **Density** 4,000/mi$^2$ (2,000/km$^2$). **Urban** 100%. **Capital** Vatican City, 800. **Ethnic groups** Italian, Swiss. **Languages** Italian, Latin. **Religions** Roman Catholic. **Literacy** 100%.
**POLITICS**
**Government** Ecclesiastical city-state. **Parties** None. **Suffrage** Roman Catholic cardinals less than 80 years old. **Memberships** None. **Subdivisions** None. **Monetary unit** Italian lira.
**LAND**
**Description** Southern Europe, landlocked (within the city of Rome, Italy). **Area** 0.2 mi$^2$ (0.4 km$^2$). **Highest point** 249 ft (76 m). **Lowest point** 62 ft (19 m).

**People.** The Vatican City, the smallest independent state in the world, is the administrative and spiritual center of the Roman Catholic church and home to the pope, the church's head. The population is composed of administrative and diplomatic workers of more than a dozen nationalities; Italians and Swiss predominate. A military corps known as the Swiss Guard also resides here. Roman Catholicism is the only religion. The official language is Italian, although acts of the Holy See are drawn up in Latin.

**Economy and the Land.** The Vatican City does not engage in commerce per se; however, it does issue its own coins and postage stamps. In addition, it is the destination of thousands of tourists and pilgrims each year. Lying on a hill west of the Tiber River, the Vatican City is an urban enclave in northwestern Rome, Italy. The Vatican City enjoys a mild climate moderated by the Mediterranean Sea.

**History and Politics.** For centuries the popes of the Roman Catholic church ruled the Papal States, an area across central Italy, which included Rome. The popes' temporal authority gradually was reduced to the city of Rome, which itself was eventually annexed by the Kingdom of Italy in 1870. Denying these rulings, the pope declared himself a prisoner in the Vatican, a status that lasted fifty-nine years. The Vatican City has been an independent sovereign state since 1929, when Italy signed the Treaty of the Lateran in return for papal dissolution of the Papal States. The pope heads all branches of government, though day-to-day responsibilities are delegated to staff members. ■

## VENEZUELA

**Official name** Republic of Venezuela
**PEOPLE**
**Population** 19,485,000. **Density** 55/mi$^2$ (21/km$^2$). **Urban** 87%. **Capital** Caracas, 3,041,000. **Ethnic groups** Mestizo 67%, white 21%, black 10%, Indian 2%. **Languages** Spanish, indigenous. **Religions** Roman Catholic 96%, Protestant 2%. **Life expectancy** 72 female, 66 male. **Literacy** 84%.
**POLITICS**
**Government** Republic. **Parties** Democratic Action, Movement Toward Socialism, Social Christian, others. **Suffrage** Universal, over 18. **Memberships** OAS, OPEC, UN. **Subdivisions** 20 states, 2 territories, 1 dependency, 1 district.
**ECONOMY**
**GDP** $49,604,000,000 **Per capita** $3,093. **Monetary unit** Bolivar. **Trade partners** Exports: Netherlands Antilles, U.S., Canada. Imports: U.S., Japan. **Exports** Petroleum, aluminum and other manufactures. **Imports** Machinery, manufactures, transportation equipment, food, chemicals.
**LAND**
**Description** Northern South America. **Area** 352,145 mi$^2$ (912,050 km$^2$). **Highest point** Pico Bolívar, 16,427 ft (5,007 m). **Lowest point** Sea level.

**People.** Spanish colonial rule of Venezuela is reflected in its predominantly mestizo population, people of Spanish-Indian blood, and its official language of Spanish. Minorities include Europeans, blacks, and Indians, who generally speak local languages. Nearly all Venezuelans are Roman Catholic, further evidence of former Spanish domination. Protestants and lesser numbers of Jews and Muslims compose small minorities, and traditional religious practices continue among some Indians.

**Economy and the Land.** Since the expansion of the petroleum industry in the 1920s, Venezuela has experienced rapid economic growth, but unevenly distributed wealth, a high birthrate, and fluctuations in the price of oil have hampered the economy. Partly because of the emphasis on oil production, agriculture has declined; its contribution to the gross national product is minimal, and Venezuela must import much of its food. Manufacturing and hydroelectric power are being developed. The varied Venezuelan landscape is dominated by the Andes Mountains, a coastal zone, high plateaus, and plains, or llanos. The climate is tropical, but temperatures vary with altitude. Most of the country experiences rainy and dry seasons.

**History and Politics.** The original inhabitants of modern Venezuela included Arawak and Carib Indians. In 1498 Christopher Columbus was the first European to visit Venezuela. The area became a colony of Spain and was briefly under German rule. Independence was achieved in 1821 under the guidance of Simón Bolívar, Venezuela's national hero. Venezuela became a sovereign state in 1830. The nineteenth century saw political instability and revolutionary fervor, followed by a succession of dictators in the twentieth century. Since 1958, Venezuela has tried to achieve a representational form of government and has held a number of democratic elections. The fall in oil prices, for a country heavily dependent upon oil export, has been an economic hardship in recent years. ∎

# VIETNAM

**Official name** Socialist Republic of Vietnam
**PEOPLE**
**Population** 65,475,000. **Density** 515/mi² (199/km²).
**Urban** 20%. **Capital** Hanoi, 897,500. **Ethnic groups** Vietnamese 85-90%, Chinese 3%. **Languages** Vietnamese, French, Chinese, English, Khmer, indigenous. **Religions** Buddhist, Chondoist, Roman Catholic, Animist, Muslim, Confucian. **Life expectancy** 61 female, 57 male. **Literacy** 84%.
**POLITICS**
**Government** Socialist republic. **Parties** Communist. **Suffrage** Universal, over 18. **Memberships** CEMA, UN. **Subdivisions** 37 provinces, 3 minucipalities.
**ECONOMY**
**GNP** $18,100,000,000 **Per capita** $312. **Monetary unit** Dong. **Trade partners** U.S.S.R., eastern European countries, Japan. **Exports** Agricultural products, handicrafts, coal, minerals. **Imports** Petroleum, steel, railroad equipment, chemicals, medicine, cotton, fertilizer.

**LAND**
**Description** Southeastern Asia. **Area** 127,242 mi² (329,556 km²). **Highest point** Fan Si Pan, 10,312 ft (3,143 m). **Lowest point** Sea level.

**People.** Despite centuries of foreign invasion and domination, the people of Vietnam remain remarkably homogeneous; ethnic Vietnamese compose the majority of the population. Chinese influence is seen in the major religions of Buddhism and Confucianism. The official language is Vietnamese, but a history of foreign intervention is reflected in wide use of French, English, Chinese, and Russian.

**Economy and the Land.** The Vietnamese economy has struggled to overcome the effects of war and the difficulties inherent in unifying the once-divided country. Agriculture, centered in the fertile southern plains, continues to employ nearly 70 percent of the people. Vietnam intends to expand its war-damaged mining industry, which has been slowed by lack of skilled personnel and a poor transportation network. Vietnam's economic picture is not likely to improve until the country can resolve its political and social problems. The landscape of Vietnam ranges from mountains to plains, and the climate is tropical.

**History and Politics.** The first Vietnamese lived in what is now northern Vietnam. After centuries of Chinese rule, Vietnam finally became independent in the 1400s, but civil strife continued for nearly two centuries. French missionary activity began in the early seventeenth century, and by 1883 all of present-day Vietnam, Cambodia and Laos were under French rule. When Germany occupied France during World War II, control of French Indochina passed to the Japanese until their defeat in 1945. The French presence continued until 1954, when Vietnamese Communists led by Ho Chi Minh gained control of North Vietnam. United States aid to South Vietnam began in the 1961 and ended, after years of conflict, with a cease-fire in 1973. Communist victory and unification of the country as the Socialist Republic of Vietnam was achieved in 1975. Vietnamese military policy resulted in fighting with China and the occupation of Cambodia until 1989. Political reforms have aimed at improving their impoverished economic status. ∎

# VIRGIN ISLANDS, BRITISH
See UNITED KINGDOM.

# VIRGIN ISLANDS, UNITED STATES See UNITED STATES.

# WAKE ISLAND See UNITED STATES.

# WALLIS AND FUTUNA
See FRANCE.

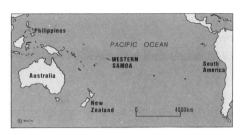

# WESTERN SAHARA

**Official name** Western Sahara
## PEOPLE
**Population** 196,000. **Density** 1.9/mi² (0.7/km²). **Urban** 53%. **Capital** El Aaiún, 93,875. **Ethnic groups** Arab, Berber. **Languages** Arabic. **Religions** Sunni Muslim. **Literacy** 20%.
## POLITICS
**Government** Occupied by Morocco. **Memberships** None. **Subdivisions** None. **Monetary unit** Moroccan dirham. **Trade partners** Morocco. **Exports** Phosphates. **Imports** Fuel, food.
## LAND
**Description** Northwestern Africa. **Area** 102,703 mi² (266,000 km²). **Highest point** 2,640 ft (805 m). **Lowest point** Sea level.

**People.** Most Western Saharans are nomadic Arabs or Berbers. Because these nomads often cross national borders in their wanderings, the population of Western Sahara is in a constant state of flux. Islam is the principal religion, and Arabic is the dominant language.

**Economy and the Land.** Most of Western Sahara is desert, with a rocky, barren soil that severely limits agriculture. Mining of phosphate deposits began in 1972, and phosphates are now the primary export. Western Sahara is almost completely arid; rainfall is negligible, except along the coast.

**History and Politics.** By the fourth century B.C. Phoenicians and Romans had visited the area. Spain explored the region in the sixteenth century and gained control of the region in 1860, but Spanish Sahara was not designated a province of Spain until 1958. When Spanish control ceased in 1976, the area became known as Western Sahara. Mauritania and Morocco subsequently divided the territory, and Morocco gained control of valuable phosphate deposits. Fighting soon broke out between an independence movement, the Polisario Front, and troops from Morocco and Mauritania. In 1979 Mauritania gave up its claim to the area and withdrew. After years of conflict, Morocco and the Polisario Front agreed in 1988 to a cease-fire and a referendum, which offered Western Saharans a choice between independence and integration with Morocco. ■

# WESTERN SAMOA

**Official name** Independent State of Western Samoa
## PEOPLE
**Population** 184,000. **Density** 168/mi² (65/km²). **Urban** 22%. **Capital** Apia, Upolu I., 33,170. **Ethnic groups** Samoan, mixed European and Polynesian. **Languages** English, Samoan. **Religions** Congregational 50%, Roman Catholic 22%, Methodist 16%, Mormon 8%. **Life expectancy** 66 female, 61 male. **Literacy** 98%.
## POLITICS
**Government** Constitutional monarchy. **Parties** Christian Democratic, Human Rights Protection. **Suffrage** Limited adult. **Memberships** CW, UN. **Subdivisions** 11 districts.
## ECONOMY
**GDP** $88,000,000 **Per capita** $550. **Monetary unit** Tala. **Trade partners** Exports: U.S., New Zealand, Australia. Imports: New Zealand, Australia, Japan. **Exports** Copra oil, fruit and vegetables, cocoa, oil seeds, aircraft. **Imports** Manufactures, food, petroleum, machinery, transportation equipment.
## LAND
**Description** South Pacific islands. **Area** 1,093 mi² (2,831 km²). **Highest point** Mt. Silisili, Savai'i I., 6,096 ft (1,858 m). **Lowest point** Sea level.

**People.** Most Western Samoans are of Polynesian descent, and a significant minority are of mixed Samoan and European heritage. Most of the population is Christian and practices a variety of faiths introduced by European missionaries and traders. Samoan and English are the principal languages.

**Economy and the Land.** The tropical climate of Western Samoa, which is composed of volcanic islands, is suited for agriculture—the country's chief economic support. Bananas, coconuts, and tropical fruits are the most important crops.

**History and Politics.** Polynesians settled the Samoan islands more than two thousand years ago. Dutch explorers visited the islands in the early 1700s, and English missionaries arrived in 1830. Rivalry between the islands' royal families increased, along with competition among the United Kingdom, the United States, and Germany. In 1900 the United States annexed Eastern Samoa, and Germany obtained Western Samoa. By the end of World War I, New Zealand had gained control of Western Samoa. Growing demand for independence led to United Nations intervention and gradual steps toward self-government. The islands became fully independent in 1962. The nation maintains friendly relations with New Zealand and neighboring Pacific islands. ■

# YEMEN

**Official name** Yemen Arab Republic
**PEOPLE**
Population 10,385,000. **Density** 138/mi² (53/km²). **Urban** 20%. **Capital** Sana, 277,818. **Ethnic groups** Arab 90%, Afro-Arab 10%. **Languages** Arabic. **Religions** Muslim 100%. **Life expectancy** 50 female, 47 male. **Literacy** 13%.
**POLITICS**
**Government** Islamic republic. **Parties** None.
**Memberships** AL, UN. **Subdivisions** 11 governorates.
**ECONOMY**
GDP $3,208,000,000 **Per capita** $522. **Monetary unit** Riyal. **Trade partners** Exports: P.D.R. of Yemen, Saudi Arabia, Italy. Imports: Japan, Saudi Arabia, France. **Exports** Machinery, pastry and other food, transportation equipment, manufactures. **Imports** Grain and other food, manufactures, machinery, transportation equipment.
**LAND**
**Description** Southwestern Asia. **Area** 75,290 mi² (195,000 km²). **Highest point** Mt. Nabi Shuayb, 12,008 ft (3,660 m). **Lowest point** Sea level.

**People.** Most inhabitants of the Yemen Arab Republic, or North Yemen, are Arab and Arabic speaking. The predominant religion is Islam, and the population is nearly equally divided into Shiite and Sunni Muslims. The Shiites populate the north, central, and east, with the Sunni community in the south and southwest. Most Yemenis are farmers.

**Economy and the Land.** Yemen has a terrain suited for agriculture, the backbone of the nation's economy. However, ineffective agricultural techniques combined with regional instability often hinder production. Industrial activity is growing slowly, with production based on domestic resources, but exploitation of oil, iron ore, and salt deposits is financially prohibitive at this time. The landscape of the Yemen Arab Republic varies from arid lowlands to the fertile, well-cultivated highlands that dominate the country's center. The climate is temperate inland and hot and dry along the coast.

**History and Politics.** From earliest times Yemen has been occupied by trade empires, and it was part of the Kingdom of Sheba in the 900s B.C. Christian and Jewish societies thrived in the pre-Islamic period, and the region's flourishing economy made it a focal point in the development of Islam. The Ottoman Empire ruled Yemen from the sixteenth century until 1918, when the Turkish military withdrew and gave control to the highland Zaidis. In 1962 the Yemeni army deposed the Imam Badr and established the Yemen Arab Republic. Civil unrest continued until a reconciliation of royalists and republicans in 1968, but a 1970 constitution was suspended in 1974 and military leaders assumed control. ∎

# YEMEN, PEOPLE'S DEMOCRATIC REPUBLIC OF

**Official name** People's Democratic Republic of Yemen
**PEOPLE**
Population 2,634,000. **Density** 20/mi² (7.8/km²). **Urban** 40%. **Capital** Aden, 176,100. **Ethnic groups** Arab. **Languages** Arabic. **Religions** Sunni Muslim, Christian, Hindu. **Life expectancy** 50 female, 47 male. **Literacy** 27%.
**POLITICS**
**Government** Socialist republic. **Parties** Socialist. **Suffrage** Universal, over 18. **Memberships** AL, UN. **Subdivisions** 6 governorates.
**ECONOMY**
GDP $900,000,000 **Per capita** $437. **Monetary unit** Dinar. **Trade partners** Exports: Japan, Yemen, Singapore. Imports: U.S.S.R., Australia, U.K.. **Exports** Petroleum, fish, cotton, textiles. **Imports** Petroleum, food, textiles, manufactures.
**LAND**
**Description** Southwestern Asia. **Area** 130,066 mi² (336,869 km²). **Highest point** 8,255 ft (2,516 m). **Lowest point** Sea level.

**People.** Most inhabitants of the People's Democratic Republic of Yemen, or South Yemen, are Arab, with small minorities of Indians, Pakistanis, and East Africans. Islam is the dominant religion, and nearly all South Yemenis belong to the Sunni sect. Small numbers of Christians, Hindus, and Jews also exist. Arabic is the official language, but Semitic variations are heard in the eastern part of the country, and English is widely understood. More than a third of the population lives in or near urban areas, particularly the capital city, Aden.

**Economy and the Land.** Arable land is limited by South Yemen's arid climate, although most Yemenis are subsistence farmers and nomadic herders. Petroleum products are South Yemen's major industrial export. However, both crude oil and food must be imported for the population, and the diminished oil market is a continuing problem. A mountainous interior and flat, sandy coast mark the terrain. The climate is hot and dry.

**History and Politics.** Between 1200 B.C. and A.D. 525, the area of present-day Yemen was at the center of the Minaean, Sabaean, and Himyarite cultures. Christian Ethiopian and Persian populations also increased before the introduction of Islam in the seventh century. British control of Yemen's coastal area began in 1839, and Aden became an important center of trade. Regional instability caused Britain to expand eastward and establish the protectorate of Aden in the 1930s. By the mid-1960s, Aden had become the focus of Arab nationalists, and in 1967 Britain granted independence to the People's Republic of South Yemen. After a coup by a Marxist faction in 1970, the country's name changed to the People's Democratic Republic of Yemen. During the 1970s, border clashes erupted with the Yemen Arab Republic, but the governments of both North and South Yemen continue to express a wish to unify Yemen. ∎

# YUGOSLAVIA

**Official name** Socialist Federal Republic of Yugoslavia
## PEOPLE
**Population** 23,765,000. **Density** 241/mi$^2$ (93/km$^2$). **Urban** 46%. **Capital** Belgrade, 936,200. **Ethnic groups** Serbian 36%, Croatian 20%, Bosnian 9%, Slovene 8%, Albanian 8%, Macedonian 6%. **Languages** Macedonian, Serbo-Croatian, Slovene, Albanian, Hungarian. **Religions** Eastern Orthodox 50%, Roman Catholic 30%, Muslim 10%, Protestant 1%. **Life expectancy** 74 female, 68 male. **Literacy** 91%.
## POLITICS
**Government** Socialist republic. **Parties** League of Communists. **Suffrage** Universal, over 18. **Memberships** UN. **Subdivisions** 6 socialist republics.
## ECONOMY
**GDP** $44,238,000,000 **Per capita** $1,917. **Monetary unit** Dinar. **Trade partners** Exports: U.S.S.R., Italy, W. Germany. Imports: U.S.S.R., W. Germany, Italy. **Exports** Shoes and other manufactures, machinery, transportation equipment, chemicals. **Imports** Machinery, petroleum, manufactures, chemcials, crude materials, chemicals.
## LAND
**Description** Eastern Europe. **Area** 98,766 mi$^2$ (255,804 km$^2$). **Highest point** Triglav, 9,396 ft (2,864 m). **Lowest point** Sea level.

**People.** The population of Yugoslavia is one of the most diverse in Eastern Europe and includes nearly twenty distinct ethnic groups, in addition to the main Serbian and Croatian groups. Serbo-Croatian, Slovene, and Macedonian are major languages. Religions are also diverse, and often divide along ethnic lines. Most Yugoslavs work in industry, resulting in a steady urban shift since World War II and a corresponding rise in the standard of living.

**Economy and the Land.** Since 1945, Yugoslavia's economy has made a successful transition from agriculture to industry. Once modeled on that of the Soviet Union, the economy today is somewhat decentralized, based on the theory of workers' self-management. Decisions on production, prices, and income are made to benefit society as a whole, though wealth has tended to concentrate in the highly industrialized north, resulting in increasing social tension. Agriculture also plays an economic part—aided by the moderate climate along the coast of the Adriatic Sea and stronger seasonal variations in the mountainous inland regions.

**History and Politics.** Yugoslavia has been inhabited for at least one hundred thousand years; its peoples have included Illyrians, Thracians, Greeks, Celts, and Romans. In A.D. 395 the Roman Empire was divided into the West Roman Empire and the Byzantine Empire, with the dividing line through present-day Yugoslavia. People in the western region became Roman Catholic and used the Roman alphabet, while Byzantines adopted the Eastern Orthodox faith and the Cyrillic alphabet. Slavic migrations led to the establishment of independent Slavic states such as Serbia and Croatia, and calls for Slavic unity began in the early 1800s. In 1914 a Slavic patriot assassinated Archduke Ferdinand of Austria-Hungary and triggered World War I. The Kingdom of Serbs, Croats, and Slovenes was formed in 1918. The fighting encouraged King Alexander I to declare himself dictator in 1929 and change the new country's name to Yugoslavia, which was retained after Alexander's assassination in 1934. Germany and the other Axis powers invaded Yugoslavia during World War II and were opposed by a partisan army organized by Josip Broz Tito, who assumed leadership when Yugoslavia became a Communist republic in 1945. Tito's policy of nonalignment, the cornerstone of Yugoslavia's foreign policy, caused the Soviet Union to break off diplomatic relations from 1948 to 1955. United States aid from the 1940s to the 1960s encouraged a shift toward Western trade and broadened political and cultural exchanges as well. Since Tito's death in 1980, the country has been governed by a presidency rotating amongst the republics. ∎

# ZAIRE

**Official name** Republic of Zaire
## PEOPLE
**Population** 35,165,000. **Density** 39/mi$^2$ (15/km$^2$). **Urban** 37%. **Capital** Kinshasa, 2,653,558. **Ethnic groups** Mongo, Luba, Kongo, Mangbetu-Azande, others. **Languages** French, Kikongo, Lingala, Swahili, Tshiluba. **Religions** Roman Catholic 50%, Protestant 20%, Kimbanguist 10%, Muslim 10%. **Life expectancy** 52 female, 48 male. **Literacy** 46%.

remained relatively unexplored until the 1870s. Belgian King Leopold II realized the potential value of the region, and in 1885 his claim was recognized. Belgium took control from Leopold in 1908, renaming the colony the Belgian Congo. Nationalist sentiment grew until rioting broke out in 1959. The country, which was then called the Congo, gained independence in 1960, and a weak government assumed control. Violent civil disorder, provincial secession, and a political assassination characterized the next five years. The country stabilized under the rule of President Mobutu Sese Seko, a former army general. However, widespread charges of corruption have strengthened the cause of rebels based in Angola. ∎

## ZAMBIA

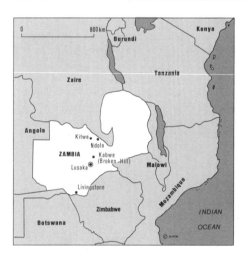

**Official name** Republic of the Zambia
### PEOPLE
**Population** 7,995,000. **Density** 28/mi² (11/km²). **Urban** 50%. **Capital** Lusaka, 535,830. **Ethnic groups** African 99%, European 1%. **Languages** English, Bemba, Nyanja, Tonga, indigenous. **Religions** Christian 70%, tribal religionist 29%, Muslim and Hindu 1%. **Life expectancy** 53 female, 50 male. **Literacy** 52%.
### POLITICS
**Government** Republic. **Parties** United National Independence. **Suffrage** Universal, over 18. **Memberships** CW, OAU, UN. **Subdivisions** 9 provinces.
### ECONOMY
GDP $2,597,000,000 **Per capita** $390. **Monetary unit** Kwacha. **Trade partners** Exports: Japan, W. Germany, U.K. Imports: South African countries, U.K., U.S.. **Exports** Copper, zinc, and other metals. **Imports** Machinery, textiles and other manufactures, petroleum, chemicals.
### LAND
**Description** Southern Africa, landlocked. **Area** 290,586 mi² (752,614 km²). **Highest point** 7,100 ft (2,164 m). **Lowest point** Zambezi River valley, 1,081 ft (329 m).

**People.** Virtually all Zambians are black Africans belonging to one of more than seventy Bantu-speaking ethnic groups. Besides the indigenous Bantu languages, many speak English, a reflection

---

### POLITICS
**Government** Republic. **Parties** Popular Movement of the Revolution. **Suffrage** Universal, over 18. **Memberships** OAS, UN. **Subdivisions** 8 regions, 1 independent town.
### ECONOMY
GDP $4,588,000,000 **Per capita** $150. **Monetary unit** Zaire. **Trade partners** Exports: Belgium, France, Switzerland. Imports: Belgium, U.S., France. **Exports** Copper and other metals, coffee and other food, crude materials. **Imports** Metals and other manufactures, machinery, food, chemicals.
### LAND
**Description** Central Africa. **Area** 905,568 mi² (2,345,095 km²). **Highest point** Margherita Pk., 16,763 ft (5,109 m). **Lowest point** Sea level.

**People.** The diverse population of Zaire is composed of over two hundred African ethnic groups, with Bantu peoples in the majority. Belgian settlers introduced French, but hundreds of indigenous languages are more widely spoken. Much of the population is Christian, another result of former European rule. Many non-Christians practice traditional or syncretic faiths such as Kimbanguism. The majority of Zairians are rural farmers.

**Economy and the Land.** Zaire is rich in mineral resources, particularly copper, cobalt, diamonds, and petroleum; mining has supplanted agriculture in economic importance and now dominates the economy. Agriculture continues to employ most Zairians, however, and subsistence farming is practiced in nearly every region. Industrial activity—especially petroleum refining and hydroelectric production—is growing. Zaire's terrain is composed of mountains and plateaus. The climate is equatorial, with hot and humid weather in the north and west, and cooler and drier conditions in the south and east.

**History and Politics.** The earliest inhabitants of modern Zaire were probably Pygmies who settled in the area thousands of years ago. By the A.D. 700s, sophisticated civilizations had developed in what is now southeastern Zaire. In the early 1500s, the Portuguese began the forced emigration of black Africans for slavery. Other Europeans came to the area as the slave trade grew, but the interior

of decades of British influence. Although most Zambians are Christian, small minorities are Hindu, Muslim, or hold indigenous beliefs. Most Zambians are subsistence farmers in small villages; however, the mining industry has caused many people to move to urban areas, where wages are rising.

**Economy and the Land.** The economy is based on copper, Zambia's major export. In an attempt to diversify the economy, the government has emphasized the development of agriculture to help achieve an acceptable balance of trade. Zambia is a subtropical nation marked by high plateaus and great rivers.

**History and Politics.** European explorers in the nineteenth century discovered an established society of Bantu-speaking inhabitants. In 1888 Cecil Rhodes and the British South Africa Company obtained a mineral-rights concession from local chiefs; and Northern and Southern Rhodesia, now Zambia and Zimbabwe, came under British influence. Northern Rhodesia became a British protectorate in 1924. In 1953 Northern Rhodesia was combined with Southern Rhodesia and Nyasaland, now Malawi, to form a federation, despite African-nationalist opposition to the white-controlled minority government in Southern Rhodesia. The federation was dissolved in 1963, and Northern Rhodesia became the independent Republic of Zambia in 1964. Zambia follows a foreign policy of nonalignment. ■

# ZIMBABWE

**Official name** Republic of Zimbabwe
**PEOPLE**
**Population** 9,252,000. **Density** 61/mi$^2$ (24/km$^2$). **Urban** 25%. **Capital** Harare, 656,011. **Ethnic groups** Shona 71%, Ndebele 16%, white 1%. **Languages** English, ChiShona, SiNdebele. **Religions** Animist, Roman Catholic, Apostolic and other Protestant. **Life expectancy** 58 female, 54 male. **Literacy** 62%.
**POLITICS**
**Government** Republic. **Parties** African National Union, African People's Union. **Suffrage** Universal, over 18.
**Memberships** CW, OAU, UN. **Subdivisions** 8 provinces.
**ECONOMY**
**GDP** $5,024,000,000 **Per capita** $613. **Monetary unit** Dollar. **Trade partners** Exports: South African countries, U.K., W. Germany. Imports: South African countries, U.K., U.S.. **Exports** Metals and other manufactures, tobacco, food, cotton, asbestos. **Imports** Machinery, petroleum, manufactures, chemicals, food.
**LAND**
**Description** Southern Africa, landlocked. **Area** 150,873 mi$^2$ (390,759 km$^2$). **Highest point** Inyangani, 8,504 ft (2,592 m). **Lowest point** Confluence of Sabi and Lundi rivers, 530 ft (162 m).

**People.** The great majority of Zimbabweans are black Africans of Bantu descent, with a small but economically significant minority of white Europeans. Most Zimbabweans are subsistence farmers who live in small villages. The influence of British colonization is seen in the official language, English, and in the influence of Christianity.

**Economy and the Land.** Zimbabwe's natural mineral resources have played a key role in the country's sustained economic growth. The subtropical climate supports the exportation of many agricultural products and makes large-scale cattle ranching feasible. Though primarily a landlocked country of high plateaus, transportation of goods is facilitated by an excellent system of paved roads and railways.

**History and Politics.** Zimbabwe was populated by Bantu groups until European exploration in the nineteenth century. British influence began in 1888, when Cecil Rhodes and the British South Africa Company obtained mineral rights to the area from local chiefs. Eventually, the region was divided under British rule as Southern Rhodesia, or present-day Zimbabwe, and Northern Rhodesia, or modern Zambia. In 1953, Southern Rhodesia, Northern Rhodesia, and Nyasaland, now Malawi, formed a federation that ended in discord after ten years; Zambia and Malawi gained their independence, and Southern Rhodesia, which remained under British control, became Rhodesia. In response to British pressure to accept black-majority rule, Rhodesian whites declared independence from the United Kingdom in 1965, which led to economic sanctions imposed by the United Nations. These sanctions and years of antigovernment violence finally forced agreement to the principle of black-majority rule. In 1980 the Zimbabwe African National Union-Patriotic Front won a majority of seats in the House of Representatives, and Rhodesia became independent Zimbabwe. Despite Zimbabwe's move toward stability since independence, some internal unrest continues. ■